The science of attachment can be daunting but, in his book, Brian Allen proves himself to be an excellent teacher. With its authoritative and practical overview of attachment-based diagnosis and intervention, this book will be a highly valuable resource for practitioners working with children, families, and adult clients.

—**Carlo Schuengel, PhD,** Professor of Clinical Child and Family Studies, Vrije Universiteit Amsterdam, Amsterdam, The Netherlands

THE SCIENCE AND CLINICAL PRACTICE OF ATTACHMENT THEORY

THE SCIENCE AND CLINICAL PRACTICE OF ATTACHMENT THEORY

A Guide From
Infancy to Adulthood

BRIAN
ALLEN

AMERICAN PSYCHOLOGICAL ASSOCIATION

Published by
American Psychological Association
750 First Street, NE
Washington, DC 20002
https://www.apa.org

Order Department
https://www.apa.org/pubs/books
order@apa.org

In the U.K., Europe, Africa, and the Middle East, copies may be ordered from Eurospan
https://www.eurospanbookstore.com/apa
info@eurospangroup.com

Typeset in Charter and Interstate by Circle Graphics, Inc., Reisterstown, MD

Printer: Gasch Printing, Odenton, MD
Cover Designer: Anthony Paular Design, Newbury Park, CA

Library of Congress Cataloging-in-Publication Data

Names: Allen, Brian, 1979- author. | American Psychological Association.
Title: The science and clinical practice of attachment theory : a guide from infancy to adulthood / by Brian Allen.
Description: Washington, DC : American Psychological Association, 2023. | Includes bibliographical references and index.
Identifiers: LCCN 2022030179 (print) | LCCN 2022030180 (ebook) | ISBN 9781433837616 (paperback) | ISBN 9781433837623 (ebook)
Subjects: LCSH: Attachment behavior. | Developmental psychology.
Classification: LCC BF575.A86 A45 2023 (print) | LCC BF575.A86 (ebook) | DDC 155.5/1241--dc23/eng/20220909
LC record available at https://lccn.loc.gov/2022030179
LC ebook record available at https://lccn.loc.gov/2022030180

https://doi.org/10.1037/0000333-000

Printed in the United States of America

10 9 8 7 6 5 4 3 2 1

Contents

Preface

When COVID-19 set in during the spring of 2020, those of us conducting psychological research found ourselves in uncharted waters. Institutional review boards at medical centers and universities across the country and overseas suspended ongoing research projects en masse. In some ways, perhaps it was a positive outcome. My focus shifted primarily to my role as a clinic director and toward how we could migrate treatment cases to telehealth, a platform we had not previously employed and that created a few headaches initially. My amazing wife stepped up in an incredible way at home, ensuring our daughters successfully made the transition to virtual schooling, which allowed me to keep my energies fixed on the patients in our clinic during an unprecedented mental health crisis and on the well-being of our program's outstanding clinicians, all of whom have families of their own.

After we began to discover a new sense of normal, my thoughts returned to my academic pursuits. In the summer of 2020, research was still not approved, and my projects lay in tatters. As I sat at home contemplating how I might produce something academically worthwhile, my thoughts went to a conversation I had many years ago with a colleague at a conference in Pittsburgh. We discussed various personal and professional topics while she drank her coffee and I drank my tea. She commented that she enjoyed reading my published papers because I was adept at taking complex empirical findings and distilling them down to their most useful components and relaying those findings to practicing clinicians. Having an interest in attachment theory herself, she proposed I write a book for practitioners to demonstrate the clinical utility of attachment research. Before I could reply, our discussion was interrupted by two people dressed in costumes, one a pierogi and the other a sausage, who entered the lobby dancing, choreographed to music (it was a sight to behold).

Earlier in my career I maintained a professional interest in attempting to bridge the often-discussed research-to-practice gap. I published theoretical discussions and reviews as well as case studies, but these efforts fell by the wayside as I advanced in academia and directed my energies to obtaining National Institutes of Health grants and conducting research. The suspension of research activities during the pandemic provided an opportunity to return to those roots, and my colleague's suggestion remained a good one. However, I was unsure if a market existed for such a book. Nonetheless, I put together a proposal and sent it to several publishers. To my surprise, only one rejected the proposal. In one way, it was quite heartening to see the potential demand for a text that provides a practical introduction to attachment. In another way, it was disappointing to learn that such a book did not already exist.

My first step in the writing process was to ask myself what practicing clinicians already know about attachment theory and research. Reviewing my memory of interactions with clinical colleagues and conference attendees, the majority of recollections involved the term "attachment" being confused for the parent–child relationship, often with little awareness that they are different concepts. Thinking about my undergraduate and graduate training experiences, I recalled only learning about Ainsworth and the Strange Situation Procedure as well as Harlow and his studies with rhesus monkeys. Even then, the coverage was minimal, and no applications to clinical practice were discussed. What I did learn, however, was that in academic clinical psychology in the United States, attachment research is typically valued only in practice with young children (i.e., under the age of 5 years). Furthermore, mentioning attachment within certain academic arenas was more likely to elicit eye rolls and sneers than any form of engaged discussion. Thus, I decided to assume no prior knowledge of attachment theory or research from the readers of this text. If you are already well-versed in some aspects, or perhaps many aspects, of attachment theory, my apologies for the repetitiveness.

My next step was to determine how to present the material in an applied yet empirically grounded way. I have often said that attachment theory is an exquisite example of the development and validation of a scientific theory. It started with clinical observations, moved to naturalistic observations and animal studies, and now finds itself possessing such a volume of empirical literature that rarely a month goes by without a new meta-analysis synthesizing a specific aspect of the field. As the scientific foundations of the field multiplied and gained widespread acceptance, a number of practitioners and researchers began testing the clinical applications of this knowledge base. Although not as advanced as the developmental science, the current state of the clinical science is sufficient for demonstrating the usefulness of attachment concepts in practice. As such, I decided to provide the reader with a coherent and functional presentation of the developmental science of attachment before considering its clinical applications. However, I stress that this is only an introduction, and the field of attachment theory and research is more developed and involved than I can convey in a volume such as this. I hope this book is both useful in the work that you do and encourages you to learn more about attachment theory and its potential role in practice.

Before concluding, I would like to return to a comment I made earlier. The perceptive reader may be asking themselves, "Why is he writing this book if he had no undergraduate or graduate training in attachment?" It's a fair question. After completing graduate school, I spent several months working my way through John Bowlby's renowned attachment trilogy, three books that provide his specification of the theory up until 1982. I was struck by the intellectual prowess of the man. I wanted to learn more, and, as I did, I realized that attachment theory was as empirically grounded as any other clinical theory I learned in graduate school and internship (which was largely cognitive behavioral). In addition, attachment theory appeared to explain key questions that went unanswered during my training, such as "How do we develop maladaptive cognitions?" and "What gives caregivers such power to shape our behaviors, beyond the obvious overwhelming amount of time we spend in their presence?" To me, these answers hold significant clinical relevance within my chosen clinical and research specialty of child maltreatment and trauma.

Through attendance at professional conferences and academic readings, and through lasting collaborations with astoundingly gifted researchers and clinicians, I found myself immersed in the attachment field in unexpected ways. My research efforts (which I am glad to say have now resumed) examine several attachment constructs, my clinical work is informed by attachment principles, and colleagues continue to ask me to present my findings at various conferences. It is safe to say that attachment theory occupies a large portion of the foundation upon which my professional work rests.

ACKNOWLEDGMENTS

Last, I want to offer sincerest expressions of gratitude to my clinical and research colleagues who provide a consistently positive presence in my life and without whom my professional experience would be quite different, and not nearly as productive. Of note, I want to thank Amanda Venta, PhD, herself an accomplished attachment researcher and busy university faculty member, for taking the time to read drafts of the chapters and provide her honest and insightful feedback. I also want to acknowledge the team at American Psychological Association Publishing for their helpful and professional shepherding of this book through to its final form. It seems only appropriate that in a book about attachment I say a few words about my own attachment figure, my wife, Kristen. The past few years presented us with numerous challenges, some COVID related and some not. Kristen provided the secure base that allowed me to write this book while juggling the many demands of my job and a steady safe haven that remained the calm throughout the storm. In closing, I want to mention that one of the great joys of my life is serving as an attachment figure for my daughters, Ashlyn and Linnea. Watching them grow, discover their interests, and explore their possibilities is awe inspiring, and knowing that I play even a small part (perhaps a large part) in that process is truly humbling. Every day they remind me why I, and you, do this work.

THE SCIENCE AND CLINICAL PRACTICE OF ATTACHMENT THEORY

INTRODUCTION

The Challenges and Promises of Attachment Theory for Mental Health Practitioners

Consider a 10-year-old child who presents for treatment alongside a caregiver but appears unwilling to discuss thoughts, emotions, or prior experiences while the caregiver is in the room. Once alone with the clinician, the child reveals a lack of trust in the caregiver and uncertainty about whether the relationship may be improved. Alternatively, imagine a married couple seeking help as their relationship is in danger of ending. As they discuss their problems in session, one partner appears particularly sensitive to critical comments while the other partner seems distant and unwilling to engage.

The issues highlighted in these two cases are not specific to any one diagnosis or problem. For instance, perhaps the 10-year-old child displayed depressive symptoms, posttraumatic stress disorder, or conduct problems. Regardless, the poor relationship with the caregiver complicates treatment. The same can be said for the married couple; perhaps one partner is struggling with a diagnoseable mental illness, or maybe infidelity occurred. It is obvious in both situations that interpersonal difficulties are at least a maintaining factor in the clinical distress being presented, if not the primary etiological cause of the problems. But, how did these individuals come to hold such perspectives, and how might they be effectively addressed in session?

https://doi.org/10.1037/0000333-001
The Science and Clinical Practice of Attachment Theory: A Guide From Infancy to Adulthood, by B. Allen

An effective understanding of attachment theory and research may prove useful in answering such clinical questions, as they provide a coherent and empirically grounded way to conceptualize interpersonal difficulties while suggesting helpful clinical directives. In addition, the current state of the knowledge is sufficiently developed that the role of attachment processes in the etiology of myriad mental health conditions are now well specified, suggesting potentially fruitful pathways for both intervention and prevention efforts. Unfortunately, training in attachment theory and research is sparse and often limited to discussions of specific research procedures, such as the Strange Situation Procedure, during a survey course in developmental psychology. This state of affairs leaves most practicing clinicians unprepared and unable to implement insights from attachment theory in clinical practice. This book aims to remedy the problem.

KEY TERMS AND CONCEPTS

It is important to recognize at the outset that attachment theory includes a number of constructs specific to the field. Certainly, it is the case that all theoretical understandings develop their own terminology to identify the concepts being described, such as "stimulus generalization" among behaviorists or "repression" among psychoanalysts, but in attachment theory one will find that many of the constructs are identified by using the term "attachment." For instance, "attachment behavior" refers to a very specific form of observable behavior, while "attachment classification" refers to a defined pattern of attachment behavior. The list goes on: "attachment script," "attachment style," and "attachment figure," to name a few. This similarity of terminology offers the potential to confuse one with little exposure to the field as the terms appear to blend together, even though each refers to a specific, albeit often related, concept. Throughout the book, I clearly define each term, provide concrete examples, and avoid using terms interchangeably.

Two specific terms deserve special mention. The first, "attachment disorder," is neither a recognized syndrome within any diagnostic nomenclature nor a term used by the vast majority of reputable researchers. Rather, it was coined by a fringe group of clinicians who often failed to test the idea or to provide a scientifically justified rationale for its usage (not to be confused with "reactive attachment disorder"; see Chapter 6 in this volume). The second, "attachment therapy," was brought into the clinical lexicon by the same group of clinicians, but it does not refer to any coherent systematic approach to treatment. Scientifically minded attachment researchers and clinicians tend to employ the term "attachment-based intervention" to distinguish their efforts from the discredited concept of "attachment therapy." The history of these two terms and the controversies they created are discussed in detail in Chapter 10.

GOALS AND APPROACH TO CONTENT

Contemporary attachment theory is a vast and ever-expanding field with cadres of researchers focused specifically on examining the structure, function, development, and clinical applications of attachment concepts. It is simply not possible to provide a comprehensive treatment of the subject. However, such an in-depth examination may serve to obscure the most clinically relevant aspects. Therefore, the goal of this book is to provide an accessible introduction to the topic of attachment theory and research that demonstrates its relevance in applied settings. Secondarily, my hope is that this book will stimulate an interest in the field of attachment theory, which may prompt you to learn more about the science of attachment and how it might be used in your specialty area of practice. If you find yourself desiring more detailed information on a particular topic, this book is designed to serve as sufficient background that will allow you to benefit from more advanced training in attachment theory as well as attachment-based clinical interventions.

A few notes of clarification are necessary to help explain the structure of the chapters and the content included. First, the specification of the developmental science of attachment is presented in Chapters 2 through 5 in a manner designed to demonstrate the evolution of attachment constructs over time (e.g., attachment behavior is discussed during the chapter on infancy and young children, internal working models are reviewed in the chapter on middle childhood). This organization should not be construed to suggest that the specific constructs examined are of relevance only to the given developmental period (e.g., attachment behavior is not only relevant during the infancy and early childhood years). Rather, the sequential ordering of these chapters largely reflects the most salient issues at a particular stage of development and methodological differences to assessing attachment constructs. I have attempted to demonstrate the interconnective nature of the various attachment-related constructs over time while maintaining a focus on presenting the material in a clear, coherent, and user-friendly manner.

Second, it is important to recognize the many different perspectives to attachment theory. The original approach of developmental scientists to understanding attachment examined the antecedents and consequences of observable behavior, which then progressed to exploring the cognitive bases underlying such behavior. In time, other constructs were added by researchers with different perspectives on examining human behavior (e.g., social psychologists). In short, the diversity of terms and constructs subsumed under the umbrella of "attachment theory" increased exponentially over the decades, many times to the chagrin of the developmentalists who originally pioneered the field. Without understanding the origins of these different perspectives and how they are (or are not) related, one may be prone to conflate terms, misunderstand and misapply empirical findings, and consequently curtail the applied value of attachment theory. As such, this book includes reviews of several different perspectives and areas of research that each claim the mantle of "attachment theory."

Third, Chapters 6 through 9 are designed to clarify and define attachment concepts commonly discussed in clinical settings as well as to demonstrate the applicability of scientifically derived attachment theory for clinical practice. Each of these chapters begins by reviewing etiologic and diagnostic issues before specifying treatment approaches. Although it is sometimes the case that attachment-based interventions directly target attachment constructs to improve a given clinical condition or presentation, this is not always the case. What qualifies as an "attachment-based intervention" is currently a hotly debated topic: Is it necessary for an intervention to specifically target an attachment construct, or is an intervention using attachment as its theoretical basis sufficient to qualify? Is an intervention "attachment based" if it was developed using a different theoretical lens (e.g., social learning) but is demonstrated to change attachment constructs? Given the lack of consensus on this definition, I selected interventions for review using a broad definition of the term "attachment-based intervention."

Finally, the chapters focused on clinical applications make liberal use of case examples. There is an inherent balance one must strike between detail and brevity when writing such vignettes. While there are always additional pieces of a clinical presentation that one may wish to know, providing richer and more thorough descriptions of the cases requires additional space and may obscure the most relevant aspects of the case. Remembering that the goal of the case illustrations is to demonstrate the application of attachment theory and research to practice, I provide sufficient material to answer the questions included with each case vignette. If you find yourself asking for additional details, it may be beneficial to refocus on the question at hand rather than the larger clinical issues that may be driving your curiosity.

INTENDED AUDIENCE

This book assumes that the reader possesses no significant knowledge of attachment theory and research; however, those with some limited background on the topic will still find it useful. The primary audience is mental health clinicians (e.g., clinical social workers, counselors, psychologists, psychiatrists), child welfare and adoption case workers, and those working in allied disciplines. Although the practical applications of the material are focused on the provision of mental health services, it is not assumed that the typical reader is a seasoned mental health professional. Researchers interested in integrating attachment constructs into their work may also benefit from the book as assessment methods are frequently discussed and the findings presented are based in peer-reviewed research.

OUTLINE OF THE CHAPTERS

If a clinician wishes to integrate attachment concepts into practice, it is first necessary to understand the scientific foundations of the field. Attempting to learn how attachment concepts can be applied to clinical techniques without spending time on the more basic research aspects is akin to wanting to learn behavior modification techniques but not taking the time to learn about operant conditioning. Part I is designed to provide this foundation.

The origins of attachment theory are reviewed in Chapter 1, focusing primarily on the work of John Bowlby, Mary Ainsworth, and their colleagues. Then, Chapters 2 through 5 provide an overview of the current state of the developmental science. Each chapter pertains to a different developmental period (infancy and early childhood, middle childhood, adolescence, and adulthood), but I urge readers to not skip directly to the period of greatest interest. As a developmental theory, attachment examines continuities across time as well as how change occurs. Skipping the chapter on infancy and early childhood, for instance, and diving directly into middle childhood may leave one confused as to how attachment scripts develop, for instance. In addition, each developmental period is directly relevant to the others. Attachment states of mind among adults are logically covered in detail when discussing adulthood in Chapter 5, but they are directly relevant to issues of parenting and infant attachment behavior as discussed in Chapter 2. I suggest reading Chapters 2 through 5 in succession.

Part II reviews the clinical implications of the science of attachment discussed in Part I. Chapters 6 through 9 allow for more flexibility, however, and are meant to be relatively freestanding. If you successfully comprehended the scientific aspects presented in the earlier chapters, the rationale for and implementation of the interventions discussed should be easily comprehended. I do want to note that I have spent a considerable portion of my career advocating for the dissemination and implementation of interventions with demonstrated efficacy, established through sound clinical trial research. I see no reason to change that perspective. As such, the clinical interventions reviewed either represent tested and validated approaches to treating the concern indicated or possess promising evidence and are presently undergoing further evaluation. Where conflicting findings are present, I review them for you.

Part III reviews notable controversies in attachment research and clinical practice and addresses common questions. Chapter 10 includes a discussion of an assortment of assessment and treatment approaches that appropriated the name "attachment theory," although, in fact, they were not based in attachment research. Many of these techniques caused serious harm and even death to children, unfortunately giving many the impression that attachment-based interventions are unethical at best and potentially lethal at worst. I hope to dispel the myths surrounding these interventions, traditionally termed "attachment therapy," and help the reader become savvier and more sophisticated in evaluating any intervention claiming attachment as its theoretical foundation. Chapter 11 answers frequently asked questions about attachment theory and its clinical applications, summarizing key points from Chapters 1 through 10.

Two special features repeatedly occur throughout this text. The first, titled "A Closer Look," provides a more focused discussion of a specific topic that may be particularly relevant for clinicians, examines a controversial topic, or highlights an important study in the field. Narrowing the subjects to showcase in these sections was a difficult task, as there are many worthy and interesting topics. For instance, I originally planned to discuss emerging research demonstrating the role of attachment processes on immunological functioning (e.g., Jones et al., 2017). To keep this book at a reasonable size, I was forced to consider those topics most relevant to practicing clinicians and, alas, the topic of immunological functioning, as well as others, did not make the cut.

The second special feature consists of the case studies provided in Chapters 6 through 10. Instead of reviewing the applications of attachment research in a didactic format, I thought it more interesting and engaging to ask you to consider for yourself how an attachment perspective might inform a given clinical presentation. Most cases are based on real-life patients directly assessed or treated by myself or by clinicians I supervised over the years. The only exceptions are the case studies related to adults, which are amalgams of several different parents and families with whom I worked. Each case study presents the pertinent clinical information before presenting a series of questions. These vignettes are not designed to demonstrate how a specific branded intervention is applied (e.g., Attachment and Biobehavioral Catch-Up) but rather to demonstrate the applicability of attachment principles in practice. I provide a discussion of each question for each case study at the end of the chapter. It should be noted that all names are fictitious and details not affecting the concepts being discussed were altered to protect patient confidentiality.

CONCLUSION

I want to emphasize that this text is meant to be an introduction to the topic of attachment theory and research. I harbor no illusions that those reading this book will afterward be fully capable of implementing attachment principles in practice. Rather, I hope this book provides you with an overview of the field that might stimulate an interest in attachment theory and research. I have included at the end of each chapter resources that might be helpful in furthering your exposure to this field, including links to reputable training resources in the assessment and treatment programs discussed. I envision that this text will be adequate background for those wishing to attain training in any specific approach.

In conclusion, I welcome you to the field of attachment theory and research. It is a field with a rich history, a promising future, and a number of complicated challenges and questions waiting to be addressed. In the hands of gifted practitioners, it also holds significant potential for improving the services we provide.

PART I THE SCIENCE OF ATTACHMENT THEORY

1 THE HISTORICAL FOUNDATIONS OF CONTEMPORARY ATTACHMENT THEORY

From John Bowlby to Mary Ainsworth

For most people, exposure to attachment theory begins with an undergraduate developmental psychology course. When the sections on social and emotional development are presented, it is not uncommon for Mary Ainsworth and the Strange Situation Procedure, and possibly Harry Harlow's famous experiments with rhesus monkeys, to be featured. Unfortunately, for many, this is where exposure to attachment research ends, resulting in numerous clinical and empirical insights being ignored. In several ways, attachment theory is a prototypical example of how the development, testing, and refinement of a scientific theory unfolds. It all began with simple clinical observations that seemed to conflict with the prevailing wisdom. Empirically minded people decided to test their ideas in a systematic manner and, in so doing, revolutionized the way we understand human development.

BOWLBY'S OBSERVATIONS AND A PIONEERING INSIGHT

John Bowlby was born in 1907, the son of a highly respected physician, and he attended the University of Cambridge intending to follow in his father's footsteps. Growing interests in the natural sciences and the burgeoning field

https://doi.org/10.1037/0000333-002
The Science and Clinical Practice of Attachment Theory: A Guide From Infancy to Adulthood, by B. Allen

of developmental psychology left Bowlby doubting medicine as a career. After graduation, he volunteered at two schools for children displaying emotional and/or behavioral concerns, and his experience at one of these schools, Priory Gates, was particularly formative. One child at Priory Gates made a lasting impression on him: a self-isolating teenage boy with significant conduct problems and no notable mother figure in his life. Bowlby contemplated how the lack of a maternal figure may serve an etiological function in the development of problematic behaviors. Encouraged by a mentor, Bowlby returned to the study of medicine and enrolled in medical school in 1929. He concurrently began training in psychoanalysis, the prevailing approach to understanding and treating mental illness at the time (Bowlby & Smuts, 1977/2020).

After completing his medical training in 1933, Bowlby began his psychiatric training at the Maudsley Hospital and began seeing child patients part-time at the London Child Guidance Clinic. The child mental health field was dominated by two perspectives at the time: social workers who were concerned mostly with the child's social environment and psychoanalysts who treated children by examining their conflicting internal fantasies. Relying on his previous experience at Priory Gates and learning from his patients at the London Clinic, Bowlby came to believe in the primacy of a third etiological explanation: mothers who were absent or emotionally distant. He saw the behaviors of the children as far more understandable when placed within this context.

Bowlby completed training in psychoanalysis in 1937 and began training in child psychoanalysis. His supervisor was Melanie Klein (1932), a renowned Freudian revisionist who argued that a child's unconscious representation of a bad mother lay at the root of mental illness. Having seen only a few patients under her supervision, Bowlby realized that his perspective was drastically different. While he was interested in examining the home life of his young patients, particularly the challenges experienced by the parents, such topics were quickly dismissed by Klein. Bowlby decided to undertake a study using cases from the London Child Guidance Clinic to test the validity of his contentions. He performed an intensive evaluation of the quality of parent–child relationships among youth referred for stealing. To increase rigor, he included a control group of patients seen at the clinic for noncriminal reasons (Bowlby, 1985/2020).

Bowlby presented his ideas to the British Psychoanalytic Society in 1939. He chose to focus more on the foundational hypothesis that real-life events were influential to the development of psychiatric concerns. His paper, "The Influence of Early Environment in the Development of Neurosis and Neurotic Character" (Bowlby, 1940), was a pointed rebuttal to established dogma. Bowlby reviewed a handful of cases from the London Child Guidance

Clinic and included a discussion of the children's early relationships, wherein each child experienced one of two factors: "(1) specific events, such as death of the mother or prolonged separation of the child from the mother; (2) The general [maladaptive] colour of the mother's emotional attitude to her child" (Bowlby, 1940, p. 157). In his conclusion, he went a step further by refuting that intrapsychic conflict is the only determinant of a child's mental well-being, stating his belief that "both good and bad mothers exist in fact as well as in fantasy, and that a child's emotional development is very dependent on his mother" (p. 178). He encountered only minor opposition and decided to press on with his larger study (Bowlby, 1985/2020). Unfortunately, his research endeavors would have to wait. Europe was thrust into war, and he was drafted into the British army in 1940.

Military service proved a transformative experience. Bowlby was assigned to a team of professionals tasked with identifying the most suitable candidates for officer positions, a process that required methodical research to identify individual characteristics that best predicted job performance. The unit included several psychologists with training and experience in assessment who placed a value on statistical judgment. Bowlby developed a deep respect for applied psychological research and learned to use statistical analyses to examine patterns within data, both of which were exceptionally rare in the psychoanalytic community (Bowlby & Smuts, 1977/2020). The opportunity to put these new skills to use came in 1943 when the editor of *The International Journal of Psychoanalysis* asked Bowlby to submit a paper. Sensing an opportunity, Bowlby returned to his examination of adolescents referred for stealing, integrated statistical analyses into his presentation of the data, and finished drafting the paper (Bowlby, 1985/2020).

"Forty-Four Juvenile Thieves: Their Characters and Home Life" was a 55-page report of exceptional depth published over the course of two issues in the journal's 1944 volume. Bowlby systematically reviewed the assessment data for each of 44 youth with a history of stealing and classified them into one of six categories. The largest group consisted of 14 youth he described as displaying "affectionless characters" marked by callousness and a lack of responsibility for their actions. These youth commonly engaged in other problematic behaviors, such as aggression, lying, and truancy, although "in a short interview, they make quite a good impression" (Bowlby, 1944a, p. 38). Of this group, 85% experienced prolonged or permanent separations from their mothers in the first 5 years of life, something experienced by only 17% of the remainder of youth with a history of stealing and 4.5% of controls. He concluded that adolescents with affectionless characters are the result of "having suffered prolonged separations from their mothers or foster-mothers in their early childhood" (Bowlby, 1944b, p. 121).

COLLEAGUES AND CLARITY

When the war ended in 1945, Bowlby was forced to make a crucial decision regarding his future: He could complete his training in child psychoanalysis or focus his time on examining the role of parental separation in the lives of children. He chose the latter and joined a number of his army colleagues at the Tavistock Clinic in London. One of his initial research projects was observing toddlers admitted to hospitals. It was not uncommon at the time for children fighting infections, such as tuberculosis, to be admitted to hospital for months with little visitation from family. There were significant medical concerns regarding the spread of infection, and it was standard practice to isolate ill patients until they recovered. The prevailing wisdom was that separations from caregivers were not particularly damaging to young children. After all, infants and toddlers were viewed as primarily motivated by physical sustenance and oral stimulation, which could be provided by nurses (Bowlby & Smuts, 1977/2020).

To assist in his project, Bowlby hired a social worker named James Robertson. The collaborators spent 2 years observing toddlers and preschoolers in hospital. Their data provided several clinical findings, including a commonly encountered three-phase pattern of response to separation. First, children initially protest through crying, reaching, and pleading for the parents' return. Once the protestations subside, children display a sad affect and listlessness that gives the appearance of being in despair. The third phase, detachment, occurs when children begin to engage with their surroundings and no longer pine for the parents (Bowlby, 1962/2020). This sequence of events was not altogether unknown to physicians of the time, as it was readily observable. However, the despair phase was viewed by many as a positive step in a child's adjustment to their circumstances as the incessant crying and pleading for the parent(s) ceased. Robertson and Bowlby's observations suggested that the emotional distress was far more detrimental than most recognized and that the despair phase resembled more a form of learned helplessness than positive adjustment.

Robertson decided to demonstrate the findings to their detractors. He and Bowlby devised a single case study in which Robertson videotaped a child's behaviors while in hospital. The child, a 2-year-old girl named Laura, was randomly selected from a list of children registered to undergo a minor surgery necessitating 8 days of inpatient recovery. In the film *A Two-Year-Old Goes to Hospital* (Robertson, 1952), the viewer watches as Laura is in obvious distress during the admission procedure and repeatedly asks for her mother.

When the parents visit on the second day, Laura pleads in anguish to go home. Throughout the rest of the week's visits, the young girl shows increasing levels of disengagement and ambivalence at seeing her mother. At other points in the film Laura is shown in a trancelike state, only to burst out in tears and plead for her mother when approached by a nurse. It was a far cry from the popular belief that a child quickly adjusts to the hospital environment (Bowlby & Robertson, 1953).

As the observations of children in hospital were underway, Bowlby was approached with an opportunity to further examine the issue of parental separation. A former army colleague who served as chief of the Mental Health Section at the nascent World Health Organization (WHO) asked Bowlby to undertake a report examining the well-being of children who were orphaned or otherwise separated from their parents, a notable problem following the war (Bowlby & Smuts, 1977/2020). In many ways, Bowlby was the ideal choice for such an investigation. In addition to his study "Forty-Four Juvenile Thieves" and his ongoing hospital observations, Bowlby saw first-hand the harmful effects of parental separation during the war. Numerous British children were evacuated from London to escape Nazi bombing and were sent to live with strangers. Bowlby treated several such children and believed the impact of parental separation was a primary factor in their emotional and behavioral concerns (Bowlby, ca. 1939–1942/2020).

Bowlby spent 6 months in 1950 reviewing the work of other investigators on the topic of parental separation and visited various European countries and the United States. He was astounded at the number of studies that examined the issue; due to language differences and physical distance, Bowlby was largely unaware that such a body of evidence existed. In 1951, the WHO released his report, *Maternal Care and Mental Health*. Bowlby methodically reviewed the evidence and noted that, with few exceptions, the evidence was quite clear: "The prolonged deprivation of the young child of maternal care may have grave and far-reaching effects on his character and so on the whole of his future life" (Bowlby, 1952, p. 46). Some of these untoward outcomes were singled out for attention, most notably the development of criminality and the "psychopathic character." He also noted that concerns such as depression, anxiety, and other forms of personality disturbance were documented in the literature. Importantly, he found evidence that sufficient mothering provided after deprivation in the first 6 to 9 months may stave off future negative consequences. The focus on maternal care led some to criticize Bowlby, and attachment theory more broadly, as being sexist, an issue explored in more detail in Box 1.1.

BOX 1.1

A CLOSER LOOK: IS ATTACHMENT THEORY SEXIST?

Feminist critics have taken Bowlby and attachment theory to task, arguing the emphasis on mothers as preferred caregivers is inherently sexist (e.g., Vicedo, 2017). These critics often point out Bowlby's repeated instances of identifying the mother as the ideal caregiver and his suggestion that maternal deprivation may be a driver of later mental illness. Indeed, some of Bowlby's most well-known and influential papers explicitly emphasized the role of the mother, often neglecting other important ecological influences, including paternal care (e.g., Bowlby, 1952, 1953, 1958). In addition, Bowlby was a prolific writer throughout the 1950s and early 1960s for popular magazines, such as *Parents* and *Ladies Home Journal*, attempting to bring his new ideas regarding child development into the mainstream. In many articles, he argued that mothers served a unique function in the lives of children and that it was most advantageous for a child's development to have the mother available at all hours of the day. Such comments from a respected authority served to reinforce gender roles and stereotypes and provided an apparent scientific rationale for discriminating against women in the workplace.

Bowlby provided additional ammunition to his critics with his introduction of the term "monotropy." Bowlby (1958) used this term in his paper "The Nature of the Child's Tie to His Mother" and defined it as "the tendency for instinctual responses to be directed towards a particular individual or group of individuals and not promiscuously towards many" (p. 370). Although he was describing the ability of a child to discriminate between adults and develop a relationship with a specific caregiver, the term itself implies the existence of a singular individual of importance (i.e., mono), and his writings suggested to critics that the individual in question was clearly the mother. Monotropy as a concept was promoted by critics as a prominent aspect of Bowlby's new approach and was used to paint the theory as clearly sexist.

Another side of Bowlby and attachment theory, however, provides a less objectionable view of the issue. In many of his academic papers, Bowlby used phrases such as "mothers or foster-mothers" or "mother substitutes." In other writings he specifically stated that various types of caregiving figures such as adoptive mothers, fathers, and even nannies may serve in the primary caregiving role. Clearly, the scientific side of Bowlby's thinking never assumed that the biological mother is the only adequate caregiver for healthy emotional development. Even the term

BOX 1.1

A CLOSER LOOK: IS ATTACHMENT THEORY SEXIST? (*Continued*)

"monotropy" was rarely mentioned by Bowlby after his initial misguided usage in 1958. Neither do attachment researchers, beginning with Ainsworth in the early 1960s, mention the term "monotropy" when examining an individual's ability to discriminate amongst caregivers and adults. In short, there is a discernible difference in the scientific writings on attachment theory and the popularized version of the field regarding the exceptionality of biological mothers to adequately fulfill the caregiving role.

The comments and assertions Bowlby made in popular magazines are an unfortunate legacy of a time at which the science was in its infancy but the desire to legitimize its implications was strong. Historian Robbie Duschinsky (2020) argued that Bowlby's comments appealed "to the obviousness and authority of popular British stereotypes about women and children and nature . . . such a strategy helped him get some core ideas heard, even if these were mostly the rind of the views he actually held" (p. 2). If Bowlby qualified his positions and popularized the view that either the mother or father may serve in the primary caregiving role, such a countervailing view of the gender stereotypes of the day may not have garnered much attention or been summarily dismissed. Bowlby's goal was to make the public mindful of the importance of real-life parent-child relationships on child development, not to confront gender bias.

As social and political forces upended the status quo, attachment researchers responded by investigating the impact of diverse forms of caregivers, including fathers, adoptive and foster caregivers, and same-sex couples, and generally found few differences in their abilities to care for children. In some small measure of redemption, attachment researchers were instrumental in providing convincing evidence that infants of working mothers who are placed in daycare are not at increased risk for poor outcomes when compared to children of stay-at-home mothers (see Belsky, 2005, for a review). In many ways, attachment research has helped dispel many gender-based misconceptions about childrearing and human development. Nonetheless, research on the role of nonmaternal caregivers (e.g., fathers) continues to receive the minority of empirical attention. In addition, evidence suggests that findings may differ based on whether the caregiver examined is male or female (see Chapter 2, this volume). Clearly, much remains to be learned with regard to the role of gender in the development and functioning of attachment processes.

True to his roots, Bowlby couched his WHO findings in psychoanalytic terminology, including discussions of how maternal deprivation may cause underdevelopment of the ego and superego and the onset of aggressive fantasies toward the mother. Nonetheless, Bowlby's assertion that real-life experiences caused the child's problems was largely rejected by psychoanalysts. In dismissing the prevailing wisdom emphasizing libidinal drive, Bowlby failed to offer an alternative motivational explanation for the behavior of an infant, which left it unclear to many how parental deprivation caused significant negative consequences.

Ethology Provides the Missing Link

The intellectual breakthrough came in 1951. Family friends recommended Bowlby read the works of Konrad Lorenz and Nikolaas Tinbergen, two researchers who were pioneering the field of ethology, the naturalistic study of animal behavior. For ethologists, a foundational principle is that evolution resulted in animals being born into the world with a set of survival instincts adapted to their environments. Lorenz (1952) was gaining notoriety for his studies demonstrating the concept of imprinting with geese, showing how a newly hatched gosling followed the first moving object it encountered, typically the mother. By identifying its caregiver and other members of its family soon after hatching, the gosling's chances of survival were significantly increased. Tinbergen (1951) elaborated on many of the ethologists' ideas by examining ways in which an animal's innate behaviors equip it for survival. Tinbergen showed that an animal adapts to its environment by changing behaviors based on the stimuli and responses encountered. In other words, evolutionarily derived instinctual behaviors could be fundamentally altered by the responses they elicited from the environment.

Bowlby immediately recognized the importance of the ethologists' research. As humans were themselves on the evolutionary chain, it seemed logical that they too entered the world with certain survival instincts. As with Lorenz's geese, human infants need their caregivers close to increase chances for survival, and they had no shortage of tools to achieve that goal, such as crying, reaching, and smiling. As Tinbergen proposed with animals, perhaps human infants begin to adapt their behaviors to the environment and potentially develop pathological alterations when deprived of suitable caregivers (Ainsworth & Bowlby, 1991).

To flesh out his ideas, Bowlby had at his disposal a sounding board of distinguished intellectuals. On the heels of his now widely circulated report, the WHO convened a "Study Group on Psychobiological Development of the Child" in 1953, which included such luminaries as Lorenz, cognitive development pioneer Jean Piaget, and renowned cultural anthropologist Margaret Mead. During one of the meetings, Lorenz referred Bowlby to a young ethologist at the University of Cambridge named Robert Hinde. By 1954, Bowlby and Hinde engaged in frequent consultations, with Hinde guiding Bowlby's thinking of how ethology can inform the understanding of human behavior (Bowlby & Smuts, 1977/2020).

Attempting to apply his new theoretical model of maladaptation to his prior research, however, proved difficult. Bowlby recognized his previous retrospective reports suffered from a major flaw: They started by identifying adolescents displaying conduct problems and looked backward. Following young children forward may show that many who endure prolonged parental separations do not develop significant behavioral problems, a caution he emphasized in the WHO report.

One member of the research team was particularly well suited to help undertake a new project. In 1950, as Robertson was observing children in hospital and Bowlby was completing his work for the WHO, the Tavistock Clinic hired Mary D. Salter Ainsworth, a psychologist, to assist with Bowlby's other projects. Ainsworth joined Bowlby in a "follow-up study" examining whether children who were separated from their parents early in life went on to develop significant conduct problems. After reviewing the records of preschool children hospitalized for tuberculous between 1940 and 1948, they selected 60 potential subjects. The researchers located the children, then ranging in age from 6 to 13 years, and completed an assessment. To further improve their methodology, they recruited a matched control sample of children attending the same schools and asked teachers to complete measures. Contrary to Bowlby's preliminary hypotheses, the primary differences between the groups were not matters of criminal behavior, but rather apathy, withdrawal, and poor emotional control. Although the children who previously experienced separations appeared to display more concerns with emotional adjustment than the control children, a number did not show significant long-term detriments (Bowlby et al., 1956).

The results of the follow-up study surprised the research team. In the conclusions of the paper Bowlby admitted that his theory regarding the development of conduct problems may be wrong:

> It is clear that some of the workers, including the present senior author, in their desire to call attention to dangers which can often be avoided have on occasion overstated their case. In particular, statements implying that children who are brought up in institutions or who suffer other forms of serious privation and deprivation in early life *commonly* develop psychopathic or affectionless characters (e.g., Bowlby, 1944) are seen to be mistaken. (Bowlby et al., 1956, p. 240)

The focus needed to turn toward a broad understanding of social and emotional development, not a simplistic association between separation and delinquency. The team offered preliminary thoughts on the issue by drawing attention to the quality of the child's relationship with the caregiver, a characteristic they termed "attachment."[1] By the time the paper was published, Ainsworth had been exploring these ideas in the field for nearly 2 years.

In 1954, Ainsworth's husband took a position in Uganda, and she began conducting home observations with 28 Ugandan families to examine the infants' behaviors toward their mothers. One group of children, which she labeled "secure," seemed to readily explore their environments and engage in social activities while their mothers were present. They sought out their mothers when upset, scared, or hungry, and began to cry when the mothers left. A second group of children, labeled "insecure" often appeared distressed even when their mothers were present, and they did not engage with their surroundings to the same extent as their secure peers. Using psychometric scales, she developed to accompany her observations, Ainsworth found significant differences in the behaviors of the mothers across the two groups. She surmised that the factors underlying differences in infant behavior were that mothers of secure infants were better able to effectively identify the cues of their children (i.e., sensitivity) and subsequently provide the necessary assistance to pacify them (i.e., responsivity; Ainsworth, 1967). For Ainsworth, the findings were concrete evidence supporting Bowlby's ethologically informed ideas, including the centrality of the mother's behavior in the emergence of childhood emotional and behavioral maladjustment. She relayed the findings from her observations to Bowlby in London (Bretherton, 2003).

Having empirical evidence to suggest that the findings of the ethologists were applicable to human infants, Bowlby decided it was time to unveil his theory to the British Psychoanalytic Society. In June 1957, he presented his paper, "The Nature of the Child's Tie to His Mother" (Bowlby, 1958). After reviewing a body of supportive ethological research, he proffered that humans too have an innate drive to maintain proximity to a caregiver because of its evolutionarily derived survival value. When threat emerges, either internal (e.g., hunger) or external (e.g., loud noises), the infant seeks comfort from a caregiver using instinctual responses (e.g., sucking, crying). The child's alarm response is terminated when the caregiver provides an appropriate reply. Other native behaviors, such as following and smiling, serve to

[1]It is specified in the paper that the term "attachment" was preferred over other terms such as "dependency," which implies that the child is interested in the caregiver only because of physical comforts such as food or warmth. "Attachment" seemed a more neutral term that allows for the relationship itself to be a primary end for the child.

keep the caregiver near to allow for a prompt response to danger. Bowlby suggested that infants likely begin the process of orienting these responses toward a specific caregiver around 6 months of age with the clear discrimination of preferred caregivers evident around 9 months, a timeline he directly derived from Piaget's postulations on the development of object permanence.

Bowlby hoped his contemporaries might be swayed by his discussions of sound scientific evidence, but it was not to be. He was roundly criticized by the psychoanalysts, especially the Kleinians, who believed his ideas were radical and misguided (Bowlby, 1985/2020). Perhaps fortunately for Bowlby, he was not in London long after delivering the paper, as he embarked on a planned trip to the United States in the autumn of 1957. Near the end of his travels, he met a researcher at the University of Wisconsin who was making a name for himself with studies utilizing rhesus monkeys, Harry Harlow.

Harry Harlow and Animal Models of Attachment

Harlow's most famous studies examined the differences in monkeys' responses to fearful situations when raised with surrogate "mothers." Two such surrogates were available: (a) a "wire mother" that provided no physical comfort but offered a bottle for feeding, and (b) a "cloth mother" that was wrapped in terry cloth and placed in front of a light bulb that provided warmth. As Harlow (1958) reported and later demonstrated in a widely viewed film, monkeys preferred to spend most of their waking time with the cloth surrogate, only venturing to the wire surrogate for feeding. To examine the fear response, Harlow devised numerous stress-inducing situations, including placing a loud and ominous-looking machine near the monkeys' cages and introducing the young monkeys to strange rooms filled with unfamiliar items. When neither of the surrogates were available during these moments, the monkeys cowered and showed indications of intense fear, such as freezing, wailing, and rocking. The same responses occurred in the presence of the wire mother. However, when the cloth mother was present, monkeys typically ran to her, gripped her tightly for a short period of time, and then confronted the feared stimulus. The implication, according to Harlow, was that "contact comfort" provided by one's caregiver was the clear determinate of emotional development, not feeding or oral stimulation. Further examination of Harlow's studies and their relation to attachment research is provided in Box 1.2.

When Bowlby arrived in Madison in June 1958, he had a basic understanding of Harlow's work, but the visit provided insight regarding the clinical implications of his new theory. At the time, Harlow was attempting to develop a surrogate mother that actively rejected the infant monkey

BOX 1.2

A CLOSER LOOK: HARRY HARLOW

Harry Harlow began a faculty position at the University of Wisconsin in 1930 intent on studying basic learning processes. To his dismay, the rat laboratory at the university had recently been discontinued, and he settled for conducting observations of monkeys at a local zoo. Harlow realized he could be more productive with his own monkeys and began importing them. Unfortunately, many arrived with diseases that spread to other monkeys, resulting in a catastrophic mortality rate. By the mid-1950s he decided to establish his own self-sustaining monkey colony. To prevent infections, he heeded veterinary advice and isolated the monkeys in their own cages and kept them separated from one another. Infants were taken from their mothers within hours following birth to prevent the mothers from teaching their babies anything that might ruin their suitability for learning studies (van Rosmalen et al., 2020).

By happenstance, Harlow noticed that infant monkeys became upset and protested when cloth diapers on the bottom of their cages were removed for cleaning. After consulting with his graduate students, his now-famous "surrogate" experiments were designed. The original intention was to refute the predominant behavioral drive reduction theory that suggested the function of behavior was the reduction of primary drives, such as obtaining food to reduce hunger (Suomi et al., 2008). A relationship with a caregiver develops because the caregiver is associated with the reduction of the primary drive (e.g., a mother feeding the child). In many respects, this theory resembles the psychoanalytic hypothesis that the mother comes to a place of importance for the child because she is associated with the breast. The finding that infant monkeys preferred the "contact comfort" of the cloth surrogate over the company of the food-providing wire surrogate shattered both the drive reduction and psychoanalytic viewpoints.

After beginning his correspondence with Bowlby and meeting him in Madison in 1958, Harlow decided to systematically examine the issue of mother-child separation. He began raising infant monkeys with their mothers and removed them at a future point, presumably after an attachment relationship was formed. The studies were modeled directly on Bowlby's previous reports with children (Suomi et al., 2008), and, not surprisingly, Harlow documented the same indications of protest, despair, and detachment with his monkeys (Seay et al., 1962). Even more concerning, the monkeys demonstrated significant social and emotional problems as they grew older, with adolescents showing no interest in social or sexual relationships (Suomi et al., 1972).

BOX 1.2

A CLOSER LOOK: HARRY HARLOW (*Continued*)

Harlow's studies occurred at a time when scientific research was poorly regulated. The fundamental scientific questions he asked were of great importance, and the information learned proved foundational for our understanding of human development. Nonetheless, Harlow faced calls for ethical scrutiny and without question his monkeys were subjected to inhumane, if not torturous, treatment. Nonhuman primate research colonies still exist today, though their studies are reviewed and monitored by boards tasked with overseeing research involving animals.

(e.g., forcefully threw it off). Harlow told Bowlby the goal was to produce psychopathology among the infants, but his attempts were failing because the rejected infants continued to return to the surrogates. Bowlby observed signs of clinical distress in many of the monkeys, such as stereotypic rocking and sucking on toes and fingers. It was common practice at the time to house monkeys individually, as infections spread quickly and were often fatal. Bowlby surmised that the isolation and social deprivation likely caused the clinical signs. He told Harlow, "I do not know what your problem is . . . you have more crazy monkeys here than probably exist any other place on the face of the earth! You do not have to produce psychopathology—you already have it!" (Suomi et al., 2008, p. 359).[2]

Bowlby Applies Attachment to Anxiety and Grief

After returning from his trip, Bowlby presented his first paper on the clinical implications of his theory to the British Psychoanalytic Society in November 1958. His topic was separation anxiety, an issue he connected to the first stage of his now well-known sequence of protest, despair, and detachment upon separation from a caregiver (Bowlby, 1960b). After reviewing psychoanalytic

[2]Harlow's student Stephen Suomi later recounted this story during a presentation at the University of Cambridge. Bowlby's long-time colleague Robert Hinde informed Suomi that it was he (Hinde) who noticed the clinical signs among the monkeys when visiting Harlow's lab and subsequently notified Harlow. In Suomi's estimation, it is likely the case that both Hinde and Bowlby made their impressions known to Harlow (Suomi et al., 2008).

theories and discussing their inadequacies, he laid out his own ethologically informed perspective. Drawing on learning theory, he noted that infants can be conditioned to anticipate the departure of a parent (e.g., putting on a coat before leaving). When these signals are present, the infant implements innate behaviors (e.g., crying, reaching) "which have become characteristic of a species because of their survival value to the species" (p. 95). When this response by the infant, termed "attachment behavior," is successful at preventing separation, the anxiety is alleviated and the behavior ceases.

The same principle applies under other conditions of perceived danger. When placed in a threatening situation, the infant seeks to escape the source of threat. Bowlby opined that "the haven of safety which terminates escape responses and brings a sense of security is proximity to the mother" (Bowlby, 1960b, p. 97). It was a concept directly reinforced by his own observations of Harlow's socially isolated monkeys and the published results of Harlow's experiments. Bowlby reasoned that the monkeys' attachment behavior was insufficient to escape their stressful situations, whether it be their cages, a frightening machine, or a strange room, and they displayed pathological behavior as a result. However, when the comforting cloth mother was present, the monkeys' attachment behavior yielded successful termination of the fear response, thus allowing a sense of security and the courage to venture away from the cloth mother. Indeed, he noted that the term "haven of safety" was borrowed from Harlow (Harlow & Zimmermann, 1958).

Bowlby (1960b) reminded the audience of the video Robertson made of young Laura in hospital. Initially, Laura would freeze when approached by Robertson and watch him with a cautious eye: He elicited fear, and her mother was not available to provide a sense of security. On at least two occasions Laura laid down in her crib pretending to be asleep when a stranger passed by her bed, and she refused to acknowledge Robertson's attempts to comfort her, even though she was well acclimated to him by that time. Bowlby suggested Laura's behavior was the functional equivalent of the types of behaviors seen in Harlow's experiments. Laura's mother was not present to provide a sense of security, and Robertson was not a suitable replacement. In effect, Laura was placed in a fear-inducing situation, but due to maternal separation her attachment behavior was ineffective at creating calming, resulting in the observed signs of distress.

In the final part of the paper, Bowlby theorized how pathological separation anxiety could occur in children not presently separated from a caregiver. First, children with a history of separations and/or loss of a caregiver may be overly sensitive to future separations. Such a perspective was supported by the findings in his report for the WHO and the follow-up study of hospitalized children. In both instances, children experiencing early separations were shown to demonstrate increased levels of emotional concerns, including anxiety. Second, an intense fear of separation may be caused by caregivers who repeatedly threaten to leave or otherwise dismiss the child. It was a perspective he first raised in 1939 when he warned that "bad mothers exist in fact as well as in fantasy" (Bowlby, 1940, p. 178) and it was a proposition he would occasionally reiterate in his writings (e.g., Bowlby, 1952, 1953). Rejecting behaviors were reflective of a disturbed form of parenting, and the child's innate attachment behavior may be altered into a pathological form as a result, just as Tinbergen (1951) suggested in his research with animals.

Nearly a year after delivering his talk on separation anxiety, Bowlby returned to the British Psychoanalytic Society and presented a paper entitled "Grief and Mourning in Infancy and Early Childhood" (Bowlby, 1960a). He described "mourning" as the process that unfolds when one is separated from an attachment figure, which ultimately leads to detachment from that caregiver, while "grief" was conceived as the emotional responses that accompany mourning. These psychological and emotional processes were the hallmark of the despair phase, following the subsiding of a child's protest to separation. It is a period of increasing hopelessness for the caregiver's return, during which the child may display signs of withdrawal. He compared such responses to the mourning seen among bereaved adults and suggested the process is similar in function.

Bowlby differentiated his views from those of René Spitz, an American psychoanalyst famous at the time for a film he made depicting reactions of sadness among infants following parental separation (Spitz & Wolf, 1947). Spitz termed the phenomenon "anaclitic depression" and suggested that the condition was the result of a child turning the anger of separation inward on the self (Spitz, 1953). Such an understanding fit firmly within a psychoanalytic model emphasizing fantasies and ineffective functioning of psychic structures. Bowlby (1960a) believed Spitz's theoretical conclusions were incongruent with the data presented. Instead, he argued that the infants filmed by Spitz were like those Robertson observed. Infants not reunited relatively soon with a caregiver went through a process of psychologically detaching from the caregiver and were then able to attach to a new caregiver. Far from the progressive clinical syndrome Spitz described, Bowlby viewed the sadness and withdrawal as grief reactions typical of the mourning process and, like mourning among adults, the reactions subside. For Bowlby, any lasting impact will be seen in the child's development.

His paper on grief and mourning was the culmination of a three-part specification of his new theory, starting with the "Nature of the Child's Tie to

His Mother" delivered nearly 2 years prior. He was certain this bombardment of empirical data, fresh ideas, and demonstrations of clinical applicability would win over the psychoanalysts. He gravely miscalculated; the condemnation grew stronger. He began pulling away from the psychoanalytic community, only attending meetings when invited, which was infrequent at best. It was likely a positive outcome, as he no longer wished to criticize dogma, choosing instead to focus his time on specifying his new theory in greater depth (Bowlby & Smuts, 1977/2020).

A SYSTEMIC MODEL OF BEHAVIOR

Following his break with the psychoanalytic community, Bowlby busied himself writing a series of comprehensive and integrative volumes that provided a detailed specification of his new understanding of human development. The three treatises, which came to be known colloquially as the "attachment trilogy" or the "attachment and loss trilogy" (Bowlby, 1969/1982, 1973, 1980), were of considerable depth and relevance for both developmental and clinical audiences. In the first book, simply entitled *Attachment*, Bowlby (1969/1982) began by reviewing the shortcomings of psychoanalytic theories before addressing the overwhelming evidence for the developmental importance of early parent–child relationships. However, the succeeding chapters provided a trove of critically important hypotheses that collectively yielded an initial theory of attachment.

Although he alluded to it in various prior papers, Bowlby (1969/1982) provided for the first time a detailed analysis of the importance of understanding the systemic nature of behavior. He argued that "what is inherited is a potential to develop certain sorts of system . . . both the nature and the forms of which differ in some measure according to the particular environment in which development takes place" (p. 45). Borrowing from the ethologists, Bowlby argued that all organisms are born with the biological equipment necessary to navigate within the environment that evolution has yielded for the particular species, what Bowlby termed the "environment of adaptedness." Human infants are born with the ability to cry, suck, and grasp, all reflexes necessary for the survival of the species.

In addition, Bowlby (1969/1982) hypothesized that humans are born with the ability to organize and adapt behavior based on feedback from other components of the system. This is critically important because, as in any system, multiple parts operate concurrently in an interactive manner. As the individual performs behaviors designed to achieve a goal, the larger system provides feedback to that individual, who must then modify the behavior accordingly to increase the likelihood of achieving the desired goal. Consequently, Bowlby termed these systems and behaviors "goal-corrected" (p. 69). Cybernetics, the perspective that automated control systems govern behavior, was widely popular at the time in the scientific disciplines. Bowlby's insight was to apply this form of thinking to understand behavior under moments of distress and to recognize the importance of such situations for human development.

In the second half of his *Attachment* volume, Bowlby (1969/1982) demonstrated how *attachment behavior* of an infant is one component of the larger *attachment system*. The evolutionarily determined set-goal of the attachment system is a sense of security; under moments of experienced threat the infant actively attempts to reestablish a sense of security by initiating attachment behavior. The newborn emerges in the world with a limited repertoire of reflexive behaviors available for use by the attachment system, such as crying when hungry or scared. Appropriate responses by a caregiver allay the infant's distress and thereby terminate the attachment behavior, teaching the young child to anticipate that certain behaviors will elicit specific responses from others (i.e., the behavior is negatively reinforced). Although these early reflexive behaviors are initially indiscriminate, within months repetitive experience allows the infant to associate certain caregivers with reliable responses, and attachment behavior becomes oriented toward select individuals. By the time the infant has developed object permanence and is able to ambulate (approximately 8–9 months of age), only clearly discriminated caregiving figures are capable of efficiently calming the child under moments of distress and thereby deactivating attachment behavior.

In a more clinical vein, if the response from the caregiver is ineffective at providing a sense of security, then the infant's attachment behavior may not be effectively terminated. Instead, attachment behavior is modified in a goal-corrected way (i.e., based on the feedback received) and is implemented accordingly in future situations. In this way, attachment behavior may eventually take on increasingly aberrant forms, although the function of the behavior remains the same: achieving a sense of security. Even attachment behavior that may be considered concerning is still considered functional and goal corrected. Given the systemic nature of attachment behavior, however, it is more accurate to say that the attachment system, largely constructed from the interactive processes between the child and caregiver, is problematic.

Bowlby (1969/1982) considered the attachment system to be a foundational mechanism for the survival of the human species. However, the attachment system does not operate in isolation, and many behaviors considered vital for development were conceptualized as functioning in partnership. Exploratory behavior, for instance, was considered crucially important for the development of any number of cognitive, social, and emotional abilities. Infants' desire to explore the environment is facilitated by a caregiver who is available and can be called upon for protection if an unexpected threat activates the attachment system. Complicating the matter, however, is that a specific form of behavior may serve various purposes depending on the situation in which it occurs. For instance, an approach behavior, such as crawling toward an individual, may be understood as occurring within the attachment system under moments of distress but also as an affiliative behavior when directed toward a nonattachment figure as a form of social interaction. Thus, the context of a given behavior is a vitally important consideration. The task of providing a more structured, scientific, and reputable way to identify and classify attachment behavior fell to Bowlby's collaborator, Mary Ainsworth.

A RESEARCH TRADITION BEGINS: AINSWORTH REFINES ATTACHMENT THEORY

Bowlby can appropriately be described as a theoretician who provided the intellectual foundation for the burgeoning theory of attachment. However, the first deliberate research efforts designed to build empirical credibility for the theory are appropriately credited to Mary Ainsworth. Before her work with Bowlby, Ainsworth already had a firm grounding in the importance of the parent–child relationship. She completed her PhD degree in psychology under the supervision of William Blatz at the University of Toronto. Blatz developed an approach he termed "security theory," which suggests children begin life in a state of total dependency on their parents and come to learn that parents provide security in the world, enabling them to feel comfortable exploring new environments and thereby learning new skills. These opportunities for growth equip children to handle similar experiences in the future without their parents. Conversely, children who do not experience secure relationships with their parents may not develop the requisite skills to become independent and, consequently, may rely on maladaptive forms of coping with challenges (van Rosmalen et al., 2016).

Ainsworth's doctoral research developed psychometric scales to assess the tenets of Blatz's security theory, and she graduated with her doctorate in 1939. Following service in the Canadian Women's Army Corps during World War II, she returned to the University of Toronto and collaborated with Blatz on further development of security theory before departing for London. Blatz's influence is observable from Ainsworth's initial publication with Bowlby. In a brief monograph in which they discussed the multitude of factors that may affect a child's reaction to separation, the duo proposed the term "secure dependency" to refer to a healthy parent–child relationship (Ainsworth & Bowlby, 1953), a term later jettisoned in favor of "attachment." In conceptualizing her findings from Uganda, Ainsworth combined the terms, describing secure and insecure attachments, and suggested that a sense of security provided by the mother was the reason that some infants freely explored their environments while others did not (Ainsworth, 1967).

Ainsworth began a clinical and teaching position at Johns Hopkins University in 1956 and continued her work. First, she more clearly defined the term "attachment behavior" as "behavior through which a discriminating, differential, affectional relationship is established with a person or object, and which tends to evoke a response from the object, and thus initiates a chain of interaction which serves to consolidate the affectional relationship" (Ainsworth, 1964, p. 51). In less technical terms, she was referring to behavior that an individual (e.g., an infant) might perform that is directed toward a specific person (e.g., a parent) with the expectation that an interaction will then occur that both is immediately beneficial and consequently builds the relationship between the two. Ainsworth's definition of "attachment behavior" here is a departure from previous works by Bowlby and herself. Whereas earlier the term was used to refer to those behaviors initiated under moments of distress for the purpose of seeking proximity to a caregiver, Ainsworth's new definition was considerably broader and focused on behaviors considered capable of building an affectionate relationship between two individuals (Ainsworth later reverted to the original, more specific definition, the reasons for which are discussed in Chapter 2, this volume).

Next, Ainsworth pored through her observations from Uganda and created a catalog of 13 behaviors that she believed were indicative of an infant who was attached to the mother. In the first 6 months of life, these behaviors primarily take the form of differential responding, such as directing crying, smiling, or cooing toward the mother. By the second half of the first year, such behavior may take new forms with the advent of locomotion, such as crawling after or climbing on top of the mother. Between 6 and 12 months of age, other forms of relevant behavior emerge, including using the mother as a "haven of safety," marked by clinging to her when scared and using her as a "secure base" from which to explore the surroundings. During this time, the infant may be observed greeting the mother after she returns from a brief absence, a common indication of a desire to engage (Ainsworth, 1964).

Ainsworth's first research project at Johns Hopkins examined infant–mother interactions using her new and more methodologically rigorous catalog of infant behaviors (Bretherton, 2003). She partnered with pediatricians in the Baltimore area to recruit 26 White, middle-class pregnant women who were followed throughout the first year of their newborns' lives. Each mother and infant were visited in the home every 3 weeks by a study team who made detailed observations, with attention focused on the child's responses to everyday separations from the mother and their subsequent reunions. The data documented the sequence in which the behaviors of interest tended to emerge, with positive greetings following reunion the earliest to show, followed by protest to separation between 5 and 6 months of age, and "actively following the mother" the last to occur after the baby was capable of locomotion (Stayton et al., 1973). The characteristics of Ainsworth's sample (White, middle-class) exposed her findings to allegations of cultural bias, a frequent criticism of attachment theory. This issue is explored further in Box 1.3.

Ainsworth attempted to identify the reasons for individual differences in infant behavior during her Baltimore study. Given previous observations and theoretical importance, the mothers' responses to their babies' behaviors were closely scrutinized. One series of analyses showed that mothers who frequently responded to crying and held their children in an affectionate manner tended to have babies who displayed positive affect; over time, their babies tended to cry relatively little. In contrast, mothers who held their children in less affectionate ways, for shorter periods of time, and who often failed to provide physical contact during crying episodes had babies who responded more negatively to being picked up as well as to being put down. These babies were more likely to cry and fuss at later points in the first year (Ainsworth et al., 1972; Bell & Ainsworth, 1972). Such findings ran contrary to longstanding psychoanalytic and behavioral beliefs that coddling and picking up an infant during crying would create a "spoiled" child who would cry more often. For Ainsworth, however, the implication was clear:

> A baby's confidence in his mother's accessibility and responsiveness is built up in the course of the first year largely through his mother's consistency and promptness in responding to his signals, including his crying, and that infants who are chronically anxious about their mother's whereabouts are those whose crying signals have fallen on deaf ears. The securely attached baby, on the other hand, because his mother has been responsive to his signals, has built up expectations that his mother, even though absent, would be accessible if

BOX 1.3

A CLOSER LOOK: IS ATTACHMENT THEORY CULTURALLY BIASED?

One of the most frequently leveled criticisms of attachment theory is that its intellectual and scientific foundations are Eurocentric and do not account sufficiently for cultural differences in, for instance, child-rearing practices and views of acceptable childhood behavior (see Keller & Bard, 2017). Much of this criticism rests on Bowlby's contention that attachment behavior was derived through evolution for the purposes of survival of the species, suggesting such behavior should be seen across cultures. Ainsworth's first observational studies of infants and mothers occurred within a communal culture in Uganda in which mothers collaborated in the care of children. Her next study in Baltimore recruited White, middle-class women in the United States, a group specifically chosen for its considerable discrepancy from her previous sample. She identified numerous similarities relating to the structure and function of infant attachment behavior across the two contexts. Such results seemed to validate Bowlby's ethological perspective and suggested attachment behavior was a universal trait. Research since these earliest observations similarly suggests attachment behavior can be identified in a diversity of cultures from every inhabited continent (Mesman et al., 2016).

To an extent, however, the critics make valid points. Much of the earliest attachment research focused on European and American samples. Cross-cultural research has increased considerably in the past 20 years and has demonstrated several important findings of the ways in which cultural context affects the expression of attachment behavior. For instance, a special issue of the journal *Attachment and Human Development* (April 2021) was devoted to the meaning and function of the concept of maternal sensitivity in seven different cultures around the world (e.g., the Gusii people in Kenya, Peruvians living in the Andes mountains). Keep in mind that Bowlby borrowed from the ethologists in constructing his view that one's environment shapes the presentation of attachment behavior, and the integration of cultural differences is easily accomplished within the framework of attachment theory. It is accurate to say that cross-cultural research examining attachment constructs is a relatively young and burgeoning field.

> searched for, responsive to signals across a distance, and reliable in returning within the time span of absences to which he has become accustomed. (Stayton & Ainsworth, 1973, p. 233)

Ainsworth (e.g., Stayton & Ainsworth, 1973) argued that security is a continuum, with infants on the secure end confident that their mothers will respond during moments of distress and infants on the insecure side unsure of the responsivity of their mothers. Although naturalistic observations in the home setting were critically important for specifying the structure and function of infant behavior in relation to caregivers, there was a noted problem: Infants did not commonly display the type of "safe haven," proximity-seeking behavior that Bowlby described as "attachment behavior." Children were commonly quite interested in and engaged with the research staff who visited the home, underlining the importance of a threatening context to elicit these types of behaviors (Tracy et al., 1976). Therefore, to study safe-haven behavior in a rigorous way, Ainsworth devised a laboratory paradigm, experienced by the 26 infants in her longitudinal study at the end of their first year, which she termed the Strange Situation Procedure. It proved to be a groundbreaking innovation and is described in detail in Chapter 2 of this volume.

CONCLUSION

Bowlby's postulations were a watershed moment in the field of child development as the content and structure of parent–child interactions were now conceptualized as of the utmost importance. His systemic view of attachment behavior generated a wide array of directions for future research, including caregiving behaviors most effective at promoting development, the impact of multiple caregivers, and the interaction of genetics and parent–child relationships, to name only a few.

However, Bowlby also left in his wake a trail of confusion and conjecture. He applied the term "attachment" to a multitude of concepts, using it to refer to everything from relationships to individual caregivers to observable behavior to a structured system, sometimes in ways that were not clearly defined. Empirical examination of Bowlby's ideas was largely left to succeeding generations of researchers. The findings they produced supported many of Bowlby's contentions and clarified others while demonstrating errors in his reasoning that necessitated theoretical revisions. It is important to recognize the work of Bowlby, Ainsworth, Harlow, and other pioneers as reviewed in this chapter; it is also imperative that science continue to progress and that clinical practice make use of the current knowledge base.

RESOURCES

Professional Societies

- **Society for Emotion and Attachment Studies (SEAS):** SEAS is a prominent international society focused on the study of attachment and its role in development. Visit their website for more information: https://seasinternational.org/
- **Society for Research in Child Development (SRCD):** SRCD is the largest professional society focused on advancing the science of child development, broadly conceived, and its applications. Attachment research is commonly presented at SRCD conferences and in publications. More information can be found at their website: https://www.srcd.org/

Suggested Further Reading

Ainsworth, M. D. S., & Bowlby, J. (1991). An ethological approach to personality development. *American Psychologist, 46*(4), 333–341. https://doi.org/10.1037/0003-066X.46.4.333

In this career retrospective, the two collaborators discuss their partnership and unique contributions to the development of attachment theory.

Bowlby, J. (1988). *A secure base: Parent–child attachment and healthy human development*. Basic Books.

This brief volume is an accessible introduction to attachment theory from Bowlby himself and is well suited to those with relatively little background in attachment.

Bowlby, J. (1982). *Attachment*. Basic Books. (Original work published 1969)

This first book of the "attachment trilogy" provides an interesting look into Bowlby's thought processes when developing the foundational tenets of attachment theory. It is rather academic and provides exceptional depth of detail that may make it less accessible to those desiring an applied discussion.

2 ATTACHMENT DURING INFANCY AND EARLY CHILDHOOD

Understanding Attachment Behavior

Attachment behavior among infants and young children is, by far, the most discussed and researched aspect of the larger theory of attachment. For many, familiarity with attachment begins and ends with the commonly described attachment classifications (e.g., secure, disorganized). There are many reasons for this. First, Bowlby's (e.g., 1969/1982) theorizing and observations, as well as Ainsworth's (e.g., 1964, 1967), largely centered on children younger than 5 years of age. Second, the majority of attachment research after Bowlby and Ainsworth focused on this age, resulting in a voluminous empirical literature and clear practical implications. Third, clinical interventions built from this developmental science with young children are now empirically supported and disseminated to practicing clinicians. Nonetheless, confusion remains amongst many as to how attachment behavior is defined and assessed, what the classifications are describing, and what antecedents predict the display of various forms of attachment behavior. Clarity on these topics is critical for understanding aspects of attachment theory relevant to later developmental periods.

https://doi.org/10.1037/0000333-003
The Science and Clinical Practice of Attachment Theory: A Guide From Infancy to Adulthood, by B. Allen

DEFINING ATTACHMENT BEHAVIOR

Bowlby's (1958, 1969/1982) original insight was that the outcome of one's proximity-seeking behavior toward a trusted companion during moments of distress, for the purposes of alleviating that distress, plays a fundamental role in development and mental health. Ainsworth provided an operational definition in her seminal volume *Patterns of Attachment*: "*Attachment behavior* is defined as a class of behaviors that have the predictable outcome of gaining or maintaining proximity to a caregiver" (Ainsworth et al., 1978/2015, p. 260). She distinguished these observable behaviors from the affectional relationship between child and caregiver, which she referred to as an *attachment bond* or *attachment relationship*. Although these two concepts are related, "the existence of an attachment bond cannot be inferred from the presence or absence of attachment behavior" (Cassidy, 2016, p. 13). One should not conclude an attachment bond exists between an infant and stranger if the infant seeks comfort from the stranger when the caregiver is unavailable. Conversely, a lack of attachment behavior from a nondistressed child does not signal the lack of a bond with a caregiver.[1]

While thus defining the observable behavior that became the focus of her studies, Ainsworth did not lose sight of Bowlby's proposal regarding the systemic nature of attachment behavior (Ainsworth et al., 1978/2015). She too emphasized that observable behavior is one part of the larger attachment system, with unobservable internal components and external social factors also at work.[2] Like Bowlby, she postulated the attachment system is activated by environmental events, such as an attachment figure moving away or the arrival of a stranger, or by internal stressors such as hunger or pain. Through experience, the organism learns the behaviors most effective for gaining proximity to a caregiver and achieving a sense of security, thereby terminating activation of the system. Thus, the attachment system works in a goal-corrected fashion, and attachment behavior is a behaviorally conditioned response to environmental cues (Bosmans et al., 2020).

[1]The concept of "attachment bonds" is revisited in Chapter 5, in the discussion of adult attachment and parenting.

[2]Among these mechanisms is the concept of the internal working model, discussed in Chapter 3.

ASSESSING ATTACHMENT BEHAVIOR: THE STRANGE SITUATION PROCEDURE

Ainsworth realized during her longitudinal study in Baltimore (see Chapter 1, this volume) that in-home observational procedures did not capture the types of proximity-seeking behavior that she and Bowlby conceptualized as attachment behavior (see Tracy et al., 1976). The presence of the observer was insufficient to create a fear response that activated a child's attachment system. She devised a laboratory-based procedure that could induce a greater level of distress in the infant than was possible during home observations, with the stated aim of evoking activation of the attachment system and, thus, observable proximity-seeking (i.e., attachment) behavior. Participants in her Baltimore longitudinal study were invited to her laboratory at 12 months of age, and the procedure was administered (Ainsworth & Wittig, 1969; see also Chapter 1, this volume, for more details).

The *Strange Situation Procedure* (SSP) is an approximately 22-minute structured observational paradigm divided into eight discrete episodes (see Table 2.1). The SSP begins with both the child and caregiver in a room with the observer administering the procedure. The observer introduces the dyad to the room, which is outfitted with various toys and other items that might appeal to an infant's curiosity (Episode 1). The observer then leaves, allowing the child to explore the items in the room at will (Episode 2). It was hypothesized that the child would explore the room and play with the toys, placing the child at ease before attempting to elicit attachment behavior. Indeed, in Ainsworth's early studies of the SSP, over 90% of infants actively engaged with the toys (Ainsworth et al., 1978/2015).

Episode 3 begins when a different observer, unknown to the child, enters the room and begins a conversation with the caregiver. After a minute, the stranger attempts to initiate a conversation with the child. In the SSP validation studies, a majority of infants appeared unbothered or displayed friendly behavior toward the stranger (Bretherton & Ainsworth, 1973). Ainsworth and colleagues (1978/2015) surmised that the continued presence of the caregiver in the room was sufficient to suppress wariness or fear for most infants and, as a result, the threshold for activating the attachment system was not reached. However, Episode 4 involves the caregiver leaving the room and the infant remaining with the stranger. As predicted, nearly half the infants cried, and most curtailed their exploration of the room. It appeared to Ainsworth that the caregiver served as a "secure base" from which to explore the room. When the secure base was no longer available, exploration (i.e., secure-base behavior) was inhibited.

TABLE 2.1. The Strange Situation Procedure

Episode	Persons in room	Behaviors to observe	Duration
1	Caregiver Child Observer	Child's initial response to the room	30 seconds
		Observer leaves the room	
2	Caregiver Child	Child's exploration of the room	3 minutes
		Stranger enters the room	
3	Caregiver Child Stranger	Child's response to the stranger's presence Whether exploration is inhibited or continues	3 minutes
		Caregiver leaves the room	
4	Child Stranger	Child's response to being left alone with the stranger Whether exploration is inhibited or continues	3 minutes
		Caregiver reenters the room; stranger leaves	
5	Caregiver Child	Caregiver's behaviors to soothe the child, if needed Child's approach or signaling behaviors toward the caregiver Child's response to caregiver and whether exploration is reinitiated	3 minutes
		Caregiver leaves the room	
6	Child	Child's response to being left alone in the room Whether exploration is inhibited or continues	3 minutes
		Stranger reenters the room	
7	Child Stranger	Child's approach or signaling behaviors toward the stranger	3 minutes
		Caregiver reenters the room; stranger leaves	
8	Caregiver Child	Caregiver's behaviors to soothe the child, if needed Child's approach or signaling behaviors toward the caregiver Child's response to caregiver and whether exploration is reinitiated	3 minutes

Episode 5 sees the caregiver return to the room and comfort the child, if needed, and attempt to engage the child in play while the stranger discreetly leaves the room. This episode affords the opportunity to observe reunion behavior and whether the child's exploration can be reinitiated. In Ainsworth's studies, 78% of infants greeted their mothers upon their return, presumably viewing their mothers as a "safe haven" to which they could retreat and regain a sense of calming and safety. With distress alleviated, 96% went on to display some form of exploration, the mother having returned to the role of a secure base (Ainsworth et al., 1978/2015).

After spending 3 minutes with the child, the caregiver is signaled to leave the room in a calm manner, thus beginning Episode 6. This separation, with the child alone in the room, yielded the greatest frequency of distress induction, with 78% of infants crying at some point in the episode (Ainsworth et al., 1978/2015). The researchers ended the episode early in 53% of the cases because the crying exceeded the built-in termination rule.

In Episode 7, the stranger reenters the room and attempts to (a) soothe the child if they are upset or (b) engage the child in play. The return of the stranger did little to soothe upset infants, leading to the conclusion that the absence of the caregiver was driving the distress, not merely being alone in the room.

Finally, the caregiver returns and engages with the child as the stranger quietly exits the room, providing one last opportunity to observe reunion behavior and the resumption of exploration (Episode 8). Not surprisingly, given the level of distress observed in Episodes 6 and 7, infants displayed more pronounced attachment behavior during Episode 8 than during the reunion that occurred in Episode 5.[3]

Criticisms of the SSP

Developmental science advanced rapidly through the 1970s, and the advent of the SSP fit firmly within the empirical emphasis on observable behavior. Consequently, the SSP became a well-known laboratory technique, and, with its acceptance, attachment theory exploded in popularity. However, the SSP is not without critics. The most common criticism falls along ethical lines, with some objecting to the intentional induction of distress in infants. Attachment researchers respond by pointing out that such experiences are not uncommon in the everyday lives of infants and the distress is fleeting, with each episode lasting only a few minutes. In addition, Ainsworth was attentive to such concerns and specifically endorsed caregivers returning

[3]Direct comparisons showed that infants displayed considerably more proximity-seeking behaviors in response to separations in the laboratory than during separations in the home (Tracy et al., 1976).

to the room before the allotted time expired if the infant displayed signs of excessive distress. Given these considerations, the SSP is typically considered ethically acceptable in research contexts and is commonly approved by university ethics review boards.

Some objected to the SSP on the grounds of cultural appropriateness. Although experience observing infants in Uganda informed Ainsworth's design of the SSP, it is true that the procedure was initially validated with a collective total of 106 White, middle-class families in the Baltimore area. One early challenge to the SSP was a study from Japan that suggested Japanese infants display more intense crying and distress upon separation than American infants. Takahashi (1986) suggested it is uncommon in Japanese culture for mothers to separate from their infants for a significant length of time, likely resulting in the heightened degree of protest observed from the infants. While some pointed out that Takahashi did not implement the discontinuation rules defined by Ainsworth in *Patterns of Attachment* and the results were, therefore, unreliable (see Duschinsky, 2020), others argued that the behavior observed likely reflected differences in parenting practices between American and Japanese cultures (Rothbaum et al., 2000). Recent findings suggest the SSP is capable of sufficiently eliciting attachment behavior among Japanese infants (Kondo-Ikemura et al., 2018). Most likely, the expression of attachment behavior is determined by both universal evolutionarily derived needs and culturally specific norms of how such behavior may be expressed (Mesman et al., 2016). As such, the SSP may be expected to elicit behavior that displays cross-cultural similarities as well as intercultural and intracultural variation.

As the frequency of studies using the SSP increased, another criticism surfaced. Given the SSP was the only standardized tool available to elicit attachment behavior and was developed by one of the field's pioneers, some researchers came to view the SSP as authoritative and unerring. As a result, the outcome of an assessment procedure was conflated with the construct it was designed to measure. Much to Ainsworth's credit, she never intended for the SSP to be a standalone index of attachment behavior. She held great respect for naturalistic and ethnographic research, and the SSP was designed to supplement the intensive home observations of her Baltimore longitudinal study (Ainsworth et al., 1978/2015). Nonetheless, the increasing acceptance of the procedure within the field, the expediency with which it could be implemented in a laboratory, and academic pressures to consistently publish resulted in data obtained from the SSP often being presented as a conclusive assessment of attachment behavior. In time, the field gained a greater awareness of the need to develop other measures and developed tools to assess attachment behavior in naturalistic settings. One such tool was the Attachment Q-Sort, which is described in Box 2.1.

BOX 2.1

A CLOSER LOOK: THE ATTACHMENT Q-SORT

Everett Waters, a former student of Ainsworth's, noted that the Strange Situation Procedure (SSP) possessed certain shortcomings that limited research on attachment behavior. Primary among these were (a) that the categorical nature of SSP coding (e.g., secure, avoidant) prevented the types of fine-grained analyses that a continuous measure might provide, (b) that the SSP was inherently a laboratory procedure that could not be implemented in more naturalistic settings, and (c) that repeated administrations may result in habituation to the procedure and thereby limit the ability to examine changes in behavior over time. The Attachment Q-Sort (AQS) was offered as a potential solution to these problems (E. Waters & Deane, 1985). Q-sort methodology is an approach to coding observational data that involves sorting a set of descriptive items into separate piles based on how characteristic the items are of the encounter observed. The AQS includes 100 items, such as "Cries in response to separation" and "Easily comforted by adult," although 75- and 90-item versions are available. The items span the full range of behaviors one tries to observe during the SSP, including the child's response to separations and reunions, and exploration, but in a more naturalistic environment.

AQS items are written on small cards easily manipulated by a trained observer who enters unobtrusively into the environment, such as a home or school. Based on several hours of observation, and potentially multiple visits, the observer sorts the cards into nine piles from least characteristic of the child to most characteristic. Through an iterative process, the sort is completed once each of the piles contains an equal number of cards (e.g., nine piles of 10 cards for the 90-item version). Scoring rules offer multiple options for analysis, but the most common involves comparing the completed sort with a prototypical sort of a securely attached child developed based on the feedback of several experts, including Ainsworth herself. As with any correlation, the level of agreement between the observer-completed sort and the prototypical secure-child sort yields a score ranging from –1.0 (least characteristic) to +1.0 (most characteristic), resulting in a continuous measure of attachment security.

Initial examination suggested that the AQS distinguished between children classified as secure and insecure in the SSP (Vaughn & Waters, 1990). A meta-analysis by van IJzendoorn and colleagues (2004), examining 139 studies, showed a significant positive correlation of AQS scores

(*continues*)

BOX 2.1

A CLOSER LOOK: THE ATTACHMENT Q-SORT (*Continued*)

with security assessed in the SSP as well as a significant positive correlation with measures of caregiver sensitivity. These findings were confirmed by a more recent meta-analysis (Cadman et al., 2018). Given such positive findings, the AQS is generally accepted as a valid assessment of attachment security and is widely used in research contexts.

The AQS is not without limitations, however. Although the continuous nature of AQS scores is a strength in many respects, it also prevents the AQS from distinguishing between the subtypes of insecure attachment (i.e., avoidant, ambivalent). Similarly, there are no consensus recommendations for identifying disorganized attachment behavior, although results from the van IJzendoorn et al. (2004) meta-analysis suggested that disorganization observed in the SSP is commonly associated with very low scores on the AQS. Nonetheless, the AQS provided a significant boon to developmental attachment research as it allowed studies to move out of the laboratory and provided an additional mechanism for assessing attachment behavior.

ATTACHMENT SECURITY VERSUS INSECURITY

Ainsworth's use of separation procedures to study infant behavior was not particularly original (see van Rosmalen et al., 2015, for a review). What was innovative was her method of classifying the behavior observed. It was common in observational research of the time to conduct frequency counts of discrete behaviors; however, Ainsworth chose to examine the overall pattern of behavior displayed across the SSP. She discovered that the children in her samples generally fell into one of three discrete groups, with reunion behavior following separations from the mother particularly important for discerning categorization.

Secure Attachment Behavior

Across the initial validation studies of the SSP, Ainsworth et al. (1978/2015) found that 66% of the infants demonstrated a pattern of reunion behavior marked by clear proximity seeking and interaction with the mother, typically through crying, reaching, and/or physically walking toward her. Interestingly, while some of these children were distressed by the mother's departures, others seemed content to patiently look toward the door as if expecting her return. During stranger encounters, many of these children looked toward their mothers as a form of social referencing, seemingly to evaluate the level of threat. In short, these children appeared to be comforted (i.e., the attachment system was sufficiently inhibited or terminated) by the knowledge that their mother was available if needed, and, therefore, physical contact and proximity were not always necessary. These findings led to a reconsideration of the set-goal of the attachment system; instead of physical *proximity* to and contact with a caregiver, the emphasis was now placed on the child's perception of the *availability* of the caregiver.

Exploratory behavior was significantly more common, and more easily reestablished following reunion, among these infants when compared with those in the other two groups. Conceptually, it was deduced that these infants were secure in the knowledge that a trustworthy caregiver was available who could help effectively manage a stress-inducing situation, which allowed them to explore their environments. Preferring to use letters to denote the groups to avoid value judgments, Ainsworth labeled this group as "B." However, it would not be long before the display of proximity seeking, social referencing, and exploratory behavior was described as "secure," and the B group was alternatively branded the *secure* group.[4]

Research after Ainsworth's has provided considerable support for her description and conceptualization of secure attachment behavior. Large-scale studies and meta-analyses generally find that 60% to 65% of infants in normative samples are coded as displaying secure behavior in the SSP (NICHD Early Child Care Research Network, 1997; van IJzendoorn et al., 1999; Verhage et al., 2016). Multiple studies examined whether secure behavior in the SSP relates to child behavior in more naturalistic settings. For instance, Bick et al. (2012) found that children classified as secure in the SSP were significantly more likely to demonstrate similar forms of reunion behavior following a day in child care. Secure behaviors in the SSP are significantly associated with the display of similar behaviors in the home environment (van IJzendoorn et al., 2004).

[4]Ainsworth's system includes four different B subgroups denoting varying forms of secure behavior. These subgroups collectively constitute the higher order B group. Ainsworth's other two primary classifications (denoted "A" and "C") are each created from two subgroups. In published papers and common parlance of attachment research and theory it is common to hear only the higher order groups discussed.

Avoidant Attachment Behavior

The second most common pattern of behavior in Ainsworth's studies was marked by either avoidance of the mother during reunion episodes or initial approach toward the mother that transitioned to avoidance before significant physical contact (Ainsworth et al., 1978/2015). This pattern, labeled "A" or *avoidant*, suggested an underactivation of the attachment system resulting in an absence or aborted implementation of attachment behavior. However, there were indications that the attachment system was, indeed, sufficiently activated amongst these children. For one, data from the home observations of her Baltimore longitudinal study showed that children classified as avoidant were more likely than children classified as secure to cry when the mother left the room and cried for longer durations, suggesting separation distress (Ainsworth et al., 1978/2015). For another, avoidant infants exhibited increased heart rate during separations in the SSP, a sign of increased arousal (Sroufe & Waters, 1977). Exploratory behavior of avoidant children rarely engaged the caregiver, although infants did not resist physical contact initiated by the mother. Ainsworth and her team (1978/2015) concluded that reticence toward proximity seeking resulted in the complete or near complete inhibition of attachment behavior (i.e., minimization of attachment behavior).

One of the more striking concomitant correlates of avoidant attachment behavior in initial studies was an increased incidence of infant frustration and anger (see Ainsworth et al., 1978/2015). This finding led to clinical interest in children classified as avoidant and the hypothesis that avoidant attachment may suggest a predisposition to behavioral problems. Early studies attempting to link avoidant behavior to externalizing problems generally met with limited success (e.g., Fagot & Kavanagh, 1990), and clinical interest in the construct was soon eclipsed by the introduction of the disorganized classification (discussed later). Still, the prevalence of avoidant attachment in normative samples generally ranges from 14% to 22.5% (NICHD Early Child Care Research Network, 1997; van IJzendoorn et al., 1999; Verhage et al., 2016), making it possible in many studies to compare these children with those classified as secure.

Resistant/Ambivalent Attachment Behavior

A third pattern of behavior suggested a different form of insecurity. These infants showed intense distress during the separation episodes and displayed proximity-seeking behavior upon reunion but appeared frustrated or angry with the mother after making contact. While clearly seeking comfort from the caregiver, these infants appeared to resist the mothers' attempts to soothe them. During home observations these children displayed the longest duration of crying but were the least likely to follow the mother when she left the room or ask to be picked up when she returned (Ainsworth et al., 1978/2015). Consequently, this pattern would be termed *ambivalent* or *resistant* attachment behavior (labeled "C").

Infants in the ambivalent group showed other differences from those in the secure and avoidant groups. An apparent hyperfocus on the mother's behavior seemingly caused significant anxiety during separation as well as a relative inability to turn attentional resources toward exploring the room during preseparation and postreunion episodes. Ainsworth et al. (1978/2015) suggested the ambivalent behaviors of these infants may reflect uncertainty regarding the mother's ability to effectively assuage distress, resulting in infants both desperately seeking to maintain proximity to her and remaining wary of her attempts to comfort (i.e., maximization of attachment behavior).

The ambivalent pattern was somewhat rare in Ainsworth's samples and in later research, accounting for approximately 9% to 17% of infants (e.g., van IJzendoorn et al., 1999; Verhage et al., 2016), and the group is considered fairly heterogeneous. As a result, although the ambivalent pattern is still coded and classified in contemporary studies, it is rarely a focus of research. Often children classified as ambivalent are grouped together with those classified as avoidant to form a superordinate "insecure" group.

ATTACHMENT ORGANIZATION VERSUS DISORGANIZATION

The three primary patterns of attachment behavior are considered structured and coherent attempts to maintain proximity to a caregiver. Although the avoidant and ambivalent patterns suggest uncertainty as to whether the caregiver is available and might respond effectively to distress, the behaviors nonetheless appear organized and goal corrected based on the responses of the caregivers (see the Determinants of Attachment Behavior section later). Mary Main, a student of Ainsworth's, hypothesized the existence of other patterns of attachment behavior that might be identified given a sufficiently large sample.

As a new faculty member at the University of California, Main initiated the Berkeley Longitudinal Study and recruited 189 infants and their caregivers from "low-risk" families (e.g., middle and upper class). To her surprise, she was unable to identify any additional coherent patterns of behavior amongst her sample. However, unlike earlier researchers, Main did not attempt to force outlying behaviors into one of the three identified categories and chose instead to consider these infants "unclassified" (Main & Weston, 1981). These nonconforming behaviors were heterogeneous and difficult to consider as a coherent classification themselves.

The breakthrough came in 1986 when Main and her student, Judith Solomon, published a chapter exploring these "unclassifiable" behaviors (Main & Solomon, 1986). They surmised that the core feature was lack of a behavioral goal, marked by a series of bizarre and often contradictory actions. They described how infants often appeared dazed, performed strange behaviors without apparent purpose (e.g., stereotypies, turning in circles), showed slowed or frozen movement, and/or attempted to seek proximity while appearing frightened. In short, as Main would later summarize,

> The most striking theme running through these behaviors was "disorganization," or an observed contradiction or lack of explicability in movement pattern. The term "disorientation" was added to describe behaviors that simply indicated a lack of orientation to the present environment (e.g., trance-like expressions). (Main et al., 2005, p. 280)

Main and Solomon (1990) published procedures for identifying *disorganized* behavior (labeled "D").[5] Rather than presenting a coherent behavioral phenotype, they presented seven different categories of disorganization based on theme (e.g., sequential display of contradictory behavior patterns, direct indices of apprehension regarding the parent). Coders make a global determination of disorganization based on the quantity and/or extremity of behaviors observed. If the resulting score reaches a threshold, then a primary classification of D is assigned; however, the coder is encouraged to provide a secondary "best-fitting" classification (i.e., A, B, C). This approach yields several analytic options for examining behavior in the SSP: the four-way scheme (A, B, C, D), organized (A, B, C) versus disorganized, or secure versus insecure (A, C, D).

In normative, "low-risk" samples (e.g., nonclinical, middle class), the prevalence of the D classification typically is 15% to 20% of infants. However, among "at-risk" groups, the percentage of cases classified D increases exponentially. A widely cited meta-analysis estimated the prevalence of D classification in lower socioeconomic samples as approximately 34%, among children of mothers with substance use problems as 43%, and among infants of maltreating parents as high as 77% (van IJzendoorn et al., 1999).

---

[5]The full term "disorganized/disoriented" is often shortened to "disorganized."

DETERMINANTS OF ATTACHMENT BEHAVIOR

Attachment classifications have become nearly synonymous with attachment theory itself; however, it is important to remember that attachment behavior in the SSP is conceived as only one component of a much more complex parent–child system. Bowlby hypothesized that the quality of the caregiving provided was the underlying factor in the emergence of attachment behavior, and Ainsworth expanded on that postulation. Ongoing research continues to refine our understanding of the development of attachment behavior and the role caregivers play.

Maternal Responsiveness and Sensitivity

Ainsworth identified numerous dimensions of caregiving with potential relevance to the development of infant attachment behavior and constructed scales to quantify these attributes. Much of her initial work centered on the concepts of parental responsiveness to signs of infant distress. During home observations in the Baltimore study, she counted the number of infant crying episodes and the number of times the mother responded. The more a mother ignored infant distress in any given quarter of the first year of life, the more crying episodes the baby displayed the following quarter. The longer it took a mother to respond to a crying infant, the longer the duration of crying in subsequent months (Bell & Ainsworth, 1972).

A second key dimension of caregiving for Ainsworth involved the type of care provided once a mother responded to a distressed infant. Physical contact (e.g., hugging, picking up) as a method of soothing a distressed child was foremost in the minds of both Bowlby and Ainsworth, partially owning to Harlow's demonstrations of the importance of contact comfort. However, the metaphorical net was cast much wider, and observers took note of whether the mother seemed to interpret the signals of the distressed child accurately, accepted the child's need for comfort, and implemented an effective means of calming. Collectively, these qualities were referred to as *sensitivity*. In the Baltimore study, mothers scoring higher for sensitivity had children who cried less during separations and were more accepting of attempts to comfort during reunions (Stayton & Ainsworth, 1973).

Ainsworth discovered that responsive and sensitive mothers were more likely to have infants classified as secure in the SSP at 12 months of age. Thus, secure attachment was hypothesized to develop through repeated experiences of having a caregiver who both responds to signals of distress and provides an effective method of alleviating that distress (Ainsworth et al., 1978/2015).

Conceptually, the infant learns that a specific caregiver is available and that soothing will be provided when needed. Being confident in such knowledge yields secure attachment behavior, a greater frequency and duration of exploratory behavior, less concern at the presence of a stranger, and quicker and more effective alleviation of distress upon reunion.

Ainsworth's data also allowed her to isolate caregiving qualities that predicted insecure forms of attachment behavior. Mothers of avoidant infants not only were less responsive and less sensitive but scored the lowest on a scale of acceptance, suggesting rejection of infant signals for comfort and interaction. There were indications these mothers were more likely to appear annoyed with a baby's cries. Viewed from this context, the infant's avoidant behavior became more understandable: Crying and other signals of distress were commonly met with a hostile response from the caregiver that may be perceived as rejection by the infant (Ainsworth et al., 1978/2015). Thus, these infants learned to minimize their displays of attachment behavior and maintain their distance from their mothers under moments of distress as the best way to promote maternal availability.

Mothers of children displaying ambivalent behavior in the SSP displayed a different pattern of caregiving. While these mothers were noted as less responsive, less sensitive, and less accepting when compared to the mothers of secure children, they were not rejecting of infant signals and did not appear bothered by their mothering role, behaviors seen in the caregivers of avoidant infants. There were, however, peculiarities in the way they interacted with their children. They did not avoid physical contact, but it was marked by a general lack of affection, and these mothers commonly seemed to implement a routinized form of caregiving rather than assessing and responding to the needs of the child. In addition, the timing was incongruent with the infant's needs, as mothers often terminated contact before their child was sufficiently calmed (Ainsworth et al., 1978/2015). Conceptually, such inconsistent caregiving resulted in exaggerated signals of distress from the infant to make needs more clearly perceptible. Uncertainty of the mother's availability prompts the infant to maximize attachment behavior and resembles a form of preoccupation with maintaining proximity, resulting in both separation anxiety and curtailing of exploration. When separations do occur, proximity seeking at reunion is tempered by uncertainty of the mother's response.

It was not long before an expanding cadre of researchers replicated Ainsworth's findings and applied her methods to more diverse populations. Many of the early reports established the relationship between parental responsiveness and sensitivity and the development of secure attachment behavior. The strength of the relationships, however, were not typically to the level seen in Ainsworth's Baltimore study ($r = .78$; Ainsworth et al., 1987/2015). De Wolff and van IJzendoorn (1997) summarized 66 studies that examined various forms of parental behavior. Results showed sensitivity was one of the parental factors most strongly related to the development of attachment security. However, the strength of the relationship was small to medium in size ($r = .22$) and led the researchers to opine that "sensitivity has lost its privileged position as the only important causal factor" (p. 585).

A more recent review suggested that De Wolff and van IJzendoorn used an overly restrictive definition of sensitivity, miscategorizing analogous constructs (i.e., mutuality, synchrony), and may have correspondingly underestimated its relationship with attachment security (Nievar & Becker, 2008). Reanalyzing the De Wolff and van IJzendoorn data with the new grouping yielded a slightly higher, though still moderate, effect for the impact of sensitivity on attachment security ($r = .30$). Regardless of how one defines sensitivity and parses the data, two clear conclusions emerge from this body of research. First, parental attention to infant cues and responding in a way that effectively soothes the distressed infant is a replicated factor that predicts attachment security. Second, parental sensitivity itself cannot account for the majority of variance in attachment security, and other factors must be explored.

Child Abuse and Frightening Parental Behavior

Ainsworth and her students' initial studies examined samples that were generally considered at low risk for aberrant parenting. However, other researchers sought to understand how various forms of risk might affect both parenting and attachment behavior. Like Ainsworth, Mary Main believed that hostility from the parent underlies avoidant attachment behavior. To explore the idea, Judith Solomon and another of Main's students, Carol George, examined 10 toddlers who experienced physical abuse and a matched control group in a day care setting. The abused children often displayed behaviors that appeared to suggest a significant approach–avoidance conflict, such as approaching a teacher but refusing to make eye contact, as if scared. In addition, data from the Berkeley Longitudinal Study suggested a relationship between maltreatment and severe conflictual behavior in the SSP. By the time that Main and her team began describing these atypical attachment behaviors as disorganized in the mid-1980s, the hypothesis was established that child abuse may be a prominent etiological cause (see Duschinsky, 2020, for a discussion of these early efforts).

Data connecting maltreatment to disorganized attachment soon emerged. Dante Cicchetti initiated a small longitudinal study at Harvard to examine the developmental impact of child maltreatment, particularly physical abuse and neglect (V. Carlson et al., 1989). His team administered the SSP to 22 maltreated infants and 22 matched controls at 12 months of age, all from low socioeconomic strata. After learning of the Main and Solomon (1990) procedures for coding disorganized behavior, they reanalyzed their observations and found that 82% of the maltreated children met criteria for a D classification while only 19% of the comparison children met the criteria.

In a key meta-analysis on disorganized attachment, researchers identified five studies that confirmed the link between maltreatment and disorganized behavior (van IJzendoorn et al., 1999). Across these studies, 48% of maltreated children and 17% of comparison children were classified as D. A more recent review, including seven samples of maltreated children ($n = 392$), found an extremely large effect for maltreatment in predicting a D classification ($d = 2.19$; Cyr et al., 2010). Because of such findings, it is generally regarded that maltreatment is a potent risk factor for the development of disorganized attachment behavior.

However, maltreatment was not the only hypothesized etiological mechanism in the development of disorganized attachment behavior. Main found it unlikely that all cases of disorganization within the Berkeley study were attributed to experiences such as physical abuse and neglect, as the sample was from fairly affluent backgrounds (Main & Hesse, 1990). This led to the examination of other potential factors that may portend significant problems with the development of organized attachment behavior. Early studies suggested a link between disorganized behavior and parental depression (Lyons-Ruth et al., 1990) and the parent's experience losing a caregiver early in life (Main & Solomon, 1990). Nonetheless, the relationship between parental depression and a D classification is exceptionally weak ($r = .06$; van IJzendoorn et al., 1999), while the relationship of a caregiver's own history of loss and/or trauma to a D classification is significantly more robust ($r = .21–.31$; van IJzendoorn, 1995).[6]

Alongside the instructions for coding disorganized behavior, Main teamed with her partner Erik Hesse (Main & Hesse, 1990) to provide a theory of how disorganized behavior develops. They proposed that a caregiver whose behavior frightens or alarms the child creates an unresolvable paradox: The child's attachment system, designed to achieve a sense of security, is directing

[6]The concept of unresolved parental loss and its relation to parenting is discussed in more detail in Chapter 5.

attachment behavior toward a caregiver who is simultaneously a source of danger. While a maltreating caregiver certainly fits within this mold, other types of *frightening behavior* may result in similar consequences. For instance, a caregiver that displays fits of rage, whether directed toward the child or not, or irrational and confusing behavior, such as might be expected from individuals with substance abuse problems, may shape disorganized attachment behavior. To spur their research, they developed a coding system for parent–child observations to identify frightening forms of caregiving, simply abbreviated FR (see Abrams et al., 2006). Karlen Lyons-Ruth expanded the FR system by including additional aspects of perceived frightening behavior in a scheme she referred to as the Atypical Maternal Behavior Instrument for Assessment and Classification (AMBIANCE; Bronfman et al., 1993).[7]

Research using the FR and AMBIANCE systems allowed for in-depth examination of the extent to which anomalous parental behavior was a direct cause of disorganized attachment behavior among infants. Across studies, these types of disconcerting parental behaviors were, indeed, related to the D classification, and the effect was medium in strength ($r = .34$; Madigan et al., 2006). A weak association of parental insensitivity with disorganization ($r = .10$; van IJzendoorn et al., 1999) suggests that the forms of atypical and alarming parenting indexed by the FR and AMBIANCE systems are not simply extreme forms of parental insensitivity but a unique construct.

Although the role of maltreating and frightening parental behavior historically occupied a prominent place in theoretical and empirical work on the etiology of disorganized behavior, it is important to emphasize that D behavior can occur in the absence of maltreatment and/or frightening parental behavior. Other explanations are mentioned later in this chapter and receive additional attention in Chapters 5 and 6 in this volume.

Nonmaternal and Multiple Caregivers

The vast majority of research examining attachment behavior has involved the child's maternal figure, but data show that administration of the SSP and the coding of attachment behavior is no more difficult with fathers than with mothers. However, studies suggest interesting results regarding the role of paternal sensitivity. A meta-analysis of 16 separate samples found a relatively weak association between paternal sensitivity and infant attachment

[7]Training in the FR system is rare, while training in the AMBIANCE system is more common. This state of affairs has led to greater dissemination and exploration of the AMBIANCE system, even though research suggests the two systems are comparable in their ability to predict disorganized behavior (Madigan et al., 2006).

security ($r = .12$; Lucassen et al., 2011), certainly weaker than the relationship commonly seen for maternal sensitivity ($r = .22 - .30$; De Wolff & van IJzendoorn, 1997; Nievar & Becker, 2008). Much of this difference appears due to disparities in time and interaction with the infant, which still trend in favor of mothers (Branger et al., 2019). Nonetheless, these studies demonstrate that fathers can serve as effective safe havens and secure bases (i.e., *attachment figures*) for young children.

Attachment research with fathers revealed another important finding: The infant's classification with the mother in the SSP is not related to classification with the father. Across 11 studies, Fox et al. (1991) found the concordance rate of mother–infant and father–infant attachment was 58%, as many children demonstrated different forms of attachment behavior (i.e., secure, avoidant, ambivalent) with different caregivers. A later review found moderate concordance across caregivers ($r = .17$; van IJzendoorn & De Wolff, 1997). As for the D classification, disorganized behavior with one caregiver appears largely independent of disorganization displayed with a different caregiver ($r = .10$; van IJzendoorn et al., 1999).

Over time, researchers expanded their focus to determine the potential influence of other individuals who are a regular part of a young child's life. Studying child care providers was a natural next step in this evolution. Studies demonstrated that infants may display attachment behavior toward child care providers; however, children are generally less likely to display secure attachment behavior toward the provider in the SSP (42%) than toward mothers (60.2%) or fathers (66.2%; Ahnert et al., 2006). Ahnert (2021) suggested that the lower likelihood of secure attachment toward a care provider may be a function of the group-based nature of child care settings and that the child's perception of the caregiver may be shaped primarily through observational learning rather than repeated experiences of one-on-one interaction. Box 2.2 reviews an influential study of the developmental impacts of early child care, conducted by the National Institute of Child Health and Human Development.

In an interesting application of attachment theory, Abraham Sagi-Schwartz and colleagues examined the development of attachment security among children living at an Israeli kibbutz. Kibbutzim are collectivistic communities with responsibilities shared amongst the members, typically numbering in the hundreds. Many daily living activities (e.g., eating meals, sleeping) occur outside of the biological family's home and are coordinated by the designated caregivers. Sagi and colleagues (1985) conducted three separate SSP observations with 86 kibbutz infants, each time with a different caregiver. They found that 56% of the children were classified as securely attached

BOX 2.2

A CLOSER LOOK: THE NICHD STUDY OF EARLY CHILD CARE

Throughout the 1980s, a growing number of children attended some form of child care, largely due to an increasing number of women entering the workforce. There was growing concern about the impact that child care might have on children and their future development. While much of the concern was the result of long-standing gender roles, attachment theory was used in some quarters to argue that the science of child development suggested the importance of mothers staying home to raise children. In 1991, the National Institute of Child Health and Human Development (NICHD) assembled a team of researchers to determine the impact, if any, that child care played in development.

The NICHD Study of Early Child Care and Youth Development (SECCYD; NICHD Early Child Care Research Network, 1997) recruited 1,364 infants approximately 1 month of age, and their families, to participate in a prospective study that continued through adolescence. The study was carried out at 10 sites across the United States and included a diverse sample to allow for an examination of various forms of family constellations, parent characteristics, and cultural factors. The research team included experts in various areas of child development, including several prominent attachment researchers.

Results from the SECCYD found no evidence that insecure attachment among 15-month-olds was directly related to being placed in child care (NICHD Early Child Care Research Network, 1997). Rather, a number of interaction effects were present. For instance, a greater number of hours in child care predicted insecure attachment only in combination with higher rates of insensitivity from the mother. Similar findings were present when attachment behavior was observed at age 3 years: Longer periods of time in child care predicted insecure attachment when combined with greater maternal insensitivity (NICHD Early Child Care Research Network, 2001). Across findings, maternal insensitivity was the linchpin in determining whether other factors contributed to attachment insecurity.

Importantly, the data from the SECCYD were made available to researchers, providing a wealth of information for the field of attachment. Incorporation of the SSP at the 15-month assessment contributed substantially to the accumulation of data on the distribution of attachment classifications, the conceptualization of attachment security, and the impact of maternal sensitivity. Studies examining the long-term impact of infant and preschool attachment on developmental and clinical outcomes, based on the SECCYD data, are still being published.

with their mothers, 65% with their fathers, and 52% with a surrogate. The percentage of infants demonstrating secure attachment with their mothers was significantly lower than a comparison sample of 36 non-kibbutz Israeli children recruited for comparison (81%). Later research qualified this finding. Sagi et al. (1994) compared infants from a kibbutz that allowed sleeping with one's parents to infants residing at a kibbutz requiring communal sleeping. Infants who slept with their parents were more likely to be securely attached to their mothers (80%) than those in the communal sleeping group (48%) and less likely to display disorganization (32% vs. 44%, respectively).

Two important lessons arise from research on nonmaternal and multiple caregivers. First, attachment behavior is not a static trait internal to the child, as is often colloquially stated, but rather is relationship specific. As such, it is technically incomplete to state that "the child displays secure attachment behavior," for instance, as it fails to identify the caregiver toward whom the child displays the behavior. Attachment researchers are often quite deliberate in identifying the caregiver included in a given study and to whom the results of the SSP, the AQS, or another metric of attachment behavior are referenced. Second, the modest concordance of attachment behavior toward two different caregivers is largely a factor of the significant differences likely to occur between the caregivers themselves, such as the quality and quantity of time spent with the child, parenting ability and sensitivity, the individualized nature of the care provided, and the accessibility of the caregiver in times of need.

Environmental Factors and the Stability of Attachment Behavior

Whether attachment behavior is stable over time is a critically important question for understanding its influence on development, the validity of the larger field of attachment theory, and the development of interventions that aim to change attachment behavior. In one of the validation studies of the SSP ($n = 23$), Ainsworth noted stability of attachment classification was 57% when the procedure was repeated 2 weeks after the initial observation (Ainsworth et al., 1978/2015). The brief period between observations and the high likelihood of habituation to the procedure was partially credited for the lack of consistency.

To address the potential influence of practice effects, other researchers examined stability of attachment classification within the SSP with longer time between assessments. Connell (1977) examined infants at 12 and 18 months and found approximately 83% of infants were classified in the same category at both assessments. E. Waters (1978) conducted a similar study and found stability to be 96% in his sample. In both the Connell and Waters samples, the stability of those originally classified as secure was higher than those classified insecure.

In the seminal Minnesota Study of Risk and Adaptation (Sroufe et al., 2005b), 100 infants from low socioeconomic strata were observed in the SSP at 12 and 18 months of age (see Box 2.3 for a more detailed discussion). The stability rate was only 62%, substantially different from the findings of the Connell or Waters samples, although the highest stability rate continued to be for those originally identified as secure (68%; Vaughn et al., 1979). Such conflicting reports led to additional investigations in the ensuing years. In general, such studies typically document overall stability estimates between 50% and 60%, with greater stability among those initially classified as secure (e.g., Belsky et al., 1996). For the D classification, results generally show a significant, though moderate, rate of concordance when observed at two different time points (van IJzendoorn et al., 1999). A later meta-analysis confirmed these findings: There is a statistically significant concordance rate of attachment classification over time (i.e., stability), the strength of that relationship is typically moderate (50.7%), and the secure classification is considerably more stable (67%) than other categories (Opie et al., 2021).

Studies investigating stability typically examine potential reasons that changes in classification might occur. Vaughn et al. (1979), in their at-risk sample, found that a change from secure to insecure after 6 months was predicted by the caregiver reporting a greater number of stressful life events. A series of studies documented a higher likelihood of being classified insecure toward the mother when the mother reported low levels of marital or social support, high stress, and depression (Atkinson, Paglia, et al., 2000). It should not be surprising that such factors are also related to low maternal sensitivity (Bernard et al., 2018; Booth et al., 2018). Such findings suggest that environmental factors are related to attachment security as a result of their impact on the quality of caregiving provided.

Changes in parenting, including sensitivity, may occur as stress alleviates or life circumstances improve. Of course, such factors may also worsen or present anew, creating a tenser home environment and reducing the quantity and/or quality of parent–child interactions. The potential for such environmental changes to affect attachment security is underlined by repeated findings that assessments of maternal sensitivity are more predictive of attachment security when they occur concurrently with the attachment observation as opposed to at some point in the past (Atkinson, Niccols, et al., 2000). As such, it is important to keep in mind that attachment behavior is a snapshot in time of a child's understanding of the caregiver as a safe haven and secure

BOX 2.3

A CLOSER LOOK: THE MINNESOTA STUDY OF RISK AND ADAPTATION

In the late 1970s, Byron Egeland and his colleagues at the University of Minnesota asked a straightforward question they knew came with an extremely complex answer: "What makes parents act in maltreating ways toward their infant children?" They recruited a sample of 240 first-time mothers receiving public assistance for medical care. Most of the mothers were unmarried, only 59% completed high school, and approximately 50% were teenagers. This high-risk sample was chosen to shine a spotlight on differences in parenting that may occur within a disadvantaged background in the hopes of identifying specific factors underlying maltreatment. They interviewed the mothers before their child's birth to assess a diversity of variables, including personality, depression, and perceptions of children and parenting, and they followed up with the children at multiple points in the first 2 years of life (Sroufe et al., 2005a).

The researchers assessed various aspects of cognitive, physical, social, and emotional development; they administered and coded the Strange Situation Procedure (SSP) when the children were 12 and 18 months of age. The findings were instructive and provided some of the earliest confirmatory evidence of Ainsworth's initial findings. Within their sample, 55% of infants were classified as secure, with 22% avoidant and 23% ambivalent (Sroufe et al., 2005a). Interestingly, they found that mothers of securely attached 12-month-olds were more sensitive and cooperative with their babies during observations at the 6-month assessment. They also found that changing from a secure attachment at 12 months to an insecure attachment at 18 months was predicted by maternal factors, such as aggressiveness and little interest when interacting with the baby. In addition, changes in life stress in the 6-month interim predicted a change to insecure, but the mother residing with a partner was a protective factor (Egeland & Farber, 1984). The results were a striking endorsement that maternal care is influential in shaping infant attachment behavior and underlined the importance of the larger ecology of the dyad.

Following the advent of the disorganized classification, the researchers reviewed their videotapes of the SSP and reclassified 35% of the observations at 12 months of age, as well as 43% of the observations that occurred at 18 months, into the D category (E. A. Carlson, 1998). Results showed that many birth-related and maternal history variables were not significant predictors of the D pattern (e.g., pregnancy or delivery complications, maternal substance use); however, poor quality of caregiving, abuse, and

BOX 2.3

A CLOSER LOOK: THE MINNESOTA STUDY OF RISK AND ADAPTATION (*Continued*)

maternal relationship status were related. These findings confirmed those emerging at the time showing frightening parental behavior, particularly abuse, was a common antecedent of disorganized attachment, with stress and lack of support as more distal causes.

Realizing the significant implications of their study, the researchers shifted focus to examine developmental progression beyond infancy (Sroufe et al., 2005a). Participants were followed and assessments were added in the preschool, school-age, and adolescent years, and attachment continued to be a prominent conceptual framework throughout the study. This study design allowed for examination of the ways in which early attachment behavior predicted later forms of social and emotional functioning, including the onset of psychopathology, and how attachment behavior was related to other attachment-related constructs.

base. To the extent that environmental factors and parenting competence remain stable, attachment behavior may be expected to remain stable; to the extent these factors change, attachment behavior also may be expected to change. Such findings provide the foundation for clinical intervention in the first years of life (see Chapter 6).

One important caveat should be added to this discussion of environmental factors. Evidence suggests that insecure and disorganized attachments are more likely to occur among infants from lower socioeconomic levels (Belsky, 1996; Cyr et al., 2010). The accumulation of stress and challenges (e.g., mental illness, substance use) may exert a detrimental effect on the caregiver's ability to remain sensitive during interactions with the child. However, maternal sensitivity is more weakly related to attachment security among low socioeconomic samples (De Wolff & van IJzendoorn, 1997), suggesting that low socioeconomic status confers additional risks outside of the quality of caregiving provided. Consider the evidence discussed earlier regarding the quality and quantity of time spent with a child. Although a caregiver may present in the SSP as sufficiently sensitive and may genuinely enjoy interacting with the child, if that caregiver is working two jobs and caring for multiple children, for instance, the child's understanding of the caregiver as a safe haven or secure base may be limited.

Temperament and Genetics

Temperament was a prominent topic of developmental research during the 1970s, and researchers quickly suggested that differences in attachment behavior may reflect a child's innate emotional reactivity more than they reflect the caregiving received. A multitude of studies were conducted to test whether differences in attachment behavior were reducible to variations in temperament. Across studies encompassing well over 11,000 children, the relationship of temperament to attachment security was found to be very small ($d = .14$), with no discernible relationship found to attachment organization ($d = .11$; Groh et al., 2017). So definitive were such findings that temperament is rarely discussed today as a significant antecedent of attachment behavior.

As research was dispelling the suggestion that attachment behavior is largely a function of temperament, genetic studies emerged. The results of the few twin studies available do not suggest significant differences in attachment security or organization between monozygotic and dizygotic siblings, implying little genetic contribution (Fearon et al., 2006; Roisman & Fraley, 2008). Rather, shared environment appears significantly more influential, and parental sensitivity is a prominent component of that shared environment. Molecular genetics research investigated the potential influence of specific candidate genes, particularly those related to the functioning of dopamine, serotonin, and oxytocin (Frigerio et al., 2009; Luijk et al., 2011). With few exceptions, these studies have not yielded replicated findings suggesting a direct link between specific alleles and attachment security or organization.

Given the well-established influence of caregiving on attachment behavior, examination of gene–environment interactions has become more common in recent years. One study suggested that infants with the short allele of the serotonin transporter gene (*5-HTTLPR*) may be more likely to develop attachment insecurity when raised with a caregiver displaying lower levels of sensitivity (Barry et al., 2008); however, this finding was not replicated when researchers examined data from the Minnesota Study of Risk and Adaptation (Raby et al., 2012) or from other longitudinal data sets (Luijk et al., 2011). Similar mixed findings are present with regard to a dopamine receptor gene (*DRD4*; e.g., van IJzendoorn & Bakermans-Kranenburg, 2006; Luijk et al., 2011).

Belsky (1997) suggested a different take on the role of genes, a concept termed *differential susceptibility*. As opposed to the more common diathesis–stress understanding of gene–environment interactions, Belsky's perspective suggests that genetic constitution determines the extent to which one's development may be influenced by the environment. For instance, the short allele of the *5-HTTLPR* may predict attachment insecurity when the child is exposed to insensitive caregiving and attachment security when the child receives sensitive caregiving; individuals with two long alleles may be relatively resistant to the influence of caregiver sensitivity. Although evidence for the differential susceptibility hypothesis is growing in relation to various developmental outcomes (Slagt et al., 2016; van IJzendoorn & Bakermans-Kranenburg, 2015), studies examining its relation to attachment behavior are few (see Bakermans-Kranenburg & van IJzendoorn, 2016, for a review).

THE DEVELOPMENT OF ATTACHMENT BEHAVIOR IN INFANCY AND EARLY CHILDHOOD

Newborn infants will accept care from practically any individual who satisfies basic biological needs, but Ainsworth's studies clearly showed that termination of the attachment system at 12 months of age requires the presence of a specific, discriminated individual. It was evident that a process of differentiation occurs at some point in the first year of life. Bowlby (1958) originally hypothesized that attachment behavior could not occur in a fully discriminated form until object permanence developed, around the age of 9 months, and identified a series of phases that occur along the path to its emergence.

Bowlby (1969/1982) proposed that babies enter the world with limited ability to discriminate amongst caregivers and will accept comforting, feeding, and interaction from whomever may provide it. To elicit care, newborn infants must rely largely on crying, with the repertoire of attachment behaviors growing over the coming months. We now know that babies are generally born equipped with other tools, including the ability to discern the voice of their own mothers (Kisilevsky et al., 2003) and to learn the smell of their mothers within days to weeks following birth (Porter & Winberg, 1999). While these sensory experiences may elicit limited behavioral responses from newborns and suggest rudimentary recognition of familiarity, any number of potential caregivers can soothe a neonate in distress, and the presence of the mother is not required. These interactions represent the newborn's initial trials of self-regulation: A need is experienced and, while some potential orienting may occur, crying is initiated to elicit an external calming response from any available individual.

By 3 months of age, the infant has begun reaching, grabbing, and smiling to provoke responses from a caregiver; these behaviors are attempts to engage in social interaction. In addition, infants are capable of recognizing faces, a skill that was limited by poor visual acuity in the first weeks of life. However, infants interact with their mothers and strangers in a similar manner (Bigelow

& DeCoste, 2003), and studies have not found a link between parental sensitivity and infant stress regulation at this age (Thompson & Trevathan, 2008). While social interaction is more prevalent, it is premature to suggest a child "is attached to" or is displaying a preference for a specific caregiver. Rather, the child is interacting in a more sociable way and learning from repeated experiences with different individuals.

The first observance of a clearly discriminated attachment figure typically occurs when the infant is between 7 and 9 months of age. At this point the infant's prior experiences yield a clear preference for certain individuals, and parental sensitivity may be a salient factor (Thompson & Trevathan, 2009). This is a time of immense growth in multiple physical and psychological capacities, including locomotion, exploration, depth perception, sociability, and communication. As the child ventures out into the world, a discriminated attachment figure is an invaluable asset as it enables greater engagement with the environment. At the same time, experiences with one's environment and the caregiver's responses to various situations provides feedback to the attachment system, which is continually undergoing refinement.

It is not a coincidence that stranger anxiety begins to emerge when the infant is around 7 to 9 months of age. As infants develop the ability to discriminate among individuals, familiarity breeds comfort and security while strangers elicit uncertainty and wariness. Repeated experiences with a sensitive caregiver allow the child to develop confidence in such situations, and stranger anxiety typically abates by 2 years of age. Separation anxiety can be understood in much the same fashion. First becoming apparent around the same time as stranger anxiety, separation anxiety suggests that the environment itself engenders a sense of threat or uneasiness that is effectively ameliorated by maintaining proximity to a discriminated caregiver. As demonstrated by Ainsworth et al. (1978/2015) and others since (e.g., Jacobson & Wille, 1984), securely attached infants are better able to tolerate separation from caregivers than their insecurely attached peers.

ATTACHMENT BEHAVIOR IN THE PRESCHOOL YEARS

Although the vast majority of research on attachment behavior occurs with children younger than 3 years of age, it is worth noting that some limited findings are available with preschool-age children. As children move out of infancy and development yields new abilities and challenges, researchers must adapt their methods to examine changes in attachment behavior. The AQS is often used with minor adaptations to examine security in various settings, but continuing to use the SSP requires more significant revision. Although the SSP was designed for children between 12 and 30 months of age, various groups developed modified forms of the SSP for use with preschoolers. The most popular version is the Preschool Attachment Classification System (PACS; Cassidy et al., 1992). Given that the intensity and duration of separation and stranger anxiety are comparatively less among preschoolers (ages 3–5 years), the PACS often omits the stranger-encounter episodes and replaces them with simply leaving the child alone in the room. In addition, the classification system focuses specifically on the behavior of the child during reunion episodes.

The PACS classifications of secure and insecure behavior display modest correlations with security scores from the AQS (van IJzendoorn et al., 2004), but attachment security and organization in PACS are related to caregiving behavior, including sensitivity, warmth, and engagement (Moss et al., 2004; NICHD Early Child Care Research Network, 2001). In addition, continuity from SSP classification in infancy to a comparable classification in the preschool years is observed, although small to moderate in strength (Pinquart et al., 2013). Studies examining stability across developmental periods identified several factors in the child's environment that predict change in classification from infancy to preschool. For instance, Levendosky and colleagues (2011) found that children who were secure at 1 year and insecure at 4 years were likely to come from a home that experienced domestic violence during the interim. Fish (2004) showed that infants initially classified as insecure at age 1 were more likely to move to secure at age 4 if living in a home with a stable caregiving presence, parental social support, and higher socioeconomic status. These findings lend credence to the hypothesis that the behavior observed during the preschool years using the PACS or AQS is, indeed, conceptually linked to the attachment behavior observed during the infancy and toddler years using the AQS or SSP.

CONCLUSION

The work of Ainsworth and scores of other investigators effectively established the field of attachment research. Their work not only demonstrated the validity of the "attachment behavior" concept but also developed psychometrically reliable forms of assessing it, identified its proximal (e.g., caregiving) and distal (e.g., caregiver stress) antecedents, and explored its genetic underpinnings. In the process, they generated significant support for the tenets of attachment as a broad theory of social–emotional development. Of course, demonstrating the utility of this work for the wider field of developmental science required not only connecting early attachment behavior to later outcomes but also providing an explanation for how it exerts a lasting effect. This topic is the focus of Chapter 3 in this volume.

RESOURCES

Training Resources

- **Attachment Training:** Training in the administration and coding of the SSP is conducted periodically through this organization. They also coordinate training on the Adult Attachment Interview (AAI). More information can be obtained on their website: https://attachment-training.com/
- **Attachment Theory & Research at Stony Brook:** The faculty webpage of Everett Waters and his colleagues at the State University of New York at Stony Brook contains a wealth of resources on attachment, including a "measurement library" containing information about the administration and scoring of the AQS. The webpage can be accessed at http://www.psychology.sunysb.edu/attachment/

Suggested Further Reading

Ainsworth, M. D. S., Blehar, M. C., Waters, E., & Wall, S. N. (2015). *Patterns of attachment: A psychological study of the strange situation*. Taylor & Francis (Psychology Press). (Original work published 1978)
This is Ainsworth's classic volume describing the administration of the SSP, the identification of the secure and insecure classifications, and the results of multiple validation studies. The book is fairly technical and provides the results of many statistical analyses.

Sroufe, L. A., Egeland, B., Carlson, E. A., & Collins, W. A. (2005). *The development of the person: The Minnesota Study of Risk and Adaptation from birth to adulthood*. Guilford Press.
This text includes a review of the planning, initiation, and results of the Minnesota Study of Risk and Adaptation. Results from infancy through young adulthood are discussed, including social, emotional, educational, and clinical outcomes. While some statistical results are discussed, they are presented in nontechnical language, and the focus is on conceptual understanding of the implications of the study.

Cassidy, J., & Shaver, P. R. (Eds.). (2016). *Handbook of attachment: Theory, research, and clinical applications* (3rd ed.). Guilford Press.
This text is a compendium of research on various aspects of attachment theory. It is both highly technical and applied but provides the single best resource for discerning the state of the empirical science of attachment. It is recommended here because many of the 43 chapters relate to infancy and caregiving, but the volume also devotes substantial space to other major topics within the field of attachment.

3 ATTACHMENT DURING MIDDLE CHILDHOOD

Internal Working Models and Developmental Trajectories

The early days of attachment research focused on the assessment, classification, and understanding of attachment behavior, primarily with infants and toddlers. As this literature developed, researchers tried to explain how early caregiving experiences might lead to lasting effects at later stages of development. Examining this issue presented many challenges, not the least of which was determining just how influential early attachment experiences are for later development. Answers came in time, and are still emerging, but contemporary attachment theory generally focuses on two primary explanatory concepts that become salient during the middle childhood years (approximately ages 5 to 12): internal working models and developmental trajectories.

INTERNAL WORKING MODELS AND ATTACHMENT REPRESENTATIONS

Bowlby (1969/1982) introduced the concept of the internal working model (IWM) in the first book of his attachment trilogy and revisited the concept in multiple writings thereafter (Bowlby, 1973, 1980, 1988). He described the

https://doi.org/10.1037/0000333-004
The Science and Clinical Practice of Attachment Theory: A Guide From Infancy to Adulthood, by B. Allen

IWM as a mental framework for interpreting information. Drawing comparisons to Piaget's concept of the schema, Bowlby talked of IWMs as organizing one's early attachment experiences in a way that yields a coherent understanding of oneself, other individuals, and the way the two interact. An infant with a sensitive and responsive caregiver, for instance, may develop an IWM of the self as lovable and valued, of others as trustworthy and helpful, and an understanding that solicitation of assistance will garner the needed support. IWMs allow for predictability in social relationships and the selection and initiation of behavioral responses. Importantly, IWMs are dynamic and capable of change based on new experiences, although they become more inflexible the longer they are reinforced by experience.

Unfortunately, Bowlby never provided a clear and detailed account of his concept of the IWM, instead often referring to it in passing or providing only a brief discussion within writings on other topics. Certainly, Bowlby viewed IWMs as complex, at various times referencing the impact of language development, the integrative and pivotal role of emotions, and conscious as well as unconscious components. However, his lack of a clear specification of the IWM concept, combined with an empirical focus on Ainsworth's attachment behavior classifications, resulted in little attention to IWMs in the earliest days of attachment research.

A remarkable paradigm shift occurred in 1985, when Mary Main and her colleagues, Nancy Kaplan and Jude Cassidy, published the groundbreaking paper "Security in Infancy, Childhood, and Adulthood: A Move to the Level of Representation." They argued for a complete reconceptualization of the understanding of attachment behavior, asserting that observable behavior was the result of acting on one's cognitive understanding of the self, the caregiver, and typical interactions, harkening back to Bowlby's concept of the IWM. They argued that repeated experiences of interacting with the caregiver yield a cognitive representation of the way in which that caregiver is likely to respond to one's behavior. As such, observable attachment behavior is an outward manifestation of one's understanding of a specific caregiver as a safe haven (i.e., attachment representation), however rudimentary it may be for an infant.

Main et al. (1985) provided an interesting bridge between Bowlby's ideas and the need for contemporary attachment researchers to explain the longitudinal impact of early attachment experiences. Observable behavior, of course, changes over time based on developmental progression; a 12-year-old will not display the types of attachment behavior that one observes from a 12-month-old. However, one's internal representations may be much more consistent over time and may explain how early attachment experiences affect a diversity of later behaviors. For instance, an infant whose behaviors are labeled as secure in the Strange Situation Procedure (SSP), hypothetically, has developed representations of the caregiver as supportive and likely to help and will carry these expectations into later interactions with peers, teachers, and others.

The remainder of Main et al.'s (1985) treatise provided concrete examples of how infant behavior in the SSP can be viewed through a representational lens, supported by data from Main's Berkeley Longitudinal Study. One of the tasks presented to the children when they were 6 years old was the Separation Anxiety Test (SAT; Klagsbrun & Bowlby, 1976). Participants looked at pictures of children undergoing various forms of parental separation (e.g., saying goodnight, first day of school) and described how the pictured child might feel and behave. Some study children provided answers suggesting negative emotions but identified potential coping strategies and completed the task with little visible personal distress. Other children provided incoherent answers, were noticeably uncomfortable, and/or were unable to provide a response. Interestingly, the first group of children were classified more frequently as secure with their mothers during the SSP at 12 months than were children in the second group. The conclusion was that early attachment experiences were manifesting at later ages and appeared to be cognitively mediated. Box 3.1 explores the connection between attachment representations and cognitive development.

Main et al. (1985) were careful not to minimize the complexity of their proposition. They reverted to Bowlby's original term and provided an expansive definition:

> We define the internal working model of attachment as a set of conscious and/or unconscious rules for the organization of information relevant to attachment and for obtaining or limiting access to that information, that is, to information regarding attachment-related experiences, feelings, and ideations. (pp. 66–67)

It was a broad definition but not the only one; other definitions followed, and the IWM became a predominant concept in attachment research (see Bretherton, 2005, for a review).

This explosion of interest in IWMs did much to stimulate research on the cognitive aspects of attachment theory and advanced the field in new and exciting directions. However, the head-first dive into the abstract world had unfortunate consequences. The different definitions of IWMs often made it difficult for researchers to compare results across studies, and some conceptualizations of IWMs were so broad that it was difficult to isolate specific facets for empirical testing. Bowlby's friend and colleague, Robert Hinde, while acknowledging the usefulness of the IWM concept, provided an important

BOX 3.1

A CLOSER LOOK: REPRESENTATIONS AND COGNITIVE DEVELOPMENT

The concept of attachment representations is inherently a cognitive approach to understanding the continuing influence of early experiences as well as the impact of later experiences, on social-emotional functioning. As such, research on cognitive development is directly relevant to the concept. In particular, findings in the areas of language development and memory are increasingly being applied to our understanding of representation formation and functioning.

In recent years, findings established that the language used by a caregiver influences attachment security. Given theoretical and empirical evidence that various forms of cognition are verbally mediated, one may expect that children with greater exposure to vocabulary-building experiences evidence higher levels of attachment security than those with less exposure. Indeed, studies now demonstrate that parental engagement in book reading or other language-based learning activities predicts attachment security among infants (e.g., Teufl et al., 2020). Evidence also suggests that infants displaying secure attachment behavior exhibit more sophisticated vocabularies than do children displaying insecure attachment behavior (Lemche et al., 2007, Teufl et al., 2020). These findings transfer to middle childhood, when children with histories of avoidant or disorganized attachment behavior in infancy are less capable of effectively engaging in discussions around emotionally laden topics (Hsiao et al., 2015) than are children with histories of secure attachment behavior.

Of course, the development of attachment representations is integrally intertwined with various constructs of memory. Infants as young as 5 months of age are capable of developing long-term implicit memories, particularly for emotionally laden interpersonal interactions (Bornstein et al., 2004), and this ability helps to explain how discriminated attachment relationships form. In addition, infants can understand and remember that the actions of others are intentional and goal directed (Skerry & Spelke, 2014) and can use these experiences to anticipate the behaviors of others (Vaish & Woodward, 2010). Findings such as these demonstrate the presence in infancy of the foundational elements needed for the development of complex and integrated representations (Sherman et al., 2015).

warning: "In the very power of such a model lies a trap: It can easily explain everything" (Hinde, 1989, p. 378). It was clear that while recognizing the multifaceted nature of IWMs was important, attachment research needed greater specificity in its constructs.

One of the most prominent aspects of the IWM concept investigated with school-age children is a specific form of representation known as the attachment script. The idea that human experience results in the development of cognitive scripts that guide future actions is a product of the cognitive revolution (e.g., Labov & Waletsky, 1967). By the 1980s, developmental scientists were examining concepts such as autobiographical memory and episodic memory to determine how children develop scripts for the completion of everyday tasks, to aid recall of important information, and to help interpret social behavior (e.g., Hudson & Nelson, 1986; Mistry & Lange, 1985). In addition, findings suggested that repetition of experiences reinforced and aided the development of cognitive scripts.

The implications of this body of work for the study of attachment were quickly recognized, and attachment scripts became a central focus of research. H. S. Waters and Waters (2006) provided a useful discussion of the concept. They proposed that repeated and consistent experiences with a sensitive and responsive caregiver are encoded in memory, which leads to a script defining the types of behaviors one can perform to effectively elicit caregiving, the manner in which help may be provided and the outcomes that will likely result. A history of insensitive or ineffective caregiving, on the other hand, may result in a script that contains elements yielding less effective forms of assuagement or, potentially, confusion and exacerbation of distress. Regardless of the type of script one develops, that script is carried forward to inform social interactions.

To demonstrate the concept more clearly, consider the examples provided in Table 3.1. In each of the scenarios the secure script demonstrates variations on a theme: Under moments of distress the child expects the caregiver to provide a soothing response, can identify behavioral responses effective at eliciting the caregiver's response, and is able to return to the previous activity after being calmed. The insecure scripts yield a different picture. In the first two scenarios (i.e., nightmare, bicycle accident), an avoidant script is presented in which the child's behavior focuses on self-care because they expect the caregiver to respond with rejection. The anticipated result is that the child experiences some continuing distress and has difficulty returning to the desired activity. The insecure script in the last scenario (i.e., stomachache) is of the ambivalent type. The child's behavior is exaggerated because the child views the mother's attention as difficult to obtain. The outcome is that

TABLE 3.1. Example Attachment Scripts

	Expectation of caregiver	Behavioral response	Likely postevent outcome
	Child awakens from a nightmare		
Secure script	Mom will be comforting.	Go to mom and request help.	Feel better and go back to sleep.
Insecure script (avoidant)	Mom will be upset if awakened.	Rely on self; stay in bed.	May not feel better; may not go back to sleep.
	Child is riding a bicycle and has an accident		
Secure script	Dad will help treat the injury and be comforting.	Return home and show dad.	Feel better and return to play outside.
Insecure script (avoidant)	Dad will be angry and will not help.	Stay outside; self-care for any injury.	May not feel better; play may not resume.
	Child experiences a stomachache		
Secure script	Mom will get medicine and will be comforting.	Find mom and tell her about the stomachache.	Feel better and resume activities.
Insecure script (avoidant)	May be difficult to get mom's attention.	Loud or angry behavior to get mom's attention.	Stay close to mom and ensure her continued attention. Activities may not resume.

the child remains close to the mother to prevent further difficulty accessing her, thus preventing a return to the previous activity. Disorganized scripts (not depicted) are characterized by disjointed and illogical sequences of events and/or integrate bizarre and unrealistic elements, suggesting the child does not possess a coherent plan of how to respond to the stress-inducing incident (Green et al., 2000). It should be reiterated that attachment scripts are largely implicit, automatically activated, and based on previous experience; the examples provided in Table 3.1 are for illustrative purposes only. There is wide variability in the ability of an individual to provide an explicit understanding and rationale for the behaviors of others, particularly among those with insecure forms of attachment (for more information on this topic, see the discussion of mentalization in Chapter 5, this volume).

Research suggests that early caregiving is instrumental in the development of attachment scripts (discussed later in this chapter; also see T. E. A. Waters & Roisman, 2019, for a review). In addition, there is evidence of both the stability of attachment scripts and openness to revision based on new experience. One informative study followed 157 children for 3 years and examined how attachment scripts changed over time (T. E. A. Waters, Facompré, Dujardin, et al., 2019). Security scores on the Attachment Script Assessment (discussed later) were moderately correlated across all four waves of data collection, which occurred annually and began when the children were approximately 11 years of age. Over time, the researchers connected higher security scores with the child experiencing more frequent mildly stressful events (e.g., academic problems at school, argument with a friend). They concluded that attachment scripts are fairly stable, and repeated implementation in response to common forms of stress may result in increasing levels of security due to practice and the feedback received.

Further supporting the contention that attachment representations are flexible to experience, a meta-analysis of attachment representations in childhood and adolescence found attachment security was associated with higher levels of concurrently assessed parental responsiveness, support for child autonomy, more frequent use of behavioral discipline skills, and less frequent use of harsh discipline and coercion (Koehn & Kerns, 2018). The results also demonstrated that lower levels of parental responsiveness and less frequent use of behavioral discipline skills were predictive of avoidant attachment. No significant results were found for ambivalent representations, and there were too few studies to assess the relationship between parenting in later childhood and disorganized representations. Taken together, a burgeoning literature suggests that attachment representations are related to both early and later caregiving experiences, suggesting both continuity and flexibility.

Assessing Attachment Representations

Much of the data for the validity of the attachment script concept comes from studies using a handful of specific assessment tools. Inge Bretherton and her colleagues (1990) developed one of the first story-stem completion procedures to assess attachment scripts, a procedure they termed the Attachment Story Completion Task (ASCT). The administrator presents the child with small dolls meant to represent members of a family and uses these dolls to set up a specific story with an obvious attachment-related theme. For instance, in the hurt knee scenario, the child doll is climbing on a rock and hurts a knee after falling. After presenting the stem, the administrator turns the story over to the child for completion. The narrative provided by the child is thought to reflect the script the child possesses for resolving the given problem. In the hurt knee scenario, coders of the narrative may examine whether the child has the doll seek comfort from a caregiver (secure) or ignore the caregiver and self-soothe (avoidant), for instance. The ASCT involves a total of five story stems, and coders look for patterns across narratives to score security. Bretherton et al. (1990) found significant and moderate-sized correlations between security in the ASCT at 37 months and security judged at both 18 months in the SSP and at 37 months in a separation-reunion procedure. Concordance between ASCT classification at 6 years of age and attachment behavior observed at 5 years of age has also been reported (Gloger-Tippelt & Kappler, 2016). Such results supported the contention that attachment scripts at older ages conceptually are related to attachment behavior observed during the first years of life.

A similar story-stem procedure gaining in popularity is the Manchester Child Attachment Story Task (MCAST; Green et al., 2000). The MCAST uses only four scenarios, each of which is designed specifically to elicit the child's script for how to respond to stress. Unlike the ASCT, the MCAST takes steps to encourage the child to identify with the child doll and includes only one caregiving figure (e.g., mother, father). Coding across scenarios yields an overall score for organization/disorganization and categorization into one of the four traditional attachment groupings. Although not validated against separation–reunion procedures, the distribution of cases across the classifications in normative samples is similar to that seen in the SSP and the Adult Attachment Interview (see Chapter 5), and disorganization is significantly more common among maltreated and clinical samples (B. Allen et al., 2018). Brown et al. (2017) found that harsh and intrusive parenting in the first 2 years of life predicted higher levels of disorganization and a greater likelihood of being classified insecure when completing the MCAST at 6 years of age.

H. S. Waters and Waters (2006) described a different form of assessment designed to assess security within attachment scripts. Originally working with adults, they provided a list of 12 words that presented an attachment theme and asked respondents to tell a story prompted by the words. Consider, for example, the word list provided in Exhibit 3.1 and read down through the

EXHIBIT 3.1. An Item Similar to Those From the Secure Base Script Assessment

	Growling dog	
James	scared	carry
walk	mother	home
dog	hug	play
growl	calm	happy

Note. Data from Waters and Waters (2006).

words in the first column before going to the second column, as instructed by the administration procedures. A narrative scoring high for security would describe a child who is out for a walk, encounters a growling dog, becomes scared, is hugged by the mother and feels calmer, is then carried home, and begins playing and feeling happy. This procedure, described as the Secure Base Script Assessment (SBSA) or the Attachment Script Assessment, has become increasingly popular in recent years given its ease of administration and scoring and strong psychometric properties. Modifications of the SBSA are available for children and are appearing with increasing frequency (e.g., T. E. A. Waters, Facompré, Dujardin, et al., 2019).

An alternative to story-stem procedures and the SBSA, which are generally considered to tap automatic or implicit processing of attachment representations, is the explicit querying of a child regarding perceptions of the caregiver as a safe haven and secure base. The most prominent child self-report measure is the Security Scale (SS; Kerns et al., 1996), which was originally developed with 10- and 11-year-olds but has been employed with samples as young as 6 years and as old as 17 years. The SS presents the child with a series of questions in a format that normalizes both secure and insecure forms of responding. For instance, one item reads, "Some kids go to their mom when upset, but other kids do not go to their mom when upset." For each item, the child is asked to choose which option is more like them and then whether that description is "sort of true" or "really true" for them. Scores are summed across items to yield a total scale for security. A meta-analysis of the SS found significant correlations in repeated assessments over time but decreasing effect sizes the longer the time between assessments, suggesting both stability and flexibility. Scores on the SS are moderately correlated with concurrently assessed maternal and paternal sensitivity (Brumariu et al., 2018).

Although the ASCT, MCAST, SBSA, and SS are some of the most commonly used assessments of child attachment representations, other metrics are found in the literature, including interview methods (see Chapter 4). However, a repeated finding suggests that narrative assessments (e.g., ASCT, MCAST, ASA) are relatively weakly associated with questionnaire measures such as the SS. For instance, attachment security assessed with the SS is strongly related to security assessed with other questionnaires ($r = .52$) but weakly correlated with security assessed with narrative methods ($r = .18$; Brumariu et al., 2018). Bosmans and Kerns (2015) suggested the discrepancy may rest largely on whether the assessment examines more strategic processes that allow the child to consciously process information and to decide how to respond (e.g., questionnaires) or automatic processes in which implicit memories and learned responses occur with little conscious processing (e.g., narrative measures).

ATTACHMENT AND DEVELOPMENTAL TRAJECTORIES

In the late 1970s, a new model emerged based on the idea that understanding the etiology of clinical problems can be enhanced by studying normative development, and vice versa. In practical terms, research that aims to identify how developmental processes emerge may provide clues as to how maladaptation occurs (Cicchetti, 1984). This field, termed developmental psychopathology, integrates findings across disciplines and levels of analysis (e.g., genetic, hormonal, familial). Attachment research, with its emphasis on the interaction of early parent–child relationships and ongoing environmental context, is a natural fit within this paradigm. Indeed, attachment theory is often integrated into studies using a developmental psychopathology framework to explain the earliest foundations of social–emotional development. In turn, such research provides considerable evidence for the validity of attachment theory and informs the ways in which attachment constructs may be used clinically.

Before discussing the specific application of attachment constructs, it is important to understand the basic principles of developmental psychopathology. First, the concept of equifinality suggests that any number of factors may lead to the development of the same outcome. Consider, for instance, the diagram provided in Figure 3.1, which shows depression as an outcome predicted by any of the three separate life events described (i.e., child abuse, a chronic medical condition, marital problems). Second, any one factor may result in the development of multiple conditions or concerns, a concept termed multifinality (Cicchetti & Rogosch, 1996). In Figure 3.1, the experience of child abuse is related to each of three different mental health outcomes provided. These principles are likely familiar to many experienced clinicians who have treated individuals with different backgrounds but

FIGURE 3.1. Equifinality and Multifinality

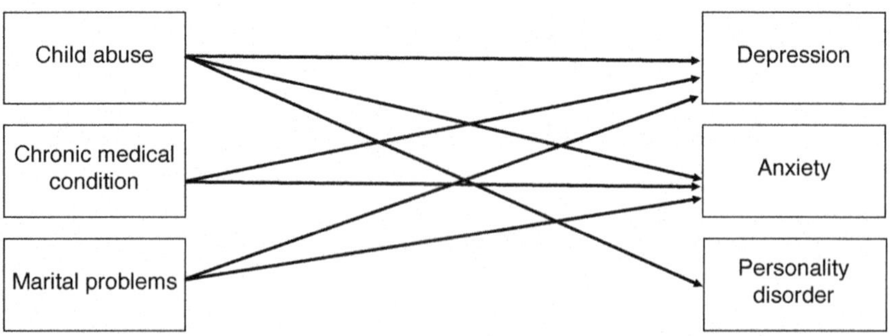

similar presenting concerns (equifinality) or who find themselves discussing similar historical events (e.g., child abuse) while treating individuals with different conditions (multifinality).

This understanding reveals that experiences such as child abuse and marital discord affect the onset of depression in different ways. Developmental psychopathology is largely concerned with understanding the routes through which various factors affect normative development and the emergence of clinical problems. Figure 3.2 offers a model examining the differential impact of the factors provided in Figure 3.1. Looking at this figure and following the pathways leads one to potential clinical implications. For instance, if one is treating a depressed adult who has battled a chronic medical condition for the past several years, the pathways suggest the greatest clinical benefit may come from targeting hopelessness and helping to manage acute stress. However, if one is working with an adult displaying symptoms of personality disorder and reporting a history of child abuse, effective treatment should enhance emotion regulation skills.

Attachment constructs often find their developmental and clinical utility in being conceptualized as one of these mechanisms between distal events and later outcomes. Bowlby (1988) drew on the work of Waddington (1957) to describe his conceptualization of how attachment fits within a larger developmental psychopathology framework. Figure 3.3 provides an example of Bowlby's logic as applied to the development of emotion regulation. The right side of the figure (solid line) is the trajectory for a child who received sensitive caregiving in the early years. When this child was observed in the SSP at approximately 18 months of age (Time 1), her responses to separation and reunion were classified as secure. Attending a high-quality preschool provided social-learning experiences and practice implementing the IWMs developed through early caregiving experiences. The secure attachment scripts

FIGURE 3.2. Mediators in the Development of Clinical Concerns

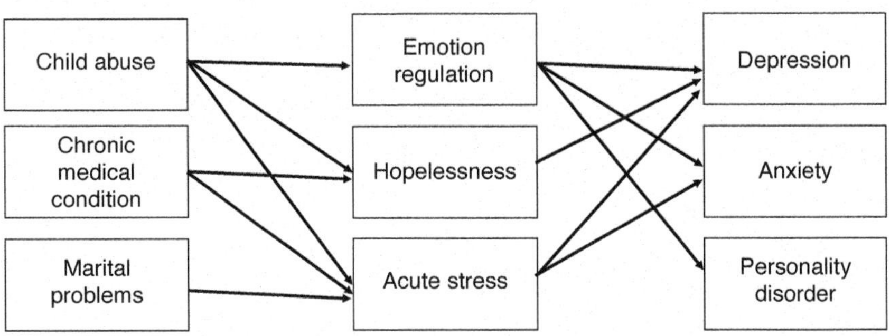

FIGURE 3.3. Developmental Trajectories

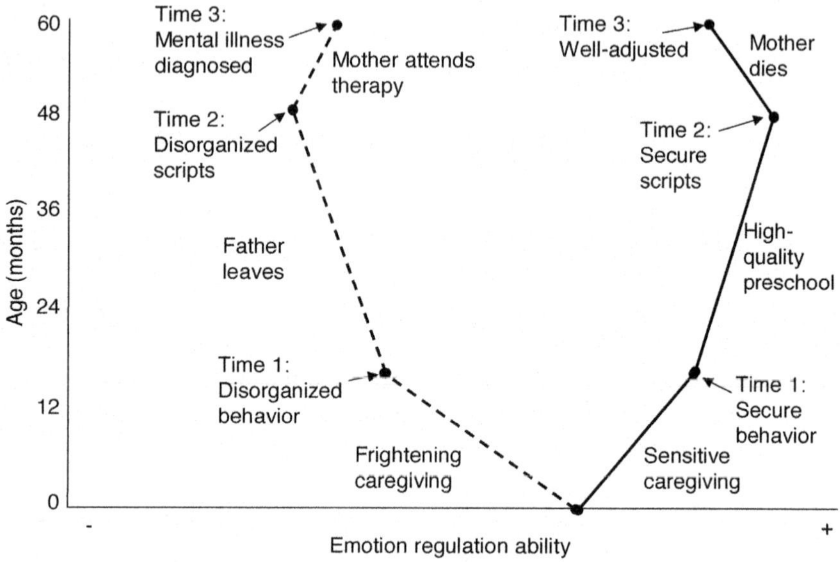

observed at age 48 months suggest an effective and coherent concept of how to access support figures in times of distress. The child whose trajectory is shown on the left (dashed line) experienced frightening parental behavior in the early years and, correspondingly, displayed disorganized behavior in the SSP at 18 months of age. The father then left the home, creating additional stress for the mother. As a result, the child's IWMs continued in an unhealthy direction, resulting in identification of disorganized scripts at 48 months of age.

This concept of developmental trajectories (i.e., pathways leading to adaptation or maladaptation) is a cornerstone of the fields of developmental science and developmental psychopathology. Such a perspective allows for the integration of an infinite number of experiences. In Figure 3.3, maternal caregiving in the first 12 months of life could be replaced with the effects of socioeconomic status, placement stability, family composition, or any number of life events. Each day presents influences that may affect development. These myriad experiences fuse together in a cumulative way to yield outcomes. For this reason, maternal sensitivity, or any factor for that matter, is only modestly related to secure attachment behavior (see Chapter 2); countless experiences may exert an effect.

Attachment constructs offer a useful index for determining the course of development up to the point at which they are assessed. As demonstrated in Figure 3.3 (solid line), possessing a coherent concept of how to access help and having confidence that such help will be effectively provided (i.e., secure attachment scripts) increases the likelihood that a child will successfully cope with stress and regulating difficult emotions. Even though this child was presented with an adverse life event at age 54 months (i.e., mother dies), the development of emotion regulation skills to that point in time allowed for effective coping and positive adjustment. The other child in Figure 3.3 (dashed line) demonstrated disorganized attachment behavior at 18 months, suggesting concerns with the ability to resolve stressful situations. If such a trajectory continues, ineffective emotion regulation skills may be strengthened and may contribute to the onset of a diagnosable mental illness. Given this perspective, attachment constructs are typically considered in the developmental literature as potent risk or protective factors on pathways to adaptation and maladaptation.

The concept of developmental trajectories offers several important considerations for attachment research. First, IMWs are dynamic constructs developed based on varied past experiences that affect the behavior, emotions, and thoughts of an individual in any given situation. As such, attachment processes contribute to the evolution of multiple core developmental capacities (e.g., emotion regulation, social skills, identity). Second, given that IWMs continue to be shaped by ongoing experiences, a bidirectional influence is observed in which various developmental capacities, by virtue of their influence on the outcome of any given situation, affect the evolution of attachment processes. As a result, it is important to consider attachment processes alongside multiple related constructs to properly appreciate development. It is precisely for this reason that neither Bowlby nor later attachment researchers ever suggested that insecure or disorganized attachment behavior in the earliest years of life was a direct cause of later psychopathology (Sroufe et al., 1999; Sroufe & Rutter, 1984).

Third, and importantly for clinicians, the concept of developmental trajectories suggests that improvements in development can occur. For instance, in Figure 3.3, the mother of the child developing on an unhealthy trajectory (dashed line) began therapy when the child was 54 months of age. Presumably, the amelioration of the mother's mental health concerns resulted in the change in direction of the child's pathway observed between the ages of 48 and 60 months.

Obviously, the trajectories displayed in Figure 3.3 are overly simplified for the purposes of demonstration; events occurring throughout development will cause the pathways constantly to twist, with influential events occurring on a frequent basis. Of course, this discussion of developmental trajectories is largely theoretical and abstract. Demonstrating the importance of attachment constructs for development requires focused empirical examination.

Early Attachment Behavior and Development in Middle Childhood

Given the definition of attachment behavior as an attempt to access a caregiver for the purposes of alleviating distress, it should not be surprising that emotion regulation was one of the first developmental outcomes examined in longitudinal attachment research. Many of the earliest studies used composites of internalizing problems (e.g., depression, anxiety) and/or externalizing problems (e.g., defiance, aggression) as proxies for dysregulated emotion. A meta-analysis by Groh and colleagues (2012) found that avoidant and disorganized attachments during infancy and the preschool years predicted later internalizing problems, although the effect sizes were generally small. Similarly, meta-analyses have demonstrated a very small effect for avoidant attachment behavior and a small-to-medium effect for disorganization in predicting later externalizing problems (Fearon et al., 2010; van IJzendoorn et al., 1999). Some evidence suggests that this relationship may be stronger for boys than girls. None of these meta-analyses found a relationship between ambivalent attachment behavior and emotional or behavioral concerns in later childhood.

Once developmental science further explicated the construct of emotion regulation independent of clinical concerns, studies examining the relation of infant attachment behavior with emotion regulation became more refined. Secure attachment behavior as a young child predicts more positive affect, better identification and understanding of emotions, a greater ability to regulate emotion, and more frequent utilization of social support and cognitive coping skills during middle childhood (Cooke et al., 2019; Pallini et al., 2018). Consequently, avoidant, ambivalent, and disorganized behaviors are associated with less positive affect and greater difficulty regulating emotions. Generally speaking, studies with older children using narrative and questionnaire-based assessments of attachment representations replicate these results, suggesting a degree of continuity from infancy into middle childhood (B. Allen, Bendixsen, et al., 2018; Cooke et al., 2016, 2019).

If the underlying assumption is correct that IWMs provide an understanding of social relationships, then attachment security should correlate with social competence. Looking across 80 independent samples encompassing over 4,000 children, Groh, Fearon, and colleagues (2014) found that children who displayed a secure attachment in the earliest years demonstrated greater social competence with peers, with a medium effect size, when compared with children classified as insecure. The age at which social behavior was assessed did not predict outcomes, suggesting that the strength between attachment security and social competence did not dissipate as the child aged. Each form of insecurity predicted less social competence when compared directly to security, with the disorganized and ambivalent forms associated with the greatest deficits. Evidence also suggested that mother–child attachment security was more influential than father–child attachment in the development of social competence.

If secure attachment behavior and IWMs suggest a greater capacity for a child to use a caregiver as a secure base from which to explore the environment, then one would expect a significant relationship between attachment security and constructs of cognitive development. Indeed, one early review found significant correlations, although small in magnitude, between secure attachment behavior and intelligence assessed with either a developmental quotient metric for infants or an intelligence quotient for older children (van IJzendoorn et al., 1995). More contemporary research largely confirms these early findings (e.g., McCormick et al., 2016) while expanding on them. For instance, Pallini and colleagues (2019) showed that children previously classified as insecure demonstrate greater attentional problems than securely attached children do, with those classified as disorganized displaying the most significant concerns.

Attachment in Context

Although bivariate relationships, such as those just discussed, suggest a place for attachment constructs in understanding varied forms of development, the concept of developmental trajectories underlines the fact that bivariate associations yield an overly simplistic understanding. Rather, the role of attachment processes is best understood by placing them within the larger developmental context. Consider the model depicted in Figure 3.4. One could easily make an attachment-based case for the development of externalizing

FIGURE 3.4. Attachment Processes in Context

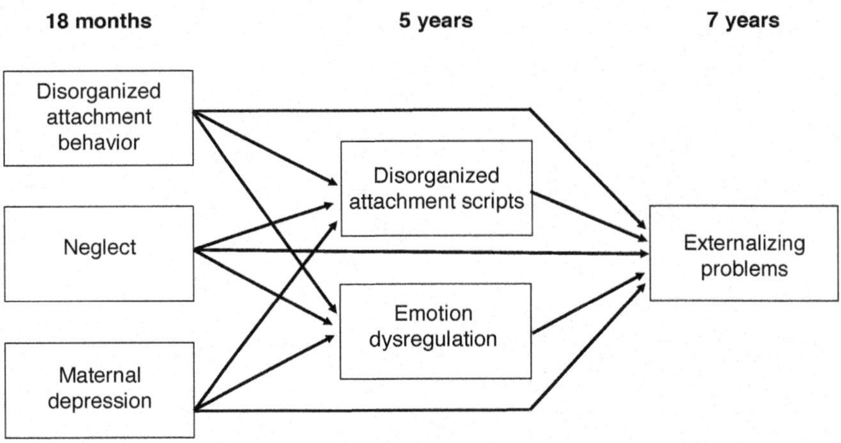

problems at age 7 by tracing the pathways from disorganized behavior at 18 months through disorganized scripts at age 5. However, other factors influence the development of externalizing problems, specifically emotion dysregulation (age 5), and factors other than disorganized attachment behavior predict the development of dysregulated emotion (e.g., neglect and maternal depression at 18 months). In fact, using this same model, one could explain the development of externalizing problems while completely disregarding attachment processes by tracing the impact of maternal depression at 18 months through the child's emotion dysregulation at age 5. Of course, looking at the model as a whole gives a much richer understanding of the development of externalizing problems. For this reason, contemporary attachment research commonly integrates other developmental constructs, and studies examining bivariate relationships between attachment constructs and a specific outcome are increasingly rare. The Minnesota Study of Risk and Adaptation (see Box 2.3) is a good example and is revisited in Box 3.2.

ATTACHMENT-RELATED BEHAVIOR IN MIDDLE CHILDHOOD

Although attachment research in middle childhood most commonly focuses on understanding the influence of early attachment behavior on later development or examining the role of various aspects of the IWM construct, some research documents the behavioral manifestations of attachment at this age. This work has its roots in Mary Main's Berkeley Longitudinal Study. Main and Cassidy (1988) separated 6-year-old children from their caregivers for approximately an hour during a laboratory visit so that each could complete other measures. After this time apart, the caregiver reentered the room with no specific instructions from the examiner. The child was given 10 to 15 minutes of free play prior to the reunification to allow for a return to normal childhood activities. The reunion episode itself lasted 3 to 5 minutes, and observers coded the child's responses to the return of the caregiver.[1] However, attempting to use separation–reunion procedures with school-age children is not without its challenges, as reviewed in Box 3.3.

[1]The use of separation–reunion procedures is rare beyond the age of 6 years given the challenge of eliciting discernible behaviors at reunion among older children. The procedures are discussed here as a bridge between the early childhood and middle childhood periods but should not be taken as indicative of how a child may respond in the later middle childhood years, such as between the ages of 10 and 12.

BOX 3.2

A CLOSER LOOK: THE MINNESOTA STUDY OF RISK AND ADAPTATION, REVISITED

The Minnesota Study provides an excellent example of the importance of considering attachment within the broad context of development. Social competence was assessed during the middle childhood years using multiple methods, including observation of peer interactions at a summer camp for participant children. Attachment security in infancy was a significant predictor of social competence at age 10, accounting for 13% of the variance. However, when caregiving behavior during the preschool years was added to the model, the explained variance doubled (27%). When social competence ratings during the preschool year were added to the model, another significant improvement was observed, accounting for 40% of the variance (Sroufe et al., 2005a).

When considering the developmental sequence of these findings, one is led down a path in which infant attachment security, developed through the caregiving received in infancy, is a moderate predictor of social competence in middle childhood. However, examining a more proximal state of development (i.e., preschool social competence) and the environment in which the child was raised during that time (i.e., caregiving during the preschool years) is far superior to considering infant attachment security alone. Of course, attachment security exerts an influence on social competence in the preschool years (Erickson et al., 1985), but so do other experiences, such as play groups. Indeed, findings from throughout the Minnesota Study demonstrate this point: Infant attachment security is an important factor in explaining later development, but its explanatory power weakens the farther out in development one looks (Sroufe et al., 2005a). It is far more instructive and empirically justified to consider the impact of infant attachment security within the context of other distal events and the current environmental setting than to ascribe a deterministic influence to early attachment behavior alone.

Attempting to model their coding system on that of Ainsworth's SSP and the preschool modifications of the SSP (see Chapter 2), Main and Cassidy (1988) identified characteristic behaviors of child responses that denoted several distinct patterns. One group of children were quite positive toward caregivers, often initiating interactions with them and describing their activities just prior to reunion (i.e., secure or B). Another group shied away

BOX 3.3

A CLOSER LOOK: STUDYING ATTACHMENT BEHAVIOR IN MIDDLE CHILDHOOD

Studying attachment behavior in middle childhood is a challenging task. Children of this age possess greater levels of cognitive sophistication and more effective emotion regulation skills, on average, than children in the infancy and preschool years. As such, school-age children commonly exhibit a greater capacity to cope with challenges independently and a subsequent decrease in frequency of turning toward a caregiver for assistance (Kerns et al., 2006). Nonetheless, when negative emotion of sufficient strength is experienced, these children report implementing attachment behavior and using caregivers as a source of support and calming (Kerns et al., 2006; Kobak et al., 2005).

Although most caregivers can provide numerous instances in which their children display attachment behavior, such as while getting a shot or when they are injured, systematically studying such behavior through direct observation is difficult. It is not ethically possible to induce the amount of stress necessary to elicit attachment behavior in children of this age during laboratory visits. Most attempts to observe such behavior in naturalistic settings (e.g., doctor's office) have failed because of the wide variability in children's perceptions of the presumed stressor. Separation-reunion paradigms with children of this age do not typically induce stress in the child. As such, the child's behavior during these observations is more accurately described as a form of social interaction directed toward the caregiver than as traditional attachment behavior. Theoretically, the child's reunification behavior is shaped by previous experiences with the caregiver and is governed by the child's internal working models of the caregiver, which helps to explain the commonly reported relationships among reunion behavior and measures of attachment representations in middle childhood, and Strange Situation Procedure classifications during infancy.

from caregivers or ignored them. These children appeared too busy with their activities to acknowledge the caregiver's presence (i.e., avoidant). A third group of children provided an exaggerated welcoming response that was quickly followed by signs of resistance to interacting with the caregiver, such as turning away or talking to the caregiver with the back turned (i.e., ambivalent).

Two additional patterns emerged that suggested active attempts by the child to control the caregiver upon reunion. In the first form, children displayed a punitive type of behavior toward the caregiver, commonly making demanding comments (e.g., "I told you to keep quiet!") or ridiculing the caregiver (e.g., "You're really clumsy."). In the second form, children were protective of the caregiver or appeared overly invested in trying to please her, such as by inviting her to play and then seeking repeated reassurances that she was having fun. Given that both approaches were focused on exerting influence over the caregiver's actions, they are often grouped together under the label of controlling, though the two subtypes are designated in some analyses as controlling–punitive and controlling–caregiving. It should be noted that this behavior is often referred to as role reversal, a concept discussed in more detail in Chapter 5 of this volume.

Main and Cassidy (1988) reported continuity of classification from the SSP observations of children at 12 months of age and their classification at 6 years of age. In the aggregate, 84% of children displayed continuity over time, significantly beyond the 35% that would be expected by chance. The controlling children (both subgroups) were grouped together as a potential form of evolved disorganized behavior given that 90% of the children displaying these types of behaviors at age 6 were classified as D (disorganized behavior) at 12 months. Looking prospectively, 75% of children classified as D at 12 months displayed controlling or unclassified behavior at 6 years. Recalling that disorganized attachment behavior is considered a response to frightening and confusing caregiving, Main and Cassidy (1988) theorized that controlling behavior evolves as an attempt to impose structure and predictability on the caregiver's behavior.

A replication of the Main and Cassidy (1988) findings was completed by Wartner et al. (1994), who found similar results, with 82% continuity from infant SSP classification at 12 to 16 months of age and classification at age 6 years. However, they went further with their analyses. They correlated 6-year attachment classification with social competence assessed the year before. Children displaying controlling behavior toward the caregiver displayed concerns in areas such as conflict resolution and tended to report hostile or confused perceptions of social interactions. Avoidant children showed significant problems in these areas as well. Solomon et al. (1995) found that children classified as controlling at age 6 were rated by their caregivers and teachers as displaying more behavioral problems, including aggression, than their less controlling peers. They also found that attachment scripts of controlling children were characterized by heightened threat and danger and often included violence or bizarre themes (e.g., objects flying out of control around a house, floating objects). The narratives of children classified as secure, however, were marked by resolution of distress and frequently involved caregivers to assist in the process.

Training in the administration and coding of separation–reunion procedures for the early years of the middle childhood period are rare and has resulted in relatively little contemporary research using these methods. One notable exception is the work of Ellen Moss and her colleagues. In a series of longitudinal studies, they showed that factors such as low maternal stress and high-quality mother–child interactions drove the display of secure behavior at age 6, while maternal stress and poor-quality interactions predicted controlling behavior (Dubois-Comtois et al., 2013). They also demonstrated the connection of attachment behavior at age 6 with attachment scripts assessed 2 years later (Dubois-Comtois et al., 2011) as well as social competence and clinical problems (Moss et al., 2004). For an excellent review of this work, refer to Moss and Lecompte (2015).

CONCLUSION

Attachment research in the middle childhood years demonstrates the complexity and usefulness of the larger theory of attachment. Not only do researchers consider the evolution of observable attachment behavior, but they also directly assess presumed underlying cognitive structures and embed multiple attachment constructs within a developmental psychopathology perspective. Through these efforts to demonstrate the short- and long-term impact of early attachment experiences and explicate the mechanisms through which this influence occurs, attachment theory has come to a place of considerable respect among developmental scientists and is considered one of the foremost theories of social-emotional development. As one ages into adolescence, the social milieu changes, as do the challenges encountered, presenting an opportunity for researchers to examine different aspects of attachment constructs and how they function in different settings. These issues are the focus of Chapter 4 in this volume.

RESOURCES

Suggested Further Reading

Bosmans, G., & Kerns, K. A. (Eds.). (2015). *Attachment in middle childhood: Theoretical advances and new directions in an emerging field*. Jossey-Bass.

This volume reviews various aspects of attachment research in middle childhood, including connections with the development of emotion regulation, information processing, and behavioral problems. The chapters examine the current research base in these areas and provide theoretical discussions. The volume is relatively nontechnical and accessible by those without a research background.

Kerns, K. A., & Richardson, R. A. (Eds.). (2005). *Attachment in middle childhood.* Guilford Press.

This volume provides a number of papers presenting data from empirical studies examining various aspects of attachment in the middle childhood years. A number of less discussed topics are examined, such as hierarchies of caregivers and the role of friendships, as well as more common topics, such as emotion regulation. Given that the volume focuses on the presentation of research data, it may be of less interest for readers interested in discussions of clinical application.

4 ATTACHMENT DURING ADOLESCENCE

Evolving Caregiver Relationships and the Role of Peers

Adolescence is often described as a period of transition during which one attempts to achieve more autonomy from caregivers. While stressful circumstances continue to occur, adolescents typically can consider multiple response options, and it is difficult to conceive of the attachment system as necessary for survival. For instance, during moments of distress, the adolescent may choose to use learned coping and problem-solving skills or to seek support from an expanded social network instead of from the caregiver. Researchers are therefore able to study how the attachment system generalizes outside of parent–child relationships to interactions with peers. At the same time, caregivers remain an important source of support for most adolescents, and determining the conditions under which an adolescent selects the caregiver or a peer for assistance provides clues to how attachment processes evolve.

https://doi.org/10.1037/0000333-005
The Science and Clinical Practice of Attachment Theory: A Guide From Infancy to Adulthood, by B. Allen

COGNITIVE STRUCTURES OF ATTACHMENT IN ADOLESCENCE

In a continuation of the theoretical and empirical work in childhood, research with adolescents is increasingly examining cognitive scripts for responding to challenges with a focus on understanding the interpersonal nature of the response. Researchers administered the adolescent version of the Secure Base Script Assessment (see Chapter 3, this volume) to participant youth in the NICHD (National Institute of Child Health and Human Development) Study of Early Child Care when they were 18 years of age (R. D. Steele et al., 2014; Vaughn et al., 2016). Results showed that child attachment security and parental sensitivity during the first 3 years predicted secure scripts at 18 years, but the relationships were weak, and effect sizes dissipated as parental support throughout the youth's life was added to the model. Analyses from the Minnesota Study of Risk and Adaptation similarly link early maternal sensitivity with secure attachment scripts in later adolescence while underlining the impact of experiences beyond the early childhood years (T. E. A. Waters et al., 2017). Such results echo those from the childhood period showing that attachment experiences in infancy continue to exert an effect, but other factors are also at play.

There is evidence, however, that the structure of attachment scripts in adolescence differs from those in middle childhood. For instance, attachment scripts are generally conceptualized as categorical in nature during the middle childhood period, typically secure or insecure, although evidence suggests that they begin to take on a more dimensional quality by the end of the middle childhood period (Psouni & Apetroaia, 2014; T. E. A. Waters, Facompré, Dujardin, et al., 2019). However, in adolescence the shift in the constitution of attachment script knowledge is quite clear, with more gradations of security being present and continuous scoring providing a better fit for the data than a categorical structure does (T. E. A. Waters, Facompré, Dujardin, et al., 2019). In addition, a significant correlation is found in adolescence for mother–child and father–child scripts ($r = .88$), and a model assuming a common latent construct influencing both scripts fits the data better than one supposing the two scripts are independent (T. E. A. Waters, Fraley, et al., 2015). This more global structure of adolescent attachment scripts is a departure from attachment behavior among young children as well as attachment scripts observed in middle childhood, when differences are often present based on the caregiver included in the assessment. In short, by the middle to end of adolescence, attachment scripts appear to have undergone a form of consolidation and refinement that yields a generalized model applicable in diverse situations.

While examination of attachment scripts in adolescence is gaining in popularity, research on attachment during this period primarily examines the concept of *state of mind.* George et al. (1996) developed the Adult Attachment Interview (AAI) to assess recollections of early attachment relationships and administered it to the caregivers in the Berkeley Longitudinal Study.[1] They noted idiosyncrasies in the ways some caregivers responded to the questions and found differences in dialogue just as important as the recalled memories. In brief, the individual's ability to access and contextualize thoughts, feelings, and memories of early parent–child relationships came to be termed a "state of mind."

Transcripts from the AAI are coded and yield three primary classifications roughly analogous to the three behavioral patterns identified by Ainsworth in the Strange Situation Procedure (SSP). The secure state of mind (denoted F) is marked by a willingness to discuss early attachment experiences and the ability to do so without avoidance, anger, or idealization of the caregiver. The insecure/dismissing (Ds) classification characterizes individuals who appear to actively avoid conversation regarding their early attachment experiences, either by refusing to discuss the topic or by providing brief answers without sufficient detail. If the individual does discuss their early experiences, they may rationalize inappropriate or harsh parenting practices or minimize the importance of such interactions. The third category, insecure/preoccupied (E), is assigned to individuals on the basis of an interview marked by significant anger toward caregivers. Narratives often include muddled or unnecessary details, incoherent mixing of memories from different time periods, and/or demeaning characterizations of the caregiver (Main et al., 1984–2003).

A fourth category was identified that delineated individuals who reported a history of childhood abuse or loss of an attachment figure and who displayed significant distress or confusion regarding the experience. Transcripts from these individuals, classified as "unresolved" (U), are marked by noticeable lapses in the discussion of such experiences, for example, being unsure of the details (e.g., "I'm not sure about when or where, but I know it happened"), denying the experiences occurred after initially reporting them, or displaying confusion and incoherence when asked for details (Main et al., 1984–2003). As with SSP classifications, it is not uncommon

---

[1]The AAI is reviewed in Chapter 5 of this volume as part of the discussion of attachment in adulthood, but the state of mind construct is discussed here because of its widespread applicability to studying attachment in adolescence. Some readers may find it advantageous to review the development of the AAI in Chapter 5 before proceeding with this chapter.

to see data analyzed using a four-way scheme (Ds, E, F, and U), a dichotomous secure versus insecure scheme with U considered a form of insecurity, or a dichotomous scheme that isolates the U transcripts from non-U transcripts. The prototypical features of the four states of mind are depicted in Table 4.1.

Given that the AAI quickly became the gold standard for assessing a form of attachment functioning with adults, early research with adolescents likewise employed the AAI, with slightly modified wording during the interview. Reviews show that 44% to 48% of adolescents in nonclinical samples are classified as secure, with 21% to 34% dismissing, 11% to 12% preoccupied, and 11% to 20% unresolved (Bakermans-Kranenburg & van IJzendoorn, 2009; van IJzendoorn & Bakermans-Kranenburg, 1996). The percentage of adolescents with a dismissing classification is higher than what is typically observed in adult populations, a finding commonly attributed to the independence strivings of adolescence that may result in minimization of the need for parental assistance. Rates of insecurity increase significantly when assessing samples at increased risk for untoward outcomes (Bakermans-Kranenburg & van IJzendoorn, 2009; Madigan et al., 2012; Roisman et al., 2017).

The Child Attachment Interview (CAI; Shmueli-Goetz et al., 2008) and the Friends and Family Interview (FFI; H. Steele & Steele, 2005), two methods designed specifically for interviewing children and adolescents, have gained in popularity in recent years. These methods display significant similarities to the AAI in their scoring of transcripts. The CAI differs from the AAI by asking about current relationships with caregivers, as opposed to memories of the distant past, and is significantly shorter in length. Although originally developed with children between 7 and 12 years old, the CAI is used with adolescents and demonstrates psychometric properties comparable to those of the AAI while largely eliminating the increased frequency of dismissing classifications observed when using the AAI with adolescents (Venta et al., 2014). The FFI was developed to assess the perceptions of current relationships with caregivers as well as other social relationships and was piloted with 11-year-old children. When applied to adolescents, the FFI displays acceptable psychometric properties and yields classification frequencies similar to those obtained with the AAI (Pace et al., 2020).

Studies attempting to predict adolescent states of mind from infant attachment classification yield interesting findings. Main and her colleagues (2005) were the first to examine this issue when they administered the AAI at the age of 19 years to youth who were originally enrolled in the Berkeley Longitudinal Study as infants. They found significant concordance between secure/insecure classifications during the SSP in infancy, the separation–reunion

TABLE 4.1. Prototypical Features of States of Mind

	State of mind			
Feature	**Secure (F)**	**Dismissing (Ds)**	**Preoccupied (E)**	**Unresolved (U)**
Content provided	Examples of supportive caregivers	Examples of rejecting caregivers	Examples of nonsupportive or irritable caregivers	Examples of abuse or loss of a caregiver
	Recognition of caregiver strengths and weaknesses	May provide overly positive views of caregivers (i.e., idealization)	May relay anger or resentment toward caregivers	May report abuse or loss and later deny it occurred
Narrative discourse	Emotions discussed	Limited emotion	Emotions varied and intense	Emotions avoided
	Sufficiently detailed	Limited detail	Overly detailed	Contradictory details
	Believable	Believability questionable	Believability unclear due to disjointedness	Poor clarity
Perception of attachment relationships	Helpful	Not helpful	Problematic	Source of emotional pain
	Valuable	Unimportant	Detrimental	Difficult to discuss
Analogous SSP classification	Secure	Avoidant	Ambivalent	Disorganized

Note. SSP = Strange Situation Procedure.

paradigm and Separation Anxiety Test (SAT) administered at age 6, and state of mind on the AAI at age 19. Examination of data from the Minnesota Study of Risk and Adaptation showed stability of infant SSP classification to AAI classification at 19 years of age was 50.9% when using a secure–insecure dichotomy (Weinfield et al., 2000). Such findings are not uniform, however. Grossmann et al. (2005) reported the results of two longitudinal studies from Germany that failed to show state of mind in later adolescence was predicted by infant SSP behavior, although it was predicted by responses to the SAT during middle childhood. Groh, Roisman, and colleagues (2014) found no continuity from the SSP at 15 months to the AAI at 18 years within the NICHD Study of Early Child Care; however, attachment insecurity assessed at 24 months with the Attachment Q-sort was related to later preoccupied and dismissing states of mind.

These same studies provide clues as to the conditions under which instability might be observed. Within the high-risk group of the Minnesota Study, maltreatment experiences, maternal depression, and indices of family functioning were predictors of continuity (i.e., stable insecure) and discontinuity (i.e., secure to insecure; Weinfield et al., 2000). Other studies generated similar conclusions; adverse events during the life course predict continuity of attachment insecurity and discontinuity of attachment security from childhood through adolescence (e.g., Booth-LaForce et al., 2014; Groh, Roisman, et al., 2014). It is also likely that the modest relation between classification in the SSP and adolescent state of mind is partially attributable to the phenomenological difference in constructs (i.e., observable behavior vs. dialogue and recollection of experiences). See Box 4.1 for an expanded discussion of the conceptualization of the state of mind concept in adolescence.

It is important to note that researchers examining attachment concepts in adolescence are cognizant of the multitude of other developmental capacities that are evolving in tandem. It should not be surprising that security in adolescence is correlated with social competence (e.g., J. P. Allen et al., 2007), effective emotion regulation skills (e.g., Zimmermann et al., 2001), and more adaptive social cognition capabilities, such as perspective taking (Hart et al., 2017). The relationship between attachment constructs and these other domains of functioning is the subject of ongoing investigation, with most studies using the developmental psychopathology model (see Chapter 3). In this manner, attachment is considered alongside other factors as a potential cause of an outcome or in developmental sequence as a mediating variable in the relationship between early life experiences and later psychosocial outcomes.

BOX 4.1

A CLOSER LOOK: CONCEPTUALIZING "STATE OF MIND" IN ADOLESCENCE

Main et al. (1985) originally conceptualized the Adult Attachment Interview (AAI) as assessing an individual's internal working model of attachment relationships. It was later recognized that classifying one's responses during an interview that probes for memories or perceptions of caregiver relationships is meaningfully different from identifying one's responses during moments of distress, which is the hallmark of attachment constructs during earlier periods of development (e.g., separation-reunion behavior, attachment scripts). As such, the construct was reframed as a "state of mind" and considered a distinct, albeit related, aspect of attachment. Nonetheless, considerable disparity among these constructs raises questions about how to examine the stability of attachment, changes in attachment system functioning, and the interrelationships among constructs. These issues are particularly salient during adolescence.

J. P. Allen (2021) argued that it is a misguided quest to examine stability of a static attachment construct from childhood through adolescence because significant changes are occurring in the development of the individual, including in the attachment system. Rather, it may be more fruitful to consider various forms of attachment-related tasks and interactions with one's environment that might be predicted by attachment constructs. While evidence clearly suggests the existence of a relatively stable latent construct that serves to cognitively organize experiences with caregivers (Jones et al., 2018), how that construct manifests will take on increasing complexity as the individual ages, creating exciting opportunities for researchers to test how such a construct (e.g., state of mind) affects various forms of relationships and outcomes associated with such relationships (e.g., academic achievement, job performance, health).

In a related vein, J. P. Allen and Miga (2010) proposed that one's state of mind may be conceptualized as a marker of emotion regulation within interpersonal contexts, given the significant correlations of the construct with conflict resolution and emotional coping skills. Such an approach offers a potential rapprochement with other attachment constructs that focus specifically on the ability to reduce distress and reinitiate exploration. However, it burdens attachment researchers with demonstrating that the state of mind concept enhances our understanding of emotion

(*continues*)

BOX 4.1

A CLOSER LOOK: CONCEPTUALIZING "STATE OF MIND" IN ADOLESCENCE (*Continued*)

regulation beyond that offered by other models. Given that interviews such as the AAI, the Child Attachment Interview, and the Friends and Family Interview take considerably more time to complete than most measures of emotion regulation, the onus is on attachment researchers to demonstrate the applicability of the state of mind concept to examination of adolescent emotion regulation research.

Despite these debates about how best to conceptualize the state of mind concept during adolescence, three conclusions are clear. First, states of mind are empirically related to earlier attachment constructs (e.g., infant Strange Situation Procedure classification, attachment scripts in middle childhood) when examined in well-controlled longitudinal studies. Second, states of mind are connected to multiple important outcomes in adolescence, including relationships with caregivers and peers, and developmental outcomes (e.g., emotion regulation, social competence). Last, the interviews administered to derive states of mind specifically cue for perceptions of relationships with individuals who previously or currently serve an attachment function, making the theoretical link of the state of mind concept to the larger body of attachment research quite clear.

ATTACHMENT TO CAREGIVERS IN ADOLESCENCE

Adolescents inherently strive for greater independence from caregivers and experience growing confidence in their self-sufficiency. When stress does occur, an expanded repertoire of emotional coping and problem-solving skills provides multiple avenues through which to reestablish a sense of calm and reinitiate engagement with desired activities and interests. As such, the threshold for activating the attachment system and thereby seeking the comfort of a discriminated attachment figure is considerably higher than at earlier points in development. Attachment behavior, when implemented, may take on noted changes given expanded communication skills and an adolescent's desire to maintain a level of independence.

Under the direst circumstances (e.g., hospitalization following a car accident), adolescents typically identify primary caregivers as the ones they most want by their side (Markiewicz et al., 2006; Rosenthal & Kobak, 2010).

Mothers are commonly identified at the top of such hierarchies, while fathers are relegated to lower positions, especially during latter periods of adolescence. These results suggest that adolescents continue to prefer primary caregivers in moments when the attachment system is most likely activated.

When adolescents turn to caregivers for assistance, effective communication is important for both accurately conveying one's needs and negotiating the balance between striving for autonomy and requesting assistance. Becker-Stoll et al. (2001) administered the AAI to a group of adolescents and observed them interacting with their mothers during a task in which they discussed disagreements about their relationship. Secure adolescents displayed more nonverbal emotional cues while adolescents with dismissing states of mind were less likely to display emotional expressions. Other studies have identified a significant relationship between attachment security and willingness and ability to engage with a caregiver during an interaction task (J. P. Allen et al., 2007; Diamond et al., 2012). Berger and colleagues (2005) found that an adolescent's preoccupied state of mind predicted disagreement between adolescents and their parents when reporting on the adolescent's internalizing (e.g., depression, anxiety) and externalizing (e.g., conduct problems, aggression) concerns, suggesting a general lack of effective communication between them regarding sources of stress.

Difficulty engaging caregivers and communicating needs may result in problems resolving conflicts, which take on increased importance in relationships during adolescence. Indeed, considerable evidence suggests that insecurity is associated with less effective forms of conflict resolution. For instance, adolescents displaying attachment insecurity often display marked difficulties negotiating a conflictual interaction task with a caregiver (Zimmermann et al., 2009). In addition, insecure attachment predicts displays of hostility within the parent–adolescent relationship, which may predict ongoing conflict (M. J. Martin et al., 2019). Collapsing across studies, a picture emerges of adolescents with an insecure state of mind being less capable of communicating with caregivers and managing conflict.

As with other stages of development, alteration of attachment processes remains possible during adolescence. In a longitudinal study, J. P. Allen et al. (2018) found that supportive maternal behavior during an interaction task at 14 years of age predicted enhanced attachment security 10 years later, while the use of psychologically controlling parenting methods (e.g., guilt induction, love withdrawal) predicted decreases in security. Other studies have similarly shown that adverse events in adolescence, such as parental depression and conflict amongst the parents, are connected to insecurity (Jones et al., 2018; Khan et al., 2020). Additionally, improved cognitive sophistication allows adolescents to evaluate the behaviors of their caregivers, including identifying caregiver flaws and areas of disagreement. When considered in the context of an otherwise positive relationship with a caregiver, this deidealization predicts improved attachment security as the youth can coherently and efficiently discuss the relationship (J. P. Allen et al., 2003).

This body of research suggests multiple conclusions. First, caregivers continue to serve an important function during adolescence as youth are prone to seek them out during situations of significant stress. Second, adolescents' ability to coherently discuss their relationships with caregivers is rooted in prior parent–child experiences and is predicted from past attachment-related constructs. Third, the concept of attachment security during adolescence demonstrates theoretically predicted stability and amenability to change based on environmental events. Fourth, bidirectional influences are evident in which adolescents' attachment security predicts their interactions with caregivers and caregivers' behavior within interactions shapes the attachment security of adolescents. Last, high levels of attachment security in adolescence signal more effective communication and conflict resolution skills that may generalize outside of the relationship with the caregiver and improve social functioning in other relationships.

ATTACHMENT AND PEER RELATIONSHIPS

Peer relationships become increasingly important throughout childhood but take on a prominent role during the adolescent years. Adolescents often report that friends are an important source of social support, and best friends may serve attachment functions (i.e., secure base, safe haven; Markiewicz et al., 2006). However, the conditions under which adolescents rely on peers are a function of the severity of a given situation. Adolescents report they are more likely to turn to friends for common forms of stress (e.g., being teased by a peer, wanting to talk about a bad day) and when looking for companions for social or pleasurable activities than they do for more significant forms of stress (e.g., hurt in a car accident; Rosenthal & Kobak, 2010). Given that adolescents are generally capable of coping with mild to moderate levels of stress without an attachment figure, it is debatable whether seeking support from peers under such circumstances qualifies as attachment behavior and whether peers qualify as attachment figures. Box 4.2 explores the difference between social support and attachment in more detail.

BOX 4.2

A CLOSER LOOK: SOCIAL SUPPORT VERSUS ATTACHMENT

There is often confusion regarding the distinction between social support and attachment behavior or relationships. As a broad concept, social support is considered any form of emotional, instrumental, or informational assistance that is provided by another individual to help cope with some form of a stressor. As such, social support may take many forms. For instance, a friend serving as a sounding board when one is frustrated, a teacher assisting a student with completing a difficult problem, or a stranger offering food and clothing to a homeless individual are forms of social support. Such actions undeniably help the individual experiencing stress to cope with the challenges being faced and result in a degree of emotional calming.

However, in the situations just described, it is unlikely that the stressor was of such intensity that the attachment system was activated and that learned attachment behavior or an attachment script was implemented to cope with the situation. This basic premise provides a line of demarcation to identify whether the social support being observed is an attachment process. Certainly, attachment processes fall under the category of social support, but not all forms of social support qualify as attachment. This distinction may seem like needless differentiation of normative interpersonal aspects of existence, but the ramifications of accurately describing the phenomenon are significant.

Consider the manner in which the word "attachment" is used in common parlance. In the academic literature one can find references to having an attachment to a specific location, an inanimate object, and pets. The conceptualization in each of these cases is that the individual holds an emotional connection or bond with the entity and that the presence of that entity provides emotional security or comfort. There is some precedent in attachment theorizing for such postulations (see the Parental Bonds and Role Reversal section in Chapter 5); however, while an individual may feel emotionally supported by being in familiar surroundings or having a favored animal companion nearby, these entities are unlikely to yield the kind of assistance and calming necessary when one is under threats of a significant magnitude. If the attachment system is activated and the individual's attachment behavior is directed toward an animal, for instance, it is unlikely in most circumstances that the animal will be capable of assisting with the resolution of whatever stimuli caused activation of the attachment system.

(*continues*)

BOX 4.2

A CLOSER LOOK: SOCIAL SUPPORT VERSUS ATTACHMENT (*Continued*)

Distinguishing between individuals who serve attachment functions and those who provide other forms of social support is critical for the study of normative and atypical development. A multitude of people may provide various forms of social support or emotional calming, as may physical locations and inanimate objects, but very few people take the role of a discriminated attachment figure who is sought out under the direst of circumstances.

Undoubtedly, peers serve a legitimate attachment function for some adolescents, perhaps because of significant strain on the relationship between the youth and the primary caregivers or the relative absence of caregivers from the youth's life. Evidence suggests that adolescents who place peers near the top of the attachment hierarchy are at increased risk for displaying emotional and behavioral problems (Rosenthal & Kobak, 2010). One potential reason is that peers, adolescents themselves, may be incapable of providing effective support under moments of significant distress. Another possibility is that the adolescent may already be at risk for displaying psychopathology given the development of ineffective emotion-regulation skills and support from a peer is likely inadequate to supersede such long-standing difficulties.

Given the theoretical contention that attachment processes in infancy and childhood form the foundation for social interactions in later life, researchers examined how early attachment affects relationships with peers. As expected, studies link insecure states of mind with poorer social skills and less supportive peer relationships during adolescence (e.g., J. P. Allen et al., 2007; Loeb et al., 2021). Given the previously reviewed results showing that early attachment experiences are linked to adolescent states of mind, it should not be surprising that early maternal sensitivity predicts social competence in early adolescence (Fraley, Roisman, & Haltigan, 2013).

The Minnesota Study provides an excellent example of how early and later attachment constructs are hypothesized to affect social relationships (Sroufe et al., 2005a). Infant attachment security significantly predicted social competence in adolescents; however, including social competence assessed during earlier points in childhood significantly increased the predictive power of the model. As depicted in Figure 4.1, infant attachment security not only

FIGURE 4.1. Developmental Progression of Social Competence

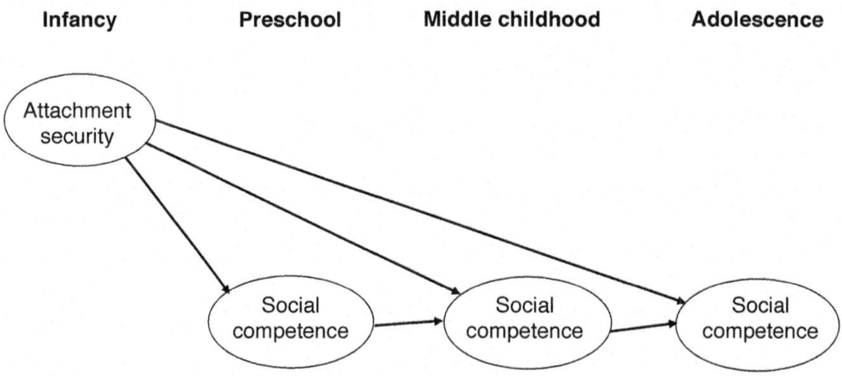

formed the foundation of early social competence, which was itself refined and improved throughout development, but also exerted an impact on adolescent social competence, likely via other mechanisms (e.g., state of mind, emotion regulation). Considering the contextual nature of attachment, the researchers found that their ability to predict social competence was better when they included a number of early care factors as well as later maternal support.

J. P. Allen and Tan (2016) argued that attachment processes might affect peer relationships for two primary reasons. The first is that experiences within attachment relationships throughout development create cognitive biases regarding interpretation of interpersonal interactions (i.e., social cognition). Dykas and Cassidy (2011) reviewed research from across the lifespan and concluded that individuals with secure forms of internal working models are capable of examining positive and negative aspects of social relationships and arriving at conclusions that allow for an adaptive response. Insecurity, on the other hand, is associated with information processing that either filters out negative characteristics of relationships to minimize emotional discomfort or interprets potentially positive aspects of interactions in a negative manner. Such maladaptive forms of social cognition appear to mediate the relationship between attachment insecurity and various forms of peer problems and psychopathology (Bosmans et al., 2010; Venta et al., 2017).

The second mechanism through which attachment processes may influence interpersonal relationships is the emotional processing of intimate experiences (J. P. Allen & Tan, 2016). For instance, secure attachment scripts related to the mother are linked during adolescence with low levels of anxiety and avoidance within close personal relationships (Dykas et al., 2006), and a dismissing state of mind on the AAI correlates with greater self-reported avoidance of emotional intimacy (Miga et al., 2010). A partial explanation for these findings may be that adolescents with dismissing states of mind are less likely than those with secure states of mind to access emotion-laden memories that occurred within attachment relationships, which inhibits their ability to engage emotionally during interpersonal interactions (Dykas et al., 2014). Such challenges with emotionally engaging in close relationships portends difficulties with romantic relationships for individuals with insecure attachment, both during adolescence and into adulthood (Bonache et al., 2017; see also Chapter 5, this volume).

Although it is well established that attachment processes affect peer relationships during adolescence, it is less clear whether peer relationships alter attachment processes. In a multiwave longitudinal study of nearly 700 youth, Khan and colleagues (2020) did not find a relationship between peer relationship quality and changes in attachment security. However, J. P. Allen et al. (2018) administered the AAI to a smaller sample of adolescents and found positive peer relationships predicted increased security over time, with relationships at later time points holding greater influence than earlier ones. A possible reason for the disparate findings is that peer relationships in general may lack the depth of emotional connection and reliance inherent in most parent–child interactions, resulting in less influence on attachment; however, as romantic relationships emerge and take on heightened salience in later adolescence and early adulthood, the possibility of noncaregiver relationships affecting attachment functioning is amplified (J. P. Allen et al., 2018).

CONCLUSION

Attachment during adolescence represents a developmental bridge between an earlier period in life during which the individual must rely on a discriminated caregiver for a sense of security and a later phase in which the individual is typically self-sufficient and turns toward individuals of their own choosing for support. Certainly, the foundations of interactions with peers are laid down during early relationships with caregivers, and caregivers continue to exert an influence during adolescence, but the attachment system is undergoing significant changes as it transitions to its role in supporting a fully independent person. Research examining attachment in adolescence is a fairly young field but provides multiple important considerations for understanding how one might navigate the interpersonal challenges awaiting in adulthood, such as being a romantic partner and a parent, which are the focus of the next chapter.

RESOURCES

Professional Societies

- **Society for Research on Adolescence (SRA):** SRA is the largest professional society focused on developmental research of the adolescent period. Attachment research is occasionally featured in the SRA's journal and in the society's biennial meeting. More information can be found at their website: https://www.s-r-a.org/

Suggested Further Reading

Allen, J. P., & Tan, J. S. (2016). The multiple facets of attachment in adolescence. In J. Cassidy & P. R. Shaver (Eds.), *Handbook of attachment: Theory, research, and clinical implications* (3rd ed., pp. 399–415). Guilford Press.

This chapter provides a succinct overview of the current state of the science regarding attachment during adolescence. The authors place the empirical findings within the larger theoretical context of attachment theory and discuss a number of fundamental questions regarding the evolution of attachment processes during this developmental period. Although the authors focus on examining the scientific literature, the chapter is relatively nontechnical and accessible to nonacademic audiences.

Scharf, M., & Mayseless, O. (2007). *Attachment in adolescence: Reflections and new angles*. Jossey-Bass.

This edited volume introduces the reader to a number of key aspects of research on attachment in adolescence, such as emotion regulation, social information processing, and the evolution of attachment representations. The individual chapters are geared toward providing a nontechnical overview of the different topics, and the goal of the chapters is to integrate scientific findings into a coherent understanding that can point the way for future research.

5 ATTACHMENT DURING ADULTHOOD

Being a Parent and a Partner

Attachment research included parents from the beginning, as assessing sensitive caregiving was vital for testing the foundational tenets of the theory. Once caregiving was established as a predictor of infant attachment behavior, it was natural to search for factors that influenced the quality of the caregiving provided. Such research required the development of new instruments, which opened new avenues to examine how attachment processes affect myriad aspects of adulthood, such as romantic relationships. However, examining individual behavior within the context of interpersonal relationships is not solely the purview of developmental scientists; social psychologists have a long history of such work. Indeed, social psychologists bring a different perspective and methodology to attachment research, yielding informative new directions.

THE ADULT ATTACHMENT INTERVIEW: A WATERSHED MOMENT

Mary Main and her colleagues (1985) introduced the Adult Attachment Interview (AAI) in a classic paper arguing for the need to examine representational constructs in attachment (i.e., internal working models; see Chapter 3

https://doi.org/10.1037/0000333-006
The Science and Clinical Practice of Attachment Theory: A Guide From Infancy to Adulthood, by B. Allen

in this volume). Tucked within a larger discussion of theoretical issues and results from the Berkeley Longitudinal Study was a relatively brief description of the AAI. Parents were asked to consider their own childhood experiences with attachment figures and "were rated for security with respect to experiences, ideas, and feelings surrounding attachment" (Main et al., 1985, p. 91). The team found a significant correlation between their ratings of a caregiver's security on the AAI and the infant's display of secure attachment behavior within the Strange Situation Procedure (SSP; for mothers, $r = .62$, $p < .001$, for fathers, $r = .37$, $p < .05$). Convinced the AAI was tapping a construct of importance for the study of differences in caregiver sensitivity, Main published several papers describing its development and use (e.g., Main & Goldwyn, 1984; Main & Hesse, 1990). In time, it was recognized that the AAI is not actually assessing a response to stress, as is the hallmark of attachment behavioral assessments and script assessments, but rather the person's overall conceptualization of attachment relationships and recall of prior attachment experiences. This broad construct is termed a *state of mind*.

The AAI begins by asking interviewees to provide basic background on their families and where they grew up. Once the primary caregivers in childhood are identified, the interviewee is asked to consider the individuals in turn and provide five adjectives to describe each. Questions then proceed in a manner that aims to identify memories of one's own attachment behaviors (e.g., when afraid or upset) and parental responses, the extent to which childhood attachment experiences continue to exert an influence, and how relationships with caregivers changed over time. In defining the sequence of questions and their presentation, the authors aimed to "surprise the unconscious" (George et al., 1996). As explained by H. Steele and Steele (2008), the AAI "poses in a calm but persistent way a series of questions that serve invariably to take the interviewee back to highly emotional events in early childhood that he or she will not ordinarily have discussed or reflected upon" (p. 8).

Main and Goldwyn (1984) noted peculiarities with the manner in which some caregivers responded to questions during the pilot of the AAI. Having the SSP classifications of the infants available, they searched for patterns among the discourse styles of caregivers when grouped based on the behavior of the infants. A general lack of coherence within the interviews was associated with avoidant behaviors from infants within the SSP, while more structured responses were found among parents of secure infants. Experience led to refinement and clarification of the coding of AAI transcript discourse (Hesse, 1999). A framework was established borrowing from British philosopher Paul Grice (1975), who opined that coherent communication involves four elements (or maxims): quality (truthful, evidence supports conclusions), quantity (complete, concise), relation (content is relevant to the topic), and manner (clear, well structured).

The current system of coding the AAI (Main et al., 1984–2003) requires reviewing the interview transcript and scoring a series of scales that collectively examine (a) the perspective of the interviewee and the content provided regarding relationships with caregivers (experiences) and (b) the extent to which the narrative ascribes to Grice's (1975) maxims of discourse (coherence). Classification rules dictate categorization of the interview into one of four primary classes: secure (F), dismissing (Ds), preoccupied (E), or unresolved (U). Each category is reviewed next based on descriptions provided by Main et al. (1984–2003), and a schematic representation of their features is presented in Chapter 4 of this volume (see Table 4.1).

States of Mind

Secure (F)[1]

A *secure state of mind* is characterized by respect for and finding value in prior caregiving relationships and acknowledgment of the need to rely on others in certain situations. However, these descriptions of caregivers are not idealized, as one can identify the flaws of caregivers and can discuss both positive and negative experiences within attachment relationships. Narratives are coherent in form and generally ascribe to Grice's (1975) maxims, suggesting that memories of prior relationships with the caregiver do not confuse, threaten, and/or overwhelm the respondent. Approximately 56% of women and 50% of men in nonclinical samples are classified secure (Bakermans-Kranenburg & van IJzendoorn, 2009).

Main's Berkeley Longitudinal Study (Main et al., 2005) provided the first evidence that a secure state of mind in adulthood was linked to attachment security assessed at earlier points in the lifespan. She found evidence that secure transcripts on the AAI at 19 years of age were significantly correlated with secure infant behavior in the SSP and with signs of security during separation and reunion procedures and the Separation Anxiety Test at 6 years of age. Replication soon followed from other longitudinal projects that

---

[1]Crowell (2021) noted that the original term, "autonomous," "was intended to reflect flexibility of attention in attachment-relevant situations and the free-flowing ability to consider and discuss attachment experiences" (p. 318). However, the term is frequently associated with the idea of independence, and some may conclude that insecure categories suggest forms of dependence. Thus, "autonomous" is used with decreasing regularity in favor of the term "secure."

integrated the AAI, with E. Waters and his colleagues (2000) finding that 64% of infants classified secure in the SSP yielded secure transcripts on the AAI 20 years later. They also found that only 33% of secure infants who later experienced at least one significant disruption in the caregiving environment (e.g., parental death, serious parental illness) were secure on the AAI, although 85% of secure infants who did not experience such events remained secure.

The most convincing evidence to date comes from the exceptionally large National Institute of Child Health and Human Development (NICHD) Study of Early Child Care. Using a sample of 819 participants, Groh, Roisman, and colleagues (2014) found that 61% of infants displaying secure attachment behavior in the SSP at 15 months were categorized with a secure state of mind on the AAI at 18 years of age. Similarly, 60% of secure children completing a modified SSP at 36 months of age were later secure on the AAI. Also using the NICHD data, Booth-LaForce et al. (2014) showed that consistent maternal sensitivity throughout infancy and later childhood predicted stability in secure status, as did fewer negative life events.

Dismissing (Ds)

Individuals who deny the importance of prior attachment experiences, minimize negative emotional experiences, and/or provide an unrealistic picture of personal independence are designated as displaying a *dismissing state of mind*. Alternatively, the individual may give an overly positive view of caregivers by refusing to acknowledge any significant flaws, suggesting excessive idealization; however, the evidence provided to support these contentions is minimal and unconvincing. Accordingly, the narratives provided are often unbelievable and lacking in detail, violating Grice's (1975) maxims of quality and quantity, respectively. A notable gender difference is often observed, as the percentage of men classified as dismissing in nonclinical samples (24%) is significantly higher than that of women (16%; Bakermans-Kranenburg & van IJzendoorn, 2009).

The dismissing state of mind is considered a vestige of avoidant forms of attachment behavior and scripts. However, the data directly linking these early childhood constructs to the dismissing classification on the AAI are fairly weak, with only 37% of avoidant infants and 29% of avoidant preschoolers classified as dismissing on the AAI at 18 years of age (Groh, Roisman, et al., 2014). Nonetheless, evidence suggests that a dismissing state of mind is associated with low levels of maternal sensitivity during infancy and childhood as well as an absent father (Haydon et al., 2014).

Preoccupied (E)

Interviews of individuals displaying a *preoccupied state of mind* typically are marked by persistent descriptions of the shortcomings of caregivers, with the individual oftentimes appearing angry and resentful and providing contradictory praise of the caregivers and suggestions that attachment experiences were positive. The discourse throughout the interview is often difficult to follow, as the individual may provide long answers to questions and cycle through numerous themes or thoughts while responding, often appearing lost in thought or confused about what experiences and emotions to convey. The preoccupied state of mind is the most rarely used classification, with approximately 9% of women and 11% of men providing such transcripts (Bakermans-Kranenburg & van IJzendoorn, 2009).

The preoccupied state of mind is analogous to the ambivalent attachment behavior seen in the SSP, but continuity of this category is not demonstrated in longitudinal research. Of 63 infants displaying ambivalent behavior in the SSP at 18 months of age, Groh, Roisman, and colleagues (2014) found only one to be classified as preoccupied on the AAI at 18 years. However, as with the dismissing state of mind, lower levels of maternal sensitivity throughout life were associated with a greater likelihood of displaying preoccupied features within the AAI transcript (Haydon et al., 2014). Findings such as these underlie much of the preferred approach to analyzing AAI transcripts, with preoccupied and dismissing states of mind categorized together as insecure and contrasted with those categorized secure.

Unresolved in Relation to Trauma and Loss (U)

Main and her colleagues noticed early in the development of the AAI that the mothers of infants categorized as disorganized often provided responses that demonstrated "lapses" in their ability to speak coherently about their attachment experiences (Hesse, 2016). For instance, some individuals spoke as though a deceased loved one were still alive or provided a coherent account of an abuse experience only to later deny any abuse occurred. Other individuals reported that negative early experiences continued to exert a profound impact on their lives, suggesting significant and persistent adverse effects. Such findings led to the development of two additional scales for scoring the AAI, one related to an *unresolved state of mind* with respect to abuse (e.g., sexual abuse, physical abuse) and another with respect to loss (e.g., parental death, abandonment). Interviewees may be categorized as unresolved if the score for either of the scales reaches a cutoff point. Among nonclinical samples, approximately 18% of women and 15% of men are classified as unresolved (Bakermans-Kranenburg & van IJzendoorn, 2009). It is not uncommon to see the unresolved category grouped with the dismissing and preoccupied categories to yield a secure versus insecure analysis. It is also commonplace to isolate unresolved transcripts from those in the other three groups to examine features associated specifically with an unresolved state of mind.

There is currently a reformulation of the unresolved category occurring within the attachment literature. Originally, the classification included individuals scoring above the cutoff on either the abuse or loss scale; however, research is highlighting significant differences between individuals unresolved for loss and those unresolved for abuse. For instance, one study found that controlling for trauma exposure resulted in no significant differences between those classified as U versus non-U related to a history of parental loss, while also finding that hostile or helpless responses on the AAI were related to trauma exposure and not parental loss (Lyons-Ruth et al., 2003). Indeed, Hesse and Main (2000) proposed that the fundamental deficit of individuals with an unresolved state of mind (as well as disorganized infants) is the inability to coherently structure attentional resources and behavioral responses to address a demanding situation. Such challenges are commonly noted among adults who experienced severe abuse in childhood (B. Allen & Lauterbach, 2007; Vonderlin et al., 2018) but are uncommon in situations of parental loss. As such, the concepts of unresolved loss and unresolved abuse are increasingly differentiated in the literature.

Earned Secure

It is important to note the concept of *earned security*. In brief, this categorization is given to individuals who identify significant experiences of abuse or substandard parenting during childhood but exhibit a secure state of mind during the AAI. Theoretically, the concept of earned security reflects the proposition that change is possible and that prior experiences do not necessarily dictate future states (Hesse, 2016). However, the clinical utility of the earned secure concept is questionable. Some evidence suggests that individuals classified as earned secure exhibit lower levels of security when using dimensional scoring than those identified as continuously secure (Venta et al., 2015) and potentially display higher levels of internalizing symptoms (Roisman et al., 2014), which may result in reporting biases when recounting childhood experiences. Longitudinal analyses suggest that individuals identified as earned secure may have experienced less severe or prolonged substandard parenting than reported during the interview (Roisman et al., 2014). As such, it is unclear whether earned secure individuals constitute a unique group displaying resiliency or an intermediate point on a continuum between security and insecurity (van IJzendoorn & Bakermans-Kranenburg, 2014).

Alternative Forms of Scoring the AAI

Research and experience since the development of the original AAI coding scheme have yielded useful alternative methods for scoring and analyzing the interview. One of the most prominent approaches forgoes the classification scheme and instead focuses on the total coherence score for the transcript, as it is the factor most strongly related to overall security on the AAI (Crowell, 2021). Some evidence suggests the coherence construct is a key factor in understanding differences in parenting quality (Shlafer et al., 2015), problem solving within intimate relationships (Crowell et al., 2002), and personality disorders in adulthood (Barone, 2003). One hypothesis is that coherence largely reflects the quality of one's attachment scripts, and vice versa. Following development of the Secure Base Script Assessment (SBSA; see Chapter 3, this volume), Theodore Waters and colleagues devised a coding scheme to assess the security of scripts within AAI transcripts (T. E. A. Waters et al., 2013; T. E. A. Waters & Facompré, 2021). Convincing evidence with this approach suggests scoring secure-base knowledge on the AAI will likely become more prevalent in the years ahead. Box 5.1 presents the relationship between attachment scripts and states of mind.

ADULT ATTACHMENT AND CAREGIVING BEHAVIOR

Ainsworth's early studies clearly pointed to caregiving as an important antecedent for attachment behavior among infants. Main's hypothesis that one's own attachment experiences during childhood informed the type of caregiving provided to one's own children was the catalyst for developing the AAI. Initial examination within the Berkeley Longitudinal Study confirmed Main's proposition, with mothers secure on the AAI more likely to have infants classified as secure in the SSP (Main et al., 1985). In addition, avoidant behavior among infants was associated with a mother's low coherence on the AAI and reports of being rejected by a caregiver when young (Main & Goldwyn, 1984).

Attempts to replicate began soon after, as demonstrating the intergenerational transmission of attachment promised significant theoretical insights and clinical applications. van IJzendoorn (1995) meta-analyzed

BOX 5.1

A CLOSER LOOK: FROM ATTACHMENT SCRIPTS TO A STATE OF MIND

Studies evaluating attachment scripts are converging on the finding that relationship-specific models present from infancy through middle childhood undergo a process of consolidation, yielding a more unified underlying model by the end of adolescence. What is unclear, however, is how this occurs. T. E. A. Waters (2021) argued that scripts developed throughout childhood and related to a specific individual (e.g., mother) are, by necessity, tested with other individuals (e.g., peers, romantic partners). He also suggested that elaboration of the scripts occurs through repeated usage and that individuals identify important contextual cues to guide their selection of responses. For instance, enacting the script will likely result in different behaviors based on whether the other individual involved is a romantic partner or a sibling.

Although attachment scripts are generally considered a specific aspect of the internal working model (i.e., how to respond under moments of distress), states of mind primarily describe one's ability to coherently recall and discuss prior attachment experiences. This is not to suggest the two concepts are unrelated, however. Recalling previous attachment experiences during the Adult Attachment Interview (AAI) inherently requires accessing autobiographical memories from childhood. The construction of life scripts based on past experiences is a key component underlying autobiographical memory (e.g., Bohn & Berntsen, 2013). Not surprisingly, findings suggest that attachment scripts form the foundation of autobiographical narratives of child–caregiver experiences (T. E. A. Waters et al., 2017), which underlie one's ability to coherently discuss such experiences during the AAI (Köber et al., 2019). Certainly, the state of mind construct integrates several cognitive, emotional, and developmental capabilities, and attachment scripts appear to be a prominent feature.

the first decade of research examining the connection between caregiver AAI and child behavior in the SSP, encompassing more than 850 dyads across 18 samples. Parsing the data into the traditional three-way scheme, he found a nearly 70% concordance rate between parental state of mind on the AAI and the hypothesized matching SSP classification of the infant (i.e., secure–secure, dismissive–avoidant, preoccupied–ambivalent); when collapsed into the dichotomous secure/insecure scheme, the concordance rate increased to 75%. Including the unresolved and disorganized classifications of the AAI and SSP, respectively, the four-way concordance rate was 63%. A later meta-analysis incorporating over 2,600 parent–child dyads found a three-way correspondence of 58% (dichotomous secure/insecure = 65%) and a four-way correspondence of 51% (Verhage et al., 2016). Such results provided convincing evidence that attachment was, to a significant degree, transmitted from the caregiver to the child.

The next task for attachment researchers was identifying the ways in which caregiver states of mind influence the display of attachment behavior among infants. It was assumed that caregivers with a secure state of mind possessed more coherent memories of childhood experiences and a more adaptive appreciation for the importance of caregivers to children, factors that might predict high sensitivity to infant cues (Main et al., 1985). Given the historical and theoretical focus on caregiver sensitivity and the fact that it was already established as an important factor in the development of secure attachment behavior, it was a logical first target of research. van IJzendoorn (1995) provided some initial support as, indeed, he found a secure state of mind on the AAI correlated with sensitive caregiving behavior. Over the next 20 years, research continued to confirm the proposition, finding that caregivers with a secure state of mind demonstrate, in general, more adaptive parenting abilities than are seen in caregivers with an insecure state of mind (Verhage et al., 2016). However, attempting to test the full model in which state of mind predicts caregiver sensitivity, which in turn predicts infant attachment behavior, has met with limited success. Both van IJzendoorn (1995) and Verhage and colleagues (2016) found that 50% to 75% of the variance between parental state of mind and infant attachment behavior was not attributable to differences in caregiver sensitivity, creating a phenomenon known as the *transmission gap* (see Box 5.2 for more details).

Security of attachment scripts is gaining popularity as a potential factor in explaining the transmission of attachment from a caregiver to a child. For instance, several studies have demonstrated that caregivers with secure scripts, marked by an expectation of comfort-seeking under moments of distress, are most likely to display sensitive caregiving (Coppola et al., 2006; Hawkins et al., 2015). In addition, this finding appears robust, as secure attachment scripts are associated with improved parenting quality among mothers from at-risk samples, such as mothers with trauma-exposure histories (Huth-Bocks et al., 2014) and from lower socioeconomic strata (T. E. A. Waters et al., 2018). Increasing evidence links secure attachment scripts among caregivers to secure attachment behavior among infants and toddlers (e.g., Vaughn et al., 2007; T. E. A. Waters et al., 2018) and secure attachment

BOX 5.2

A CLOSER LOOK: BRIDGING THE "TRANSMISSION GAP"

It is clear from the accumulated evidence that parental state of mind on the Adult Attachment Interview predicts infant attachment behavior in the SSP. However, only a portion of this relationship, approximately 25% to 50%, appears attributable to differences in caregiver sensitivity, leaving a large discrepancy in attachment theorizing, a phenomenon van IJzendoorn (1995) termed the "transmission gap." No shortage of theories emerged proposing other mechanisms through which a caregiver's state of mind influences the development of a child's attachment behavior.

One of the initial hypotheses to emerge suggested a genetic predisposition on the part of the child that interacts with the caregiving provided to yield attachment behavior (e.g., Fearon et al., 2006). However, much of the evidence related to temperament and candidate genes does not suggest significant variance in attachment behavior is attributable to such factors, although research continues (see Chapter 2, this volume). An alternative perspective suggests examining an expanded realm of parenting behaviors beyond sensitivity, such as supporting the autonomy of the child (Bernier et al., 2014) or understanding the perspectives of the child (i.e., mind-mindedness; Bernier & Dozier, 2003). One must also recognize that the multitude of developmental factors evolving in concert with attachment representations (e.g., emotion regulation, behavior regulation) exert an influence on one's later caregiving behavior. In other words, parents with better self-control and ability to tolerate and/or modulate stress may transmit such capacities to their children, which are reflected in the child's attachment behavior.

As with so many other areas of attachment theory, it is likely the case that transmission of attachment from parent to the child is dependent on environmental factors (e.g., Tarabulsy et al., 2005). Van IJzendoorn and Bakermans-Kranenburg (2019) recently proposed a model wherein caregiver state of mind is considered within either a supportive or a stressful environmental context to yield either sensitive or insensitive parenting behavior, which then interacts with the child's level of susceptibility to environmental influence and results in infant attachment behavior. It is an intriguing model that integrates many of the established influences, but the authors were quick to point out that even such a model, if validated, would not completely close the transmission gap. Undoubtedly, multiple other influences are yet to be identified and empirically examined.

scripts among older children (e.g., T. E. A. Waters, Bosmans, et al., 2015; Wong et al., 2011). Conceptually, a caregiver with secure attachment scripts possesses an adaptive mental framework, a sort of cognitive roadmap, which aids in accurately interpreting infant signals and implementing effective responses. Caregivers with insecure scripts may either miss important cues from their children or be unsure how to respond.

Unresolved State of Mind and Disorganized Attachment Behavior

Given the theoretical and practical similarities between the unresolved state of mind in adults and disorganized attachment behavior among infants, links between the two constructs emerged quickly. Main and Hesse (1990) first established the relationship within the Berkeley Longitudinal Study. Multiple follow-up studies likewise appeared to confirm such a connection, with the established relationship between small and medium in strength (r = .21–.31; Madigan et al., 2006; van IJzendoorn, 1995). These findings suggest that caregivers exhibiting an unresolved state of mind place their children at significant risk for displaying disorganized attachment behavior, but identifying the cause of such a connection is difficult.

Main and Hesse (1990) hypothesized that frightening behavior (FR) from the caregiver is the most likely mediating mechanism. More specifically, they opined that lapses in cognitive and attentional processes, ongoing trauma-related fear, and erratic behavior characteristic of the unresolved state of mind constitute FR, which places the child in an approach–avoidance conflict and results in disorganized behavior (see Chapter 3, this volume). Research since this original postulation offers only partial support for this perspective. Certainly, compelling evidence links an unresolved state of mind to the display of FR (e.g., Madigan et al., 2007); however, relatively little variance in the connection between unresolved state of mind and disorganized attachment behavior is accounted for by FR (Madigan et al., 2006).

These findings suggest another transmission gap, and researchers are searching for other mechanisms linking unresolved state of mind with disorganized attachment behavior. One approach examines the heterogeneity observed within the unresolved classification, such as homing in specifically on AAI content suggestive of hostility or helplessness on the part of the parent (Lyons-Ruth et al., 2003). Another avenue involves looking at deficits in other aspects of parenting that may be more prevalent among those with an unresolved state of mind, such as displaying less positive emotion during interactions with the child (Busch et al., 2008) or difficulty regulating the stresses associated with parenting (Lionetti et al., 2015).

Mentalization

A relatively new approach in the attachment field holding promise for explaining how state of mind affects parenting is the construct of mentalization. In the 1990s, some attachment and developmental researchers began examining the hypothesis that parenting ability may be influenced largely by a caregiver's ability to understand their own mental states and processes as well as those of others, including the child. Peter Fonagy and colleagues (1991) reviewed the AAI transcripts of 200 pregnant women recruited as part of the London Parent–Child Project to identify the extent to which interviewees discussed the motivations and intentions of both their own behaviors and those of their parents. High levels of insight and consideration of psychological factors, what they termed "reflective-self functioning" or more simply *reflective functioning*, predicted ratings of infant attachment security during the SSP at 12 and 18 months of age. Further research demonstrated that lower scores for reflective functioning are associated with higher levels of FR parenting behavior, which in turn predict disorganized attachment behavior from the child (K. Kelly et al., 2005), while higher scores for reflective functioning are associated with caregiver sensitivity and secure infant attachment behavior during the SSP (Stacks et al., 2014).

In a related vein, Elizabeth Meins focused on the language used by caregivers during interaction with their children and the extent to which it conveyed caregivers' ability to view their children as separate entities with their own thoughts and perspectives, a trait she labeled "mind-mindedness." She discovered that the more frequently a mother verbalized an age-appropriate understanding of the child's mental capacities during the first 3 years of life, the greater the child's ability to similarly understand the perspectives of others at 4 to 5 years of age (Meins & Fernyhough, 1999; Meins et al., 2003). Studies emerged suggesting that mind-mindedness accounted for a significant proportion of the variance between maternal state of mind on the AAI and attachment security of the child in the SSP (Arnott & Meins, 2007; Bernier & Dozier, 2003).

Concepts such as reflective functioning and mind-mindedness are often subsumed under the broad construct *mentalization*. Mentalization is a higher order classification for various facets of one's ability to understand and consider the role of mental processes in shaping interpersonal behavior, including cognitively reflecting on what may be motivating one's behavior, accurately describing what another is experiencing in a given moment, considering the cognitive bases of emotions, and attending to both internal and external elements that may provide useful information (Fonagy et al., 2016).[2] In relation to parenting, much of the available research on mentalization reflects the findings examining the more circumscribed constructs of reflective functioning and mind-mindedness, namely that parental capacity for mentalization predicts both attachment security for the child and caregiver sensitivity (Zeegers et al., 2017).

To concretize this rather abstract concept, consider the example of a crying child who approaches his mother after being scared by a loud noise. One mother may interpret the cues as signaling the child is afraid, conclude the crying is motivated by a desire for comfort, and interact with the child by both providing physical comfort and accurately labeling the child's mental state (e.g., "I know, that loud noise scared you"). This mother demonstrates a high level of mentalizing ability and provides a response that both fosters a secure attachment and promotes the child's own ability to mentalize. A second mother, displaying much lower mentalizing ability, may view the child as overly sensitive, believe the child's crying is motivated by a desire to bother her, and respond by telling him to "Stop whining and go play." This second mother's rejecting response may engender avoidant attachment behavior and do little to promote the child's mentalizing ability.

Parental Bonds and Role Reversal

In her landmark volume, *Patterns of Attachment*, Ainsworth provided an alternative broader definition of attachment as "a bond, tie, or enduring relationship between a young child and his mother" (Ainsworth et al., 1978/2015, p. 17), echoing earlier sentiments by Bowlby (1969/1982). A decade later she clarified that she views attachment as a form of *affectional bond*, which she defined as "a relatively long-enduring tie in which a partner is important as a unique individual and is interchangeable with none other" (Ainsworth, 1989, p. 711). She argued that what distinguishes an *attachment bond* from other forms of affectional bonds is the "experience of security and comfort obtained from the relationship with the partner" (p. 711). Consequently, it can justly be said that attachment theorists recognized early that a lasting emotional connection is made between a child and caregiver; however, studying such an abstract concept is difficult, and attachment research,

---

[2]Although mentalization is a relatively complex concept, it is often referred to in simplistic terms that make it indistinguishable from the concept of reflective functioning. Indeed, the two terms are often used interchangeably.

by necessity, focuses on observable behavior, scripts, and states of mind, which are more operationally definable.

The concept of affectional bonds has found a significant place, however, in examining the caregiver's perspective of the parent–child relationship. It is certainly acknowledged that caregivers develop a "long-enduring tie" of an emotional nature with their children and that such a bond can activate what is typically referred to as the *caregiving system*, the complex array of cognitive, emotional, and behavioral responses that result in observable caregiving behavior. However, this form of affectional bond does not qualify as an attachment bond precisely because the presence of the child is not expected to create a sense of emotional security and comfort for the caregiver. As such, the caregiver's affectional tie to the child is commonly referred to as a *parental bond* (Cassidy, 2016).

This distinction between an attachment bond and a parental bond allows for the specification of a potentially problematic characteristic of parent–child relationships, a phenomenon referred to as "role reversal." In these instances, the normal hierarchical structure of the parent–child relationship, namely that the child seeks security from the caregiver, is reversed, and the caregiver relies on the child for a sense of security. Mothers who report more experiences of role reversal in their own childhoods during the AAI demonstrate more role-reversing behaviors during interactions with their own toddlers (Macfie et al., 2005), suggesting a form of intergenerational transmission. In addition, mothers reporting elevated levels of depression and stress are more likely to report helplessness in their role as a caregiver and, correspondingly, more caregiving displayed by the child (George & Solomon, 2011). Disorganized attachment behavior appears to predict the later display of a child's caregiving behavior toward the mother (Macfie et al., 2008), an unsurprising finding given the relation of disorganized attachment behavior in infancy to controlling forms of behavior during middle childhood (see Chapter 3, this volume). Such signs of role reversal may portend significant behavioral problems for youth (Lecompte & Moss, 2014).

A SOCIAL PSYCHOLOGICAL PERSPECTIVE ON ATTACHMENT

Although Bowlby suggested that attachment processes play a crucial role "in the life of a man from the cradle to the grave" (Bowlby, 1969/1982, p. 208), developmental researchers throughout the 1980s and 1990s rarely examined attachment functioning in adulthood. Measures such as the AAI were developed to examine parental antecedents of caregiving, and research included adults because of their central role in the development of attachment behavior among infants. Social psychologists stepped in to fill this void as Bowlby's and Ainsworth's insights were considered helpful for understanding mature intimate relationships.

Phillip Shaver is often credited as the first social psychologist to apply attachment concepts to adult relationships. Shaver, along with graduate student Cindy Hazan, developed a "love quiz," published it in a local newspaper, and solicited readers to reply (Hazan & Shaver, 1987). Respondents identified which of three different interpersonal styles "best describe your feelings" regarding intimate relationships.[3] The options were modeled on Shaver and Hazan's understanding of how Ainsworth's primary classifications of infant behavior might present in adult romantic relationships: secure (easy to get close to others, comfortable depending on others), avoidant (uncomfortable getting close to others, difficult to trust or depend on others), and anxious/ambivalent (wants to be closer than others do, worries about being abandoned). In their sample of more than 500 people, 56% self-reported a secure style, 25% identified being avoidant, and 19% endorsed the anxious/ambivalent type. In addition, individuals who reported being secure scored higher on measures of relationship satisfaction, happiness, and trust.

Mario Mikulincer adopted the "love quiz" in his own research, with one significant modification. He and his team developed a 15-item questionnaire, with five items crafted to reflect each of the three styles, and asked participants to rate the items on a 7-point scale (Mikulincer et al., 1990). When they categorized participants into the three groups based on the highest scoring scale, they found a 94% concordance rate with self-categorization using the "love quiz." In the same year, Simpson (1990) devised a series of scales assessing the three styles. A higher score on his secure scale was associated with the display of more positive emotions and fewer negative emotions within a romantic relationship as well as with greater trust and relationship satisfaction, while a higher score on the avoidant and anxious/ambivalent scales was associated with the opposite results.

Studies employing such continuous and categorical methods convincingly linked self-reported *attachment style* to diverse outcomes, including self-image, perceptions of social support, and coping during stressful situations (for a review, see Mikulincer & Shaver, 2016). The problem, however, was the

---

[3]Social psychological literature most often denotes results of self-report measures of attachment as "style." Social psychologists recognize they are not assessing behaviors, scripts, or states of mind, nor are they assessing Bowlby's conceptualization of the internal working model. Rather, they are assessing respondents' self-perception of how they interact with others and, thus, "style" (Mikulincer & Shaver, 2016, pp. 78–79).

significant proliferation of scales and measurement approaches that followed in the wake of Hazan and Shaver's original "love quiz" (e.g., Bartholomew & Horowitz, 1991; Feeney et al., 1994). The diversity of terminology and methods created a confusing picture of the results and their potential applications.

To consolidate the different approaches to assessment and bring clarity to the construct of attachment style, Brennan et al. (1998) combined all items from the various questionnaires then in existence, removed redundancies, and administered them to a sample of more than 1,000 college students. They distilled a 36-item measure that included two subscales, one assessing avoidance in relationships and one assessing relationship-specific forms of anxiety. This new measure, termed the Experiences in Close Relationships (ECR) Scale, quickly became the standard for examining adult romantic attachment style. Meta-analyses demonstrate excellent psychometric properties for the ECR, with negligible gender differences (Del Giudice, 2011), and the two subscales are largely independent of one another (Graham & Unterschute, 2015).

Fraley et al. (2000) directly compared the ECR with other continuous measures and found that the ECR performed the best. However, they noted the ECR did not sufficiently detect gradations among people who reported low levels of interpersonal avoidance and/or anxiety. To address this problem, they returned to the original item pool of Brennan et al. (1998) and empirically identified items that functioned more adequately, replacing 5 of the 18 Anxiety subscale items and 11 of the 18 Avoidance subscale items. They termed the new measure the ECR-Revised (ECR-R) Scale. Reviews show relatively few differences between the ECR and the ECR-R, likely because they share many of the same items, but there is some suggestion that the ECR-R possesses slightly better psychometric properties (Graham & Unterschute, 2015). Regardless, both are commonly used in contemporary social psychological research, and it is generally agreed that they assess the same constructs.

In conceptualizing the meaning of the avoidance and anxiety dimensions, as found on the ECR/ECR-R and other measures, Mikulincer and Shaver (2016) suggested that deactivation of the attachment system (i.e., minimization/avoidance) is employed when support is perceived as either unavailable or likely ineffective, while hyperactivation (i.e., maximization/anxiety) aims to demand a response from an individual viewed as unreliable. Viewed through this lens, self-reported attachment style is often conceived as a cognitive perspective on interpersonal forms of emotion regulation. Individuals reporting high anxiety and/or avoidance report higher levels of loneliness (Manthos et al., 2014), difficulty managing relationship conflict

(Jenkins-Guarnieri et al., 2012), and poor social skills (Oldmeadow et al., 2013). Not surprisingly, attachment avoidance and anxiety are linked with increased risk for substance use (Brennan & Shaver, 1995), risky sexual behavior (Manthos et al., 2014), and suicide (Levi-Belz et al., 2013).

DIFFERENTIATING SOCIAL AND DEVELOPMENTAL PERSPECTIVES ON ATTACHMENT

The social psychological approach of quantifying self-reported attachment style on scales of interpersonal avoidance and anxiety popularized a relatively little-discussed developmental hypothesis. Ainsworth et al. (1978/2015), to condense the behaviors of infants in the SSP, statistically identified two discrete functions. The first, labeled "A versus non-A," identified behaviors that distinguished avoidant infants from secure and ambivalent ones, while the second, labeled "C versus non-C," included behaviors characteristic of ambivalent infants. Cassidy and Kobak (1988) conceptualized these two factors as emotion regulation strategies, and Kobak went on to develop a widely used Q-sort scoring system for the AAI that largely uses the minimization versus maximization framework (Kobak et al., 1993). In addition, a recent meta-analysis suggests that viewing the AAI in a dimensional manner based on these two factors is preferable to the categorical approach (Raby et al., 2022; see also Box 5.3 for a discussion of whether attachment is categorically or dimensionally distributed). As such, the social and developmental approaches to attachment appear to share important qualities.

Studies investigated how the social psychological concept of attachment style corresponds with other aspects of attachment theory. Using the NICHD Study of Early Child Care, researchers found mixed results connecting infant attachment security and maternal sensitivity during childhood with self-reported avoidance and anxiety in young adulthood; when relationships were found, they were usually weak (Fraley, Roisman, Booth-LaForce, et al., 2013; R. D. Steele et al., 2014). However, a higher level of stability was found when using self-report measures of attachment anxiety and avoidance from childhood through young adulthood (Khan et al., 2020). Notably, important life events predict changes in self-reported attachment style, as postulated by attachment theory (Fraley et al., 2021; Khan et al., 2020).

Regardless, the social psychological construct of attachment style does not typically relate to attachment metrics from the developmental tradition. Decades of research comparing self-report measures of attachment style to the AAI demonstrates practically no relationship between the assessments (e.g., Roisman et al., 2007), nor does there appear to be a relationship

BOX 5.3

A CLOSER LOOK: IS ATTACHMENT CATEGORICALLY OR DIMENSIONALLY DISTRIBUTED?

Initial attempts to assess attachment relied on categorical descriptions, such as Ainsworth's classification of attachment behaviors, Main's state of mind categories, and Hazan and Shaver's attachment styles. Using such an approach demonstrated the relevance of attachment research for understanding development. However, the traditional criticism of categorical approaches to assessment is that they obscure important differences within groups and eliminate gradations often found between the groups. These criticisms are applicable and important for considering the assessment of attachment.

Ainsworth herself identified two primary dimensions of child behavior (i.e., avoidant and ambivalent) and found that they effectively delineated each of the three primary categories (Ainsworth et al., 1978/2015). Fraley and Spieker (2003) examined Strange Situation Procedure observations from the National Institute of Child Health and Human Development (NICHD) Early Child Care study and discovered precisely the same two-factor structure. Similar results show the same two dimensions underlie Adult Attachment Interview transcripts (Raby et al., 2022) and self-report measures of attachment (Fraley et al., 2015). From a methodological standpoint, embracing a dimensional approach allows for more fine-grained statistical analyses and removes the somewhat artificial process of determining on which side of a categorical dividing line an individual falls.

H. Steele and Steele (2021) argued that the categorical approach provides multiple benefits, primary among them the ease at which an individual can use the information. Decision making often uses a categorical approach to allow for efficient processing of data (e.g., sick vs. healthy, normative vs. problematic). They suggested labeling attachment in categorical ways offers similar benefits. They also pointed out that some of the clinically useful aspects of attachment theory, specifically the disorganized and unresolved classifications, are not sufficiently captured in current dimensional approaches. Raby et al. (2021) suggested that high scores on both anxiety and avoidance should correspond with the traditional ideas of disorganization/unresolved, but H. Steele and Steele (2021) suggested such concerns are inherently focused on quality, not quantity. As it currently stands, categorical approaches continue to prevail in the literature, but dimensional approaches are becoming increasingly commonplace.

between the ECR subscales and the security of attachment scripts assessed with the SBSA (R. D. Steele et al., 2014; Waters et al., 2002). Such findings appear to validate early criticisms of the social psychological constructs by developmental researchers, who asserted that the self-report measures were not assessing attachment constructs, such as attachment behavior or internal working models (Crowell & Waters, 1994). In effect, developmentalists accused social psychologists of studying unrelated constructs, inappropriately applying Bowlby and Ainsworth's theory, and they dismissed the relative ease of self-report questionnaires.

Social psychologists responded by demonstrating that their work filled an important niche. For instance, in conceding that the AAI and self-report measures are assessing different constructs, Roisman et al. (2007) demonstrated that various aspects of interpersonal relationships are better predicted by self-report measures than by results from the AAI. In a separate analysis, Fortuna and Roisman (2008) showed that the AAI predicted mental health outcomes only when the individuals experienced high levels of stress, while a self-report measure predicted such outcomes under conditions of high and low stress. It is likely the case that social psychological measures correlate better with these outcomes, to an extent, because of common method variance (i.e., they both rely on self-report), but it can be argued that such metrics are more practical in diverse research and clinical settings, increasing the potential utility of attachment ideas.

A rapprochement between developmental and social psychological attachment researchers has occurred over the past decade (see Duschinsky, 2020, for an excellent review). Although not the norm, the integration of metrics from the two traditions is becoming more deliberate and studies using the social psychological approach are increasing (Schuengel et al., 2021). Nonetheless, the two camps are largely content researching the topics corresponding with their fields. For instance, although some data suggest self-report metrics may predict parenting behavior (Jones et al., 2015), the social psychologists primarily leave those issues to the developmental scientists. In turn, although measures such as the AAI appear related to functioning within romantic relationships (Tarabulsy et al., 2012), the bulk of research on this topic comes from the social psychologists.

ATTACHMENT WITHIN ROMANTIC RELATIONSHIPS

Starting in adolescence, romantic partners take on the characteristics of an attachment figure as they are increasingly relied upon for support in mild to moderate stress situations (Kobak et al., 2005). As the individual ages and becomes less reliant on caregivers for support, romantic partners take on increased salience, and the attachment system is believed to orient largely toward these individuals under moments of distress. As such, attachment processes are relevant to understanding individual functioning within intimate relationships.

From the beginning of romantic relationships, attachment style appears to be an operative factor. In a series of studies, McClure and Lydon (2014) showed that attachment anxiety resulted in more frequent episodes of awkward interpersonal behaviors and difficulties with effective communication when first meeting an attractive, and potential, dating partner. Not surprisingly, higher levels of attachment avoidance correlate with aversion to initiating significant intimate relationships, thereby resulting in poorer commitment when dating (Birnie et al., 2009).

When insecure individuals enter committed relationships, they may experience difficulties interacting effectively with their partner. For instance, high levels of attachment anxiety are commonly associated with conflictual relationships (Li & Chan, 2012) as well as frequent displays of negative emotions and a low frequency of constructive problem-solving strategies when managing conflict (Tran & Simpson, 2009). Avoidant individuals typically demonstrate problems with effectively communicating and resolving conflict, although their responses more commonly take the shape of angry and withdrawing responses (Overall et al., 2013).

Given such problems with interpersonal functioning, it is not surprising that insecure individuals, particularly those highest on avoidance, report feeling disconnected from partners and dissatisfied with their relationships (Li & Chan, 2012). Over time, relationship satisfaction may continue to deteriorate and, with it, commitment to the partner, resulting in more frequent relationship dissolution for individuals with high insecurity scores (Hadden et al., 2014). Unfortunately, some evidence suggests that insecure individuals are more likely to choose insecure partners (e.g., C. Strauss et al., 2012), resulting in uncertain prospects for the viability of the relationship (Gallo & Smith, 2001).

CONCLUSION

Appreciating the importance of adults for understanding the attachment behavior of infants, researchers developed the AAI to examine caregivers' memories of their own childhoods. The validation of this measure in many ways directed the research agenda on adult attachment and resulted in examinations of states of mind. The social psychological tradition expanded on this prospect by designing measures to assess self-reported perceptions of interpersonal anxiety or avoidance, presuming that such constructs were related to prior attachment experiences and the logical analogue of attachment behavior in adulthood. While the development of the AAI and measures such as the ECR provided significant insights into social relationships, particularly caregiving and romantic relationships, respectively, the purview of attachment theory was significantly stretched to include constructs outside of the original conceptualizations of Bowlby and Ainsworth. Nonetheless, decades of research into the clinical applications of varied attachment constructs, both developmental and social psychological, provide important insights for understanding the development of mental illness and its treatment. The clinical applications of attachment theory and research is the focus of the next part of this volume.

RESOURCES

Training Resources

- **Attachment Training:** Training in the administration and coding of the AAI is available periodically through this organization. They also coordinate training on the Strange Situation Procedure (SSP). More information can be obtained on their website: https://attachment-training.com/
- **Attachment Lab at the University of Illinois:** The faculty lab webpage of R. Chris Fraley at the University of Illinois contains multiple papers on adult attachment styles, the ECR/ECR-R, and copies of the ECR-R available free of charge for general use. The webpage can be accessed at https://labs.psychology.illinois.edu/~rcfraley/resources.html

Suggested Further Reading

Mikulincer, M., & Shaver, P. R. (2016). *Attachment in adulthood: Structure, dynamics, and change* (2nd ed.). Guilford Press.

This volume provides a comprehensive overview of attachment theory in adulthood from two pioneers of the topic. The perspective is decidedly social psychological, given the background of the authors, but the book also includes findings from the developmental tradition and provides theoretical and empirical discussions of a variety of germane issues.

PART II THE CLINICAL APPLICATION OF ATTACHMENT THEORY AND RESEARCH

6 ATTACHMENT AND CLINICAL PRACTICE WITH INFANTS AND YOUNG CHILDREN

The Field of Infant Mental Health

During the 1990s, considerable empirical and clinical focus, as well as public policy directives, turned to identifying infants and young children displaying anomalous social–emotional development and providing appropriate methods of intervention. Much of the foundation for these initiatives derived from the work of attachment researchers. Indeed, the field of infant mental health largely rests on the clinical application of contemporary attachment theory and research. As a result, various efforts have sought to identify and classify pathological forms of attachment behavior, design and evaluate clinical interventions to improve attachment behavior, and apply attachment principles in the child welfare context.

ATTACHMENT AND DIAGNOSTIC APPROACHES

Traditional conceptualizations of aberrant attachment behavior (i.e., insecure, disorganized) are not clinical syndromes but rather risk factors that suggest potentially problematic development. These constructs are typically discussed in the developmental literature (see Chapter 2, this volume). Clinicians

---

https://doi.org/10.1037/0000333-007
The Science and Clinical Practice of Attachment Theory: A Guide From Infancy to Adulthood, by B. Allen

seeking to apply findings from the attachment field have attempted to extrapolate attachment theorizing and research to clinical presentations with varying degrees of success.

Reactive Attachment Disorder

The most recognized attempt at applying attachment concepts is the diagnosis of reactive attachment disorder (RAD). RAD first appeared in the third edition of the American Psychiatric Association's *Diagnostic and Statistical Manual of Mental Disorders* (*DSM-III*; American Psychiatric Association, 1980) shortly after Ainsworth's studies on attachment behavior were popularized in the field of developmental science. Originally termed "reactive attachment disorder of infancy," RAD described a lack of social responsivity (e.g., smiling, reaching for mother) and poor physical development, such as difficulty maintaining or gaining weight, among infants younger than 8 months of age. Problems within the primary attachment relationship were the presumed etiological cause; that is, the symptoms were believed to be "reactive" to a problematic attachment relationship. Criticism of the diagnosis was immediate, as it neither diagnosed attachment behavior nor accurately employed attachment research (Rutter & Shaffer, 1980). For instance, some of the diagnostic criteria were considered applicable if the child was at least 2 months of age, a period during which no child possesses a discriminated attachment figure.[1]

With the publication of the revised third edition of the *DSM* (*DSM-III-R*; American Psychiatric Association, 1987), the diagnostic criteria for RAD were overhauled. In this revision, the diagnosis referred to disturbances of social relatedness in which the young child failed to engage in social interactions (inhibited) or displayed near-absent social boundaries characterized by a lack of age-appropriate reticence toward unfamiliar adults (disinhibited; see p. 91 of the *DSM-III-R*). This reformulation relied on observations of young children in institutions (i.e., orphanages). For example, Tizard and Rees (1975) observed both extreme self-isolating behavior (inhibited) and lack of appropriate social boundaries (disinhibited) among 4-year-old children raised in institutions but not among children raised with biological parents or children adopted out of the institution. Such findings led to the conclusion that these extremes of social relatedness occur only within the most deprived of conditions, resulting in the *DSM-III-R* adding the criterion that the disturbances must be caused by "grossly pathological care" (p. 91). In addition, the age of first diagnosis was revised upward to 5 years, and the diagnosis was referred to as RAD of infancy or early childhood.

[1]This condition is now commonly referred to as "nonorganic failure to thrive."

The diagnostic criteria in the *DSM-III-R* did little to stimulate research or clinical interest. Developmental researchers were unimpressed, as the condition still did not describe disordered attachment behavior. Given that the problems were isolated almost exclusively to children in institutions, most practicing clinicians had no need for the diagnosis. The release of the *DSM-IV* (American Psychiatric Association, 1994/2000) largely left the criteria unchanged. The only notable revision was the insertion of the word "attachment" into the criteria; for example, the indiscriminate sociability of the disinhibited subtype was described as "diffuse attachments" (p. 130). As before, the new criteria were criticized because they continued to diagnose aberrant social behavior, not attachment behavior, and misapplied attachment research (Richters & Volkmar, 1994; Zeanah & Boris, 2000). For instance, the term "diffuse attachments" suggests that a child seeks comfort from any individual under moments of distress, but the diagnostic criteria remained focused on poor social boundaries.

Starting in the early 1990s, a number of opportunities presented themselves for conducting research on RAD as defined in the *DSM*. The fall of communism in Eastern Europe revealed an epidemic of young children warehoused in understaffed state-administered institutions. Adults in Western countries, most notably England and Canada, adopted these infants and preschoolers, allowing for evaluation of their cognitive, socioemotional, and physical state and of the ways in which development changed over time in their enriched adoptive environments. In addition, large-scale studies within Eastern Europe allowed for comparisons of foster care to ongoing institutionalization.

The inhibited subtype of RAD was rare within samples of institutionalized children, occurring in less than 5% in one sample in Bucharest (Smyke et al., 2002). Within this study, infants and toddlers were randomized either to remain in the institution or to be placed with a foster home. Symptoms of inhibited RAD dissipated quickly for children placed in foster care, and by 30 months of age, they resembled a control group of never-institutionalized children residing with their biological families (Smyke et al., 2012). Among the children placed into foster care, none met criteria for inhibited RAD following placement. Findings from other studies of adoptees showed similar results, leading Zeanah and Gleason (2015) to conclude that "signs of (inhibited) RAD diminish or disappear once the child is placed in a more normative caregiving environment" (p. 217).

Children in these same studies diagnosed with the disinhibited subtype of RAD, however, displayed different outcomes. Disinhibited social behavior was much more prevalent among the institutionalized children, with one estimate finding such behavior in 31.8% of the sample (Smyke et al., 2002).

In addition, the disinhibited behavior was commonly identified long after the children were adopted into families (Chisholm, 1998; Rutter et al., 2007), creating a problem for the *DSM* definition of RAD, as it was increasingly apparent that children continued to display indiscriminate sociability long after developing appropriate attachment behavior toward the new caregiver (e.g., Chisholm et al., 1995). As such, it was contrary to the evidence to claim that the disinhibited form of RAD was related to ongoing problems of attachment.

With the publication of the *DSM-5* (American Psychiatric Association, 2013), the RAD diagnosis underwent significant revision.[2] First, the inhibited form of RAD was revised to explicitly reflect that a child fails to display attachment behavior (i.e., seeking or accepting comfort when in distress) during appropriate situations (see p. 265 of the *DSM-5*). In other words, RAD in the *DSM-5* refers to the complete absence of any discernible attachment to a caregiver (Lyons-Ruth et al., 2014). This consideration is important as it implicitly denotes that children displaying insecure or disorganized forms of attachment behavior do not qualify for a RAD diagnosis because they are clearly demonstrating attachment behavior toward a discriminated attachment figure, albeit in a concerning manner. Second, the disinhibited form was split off and made a separate diagnosis, *disinhibited social engagement disorder* (DSED; see p. 268 of the *DSM-5*). Although DSED is still considered to be the result of living in a severely deprived environment, it is clearly indicated that DSED is not related to attachment behavior.[3] For both RAD and DSED, the child must first be diagnosed between the ages of 9 months and 5 years.

Children with RAD are at risk for elevated rates of internalizing concerns (e.g., anxiety, depression) but not externalizing concerns (e.g., aggression, conduct problems; Atkinson, 2019). Of clinical importance, children placed in a suitable caregiving environment earlier in life show a steeper decline in RAD behaviors after placement than those placed later in life (Guyon-Harris et al., 2019), although subsyndromal signs of RAD may persist and predict a host of negative mental health outcomes and concerning internal working models (Zimmermann & Iwanski, 2019).

---

[2]Note that the *Diagnostic and Statistical Manual of Mental Disorders* (5th ed.; *DSM-5;* American Psychiatric Association, 2013) and the *International Statistical Classification of Diseases and Related Health Problems* (10th ed.; *ICD-10*; World Health Organization, 1993) used different definitions and terms; however, with the release of the *ICD-11* (World Health Organization, 2019), the two systems are practically the same in their description of these conditions.

[3]This presentation of the RAD and DSED criteria may seem foreign to some clinicians who understand RAD as a form of severe conduct problem. The reasons for this common misconception are discussed in Chapter 10 of this volume.

Several studies now document that the relationships between the disinhibited social behavior of DSED and both attachment security and organization are relatively weak (Zephyr et al., 2021). Rather, DSED behaviors are more strongly related to concerns of impulse control and attention problems (Gleason et al., 2011; Pears et al., 2010). Poor inhibitory control is generally considered a transdiagnostic mechanism that underlies an assortment of externalizing problems (e.g., aggression, ADHD) and is a common finding among children raised within institutions and/or suffering from prolonged maltreatment. As such, DSED is commonly viewed in contemporary research as a form of externalizing problem that is conceptually and etiologically distinct from problematic attachment behavior.

Assessment for RAD and DSED, as performed in controlled research, involves intensive observations and structured interviews. Use of these tools is typically infeasible in general clinical settings because of the time and effort necessary to administer and score them reliably. In addition, the exceptionally low base rate of RAD and DSED in such settings creates little impetus to invest an agency's limited time and resources in such procedures. Efforts are ongoing to develop more portable metrics, such as caregiver-report measures and brief observational paradigms, but the psychometric properties of these tools are not well established, and large-scale dissemination efforts do not appear imminent. For the time being, reputable and comprehensive assessments of RAD and DSED are primarily found in specialized programs, such as adoption or maltreatment programs based in university clinics and medical centers.

Research examining treatment options for RAD and DSED is difficult owing to the relatively rare presentation of these conditions. In addition, the somewhat rapid amelioration of RAD following placement in a suitable home environment makes it uncertain "whether additional interventions beyond family placement may be necessary" (Zeanah & Gleason, 2015, p. 217). At the least, best practices dictate offering such families support and potentially an intervention (such as those discussed later in this chapter) to increase the likelihood that a caregiver would be sensitive and supportive. As for DSED, some evidence suggests that treating it as a special form of externalizing behavior problem may be advantageous. Multiple case reports suggest that implementation of a social-learning/behavioral parent-training intervention (see Chapter 7, this volume) may result in significant improvement (Buckner et al., 2008; Dickmann & Allen, 2017). Boxes 6.1 and 6.2 present two case studies—one about a 2-year-old girl and the other about a 3-year-old boy—who potentially meet criteria for RAD or DSED.[4]

[4]To protect patient confidentiality, proper steps have been taken to disguise the identities of the individuals in this chapter's case examples.

BOX 6.1

THE CASE OF GEMMA

Gemma is a 2-year-old African American girl discovered by Child Protective Services (CPS) when they entered her home following a tip alleging severe child neglect. Her older brother was found near death as a result of malnutrition, and both of her parents were unconscious due to drug overdoses. Gemma was significantly underweight. When approached by a CPS worker, Gemma displayed no significant emotional reaction and turned toward a corner, as if wishing to be left alone. When the worker attempted to speak with her, Gemma put her hands over her ears and shook her head. Upon being admitted to hospital, Gemma's nurses reported no significant emotional reactions from her in response to painful medical procedures, such as blood draws, and none recalled her asking for her parents. Gemma understood nurse instructions and communicated her wishes, such as selecting meals or programs to watch on television. Gemma's grandmother, whom she had not seen in 6 months, was identified as a suitable placement. When the grandmother arrived at the hospital, Gemma briefly waved at her and continued watching television.

Approximately 3 months later, Gemma presented to an outpatient treatment clinic alongside her grandmother. She was physically stronger and entered the clinic holding her grandmother's hand. During the assessment interview, Gemma displayed some hesitation interacting with the clinician and often looked at her grandmother when asked a question. The grandmother rubbed her back as a form of reassurance and Gemma provided head nods and shakes as answers. The clinician left the room and observed Gemma and her grandmother playing together from behind a one-way mirror. The two easily engaged in play and, although Gemma did not speak much, she smiled at her grandmother multiple times during the observation.

Discussion Questions

1. What evidence for a diagnosis of reactive attachment disorder (RAD) is evident when Gemma was first identified by protective services and admitted to hospital?
2. Why do you think the diagnostic criteria for RAD requires the child be between 9 months and 5 years of age?
3. Did Gemma display RAD symptoms when seen later in the clinic? What changed, and why did these changes occur?
4. What treatment options might be most helpful for Gemma?

BOX 6.2

THE CASE OF SOO

Soo is a 3-year-old boy who was adopted at the age of 2 years from an orphanage in Asia and presented to an outpatient clinic for his first treatment session. When the clinician entered the waiting room to meet the child for the first time, Soo jumped off the lap of a man, ran toward the clinician, and gave her a hug. Soo's mother approached and introduced herself. The clinician asked if Soo's father would be joining the session and motioned toward the man on whose lap Soo had been sitting. The mother's eyes grew large with apparent shock before stating, "Oh, we don't know him." The man responded, "I'm just here for my appointment, and he climbed up and asked me to read him a book." The mother then relayed that such behaviors are a common problem with Soo, who will talk to and go off with complete strangers. She further explained that she and her husband were the recipients of such affection when they first visited Soo at the orphanage. They found this behavior endearing but now fear he may go off with strangers. During observation, Soo presented as an impulsive child who tipped backward in his chair and fell on the floor. He immediately began crying and ran around the table to his mother, who hugged and comforted him. The two then played collaboratively for the remainder of the time.

Discussion Questions

1. What evidence is present for a diagnosis of disinhibited social engagement disorder (DSED) for Soo?
2. What evidence is there regarding Soo's attachment to his mother, and does this evidence inform your determination of whether he meets the diagnostic criteria for DSED?
3. What treatment options might be most helpful for Soo?

Diagnostic Classification of Mental Health and Developmental Disorders of Infancy and Early Childhood (DC:0-5)

Because attachment behavior is relationship specific (i.e., different behavior may manifest with different caregivers), there is an inherent challenge in employing common psychiatric nosologies, such as the *DSM-5*, that view psychopathology as residing "within the child." With this in mind, the National Center for Infants, Toddlers, and Families (also known as ZERO TO THREE) published a supplement to the *DSM-IV* in 1994 to improve assessment and diagnosis with infants and young children. The *Diagnostic Classification of Mental Health and Developmental Disorders of Infancy and Early Childhood,* revised in 2005 (*DC:0-3-R*; ZERO TO THREE, 2005), prescribed assessing the global quality of the child–caregiver relationship on a scale from 1 (*documented maltreatment*) to 100 (*well adapted*) as part of the diagnostic process.

The latest version of the manual extends the age range up to 5 years and is correspondingly referred to as the *DC:0-5* (ZERO TO THREE, 2020). Of note, the *DC:0-5* includes a diagnosable "relationship-specific disorder of infancy/early childhood," which is defined as "symptomatic behavior in the infant/young child that is limited to one relationship context" (p. 135). Behaviors of concern range from aggression and oppositionality to controlling behavior toward the caregiver. This diagnosis reflects the understanding that the behavior and emotions of the young child may differ based on the caregiver present and that dysfunction resides at the relationship level. In addition, the *DC:0-5* expanded on the assessment of a specific child–caregiver relationship, separating the process into descriptions of the caregiving provided along several dimensions (e.g., ensuring physical safety, providing comfort for distress) and the ways in which characteristics of the child (e.g., temperament, physical health) contribute to the quality of the relationship. While a positive step in conceptualizing psychopathology from an attachment perspective, the *DC:0-5* is little known outside of the infant mental health field.

Lesser Known Conceptualizations

Other conceptualizations of attachment problems are infrequently discussed in the literature. For instance, Zeanah and Boris (2000) proposed three additional classifications of attachment diagnoses: *nonattachment*, in which no preferential and discriminated attachment figure is established (similar in many ways to *DSM-5* criteria for RAD); *secure-base distortions*, in which an attachment figure is present but appears to be the source of problems, such as role reversal; and *disrupted attachment*, in which a child experiences the loss of an attachment figure, such as through the death of the caregiver or placement in foster care. In a revision, Zeanah and Smyke (2009) mentioned these concepts only briefly before concluding that problems of attachment must be diagnosed at the relationship level. B. Allen (2011a) suggested supplementing the standard diagnostic system by denoting the existence of an *attachment disturbance* that complicates treatment efforts. For instance, exposure-based therapy for a young child with anxiety or posttraumatic stress may be hindered if the child does not view the caregiver as providing a safe haven that might offer emotional calming or a secure base that supports confronting threatening stimuli.

ATTACHMENT-BASED INTERVENTIONS WITH INFANTS AND YOUNG CHILDREN

Given the innumerable difficulties with defining what qualifies as pathological forms of attachment behavior, *attachment-based interventions*[5] for infants, toddlers, and preschoolers most often focus on improving the security and organization of attachment behavior through enhancement of caregiver sensitivity. These protocols display remarkable similarities owing to their derivation from contemporary attachment research. For instance, they typically focus on improving caregiver understanding of infant cues (e.g., signs of safe-haven and secure-base behavior), teach caregivers more sensitive ways of responding to a child's cues, and stress the importance of consistency in caregiving behavior.

Although the goal of these interventions is to improve developmental outcomes and prevent later psychopathology, long-term follow-up studies demonstrating such downstream benefits are rare. In addition, studies demonstrating that improvement of attachment constructs mediates the relationship between such interventions and long-term outcomes are equally scarce. Nonetheless, the compelling evidence that attachment constructs predict later adaptation and maladaptation sufficiently justifies using attachment outcomes in clinical trials among infants and young children. Four of the most popular attachment-based interventions for children under the age of 5 years are discussed here.

Attachment and Biobehavioral Catch-Up

Attachment and Biobehavioral Catch-Up (ABC) is a 10-session intervention administered by a trained "parent coach" who implements the protocol within the caregiver's home (Dozier & Bernard, 2019). Sessions focus on helping caregivers follow the lead of the child and provide nurturing comments while eliminating caregiving behavior that may inadvertently frighten the child. During later sessions caregivers are asked to evaluate their own childhoods and the type of parenting they received as a way of processing and

[5]As discussed in the Introduction to this book, the term "attachment-based intervention" is the preferred term for this class of interventions and the most often used in the literature.

restructuring the thought processes that might contribute to concerning forms of caregiving behavior. The hallmark of ABC is the coach shadowing caregivers during interactions with the child and providing "in-the-moment" comments that help caregivers connect the discussed material with the patterns of interaction occurring with the child in real time. Such comments also serve to promote caregiving confidence and efficacy.

A randomized controlled trial (RCT) of infants and their caregivers referred by CPS showed that ABC outperformed a psychoeducational control intervention in reducing attachment disorganization and increasing security when assessed in the Strange Situation Procedure (SSP; Bernard et al., 2012), and evidence suggests that these effects may last well into middle childhood (Dozier & Bernard, 2019). Caregivers receiving ABC demonstrate higher levels of sensitivity and responsiveness than caregivers in control conditions, both immediately and when followed over a number of years (Bick & Dozier, 2013; Yarger et al., 2020). There are indications that ABC prompts improvement in several developmental areas, such as more normalized diurnal cortisol regulation (a stress hormone; Bernard et al., 2015), greater social–emotional competence (Lind et al., 2021), and better inhibitory control (Lind et al., 2020).

Video Intervention for Positive Parenting and Sensitive Discipline

Video Intervention for Positive Parenting and Sensitive Discipline (VIPP-SD) was originally developed as an intervention targeting caregivers of infants less than a year old and at risk for poor psychosocial outcomes (Juffer et al., 2008). With these young samples the intervention focuses largely on enhancing caregiver sensitivity and understanding the needs of the child. For children between the ages of 1 and 6 years, the program integrates instruction on nonviolent forms of discipline designed to disrupt and/or prevent coercive cycles that may promote child behavioral problems. During VIPP-SD, the clinician video records the caregiver interacting with their child in the home and later reviews selected segments of the videos with the caregiver. Over the course of six sessions, the clinician helps the caregiver distinguish between secure-base and safe-haven behavior, respond sensitively to emotions, use positive reinforcement, and deliver an effective timeout procedure.

Initial evidence for VIPP-SD derived from an RCT of adoptive mothers and their infants showed that mothers who received VIPP-SD demonstrated greater sensitivity after treatment than did mothers who received a psychoeducational intervention, and their children were more likely to display organized attachment behavior (Juffer et al., 2005). Additional RCTs soon followed examining the efficacy of VIPP-SD with other populations. A recent meta-analysis of 25 RCTs found significant positive effects for VIPP-SD on caregiving behavior and child attachment outcomes but not on externalizing problems (van IJzendoorn et al., 2022).

Child–Parent Psychotherapy

Child–Parent Psychotherapy (CPP) is somewhat unique among attachment-based interventions, as it was developed based on both attachment theory and the emerging research on the impact of trauma on infants. CPP derived from Fraiberg's (1980) infant–parent psychotherapy, an intervention designed to help mothers examine how thoughts and feelings related to their own traumatic experiences may affect interactions with the infant. Current CPP integrates these components with a contemporary understanding of the ways in which trauma affects children and the role caregivers may play in mitigating its effects. Treatment typically occurs with the child and caregiver together and the clinician providing feedback directly to caregivers to help them consider issues such as safety, the ways in which caregiving behavior may be perceived by the child, and how the caregiver's own experiences may be manifesting within session. In other instances, the clinician may "speak for baby" by putting words to a child's behaviors or emotions to help the caregiver understand their meaning (Lieberman & Van Horn, 2008). Through weekly sessions delivered over the course of 10 to 12 months, CPP aims to improve infant safety within the child–caregiver relationship, enhance parental sensitivity and responsiveness, and alter maladaptive cognitions of both the caregiver and the child (Toth et al., 2018).

Early RCTs suggested that CPP performed well at promoting improvements in attachment security among insecurely attached infants (Lieberman et al., 1991) and infants of depressed mothers (Toth et al., 2006). CPP outperformed a psychoeducational program for improving attachment representations among preschool children, most notably their perceptions of the mother and the parent–child relationship (Toth et al., 2002). There is evidence that completion of CPP prompts improved diurnal cortisol regulation and that such effects are sustained at least a year after treatment completion (Cicchetti et al., 2011). Across studies, CPP is found to be efficacious with a diversity of caregivers at risk for negative outcomes, including caregivers known to commit maltreating acts against their children, survivors of interpartner violence, and depressed mothers.

Circle of Security

The original Circle of Security (COS) model is a 20-session group-based program in which five or six parents meet collectively with the facilitator in a clinic or other setting (Powell et al., 2014). Prior to beginning the group, caregivers are video recorded interacting with their infants. These recordings are edited and then used during the group to help concretize the concepts. Caregivers are recorded with their children at intervals throughout the course of treatment to demonstrate improvement and areas in need of additional focus. Specific goals of the sessions include helping caregivers understand the secure-base and safe-haven behaviors of children (i.e., the "Circle"), recognize children's needs and cues, identify emotional responses they display toward their children, and learn strategies to better regulate these emotions. Modifications of the original COS program are available, including one designated for pregnant mothers who are incarcerated and another that is an intensive four-session home-based program.

COS is, perhaps, the most well known of the infant mental health interventions, owing to successful dissemination efforts. Empirically speaking, however, no available RCTs demonstrate the efficacy of standard COS when compared with an appropriate control condition. Pre–post comparisons suggest COS may yield improved attachment organization and security as well as reductions in parenting stress and increases in parenting efficacy (Hoffman et al., 2006; Huber et al., 2015). As for the modifications, RCTs are available but show mixed results, and whether these modifications outperform standard services-as-usual is unclear at this time (Cassidy et al., 2011, 2017).

A Note on the Length of Attachment-Based Interventions

It is often surprising to individuals unfamiliar with the attachment literature that brief interventions (i.e., fewer than 12 sessions), such as ABC and VIPP-SD, can improve not only caregiver sensitivity but also attachment security. This effect was most clearly demonstrated in a widely cited meta-analysis by Bakermans-Kranenburg et al. (2003). In reviewing over 80 intervention studies, they found clear evidence that (a) interventions are effective at improving caregiver sensitivity, (b) interventions focused solely on improving caregiver sensitivity are more effective than interventions that include multiple other components (e.g., providing support, altering caregiver representations), and (c) interventions involving fewer than five sessions were equally as effective as interventions requiring between five and 16 sessions, while interventions requiring more than 16 sessions were less effective. These findings held even when the data were restricted to caregivers from "at-risk" backgrounds. The conclusion was that brief, focused interventions are more effective for improving caregiver sensitivity than longer, more comprehensive programs.

Bakermans-Kranenburg et al. (2003) also examined attachment security as an outcome in their meta-analysis. Across 29 studies, evidence indicated that the interventions exerted a small effect on improving attachment security. However, regarding the type of intervention, those focused specifically on enhancing caregiver sensitivity exerted a much stronger effect, suggesting that more comprehensive programs were largely ineffective and weighed down the summary effect size. Not surprisingly, the interventions more effective at improving caregiver sensitivity were also more effective at improving infant attachment security.

Regarding the issue of disorganized attachment, Facompré et al. (2018) sought to determine whether attachment-based interventions during infancy might improve this construct. They reviewed 16 studies and found attachment-based interventions exerted a moderate effect in improving or preventing attachment disorganization. Results showed that interventions were more effective with maltreated samples than with other populations, but no significant effect was found for the target of a given intervention (i.e., parental sensitivity only vs. combined) or the length of the intervention. While these results do not suggest superiority of briefer and more focused programs, they do suggest that longer and more comprehensive programs are unlikely to yield additional benefit.

There are no definitive conclusions as to why briefer interventions focused on caregiver sensitivity are preferable to longer and more involved approaches. One likely culprit is higher rates of attrition that occur with longer interventions. Participants may discontinue with services before the most critical aspects are delivered. An alternative hypothesis is that increasing the complexity of a program inherently requires a clinician to learn a greater number of techniques, creating concerns regarding treatment fidelity, clinical skill acquisition, and time constraints related to training and monitoring (van IJzendoorn et al., 2005). In short, defining a clear goal (i.e., caregiver sensitivity) and achieving quality results for that goal is preferable to achieving mediocre results in multiple areas. An added benefit, then, is that more effective interventions are of briefer duration. The case example in Box 6.3 offers practice examining how an attachment-based intervention might benefit a 20-month-old girl and her mother, who had recently left an abusive relationship with the girl's father.

BOX 6.3

THE CASE OF ALLISON

Ms. Adams, a White 25-year-old woman, and her 20-month-old daughter, Allison, presented to a specialized infant mental health program following the recommendation of a Child Protective Services (CPS) caseworker. For the past several years Ms. Adams was the victim of interpartner violence perpetrated by Allison's father. She recently left that relationship, resulting in significant financial difficulties that necessitated living with Allison's grandparents. Ms. Adams described Allison as a sweet child who frequently smiles and loves to play, but "she has a mean streak that comes out on occasion."

Allison sat on Ms. Adams's lap throughout most of the assessment but became upset when Ms. Adams put her down to complete a form. What initially began as crying quickly turned into head banging on the floor, prompting Ms. Adams to pick Allison up once again. Allison responded by squirming and flailing her arms, one of which hit Ms. Adams across the face. Ms. Adams was visibly upset following this interaction with Allison and disclosed that such incidents remind her of Allison's father. She noted that she worries that Allison "has too much of her father in her." When asked about the frequency of these behaviors, Ms. Adams reported that Allison displays such "meltdowns" multiple times in a day and one was observed by the CPS worker, prompting the referral.

Throughout the assessment Allison showed little interest in engaging with the age-appropriate toys in the room, although no significant developmental or physical delays were identified. Ms. Adams was somewhat surprised by this behavior because Allison enjoys playing with toys. During a structured 5-minute observation session that occurred near the end of the assessment, Allison showed little interest in engaging with Ms. Adams or the toys and mostly sat quietly. Ms. Adams primarily busied herself with her smartphone.

Discussion Questions

1. What indications of attachment behavior are present in this scenario?
2. What factors likely led to Allison's current concerns?
3. Given the information presented, what might an appropriate intervention entail?

ATTACHMENT AND THE CHILD WELFARE SYSTEM

The traditional focus of attachment theory on the parent–child relationship resulted in various aspects of the child welfare system focused on implementing insights from the field. Some child protection social workers incorporate attachment theory as a primary influence in their decision-making process because it seems to offer a rich understanding of the child and a research-based perspective on the types of services most indicated (Wilkins, 2017). However, countless observations, as well as published papers, suggest attachment theory is often misapplied in the child welfare context (see Granqvist, 2016). As such, ill-informed decisions may be recommended or implemented in the mistaken belief that attachment theory supports the course decided by the caseworker. Two of the more common situations are highlighted here.

Parenting Evaluations

Courts often turn to child welfare workers for help determining issues of parental custody, particularly when concerns are raised regarding the fitness of a parent or during a conflictual divorce in which allegations of maltreatment arise. In such situations, it is not uncommon that caseworkers seek to determine the quality of the attachment relationship as part of an evaluation. Some caseworkers undertake this assessment of the attachment relationship themselves, whereas others seek an evaluation by a mental health professional.

A common recommendation appearing in the literature is to assess whether the child displays disorganized attachment behavior; the recommendation is based on the idea that such behavior is indicative of maltreatment on the part of the caregiver (Shemmings & Shemmings, 2011; Wilkins, 2012). Indeed, there are documented cases in which a child's display of disorganized attachment behavior was deemed suggestive of maltreatment and the child was removed from a caregiver (Granqvist, 2016). This recommendation, however, is directly refuted by the scientific evidence. Although child maltreatment is a predictor of disorganization, it is not the only predictor. For instance, Cyr et al. (2010) demonstrated that an accumulation of socioeconomic risk factors may confer the same risk as maltreatment for displaying disorganization. Relying on the presence of disorganized behaviors to discern maltreatment may result in caregivers from lower socioeconomic strata being unfairly identified as perpetrators.

Using the disorganized (D) classification in parenting evaluations obscures important information that may be relevant for the assessment at hand.

Manifestly, the question to be answered typically deals with the suitability of a specific caregiver to parent the child. A determination that the caregiver is experiencing financial hardship, resulting in socioeconomic risk, leads one to a different conclusion regarding the services required than a determination that the caregiver is physically abusive. Similarly, understanding that a caregiver struggles to cope with a history of loss suggests the importance of seeking treatment for the caregiver. Ill-advised uses of the D classification resulted in more than 40 of the world's leading attachment researchers issuing a joint statement proclaiming that the presence of disorganized attachment behavior allows caseworkers or clinicians to "only infer that this infant has experienced alarm in relation to the caregiver for some reason" and that it is not a conclusive test for maltreatment (Granqvist et al., 2017, p. 542). In addition, some who previously argued for considering disorganized attachment behaviors as indicative of maltreatment no longer support such a practice (Wilkins, 2021).

Other problems are frequently noted with the use of attachment theory in the context of parenting evaluations, not the least of which is terminology. Caseworkers and clinicians commonly reference the quality of the parent–child attachment; however, "quality of attachment" refers in the scientific literature to the security and organization of a child's behavior under moments of distress (i.e., safe-haven and secure-base behavior). Assessments of parental competence do not typically examine attachment behavior and, instead, provide a general conclusion regarding the quality of the parent–child relationship. While it is appropriate, of course, to examine various aspects of the parent–child relationship, such as communication, discipline skills, or engagement in activities, it is inaccurate to conclude these characteristics translate into "quality of attachment." More confusing, caseworkers and clinicians often reference attachment terms, such as "secure" or "insecure," when referring to the parent–child relationship. Utilizing attachment language to describe the parent–child relationship confers a sense of scientific clarity and confidence in the recommendations that is inaccurate and misleading.

In the context of high-conflict divorce, evaluators may be tasked with determining which parent shall have primary custody of the child. In such situations it is not unusual for judges or caseworkers to ask an evaluator to determine the parent to whom the child is "most attached" or "more strongly attached." Such statements demonstrate a limited knowledge of attachment research, as classifications of attachment behavior relate to quality, not strength. In fact, no system or coding scheme for determining the strength of a child's attachment to a caregiver is psychometrically valid. Even continuous measures, such as the Attachment Q-sort (AQS), provide a rating of how clearly secure behaviors were observed during an interaction, not the strength with which a child performed the behaviors or the strength of the emotional connection between parent and child.

Highlighting these concerns is not to suggest that scientific attachment theory has little to offer in the context of parenting determinations. The key, however, is appreciating what attachment research supports and does not support. The general consensus is that attachment theory yields three primary principles relevant to child welfare applications: (a) children need familiar and nonmaltreating caregivers; (b) continuity of caregiver relationships is important, and severing such relationships should be handled with great care after judicious deliberation; and (c) fostering multiple attachment relationships is beneficial, not detrimental, to child well-being (Forslund et al., 2022). These principles have numerous implications in the context of parenting evaluations. For instance, encouraging a child to maintain attachment relationships with multiple nonmaltreating caregivers is preferable to singling out a "primary" caregiver for preferential treatment based on the thought that such an arrangement is more beneficial for the child. Another suggestion is that maintaining placement in a nonmaltreating caregiver's home is preferable to repeated and prolonged changes in attempts to create fairness or equity for the parents.

Researchers in the field disagree about the extent to which attachment metrics should be included in parenting evaluations. Some point out that attachment measures are untested for forensic uses and the research base is insufficient for determining how they might inform parenting capacity or custody decisions. Others argue these measures may be informative when administered by appropriately trained clinicians who consider the results within the context of a larger evaluation. However, even in such situations there is a noted concern that untrained judges and/or caseworkers may misunderstand what is being assessed and assign too much weight to the results of the metric described as assessing attachment (Forslund et al., 2022).

Perhaps the most useful, and least controversial, application of attachment theory in the context of parenting evaluations is determining the types of services that might be most helpful. For instance, observation of the child and caregiver together, even if not in a formal paradigm such as the SSP, may suggest the extent to which the caregiver is sensitive in responding to the child's needs or understands concepts such as safe-haven and secure-base behaviors. Identifying concerns in these areas may prompt a clinician to make a referral to one of the attachment-based interventions discussed previously. Alternatively, use of an interview probing for attachment experiences may reveal concerns related to housing, food, and/or stress within the home and suggest the need for practical financial assistance. Similarly, such an interview may suggest ongoing concerns with mental illness or an unresolved history of abuse during the caregiver's childhood, and a referral for mental health treatment may be indicated.

Foster Care and Adoption

It is an unfortunate reality that children must sometimes be placed in surrogate care as a result of abandonment, maltreatment, or any number of other events, thus creating an important question regarding the impact such changes of placement might have on the attachment of a child. Given that attachment formation is occurring throughout the first year of life, some commentators claimed that removing a child during this time held the potential for causing irreparable harm to the young child's ability to form attachments. Stovall-McClough and Dozier (2004) examined a group of infants, ranging in age from 5 to 28 months, who were placed in foster care as a result of maltreatment. Within 3 to 4 months following placement, 60% of the infants were classified as secure in the SSP with the foster parent while none were classified as disorganized. Other studies soon emerged and, across findings, adopted children and those in foster care appear to show approximately the same rates of attachment security as children raised in biological families (van den Dries et al., 2009). However, foster and adoptive children appear to demonstrate higher levels of disorganization than their biologically reared peers do.

Researchers attempted to identify factors that predict secure and organized attachment among fostered and adopted infants. One replicated finding is that children placed prior to 12 months of age typically fare better than those brought into care later (Stovall-McClough & Dozier, 2004; van den Dries et al., 2009). Many of these youngest children begin demonstrating attachment behaviors toward their new caregivers within days of placement (Stovall & Dozier, 2000). For those placed later, however, the longer period of adversity faced in their preplacement setting likely contributes to increased difficulties establishing a secure attachment with the new caregiver. Nonetheless, it is generally regarded that, with sufficient time, children are capable of developing secure attachment relationships with surrogate caregivers regardless of the age of placement, including those first placed in care as adolescents (Joseph et al., 2014).

Another replicated factor predicting the development of attachment among foster and adoptive children is the perspective of the caregiver. Research established that concordance between caregiver state of mind and infant attachment behavior is similar between foster dyads and biologically related dyads (Dozier et al., 2001). In a follow-up investigation, Stovall-McClough and Dozier (2004) showed that the infants of foster caregivers rated secure on the AAI displayed greater levels of security and organization than those rated insecure. Other studies exploring caregiver state of mind similarly have documented this relationship, even among older adopted children (Pace et al., 2015).

Studies examining how parental state of mind might influence attachment outcomes among foster and adopted children largely converge on two related factors: commitment to the child and quality of the caregiving provided. Caregivers with an insecure state of mind tend to show lower levels of commitment to the child and are less likely to believe they can have a significant impact on the child's life (Bates & Dozier, 2002). In turn, less caregiver emotional investment predicts parent–child interactions of lower quality (Dubois-Comtois et al., 2015). Both caregiver commitment and the quality of parent–child interactions predict child emotional and behavioral problems (Dubois-Comtois et al., 2015; Lindhiem & Dozier, 2007). In addition, caregiver state of mind predicts the quality of parenting provided (see Chapter 5, this volume).

Caseworkers and clinicians understand that children in foster and adoptive care are at increased risk for displaying emotional and behavioral problems and often attribute problems within the parent–child relationship to the child's preplacement experiences. Indeed, children with placement instability are at increased risk for behavioral problems, as are children who experienced a long duration of deprivation, such as those adopted from institutions (Almas et al., 2020). Nonetheless, emotional and behavioral concerns are amenable to change once placement stability is achieved. Attempting to intervene directly with children, particularly children under the age of 5 years, is often unsuccessful. Rather, a more effective route focuses on improving the caregiving provided by working specifically with the caregiver. This approach aims to restructure the child's environment in such a way that sensitive and effective responses become the norm and developmental recovery can occur. RCTs testing interventions such as ABC (Bick & Dozier, 2013) and VIPP-SD (Juffer et al., 2005) demonstrate that sensitivity of foster and adoptive caregivers may be improved with short-term interventions and result in improved child attachment security and organization. Even among children from the most deprived environments, improvements in caregiver sensitivity enhance child attachment security, which in turn predicts improved emotional and behavioral concerns (McGoron et al., 2012).

This body of research leads to several conclusions regarding the development of children in surrogate care and the best ways to intervene. First, children placed in care, regardless of age, are capable of developing secure and organized attachments to new caregivers. Second, the time required to develop attachments may vary, depending on several factors, including the number of placements experienced, the extent of the preplacement maltreatment and/or deprivation, and the quality of caregiving provided by the surrogate caregiver. Third, the most effective approach to intervention aims to improve the quality of the caregiving. Many foster and adoptive parents have a history of successfully raising children, but parenting a child who experienced disruptions in attachment and/or displays behavioral problems may present significant challenges. Interventions such as ABC and VIPP-SD may help surrogate caregivers understand the child's behaviors and provide strategies to support them in developing healthy attachments. Box 6.4 presents a case example in which a 4-year-old boy goes back and forth between his biological mother and a foster family and presents with behavioral problems.

BOX 6.4

THE CASE OF HECTOR

Hector is a 4-year-old Latino boy who presented for assessment with his foster mother, Ms. Young. Hector stomped into the room and declared, "I already hate this place." Ms. Young described how Hector came to their home when he was 15 months old, and the initial plan was to adopt him. However, the process has dragged on because of multiple attempts to reunite him with his biological mother, all of which failed and have since been discontinued. They are now approaching the deadline to finalize the adoption, but she and her husband are unsure they wish to adopt Hector. Ms. Young stated that his behavioral problems have worsened over the past 12 months, and she blames the constant back and forth between her house and that of his biological mother. She is skeptical about receiving treatment services because previous therapists spent most of the treatment time talking with her and not helping Hector deal with his problems.

During a structured observation Hector and Ms. Young sat at a table with a number of toys available. Hector played with the toys while Ms. Young sat quietly. Hector made overtures attempting to engage Ms. Young in the play, but she responded with brief and dismissive comments. Hector then left the table and began skipping around the room, pretending he was flying a toy airplane. Ms. Young became upset, told the boy to sit

BOX 6.4

THE CASE OF HECTOR (*Continued*)

down, and threatened to remove movie night with the family if he did not comply. Hector returned to his seat, at which time Ms. Young commented, "Hey, look at that, you finally followed directions." Hector sat with his eyes looking down for a few seconds before reengaging with the toys.

Discussion Questions

1. What do you suspect are the causes of Hector's behavioral concerns?
2. What aspects of the current parent-child relationship seem important to target during intervention?
3. How might you approach Ms. Young in hopes of attaining her buy-in for participating in an attachment-based intervention?

CONCLUSION

The considerable research completed with children younger than 5 years of age provides ample directions for clinical practice. Although attempts to classify disordered attachment have met with limited success, interventions aiming to improve attachment security, organization, and caregiver sensitivity are now well established. In addition, dissemination efforts to increase the implementation of these programs in general practice are speeding forward. Such efforts hold promise for improving the well-being and development of children, including improving the application of attachment concepts within the child welfare system.

BOX 6.5

DISCUSSIONS OF CASE STUDIES

Box 6.1: The Case of Gemma

Question 1

At the hospital, Gemma did not ask for or seek out a caregiver even though she was in a strange setting and was subjected to a painful medical procedure. The arrival of her grandmother seemingly made little difference.

(continues)

BOX 6.5

DISCUSSIONS OF CASE STUDIES (*Continued*)

Gemma displayed no significant social or emotional response when approached by nurses or a CPS worker and generally displayed a flat affect. Certainly, her home environment can be classified as emotionally and socially deprived, resulting in all diagnostic criteria being met for RAD.

Question 2

Recall that discriminated attachment behavior is not commonly present prior to 9 months of age and, as such, it is inappropriate to suggest that a lack of attachment behavior for younger children is indicative of RAD. Eliciting attachment behavior from children older than 5 years is difficult owing to expanded self-regulatory skills, and this difficulty has resulted in a research base that provides little direction on how RAD might present with older children. Also, the likelihood is high of misdiagnosing a maltreated child who developed exceptional self-sufficiency with RAD.

Question 3

There are clear indications that Gemma displayed attachment behavior toward her grandmother in clinic. Gemma displayed hesitancy interacting with the unknown clinician and made eye contact with her grandmother when asked a question. Following the grandmother's reassurance, Gemma was able to provide answers to the questions. Reflecting the available research, Gemma appeared to develop attachment behavior toward her grandmother after having been provided stability in her home. She did not appear to display RAD in clinic.

Question 4

Although evidence suggests Gemma will likely fare well with her grandmother, offering an effective attachment-based intervention may be helpful. Such an intervention should focus on helping the grandmother understand Gemma's behaviors and develop strategies to respond in a sensitive manner.

Box 6.2: The Case of Soo

Question 1

Soo displayed multiple DSED behaviors, including sitting on the lap of a stranger and hugging the unknown clinician upon meeting her, and the mother reported fear he might go off with a stranger. Although Soo also displayed significant impulsivity, the disinhibited social behavior does not appear isolated to impulsivity. Given Soo's experience in an institutional setting in Asia, all criteria for DSED are met.

BOX 6.5

DISCUSSIONS OF CASE STUDIES (*Continued*)

Question 2

Soo sought out his mother after he fell to the floor and began crying, suggesting a form of secure attachment behavior. However, attachment behavior has no bearing on the diagnosis of DSED, as DSED is no longer considered a form of problematic attachment.

Question 3

The best available evidence suggests that the most effective treatment approach for Soo should make use of appropriate limit setting and non-violent discipline procedures, such as those typically taught in social-learning/behavioral parent-training interventions. In other words, rules of social behavior should be clearly explained to Soo, positive reinforcement (e.g., praise) delivered for adhering to the rules, and appropriate consequences implemented when he breaks the rules (see Chapter 7 of this volume).

Box 6.3: The Case of Allison

Question 1

Allison clearly showed signs of attachment behavior, such as crying when she was put down and wanting to be picked up again. However, after Ms. Adams picked her up, Allison began squirming and flailing as if resisting the mother's overtures. Her behavior suggests the likelihood of an ambivalent classification, if the SSP were administered. However, her crying after being put down quickly turned into self-injurious behavior, which may be suggestive of disorganization. Her resistance to be being picked up by the mother may also be indicative of disorganization. Although the exact classification of her behavior is unclear, the evidence clearly suggests insecurity of some sort.

Question 2

Although there are no indications of maltreatment directed toward Allison, the home environment was recently marked by violence, and a number of socioeconomic risks are present, including financial and housing difficulties. Stress may be taxing Ms. Adams, thereby affecting her caregiving abilities. Ms. Adams also makes a comment suggesting potentially maladaptive representations she holds of Allison (i.e., she "has too much of her father in her"). In addition, the social modeling of violence within her home cannot be overlooked.

(*continues*)

BOX 6.5

DISCUSSIONS OF CASE STUDIES (*Continued*)

Question 3

Ms. Adams appears to display significant difficulties with understanding Allison's behaviors and responding in a sensitive manner. An attachment-based intervention can help her identify Allison's cues and provide practice responding in a more adaptive manner while receiving feedback from the clinician. In addition, the clinician can help Ms. Adams understand how her experiences of interpartner violence are shaping her perceptions of Allison and can encourage Ms. Adams to develop developmentally appropriate attributions for her child's behavior.

Box 6.4: The Case of Hector

Question 1

Undoubtedly, the lack of placement stability exerted a negative impact on Hector's behavioral functioning. However, a clear pattern evident in the parent-child interactions suggests Ms. Young's commitment to parenting Hector is low. Attempts by Hector to engage in pleasant activities with Ms. Young were rebuffed, resulting in an emotionally negative exchange between the two.

Question 2

Certainly, an intervention must target the problematic exchange between Hector and Ms. Young, and this is best accomplished by assisting Ms. Young in identifying ways that she can follow Hector's lead and foster a positive emotional climate. A video-feedback intervention may be particularly helpful to show Ms. Young the attempts Hector made to engage her and how her responses may have perpetuated the frustrating dynamic. It may be worthwhile to further probe Ms. Young's representations of Hector and determine how they might be sustaining her manner of interacting with him.

Question 3

The clinician may want to empathize with Ms. Young that the placement instability was likely a contributing factor to the onset of Hector's behaviors. However, this unfortunate situation has now ceased, and Ms. Young can start fresh with Hector by establishing a permanent relationship from this point. Given his young age, it is not too late to shape more positive behaviors from Hector and improve family functioning at the same time.

RESOURCES

Training Resources

- **Attachment and Biobehavioral Catch-Up (ABC):** Training in ABC and further information is available at https://www.abcintervention.org/
- **Video Intervention for Positive Parenting and Sensitive Discipline (VIPP-SD):** Training in VIPP-SD and further information is available at https://www.universiteitleiden.nl/en/vipp
- **Child–Parent Psychotherapy (CPP):** Training in CPP and further information is available at https://childparentpsychotherapy.com/
- **Circle of Security (COS):** Training in COS and further information is available at https://www.circleofsecurityinternational.com/

Suggested Further Reading

Steele, H., & Steele, M. (Eds.). (2018). *Handbook of attachment-based interventions*. Guilford Press.

This edited volume provides introductions to 21 different attachment-based interventions, the vast majority of which are focused on aiding children under the age of 5 years and their caregivers. This book is an appropriate introduction to the diversity of programs available and an excellent resource for identifying a program best suited to an agency's specific needs.

7 ATTACHMENT AND CLINICAL PRACTICE WITH SCHOOL-AGE CHILDREN

At the Intersection of Clinical and Developmental Science

The application of attachment to clinical practice with school-age children is fraught with challenges. Researchers turn their attention during this age primarily to considering developmental trajectories and attachment representations, as opposed to attachment behavior. This empirical expanding of the lens requires clinical researchers to posit how attachment-based interventions may affect various developmental constructs. At the same time, children may be more actively engaged in treatment than infants are but generally may lack the cognitive sophistication to consider abstract concepts. Nonetheless, attachment theory yields a number of useful insights for the assessment and treatment of school-age children and their caregivers.

ATTACHMENT AND CHILD PSYCHOPATHOLOGY

Recognized diagnostic nosologies (e.g., American Psychiatric Association's, 2013, *Diagnostic and Statistical Manual of Mental Disorders* [5th ed.]; World Health Organization's, 2019, *International Statistical Classification of Diseases*

https://doi.org/10.1037/0000333-008
The Science and Clinical Practice of Attachment Theory: A Guide From Infancy to Adulthood, by B. Allen

and Related Health Problems [11th ed.]) do not include any discernible classification of disordered attachment among school-age children, largely because of the difficulties with observing and classifying attachment behavior beyond the first years of life. However, developmental and clinical scientists have examined the ways in which attachment representations relate to emotional and behavioral concerns of children. In addition, developmental factors of interest to attachment researchers, such as emotion regulation and social skills, are frequently examined in etiological research.

Internalizing Problems

Bowlby (1973, 1980) devoted significant time to theorizing about the application of attachment theory to internalizing concerns, such as anxiety and depression (see Chapter 1, this volume). Not surprisingly, then, attachment researchers examined the extent to which insecure attachment behavior in the SSP might predict later internalizing problems. More than 40 studies examining this link converged on the finding that secure attachment behavior in infancy and early childhood predicts low rates of internalizing problems both concurrently and into the middle childhood years, although the size of the relationship is small (Groh et al., 2012). Interestingly, the presence of internalizing concerns was predicted by avoidant attachment behavior during infancy but not by ambivalent or disorganized behavior. Although this review focused on attachment in relation to the mother, a recent meta-analysis focused on fathers found similar results (Deneault et al., 2021). In the context of children with two parents, studies suggest a singular insecure attachment increases the risk for internalizing symptoms, with children displaying insecure attachment to both parents at the highest level of risk (Dagan et al., 2021).

Another review confirmed this relationship: Madigan and colleagues (2013), using slightly different criteria, included more than 60 studies and obtained a similar small effect for the relationship between infant attachment security and internalizing problems. They likewise found the strength of the relationship was similar whether internalizing problems were assessed concurrently with attachment behavior or years later. Again, avoidant attachment behavior predicted internalizing problems while ambivalent behavior did not. However, in their analyses, disorganized behavior did predict higher levels of internalizing problems.

Moving into the middle childhood years, assessment of attachment primarily relies on questionnaire and narrative (e.g., interviews, story stems) forms of assessment. Attachment security assessed with these instruments generally predicts the concurrent and future display of internalizing concerns

(Madigan et al., 2016), with questionnaire measures more strongly predictive than narrative measures. It should be noted that the relationships between questionnaire and narrative measures and internalizing concerns are significantly stronger than those connecting observed behavior in infancy to later internalizing concerns. Multiple reasons for these findings are possible. For one, common method variance is a likely factor, as the relationship between attachment security and internalizing concerns is strongest when the child is the reporter of both outcomes. Another factor seems to be the age of the child, as the relationship between attachment and internalizing concerns is stronger for older children than for younger children.

Examining internalizing symptoms as a broad category may obscure important differences between subtype. Madigan and colleagues (2016) noted that attachment security was a significantly better predictor of depression than of anxiety. However, other meta-analyses focused solely on one outcome suggest the influence of attachment security on depression (Spruit et al., 2020) may be similar to its influence on anxiety (Colonnesi et al., 2011). Echoing previous findings, these studies showed that the relationship was stronger when clinical outcomes were evaluated by the child and when questionnaire measures were used.

These results speak to the potential utility of attachment metrics in clinical assessment. For instance, standard self-report questionnaires assessing depression do not commonly ask the child whether they perceive their caregiver as supportive during moments of sadness. However, treatments for childhood depression commonly include caregivers as a component of the treatment process. Including an assessment of a child's attachment security, whether in a narrative or questionnaire format, may provide useful information that can inform treatment delivery. Box 7.1 presents a case example of a 9-year-old girl exhibiting signs of depression.[1]

Externalizing Problems

Research examining the relationship of attachment constructs to externalizing problems, such as oppositionality and aggression, emerged relatively independent of research on internalizing problems. Interestingly, the patterns of findings related to the two different clinical outcomes significantly diverge. When attachment is evaluated with the mother, children who display insecure attachment behavior (inclusive of disorganized attachment)

[1]To protect patient confidentiality, proper steps have been taken to disguise the identities of the individuals in this chapter's case examples.

BOX 7.1

THE CASE OF MADDIE

Maddie is a White, 9-year-old girl referred for treatment by a school counselor who noticed that she often seemed sad and unable to focus on her schoolwork. When the counselor asked if anything was bothering her, Maddie only shrugged her shoulders and said, "I don't know." Although she was historically a good student, her grades slowly declined over the past 12 months, and both her teacher and the counselor surmised that this decline is the result of a depressed mood. The counselor contacted Maddie's mother, Ms. Williams, to express her concerns and provide the referral. Ms. Williams was surprised to hear that Maddie was not doing well academically and stated that she had not noticed any concerns with Maddie's mood at home.

Maddie displayed a depressed affect when presenting to the clinic for the initial evaluation and was generally quiet throughout the session. She spoke little and provided one-word answers to questions. The clinician asked Ms. Williams if the behavior displayed was typical for Maddie, to which Ms. Williams replied, "Yes, she is a very calm child." When meeting with Maddie alone the clinician tried to ascertain Maddie's perception of her mother. When asked the kind of activities she and her mother engage in together, Maddie responded by saying they watch television and eat meals. Maddie reported she does not live around other children and her mother will not drive her to play at parks or the homes of other friends. Similarly, she is not enrolled in any extracurricular activities, such as sports, art, or dance.

Discussion Questions

1. Maddie presents as a child struggling with depression. What may be the primary etiological factors?
2. What attachment-related concepts appear relevant to understanding Maddie's condition?
3. What types of experiences do you think may be necessary for Maddie given your conceptualization of her case?

typically demonstrate more externalizing problems than children with secure behavior do (Fearon et al., 2010). Similar findings are also found when attachment is assessed in relation to the father (Deneault et al., 2021). However, Fearon and colleagues (2010) found little difference between children who displayed avoidant or ambivalent behavior; rather, the best predictor of externalizing concerns was the display of disorganized behavior. Interestingly, the risk of externalizing problems is reduced in children with disorganized attachment to one caregiver if they have organized attachment to another caregiver (Dagan et al., 2021). The strength of the relationship between attachment behavior and externalizing problems did not dissipate over time in the Fearon et al. (2010) meta-analysis, suggesting a role for attachment in understanding current as well as future behavioral concerns.

Further evidence emerged when researchers evaluated the relationship between externalizing problems and attachment assessed through questionnaire and narrative measures (Madigan et al., 2016). In general, insecurity predicted high levels of externalizing problems, and, unlike with internalizing problems, no significant differences were noted based on whether the attachment construct was assessed using a questionnaire or a narrative approach. However, the strength of the relationship was significantly higher when the child reported on externalizing problems than when the reports came from parents or teachers. Although neither ambivalent nor avoidant representations predicted externalizing problems, disorganized representations were significantly associated with the display of externalizing problems.

Across studies, the primary factor connecting attachment to externalizing problems appears to be disorganization. Early research documenting the role of adversity and trauma in the development of both disorganized behavior and externalizing problems suggested the relationship between the two may be spurious. However, reviews either indicated no effect for socioeconomic status (Fearon et al., 2010) or suggested the relationship between disorganization and externalizing concerns was stronger among children living in more advantageous settings (Madigan et al., 2016). It is important to consider that disorganized attachment behavior in infancy may emerge before most types of externalizing problems, suggesting that it plays a role as an early risk factor for the onset of externalizing problems.

The Role of Attachment in the Etiology of Childhood Disorders

Research documenting a relationship between attachment processes and internalizing and externalizing problems in childhood suggests a role for attachment in the etiology of these concerns. Two primary explanations are available. One proposition is that a direct path exists between attachment representations and emotional and behavioral concerns. Evidence for such a direct path is abundant, most particularly the meta-analytic results discussed previously that show concurrent relationships (e.g., Fearon et al., 2010; Groh et al., 2012), especially between avoidant attachment and internalizing concerns and disorganized attachment and externalizing concerns. For instance, a child possessing an avoidant attachment representation may expect an unhelpful and potentially rejecting caregiver response to overtures for comfort and so, instead of seeking comfort, may rely on personal coping skills that may be ineffective. As a result, the child may develop anxiety or depression. A child with disorganized representations may be overwhelmed with a given situation and unable to construct a coherent response. This child may appear to most observers as distracted, oppositional, or potentially violent.

In many respects, this model is the traditional attachment theory explanation and the one most commonly considered by clinicians when assessing or treating children, as it yields clear and direct clinical implications. Assessment may incorporate questionnaires, interviews, or story-stem procedures to assess the child's representations, and treatment goals may include altering the child's maladaptive attachment representations or improving the quality of parent–child interactions by enhancing caregiving sensitivity. In this way, treatment generally reflects goals and procedures similar to attachment-based interventions with infants and young children.

The second explanation for the relationship between attachment and clinical concerns is often more compelling from a research perspective. In this developmental psychopathology approach, attachment serves as an antecedent for developmental capacities that are closer in etiological timing to externalizing and internalizing concerns. Significant evidence suggests that attachment predicts the emergence of myriad competencies, such as emotion regulation and social competence (see Chapter 3, this volume), which are well established in the literature as direct causes of psychopathology among children. Multiple studies find that attachment security and organization no longer predict many clinical concerns after accounting for such developmental factors (e.g., Brumariu & Kerns, 2013; Frick et al., 2022).

Conceptualizing the impact of attachment from this perspective suggests an indirect effect on the presentation of externalizing and internalizing problems. A corollary, then, is that instead of focusing on changing an attachment construct, treatment should aim at improving emotion regulation, impulse control, social skills, and so on. This type of treatment approach benefits from a sizable clinical literature that demonstrates a host of interventions capable of achieving such outcomes. A question that arises, however, is whether a treatment employing an attachment theoretical rationale and focused on improving emotion regulation, for instance, as opposed to an attachment construct, can be described as "attachment based." In reality, there is no consensus in the academic or clinical literature as to what exactly constitutes an "attachment-based intervention" (Duschinsky et al., 2021; H. Steele & Steele, 2018).

It must also be mentioned that these two explanations for the relationship between attachment processes and child emotional and behavioral problems are not mutually exclusive. One may experience aberrant development of a particular developmental competency (e.g., emotion regulation) that is compounded by ongoing insecurity within an attachment relationship. Enlisting the caregiver in treatment may not only assist with improving the developmental capacity targeted by an intervention but also provide the child with caregiving experiences that serve to alter maladaptive attachment representations. The case study in Box 7.2 presents an opportunity to explore how attachment may affect the assessment of behavioral problems in a 7-year-old boy.

ATTACHMENT-INFORMED TREATMENT WITH SCHOOL-AGE CHILDREN

Attachment researchers interested in clinical applications with school-age children struggle to define the specific attachment construct to target with an intervention. It may be unrealistic to expect significant changes in attachment representations in the relatively short window of time during which a clinical trial occurs, and long-term follow-ups are costly, time consuming, and susceptible to the influence of numerous extraneous factors. In addition, developmental attachment research most frequently focuses on infancy, resulting in comparatively little research on which to build interventions for school-age children. Although these challenges are slowly being addressed, there are currently no widely accepted attachment-based interventions with school-age children. Instead, attachment-based practice rests primarily on application of principles derived from attachment theory and research.

Attachment-Based Principles for the Treatment of School-Age Children

B. Allen (2011b) identified four primary directives prescribed by attachment theory relevant to the treatment of school-age children. First, treatment must

BOX 7.2

THE CASE OF JASON

Jason is an African American 7-year-old boy who entered the clinic screaming at his father and arguing about where to sit. His father, Mr. Abood, argued back and eventually threatened to spank Jason if he did not sit down. When it was time for their appointment, Mr. Abood grabbed Jason by the arm and led him back to the consulting room. Mr. Abood proceeded to report a litany of problems with Jason, including oppositionality, aggression, and disrespectful behavior toward both him and his wife as well as toward school staff. Jason recently hit another child at school, prompting a number of disciplinary actions and leading Mr. Abood to contact the clinic for treatment.

Jason continued to display significant behavioral concerns while meeting with the clinician alone. To assess attachment narratives, the clinician implemented a story-stem completion task. Jason was attentive throughout the administration of each stem and displayed facial expressions suggesting both comprehension and engagement with the task. However, when the procedure was turned over to him for completion, he often appeared confused as to how to resolve the stem and subsequently provided unusual responses that variously included the house burning down, aliens descending from space, and caregivers flying around picking up the children. After the end of the procedure, Jason asked where his father was. The clinician told him that Mr. Abood was in the waiting room and asked whether he wanted him to return to the room, to which Jason responded, "Yes . . . well, really, I don't care." He then walked to the window and described a car on the street below.

Discussion Questions

1. Jason displays obvious externalizing problems. What etiological factors appear most prominent within the vignette?
2. In considering Jason's responses to the story-stem procedure and the events that occurred immediately after, what can we deduce about his attachment narratives, in particular their classification and etiology?
3. How might Jason's attachment narratives be related to his externalizing problems?

focus on helping the child establish a trusting relationship with a supportive caregiver. Repeated experiences of a responsive caregiver under moments of stress can lead to revision of the child's internal working models, resulting in more adaptive representations of the self, others, and social interaction. In addition, a reliable caregiver provides a sense of structure and predictability that can reduce the frequency with which the child's attachment system is activated and can help terminate activation when it does occur through the provision of a safe haven. Consequently, the child may display improvements in numerous developmental capacities, such as emotion regulation, social skills, and self-perception. Individual therapy with the child, if implemented, should focus on the development of such competencies through focused training and actively include the caregiver, who can help ensure retention and progress by reinforcing the use of learned skills outside of sessions. In addition, the caregiver assisting in this manner may itself improve the parent–child relationship.

Second, treatment should focus on enhancing the caregiver's ability to respond to the child in a consistently sensitive manner. Two primary treatment techniques are evident:

- The clinician must provide the caregiver with focused training in delineating attachment behaviors from other forms of child behavior (e.g., exploring, playing, having a tantrum). This process typically requires helping the caregiver evaluate their perceptions of the child, including the child's motivations for different types of behaviors, and understand how such views affect their relationship with the child. This process may involve examining previous experiences with the child while helping the caregiver place the child's behavior in a new light or, potentially, examining the caregiver's own experiences with their parents during childhood. It may be necessary for clinicians to refer caregivers for their own mental health treatment.
- The clinician should instruct the caregiver in delivering calm and reassuring responses to a child's attachment behaviors and engaging in a positive manner during general interactions with the child. It is critical this instruction provide ample opportunities for the caregiver to practice these skills and receive feedback from the clinician, including troubleshooting various situations, potentially by recording videos of the caregiver's interactions with the child and reviewing them in session.

Third, the delivery of interventions should be present focused and geared toward improving the child's developmental trajectory through enhancement of the current environment (for an example, see Figure 3.3). It must be remembered that although the child's presenting concerns may be the result of a history of substandard caregiving, development progressed nonetheless. While the child may demonstrate difficulties in certain areas, such as emotion regulation, they may possess age-appropriate capabilities in other areas, such as intelligence. A corollary of this understanding is that successfully changing the course of years of troublesome development will not occur in the span of weeks or potentially even months. It is important for clinicians to provide a realistic understanding of the process and timing of change to build rapport with caregivers and guard against treatment dropout.

Fourth, in keeping with Bowlby's attention to issues of cognitive development, it is important that interventions be tailored to the cognitive ability of the child being treated. School-age children demonstrate a range of cognitive abilities, and it is incumbent upon the clinician to modify techniques accordingly. For instance, children with severe intellectual disabilities demonstrate attachment behavior and differentiate between discriminated attachment figures and strangers (Vandesande et al., 2020). Under such circumstances the clinician must help the caregiver distinguish between behaviors signifying an attachment function and those attempting to communicate other needs (e.g., nonverbal gestures). In a similar vein, implementing an intervention in the manner one would with a 6-year-old child may be viewed by an 11-year-old child as condescending and frustrating.

Bosmans and colleagues (2022) proposed an additional aspect of treatment that may be necessary for successfully improving attachment representations among school-age children. In short, they opined that treatment must involve an exposure component in which the child experiences a stimulus sufficiently stressful to activate the attachment system as well as a sensitive caregiver who provides emotional support and practical assistance in coping with the situation. They suggested in-session discussions of emotionally laden topics (e.g., academic problems, past conflicts within the family) as exposure exercises. B. Allen and Brown (2021) recently examined this contention in a small study of youth receiving exposure therapy for the treatment of posttraumatic stress secondary to experiences of child abuse. Nonoffending caregivers were actively involved in treatment, which included a conjoint session in which the youth discussed their accounts of abuse while caregivers remained validating and supportive. Youth who self-reported poor attachment security at the onset of treatment identified a drastic improvement in attachment security by the end of the 12-session protocol.

Parent-Training Interventions: Expanding the Lens

The proposition that altering caregiver responses to child behaviors may result in the amelioration of child emotional and behavioral concerns is not unique to attachment theory. At the time that Bowlby and Ainsworth were popularizing the developmental understanding of attachment in the 1960s, American psychologist Constance Hanf was developing a caregiver-focused treatment model designed to alter problematic child behavior. Relying on the science of behavior modification, Hanf proposed a two-stage model of intervention (Hanf & Kling, 1973). In the first stage (Child Game), the child selects the activities of the session, and the caregiver is instructed to provide attention and praises for desired behaviors while ignoring undesired behaviors. In the second stage (Mother's Game), the caregiver assumes control of the activities and provides directions to the child. The caregiver is instructed in the use of timeout procedures to implement for noncompliance. Many of the contemporary social-learning/behavioral parent-training interventions are derivatives of the original Hanf model. Two of the most prominent, both of which are gaining the attention of attachment researchers, are Parent–Child Interaction Therapy (PCIT) and the Incredible Years (IY).

Parent–Child Interaction Therapy

PCIT (McNeil & Hembree-Kigin, 2011) incorporates Hanf's two-stage model by emphasizing the development of a caregiver's positive attending skills before addressing active discipline skills. In the first phase, caregivers are taught to praise and describe the child's desired behavior, reflect the child's verbalizations, and engage in the child's play, all while demonstrating a sense of enjoyment with the interactions. In addition, caregivers are instructed to remove attention in response to undesired behavior (i.e., ignore). In the second phase, clinicians teach caregivers how to deliver clear commands and effective consequences for noncompliance, including a defined timeout sequence and/or removal of privileges. The parent interacts with the child during sessions while the clinician observes from an adjoining room using either a closed-circuit video system or a one-way mirror. The caregiver wears a remote speaker ("bug-in-the-ear"), and the clinician coaches the caregiver in the delivery of the techniques using a connected microphone. This arrangement allows the clinician to provide in-the-moment feedback to the caregiver while ensuring that the child receives all responses and directives from the caregiver. PCIT was originally developed for children between the ages of 3 and 6 years, but modifications are available that extend the upper end of the age range to 12 years (Chaffin et al., 2004; McNeil & Hembree-Kigin, 2011).

Clinical trials demonstrate superior results for PCIT when compared with control groups, including reductions in externalizing behaviors and parenting stress as well as increased frequency of target skills (e.g., praises, reflections; R. Thomas et al., 2017). B. Allen et al. (2014) argued that PCIT ascribes to attachment-derived treatment directives, including focusing on the parent–child relationship, enhancing caregiver sensitivity, and working within the current environment to improve a child's developmental trajectory. Indeed, studies document that caregivers completing PCIT show increased sensitivity to child cues as well as more emotionally engaged responses (R. Thomas & Zimmer-Gembeck, 2012; Timmer et al., 2011). Across these same studies, PCIT is found to be efficacious with a number of populations at risk for insecure or disorganized attachment, including maltreating, depressed, and foster/adoptive caregivers.

PCIT researchers are increasingly highlighting the attachment underpinnings of the intervention. Nonetheless, important questions remain, not the least of which is whether PCIT may improve child attachment representations. Some evidence suggests that children display greater responsivity to and engagement with the caregiver following PCIT (Timmer et al., 2011), which may suggest improved representations of the caregiver. A related question is whether caregiver-focused attachment constructs improve following PCIT, as these are not specifically targeted by the intervention. Zimmer-Gembeck and colleagues (2019) reported improvements in parenting-related reflective functioning (i.e., understanding the mental states of children) following PCIT, but the effect was small and has not been replicated. Research is ongoing, including determining whether supplementing PCIT with a limited number of sessions focused on improving parental reflective functioning may enhance outcomes. Box 7.3 continues the case example from Box 7.2, examining the role of attachment in the delivery of PCIT.

The Incredible Years

IY is another Hanf-inspired parent-training intervention that is popular for its group-based administration. In this model, a group of caregivers review videotaped demonstrations of parenting skills similar to those taught during PCIT. Caregivers then practice these skills with one another while the clinician facilitates acquisition of the skills by providing feedback during the role plays. Participants are encouraged to consider the unique challenges involved with parenting their own children and how the techniques might be implemented to address those challenges. Members of the group are encouraged to provide their thoughts or reactions during the role plays to help one another better understand the perspectives of the children. IY programs are available for the preschool (ages 3–6 years) and school-age (ages 6–12 years) periods.

IY is supported by a number of clinical trials demonstrating significant improvement of externalizing behaviors (Leijten et al., 2020). From an attachment perspective, O'Connor and colleagues (2013) found that caregivers

BOX 7.3

THE CASE OF JASON, REVISITED

The clinician decided to implement Parent-Child Interaction Therapy (PCIT) with Jason, the 7-year-old boy who presented with externalizing problems (see Box 7.2), and his father. However, Mr. Abood was skeptical at the outset of treatment because he attributed Jason's behavior to willful defiance, and he suggested that treatment needed to focus on helping Jason "figure out his issues." The clinician inquired as to how effective Mr. Abood felt his parenting techniques were, to which Mr. Abood replied that his techniques were the same ones used on him by his own parents. The clinician restated the question by asking whether he viewed the techniques as effective for changing Jason's behavior. After some reflection, Mr. Abood conceded that the techniques were seemingly ineffective. The clinician then conceptualized the skills learned through PCIT as alternatives that may yield better results.

During the initial phases of treatment, the clinician provided focused coaching in the use of praises and providing attention to desired behavior while ignoring unwanted behavior. At moments Mr. Abood appeared frustrated with Jason's behavior and relayed to the clinician that Jason was intentionally trying to manipulate him. The clinician reframed Jason's behaviors as reflecting poor ability to regulate emotions and behaviors and encouraged the father to implement the skills as coached. After a number of sessions, Mr. Abood was able to identify positive changes in Jason, including ceasing problematic behavior more quickly after removing attention. He also noticed that Jason was deliberately offering to engage him in play, something that was rare in the past. The clinician noted that Mr. Abood displayed less frustration during interactions and by the midpoint of treatment no longer suggested that Jason's problems were the result of manipulation or "his issues."

Discussion Questions

1. How would you describe Mr. Abood's mentalizing ability at the beginning of treatment, and how did it affect his parenting? Are there indications that his mentalizing ability changed over the course of treatment?
2. How did Mr. Abood's caregiving responses change over the course of treatment, and what factors may have prompted the change(s)?
3. Are there any indications that Jason's attachment security improved?

participating in IY demonstrated significant improvements in sensitivity and, interestingly, changes in sensitivity only modestly correlated with changes in social learning-based frequency counts of parenting skills (e.g., praises delivered). These latter findings suggest the two coding systems were indexing distinct aspects of caregiving. The authors did not find that IY changed attachment representations immediately following the 12-week protocol; however, using the same sample, the researchers demonstrated that secure child representations were predicted by caregiving coded using the attachment-based scheme but not when coded with the social learning-based scheme (Matias et al., 2014). Assuming retention of the parenting skills learned in the IY program, this finding suggests children of parents completing IY may demonstrate more secure representations over time.

Future Prospects for Social Learning-Based Parenting Interventions
Implementation of social learning-based parenting interventions for the purposes of enhancing attachment is an exciting new development. Such interventions already possess considerable support for the treatment of externalizing problems among children, and emerging evidence is showing similar positive outcomes for the treatment of child internalizing concerns (e.g., Phillips & Mychailyszyn, 2021). Traditional explanations are that such interventions shape adaptive behaviors using behavior modification techniques and/or foster the development of improved emotion regulation, impulse control, and social skills. Such reasoning coincides with the view that attachment behavior and representations are shaped by parental responses and attachment constructs influence the emergence of developmental capacities. To prevent "reinventing the wheel," it appears warranted to continue exploring these interventions using an attachment lens.

A Note on Discipline Techniques

There is a common misperception among many in the clinical community, as well as in allied disciplines, that attachment theory dictates empathically attending to any and all negative emotions a child displays. For instance, some foster and adoption agencies prohibit surrogate caregivers from diverting attention away from tantrum behavior, and some clinicians are known to intentionally remove timeout procedures from parenting interventions. They argue that attachment theory suggests such discipline techniques may damage the relationship between the child and caregiver and propose instead to sit with an upset child and provide reassuring comments (e.g., Siegel & Bryson, 2014).

In actuality, attachment research does not support such an idea, nor did Bowlby or Ainsworth ever make such arguments. Quite the opposite. Attachment researchers generally respect the established science of behavior modification, and behavioral theory increasingly forms the foundation for understanding how a child's attachment behavior and representations develop (Bosmans et al., 2020). It is a clearly demonstrated principle that providing attention to problematic behaviors and their concurrent emotions may be reinforcing and result in more frequent displays of the behavior. For this reason, many attachment-based interventions, such as Video Intervention for Positive Parenting and Sensitive Discipline (see Chapter 6, this volume), explicitly incorporate instruction on the implementation of timeout procedures.

When it comes to discipline techniques, the important feature from an attachment perspective is that the administration of consequences is done in a nonmaltreating, sensitive, and empathic manner (see Dadds & Tully, 2019, for an excellent discussion). Many social learning parent-training interventions, such as PCIT and IY, teach discipline procedures that coincide with these directives, and evidence suggests they may drastically reduce the frequency with which caregivers use physically coercive forms of discipline (e.g., Chaffin et al., 2004). In addition, attachment theory supports teaching caregivers to decipher the causes of a child's behavior in order to respond most effectively. For instance, a caregiver should soothe a child who cries during moments of fear (i.e., attachment behavior), but this caregiving response reinforces undesired behavior if the child is crying because they are upset at not receiving a treat.

ATTACHMENT AND TRAUMA

The roles of maltreatment and trauma in the development of attachment are discussed throughout this volume, but the ways in which attachment-based intervention may address the effects of trauma deserves consideration. Trauma may affect the developing individual through two primary routes. The first employs the developmental psychopathology framework. According to this view, trauma causes aberrant development of emotion regulation, social skills, or any number of other capacities, and attachment may be a mediating factor in the process. As such, improving attachment may aid in the process of improving developmental trajectories.

Research examining attachment-based interventions with infants demonstrates this principle (see Chapter 6). Many of the currently supported attachment-based interventions were developed and tested with maltreated and/or foster/adopted children precisely because of the high risk in such populations for insecure and disorganized attachment. For instance, Attachment and Biobehavioral Catch-Up (ABC; e.g., Bernard et al., 2012; see Chapter 6, this volume) is shown to improve attachment security and organization, as well as emotion regulation, impulse control, and diurnal regulation of a stress hormone (i.e., cortisol). In addition, as mentioned previously, social learning-derived parent-training interventions with school-age children, such as PCIT and IY, similarly demonstrate improvement of attachment constructs and effectiveness with maltreated and foster/adopted populations. These findings suggest that interventions supported by attachment theory and research can improve anomalous developmental trajectories resulting from the impact of trauma.

The second mechanism through which trauma may affect the individual is the development of posttraumatic stress (PTS), a cluster of symptoms characterized by intrusive memories of a traumatic event (e.g., nightmares), avoidance of stimuli associated with the traumatic event, altered moods and cognitions (e.g., viewing the world as dangerous, experiencing shame), and physiological hyperarousal (American Psychiatric Association, 2013). Front-line intervention for the treatment of PTS typically involves some form of exposure therapy in which the child is confronted with the feared stimuli in graduated doses, either imaginal or in vivo, to extinguish the PTS responses. Given that such an intervention inherently requires the induction of manageable forms of stress, it is hypothesized that attachment security should enhance the effectiveness of the intervention by allowing the child to engage more fully in the treatment as a result of knowing a trusted caregiver is available to help manage the stress. However, the only known trial testing this contention did not find that attachment security predicted the outcome of exposure therapy among youth with PTS (B. Allen & Brown, 2021). Another trial testing a similar hypothesis with youth receiving cognitive behavior therapy for an anxiety disorder also did not find that attachment security predicted outcomes (Walczak et al., 2017). Given that both trials demonstrated positive results of the interventions, it seems likely that the treatments' mechanisms of action are effective regardless of one's attachment security.

An alternative approach supposes that improving attachment security may ameliorate PTS even in the absence of focused exposure exercises. Given that children are often forced to confront reminders of their trauma(s) in their daily lives as well as experience intrusive memories and other PTS symptoms, improving attachment security may allow them to cope with these occurrences better, thereby providing a form of naturalistic exposure therapy. Although investigation of this hypothesis is rare, evidence suggests that Child–Parent Psychotherapy (see Chapter 6) may reduce PTS symptoms among preschoolers exposed to interpartner violence (Lieberman et al., 2005) and that PCIT may reduce PTS among preschoolers and school-age children with maltreatment histories (B. Allen et al., 2016). Further research on this possibility is warranted as it suggests an alternative treatment option for children who do not respond well to standard forms of exposure therapy. Box 7.4 presents a case study of a 7-year-old in foster care who exhibits behavioral problems secondary to trauma exposure and disruption of attachment relationships.

BOX 7.4

THE CASE OF HANNAH

Hannah is a White, 7-year-old girl referred for treatment by a Child Protective Services (CPS) worker after she was removed from her biological mother because of severe neglect, physical abuse, and interpartner violence. Her current foster mother of 3 months, Ms. Halter, attended the initial assessment with her and reported that Hannah struggles with anxiety, sadness, difficulty sleeping, oppositional behavior, and tantrums. These behaviors occur most frequently before and after visits with her biological mother. The clinician recommended a parent-training intervention, and Ms. Halter agreed to participate. However, shortly after the assessment the CPS worker called to inquire about the recommended treatment course. The CPS worker voiced strong objections to the parent-training intervention because Ms. Halter is Hannah's third caregiver in the past 12 months (after her biological mother and one previous foster caregiver) and the plan is for Hannah to be reunited eventually with her biological mother. The CPS worker does not want Hannah developing an attachment to Ms. Halter because of a high likelihood that she will be moved to another placement in the coming months. The worker worried that multiple attachment disruptions might have an irreversible impact on Hannah's well-being.

Discussion Questions

1. Hannah's behaviors included both internalizing and externalizing problems, and her history is quite complex. How might you explain the etiology of her problems?
2. How would you respond to the CPS worker's concerns related to multiple attachment disruptions?
3. If the CPS worker withholds consent for the parent-training intervention, how might you respond from an attachment perspective?

CONCLUSION

The relative dearth of attachment research during the school-age period has resulted in a lack of empirically tested protocols derived from the attachment tradition. Nonetheless, the available evidence, including the results of trials with infants and preschoolers, provides clear attachment-based principles for treatment. In addition, attachment-based interventions designed for school-age children would likely resemble, in many respects, any number of well-established parent-training interventions derived from social-learning/behavioral theory. Such interventions appear capable of altering attachment constructs and may be justly implemented according to both clinical indications and attachment theoretical propositions. Much work remains to determine how attachment theory and research may enhance treatment outcome with school-age children.

BOX 7.5

DISCUSSIONS OF CASE STUDIES

Box 7.1: The Case of Maddie

Question 1

One of the primary etiological explanations for the onset of depression among children emphasizes the role of problematic parent–child relationships. In Maddie's case, the activities she reported participating in with her mother are not interactive (i.e., watching TV, eating meals), and Ms. Williams displays little understanding of Maddie's challenges, going so far as to confuse Maddie's depressive symptoms with being a "calm child." This problematic parent–child relationship is compounded by a seeming lack of pleasurable activities for Maddie, who has little opportunity to play with other children or to participate in typical childhood activities. The result is a child isolated for large periods of the day with a seemingly uninterested caregiver.

Question 2

First, there is substantial evidence that Ms. Williams likely possesses poor mentalizing abilities in her parental role. She was unaware that Maddie is performing poorly in school, she confused depressive symptoms with being well-behaved, and she seems either not to understand or not to appreciate the importance of pleasurable activities for a child. Second, this poor mentalizing ability may be maintaining the apparent lack of

BOX 7.5

DISCUSSIONS OF CASE STUDIES (*Continued*)

caregiver sensitivity displayed by Ms. Williams. Third, Maddie's answers to questions suggest that she does not view her relationship with Ms. Williams in a positive light. Assessment of attachment security with Maddie may be helpful to clarify her perception of Ms. Williams as a secure base and safe haven. Given Maddie's tendency to answer questions briefly because of her depression, a questionnaire may be more effective at capturing this construct than an interview.

Question 3

Clearly, treatment will require improving the parent-child relationship. Although such a clinical direction may take many forms, it appears important to focus on Ms. Williams' ability to respond to Maddie in a more sensitive manner. Accomplishing this task may include individual treatment for Ms. Williams (see Chapter 9) and/or a parent-training intervention.

Box 7.2: The Case of Jason

Question 1

The most prominent etiological factors in Jason's externalizing problems appears to be deficits regulating emotional and behavioral responses. Mr. Abood seems to have little control over Jason's behaviors and resorts to physical coercion, potentially including corporal punishment, in efforts to manage Jason's behaviors. Such parenting approaches may perpetuate coercive cycles and fail to teach Jason more effective modes of regulation.

Question 2

Jason's responses on the story-stem procedure are classic examples of disorganized attachment narratives. He appeared focused on the task, at least initially, before demonstrating an inability to muster a coherent response to the story stem, which resulted in confused, eccentric, and, ultimately, incoherent responses. In addition, Jason asking for his father suggests potential attachment behavior as it immediately followed a story-stem completion task assessing responses to stressful situations. However, he quickly pivoted to saying that he did not care if his father returned to the room, then distracted himself with events out the window. This approach-avoidance behavior is also suggestive of disorganized representations. Mr. Abood demonstrates a propensity toward frightening forms of caregiving, including arguing, threatening corporal punishment,

(*continues*)

BOX 7.5

DISCUSSIONS OF CASE STUDIES (*Continued*)

and physically pulling Jason to prompt his movement. Such frightening behavior is well established as a cause of disorganized attachment.

Question 3

Disorganized attachment representations are related to difficulty regulating emotions and behaviors and may be the result of developmental progression, as proposed by the developmental psychopathology framework. In addition, disorganized representations suggest that Jason has difficulty developing coherent responses to stressful situations, which may portend the onset of dysregulated behavior. Last, such narratives convey either a perceived uncertainty or an inability to access caregivers for help resolving difficulties, resulting in Jason being forced to confront such situations by himself.

Box 7.3: The Case of Jason, Revisited

Question 1

Mr. Abood's mentalizing ability at the beginning of treatment appeared generally poor. He attributed Jason's externalizing concerns to factors internal to Jason (i.e., framing them as "his issues") and believed his behavior was deliberate. As a result, Mr. Abood responded angrily to Jason's behaviors. The clinician pointed out that Jason's behaviors may reflect poor regulatory ability and highlighted how Jason's behavior changed in response to Mr. Abood's change in caregiving approach. Mr. Abood came to see Jason's troublesome behavior through a new lens and was no longer making blaming comments by the middle of treatment.

Question 2

Mr. Abood's caregiving approach was marked by greater self-control and increased utilization of nonviolent techniques. Certainly, a portion of this improvement may be ascribed to improvements in mentalizing ability, as just discussed. However, Mr. Abood received focused training in the implementation of various parenting skills that likely changed the contingencies of response to Jason's behavior (social learning-based) as well as the relationship-related emotional climate in the room (attachment-based). Both attachment and social-learning models emphasize feedback as a key component of skill acquisition, whether it is done "in the moment" as occurred here or through review of videotapes.

BOX 7.5

DISCUSSIONS OF CASE STUDIES (*Continued*)

Question 3

Although this vignette includes no observations of attachment behavior, there are indications that Jason desires to engage with his father in play. This change may suggest fear of his father is receding, and, therefore, the potential exists that greater organization of attachment representations may be possible. At least, such willingness to interact with his father is a positive sign from an attachment perspective and offers hope for improved security.

Box 7.4: The Case of Hannah

Question 1

Hannah's concerns are likely the result of poor developmental experiences, particularly within attachment relationships, and she now displays significant problems with emotional and behavioral regulation. In addition, her experience of physical abuse and interpartner violence appears to have prompted the onset of posttraumatic stress (PTS) symptoms (e.g., trouble sleeping, visits with biological mother serve as trauma reminders and exacerbate the symptoms).

Question 2

The Child Protective Services (CPS) worker's concern is not uncommon among those unfamiliar with attachment theory and research. Certainly, multiple attachment disruptions are unfortunate and a cause for concern; however, the disruptions already occurred and seem likely to occur again. This situation presented two choices. The first choice is having the child reside in a home, potentially for a number of months, with a foster mother instructed to maintain an emotionally distant posture, to not comfort the child when she is distressed, and to not engage in pleasurable activities with her. Unless such a caregiving approach is provided, it is a high likelihood that the foster mother will begin to take on the characteristics of an attachment figure for the child. Of course, most will recognize such caregiving is not realistic and is likely emotional maltreatment. In addition, the CPS worker's desire that Hannah not develop an attachment to Ms. Halter overlooks the fact that development will continue for Hannah, and her preferred course of action implies that it is better for that development to occur in an emotional void as opposed to an environment conducive to healthy progress.

(*continues*)

BOX 7.5

DISCUSSIONS OF CASE STUDIES (*Continued*)

The second choice is having Ms. Halter try to provide a sensitive and responsive home environment for Hannah and help improve her socioemotional development. Whatever progress may be made in the time Hannah spends with Ms. Halter may better equip her for the future challenges she is sure to face. The loss of Ms. Halter may be a blow to Hannah, but it is unlikely to create lifelong, irreparable damage. Research suggests that children with a history of placement instability are capable of forming secure attachments once stability is achieved.

Question 3

If the CPS worker persists in her objections, attachment-based principles still support an attempt to improve developmental trajectories within Hannah's current environment. The clinician may provide focused training in emotion regulation, behavior regulation, and/or social skills as well as exposure therapy for PTS. Ms. Halter is still expected to be an active participant in treatment to reinforce usage of the learned skills in the home environment. It would not be surprising if the parent-child relationship, including attachment security and organization, improved through this form of treatment, consequently furthering the therapeutic goals of an attachment-based intervention.

RESOURCES

Training Resources

- **Parent–Child Interaction Therapy:** Training in PCIT and further information is available at https://www.pcit.org/ and https://pcit.ucdavis.edu/
- **The Incredible Years:** Training in IY and further information is available at https://incredibleyears.com/

8 ATTACHMENT AND CLINICAL PRACTICE WITH ADOLESCENTS

Building Autonomy and Connectedness

Significant shifts are perceptible in the literature regarding the ways in which attachment theory and research can be applied to clinical work with adolescents. Most evident among these changes is the conceptualization of how attachment constructs relate to psychopathology. The cognitive maturation of adolescents necessitates an interactional understanding of the etiology of internalizing and externalizing concerns, as opposed to the caregiver-focused model predominating earlier stages of development. Treatment approaches offer a mixture of adolescent-focused and caregiver-focused techniques, typically with an emphasis on altering the dynamics and forms of communication within the caregiver–adolescent relationship. Although clinical research with adolescents pales in comparison with the work done with infants, sufficient evidence is available to demonstrate the clinical utility of attachment theory and research.

https://doi.org/10.1037/0000333-009
The Science and Clinical Practice of Attachment Theory: A Guide From Infancy to Adulthood, by B. Allen

ATTACHMENT PROCESSES IN ADOLESCENT PSYCHOPATHOLOGY

Examination of the role attachment processes play in the development and maintenance of clinical problems during adolescence focuses primarily on the youth's states of mind and patterns of interaction between the youth and the caregiver(s). These two factors are not mutually exclusive, however, as state of mind commonly influences the quality of the parent–adolescent relationship as well as the manner in which the youth and the caregiver convey their thoughts and feelings. In turn, interactions among the dyad affect the adolescent's state of mind.

Depression and Anxiety

Evidence suggests a link between attachment security and internalizing concerns, and this relationship is seemingly stronger during adolescence than during childhood (Brumariu & Kerns, 2010; Madigan et al., 2016). This connection is found both when the two factors are assessed concurrently and when attachment is assessed earlier in development, suggesting a potential role for attachment security in both the etiology and the maintenance of depression and anxiety. Unlike in childhood when avoidant/dismissing attachment is the best predictor of internalizing symptoms, reviews suggest that preoccupied/ambivalent attachment is the most predictive form of insecurity during adolescence (Dagan et al., 2020; Spruit et al., 2020).

Dagan et al. (2021) postulated this shift in how insecurity predicts internalizing symptoms is likely a result of a changing environment mixed with evolutionary demands. The individual relies primarily on caregivers to manage stress during earlier stages of development, and ambivalent/preoccupied attachment behaviors serve to keep the caregiver nearby but suggest the child is uncertain of the caregiver's response. Avoidance/dismissing behavior, on the other hand, keeps the caregiver at a distance and potentially creates internal distress at the lack of protection and assistance. However, during adolescence the individual is expected to achieve a level of autonomy, and, to an extent, the self-reliance of avoidant/dismissing individuals is more functional. Their learned ability to independently handle stress results in less anxiety and depression. Ambivalent/preoccupied individuals, however, increasingly find themselves in situations that demand autonomy, such as interacting with peer groups and resolving conflicts. Under such situations, an ambivalent/preoccupied individual may experience increased stress, uncertainty, and subsequent withdrawal from social settings.

While this perspective underlines the hypothesis that state of mind and attachment security serve an emotion regulation function, it is important to remember that adolescent attachment is related to multiple aspects of the parent–youth relationship. Compared with secure attachment, insecure attachment in adolescence predicts higher levels of conflict between parent and youth (see Chapter 4, this volume), which in turn predicts the onset of depression and anxiety (Yap et al., 2007). These findings are in addition to studies showing that insecurity-fostering parental behavior, such as rejecting comments and disinterest, predict the onset of such problems (Johnco et al., 2021).

A picture emerges of problematic parent–youth interactions resulting in the development of insecure attachment, with the adolescent viewing the caregiver as either unhelpful or inconsistently available and prompting difficulty expressing thoughts and emotions within the dyad. This poor communication coupled with emotionally tense interactions maintains, and potentially exacerbates, problems with the parent–youth relationship while reinforcing the adolescent's insecure state of mind. When stressful circumstances arise (e.g., relationship break-ups, problems with peers), the youth finds it difficult to access the caregiver for assistance, resulting in the potential for spiraling emotional well-being and the emergence of anxiety and/or depression.

Suicidal and Self-Injurious Behavior

In extreme cases, the adolescent's inability to resolve sources of stress combines with the troublesome parent–adolescent relationship to predict self-injurious or suicidal behavior. One of the most prominent explanations of suicide, the interpersonal theory, proposes that one's decision to attempt such an action is predicted by (a) perceived burdensomeness and (b) a sense of not belonging/social alienation (Joiner et al., 2009). Problematic relationships within the family drive these perceptions, which may be further exacerbated by interactions with peers (Buchman-Schmitt et al., 2014). This perspective helps explain how attachment insecurity is connected to adolescent suicidal ideation.

Studies seeking to explain the relationship between attachment and suicide among adolescents largely isolate caregiver availability as a key factor (Adam et al., 1996; Zisk et al., 2017). In essence, if one views the caregiver as inaccessible, one is challenged with a sense of social alienation while simultaneously interpreting the stresses that are encountered as burdensome to others. In other words, this one factor from attachment theory encompasses both vital aspects of the interpersonal theory. Implied in these findings is a significant level of dysfunction within families of suicidal adolescents.

Indeed, adolescents with prior suicide attempts are more likely than their peers to rate their families low on scales of cohesion and adaptability (Sheftall et al., 2013). Parental perceptions of these aspects of the family are generally unrelated to adolescent suicidal ideation, suggesting that changing the adolescent's perception of the family and caregivers is critical for successful intervention.

A related, although distinct, concept is that of nonsuicidal self-injurious (NSSI) behavior (e.g., cutting). In cases of NSSI, the goal is not typically to complete suicide. Rather, Nock (2009) proposed that an individual intentionally self-injures as a means of either resolving a form of internal distress (e.g., emotion regulation) or communicating distress to another (i.e., "a cry for help"). Indeed, many of the studies examining NSSI among adolescents focus on the etiological role of emotion regulation and assorted forms of family dysfunction. These proposed pathways led to examinations of how attachment theory may help identify those most at risk for NSSI.

As might be expected, research establishes a link between insecure forms of attachment and NSSI (Woo et al., 2020). A number of explanations are available to explain this relationship. For instance, the interpersonal theory of suicide is often applied to NSSI, in that adolescents may turn to NSSI as a form of regulating emotion and/or communicating their distress to others when they feel alienated and burdensome to family members. Attachment is also viewed as a mediator in the link between stressful life events and the later display of NSSI and/or suicidal behavior (B. Allen et al., 2013; J. Martin et al., 2017). This perspective invokes attachment theory as an explanation for the development of emotion dysregulation and problematic interpersonal relationships. As such, although NSSI and suicidal ideation are distinct concepts, they share proposed etiological mechanisms and are both targeted by similar interventions. Box 8.1 presents a case example in which attachment may have a played a role in a 16-year-old girl's suicide attempt.[1]

Aggression and Callous/Unemotional Traits

Given that attachment disorganization is related to externalizing problems, researchers have sought to connect attachment constructs to behavioral concerns, such as aggression, during adolescence. There is some evidence for a relationship between the two concepts. For instance, Miga and colleagues (2010) found that adolescents with preoccupied states of mind were more

[1]To protect patient confidentiality, proper steps have been taken to disguise the identities of the individuals in this chapter's case examples.

BOX 8.1

THE CASE OF JASMINE

Jasmine is a 16-year-old Asian American girl admitted to an inpatient treatment facility following a suicide attempt; she tried to overdose on sertraline (i.e., Zoloft) prescribed by her primary care physician for depression. Upon presenting to the emergency department of a local hospital, she told the on-call psychiatrist that her medication did not solve her problems because she was still living at home. She went on to tell the psychiatrist that her parents frequently blame her for the problems in their marriage and make comments about her failing grades. Jasmine became irritated while talking about her mother, often accusing her of not being a "real mom," and then asked if it would be possible to live with her aunt after being released from the hospital.

The psychiatrist interviewed Jasmine's parents, Mr. and Ms. Kwan, who were surprised to hear that Jasmine wanted to leave home. The parents admitted they become frustrated with Jasmine's poor academic performance but denied having any significant problems in their marriage and did not recall ever blaming Jasmine for marital disagreements. Ms. Kwan confirmed that she is often the target of Jasmine's anger, which their doctor said is a symptom of depression. It has strained her relationship with her daughter, and Mr. Kwan noted he becomes upset with Jasmine when seeing the way she treats her mother. The parents are worried about Jasmine's well-being, as this is her third suicide attempt. The psychiatrist decided to refer Jasmine to an inpatient facility where she can receive intensive therapy for her depression.

Discussion Questions

1. What role do attachment-related factors appear to play in Jasmine's presentation?
2. There are significant discrepancies between Jasmine's report and that of her parents. Based on initial impressions, to what do you attribute these discrepancies?
3. What other pieces of information or data would you like to have, and why?

psychologically aggressive within dating relationships than those with a secure state of mind, while Kobak et al. (2009) found preoccupied states of mind predicted increased rates of caregiver-reported physical aggression throughout adolescence. The connection appears largely the result of the conflictual and angry interpersonal responses characteristic of individuals with preoccupied states of mind.

Although the evidence linking attachment processes to adolescent aggression is minimal, the developmental impact of early attachment experiences is important. Aggression in adolescence is frequently linked to problems with emotional and behavioral regulation as well as to problems with peer relationships (Card & Little, 2006), all of which are outcomes related to attachment behavior and representations (see Chapter 3, this volume). In addition, parenting approaches known to predict insecure and/or disorganized attachment, such as psychological neglect or harsh physical discipline, predict the display of aggression among children and adolescents (Kawabata et al., 2011). These findings suggest a place for attachment processes in mediating the relationship between parenting and the emergence of aggression, potentially through their impact on the growth of developmental capacities. Box 8.2 presents a case study that explores possible connections between a 14-year-old boy's aggressive, violent behavior at school and attachment functioning with his mother.

BOX 8.2

THE CASE OF MICHAEL

Michael is a 14-year-old White boy referred for treatment following a number of physical altercations with peers at school. The majority of these incidents resulted from disagreements with other males that spiraled from verbal arguments to fighting. On one occasion, however, Michael assaulted a classmate without warning, resulting in significant injuries for the classmate. Michael was hesitant to discuss the events during the initial interview, often shrugging his shoulders in response to questions. When he did answer a question, it was typically to blame the other adolescent involved. The rationales ranged from the peer being disrespectful, to competition for the favor of a female peer, to a belief that the other individual stole something belonging to him. In each instance, Michael was unable to provide concrete evidence and simply justified his responses by saying, "I know it's true." Michael often pivoted to discussing other topics and asked questions of little relevance to the issues at hand.

BOX 8.2

THE CASE OF MICHAEL (*Continued*)

When asked about his mother, Ms. Simpson, Michael just waved his hands and referenced her being in the waiting room. The clinician persisted and asked Michael to describe his relationship with her. Michael explained she goes into his room without his permission, which upsets him, before quickly turning to a discussion of his mother being an excellent cook. The clinician brought the topic back to the issue of his mother entering his room, and Michael shook his head, stating, "She doesn't really do that too much." When asked whether he can rely on his mother for help when needed, Michael nodded his head but was unable to give clear examples. Instead, he recounted a time his mother slipped on ice outside the family home.

When Ms. Simpson met with the clinician, her answers provided little context for Michael's problems. She was generally unaware that he was having such problems and blamed the school for not communicating their concerns to her earlier. The clinician asked how she responded to word of Michael's involvement in fights at school, and Ms. Simpson responded, "Oh, no. I sat him down and gave him the business. He knows he can't do stuff like that." When asked for clarification of what "the business" meant, Ms. Simpson continued to provide unclear responses that were suggestive of harsh discipline. The clinician specifically asked if she physically punished Michael in some way. She answered, "No, cause you can't do that with teenagers. Now, if he was still a younger child, you can bet that his butt would be hurting."

Discussion Questions

1. What do you make of Michael's answers to interview questions? How might he perform on an interview, such as the Child Attachment Interview or the adolescent version of the Adult Attachment Interview?
2. Considering your response to Question 1, how might your understanding of Michael's attachment functioning inform your conceptualization of his aggressive behavior?
3. What can be said of Ms. Simpson's contribution to Michaels' attachment functioning and his aggression problems?

Conduct problems may be more severe if accompanied by callous/unemotional (C/U) traits, which generally include a lack of awareness or concern for the emotions of others and a corresponding deficiency of developmentally normative empathy. Although disorganized attachment behavior at age 3 is weakly related to C/U traits (Willoughby et al., 2014), evidence suggests that disorganized attachment narratives during childhood correlate more strongly with C/U traits (Pasalich et al., 2012). However, it is important to note that children with higher C/U traits are observed to display appropriate emotional responses to attachment-related stimuli and to regulate such emotions effectively (Dadds et al., 2016). One of the few studies examining the relationship between attachment and C/U traits in adolescence found that a dismissing state of mind was related to C/U traits, but only for males (Gambin et al., 2018). These findings are limited by the fact that they are cross-sectional in nature and thus can demonstrate a relationship but cannot suggest causal mechanisms. Taubner and colleagues (2013) found that C/U traits predicted an outward display of aggression, but only when the adolescent exhibited low mentalizing ability, suggesting a potential causal role for an attachment construct.

ATTACHMENT-BASED INTERVENTIONS WITH ADOLESCENTS

Few attachment-based interventions are available for adolescents. Those that are available typically emphasize two components: respecting and boosting adolescent autonomy and building healthier relationships with caregivers who can provide support during times of stress. Although numerous efforts are underway to determine how attachment-based interventions function and might provide benefit, sufficient data is available to give particular attention to two protocols: Attachment-Based Family Therapy (ABFT) and the Connect program.[2]

Attachment-Based Family Therapy

ABFT is a 12- to 16-session intervention designed for adolescents struggling with depression and/or suicidal ideation (Diamond et al., 2014). Individual sessions with the adolescent focus on eliciting and discussing prior attachment experiences with the caregivers, including identifying the reasons why

[2]A third intervention with a growing evidence base for adolescents is mentalization-based therapy (MBT). MBT was originally developed with adults and is discussed in Chapter 9 of this volume.

the adolescent may not approach caregivers for support. Individual sessions with caregivers encourage self-reflection to consider how parenting approaches may have contributed to the state of the relationship and then teach caregivers more validating and sensitive ways to interact with the adolescent. Following these sessions, youth and caregivers are brought together for a series of conjoint sessions. The adolescent is encouraged to discuss prior attachment experiences, including thoughts and feelings related to the caregiver's behavior, and the caregiver responds in an empathic and supportive manner. Final sessions focus on other aspects of the adolescent's world that may be related to the onset and continuance of depression, such as peer relationships or academic difficulties. These tasks allow the adolescent to practice relying on the caregiver for support and help the caregiver engage in a developmentally expected caregiving role, thus encouraging both autonomy and help-seeking.

Initial examinations of ABFT suggested significant improvement in depression and reduction of suicidal ideation for adolescents receiving the intervention, who performed better than individuals on a waitlist or who received usual community-based care (Diamond et al., 2002, 2010). The family nature of ABFT is distinct among interventions for adolescent depression, in which most established protocols stress individual sessions with the adolescent while the caregivers play a secondary role. This emphasis on the youth–parent relationship led to ABFT receiving significant attention as a potential alternative to cognitive behavior therapy (CBT) for adolescent depression, particularly in situations in which an adolescent did not respond to CBT. However, a randomized controlled trial comparing ABFT with nondirective supportive (i.e., Rogerian) therapy among suicidal adolescents suggested tempering expectations (Diamond et al., 2019): While adolescents receiving ABFT showed substantial improvement in depression and suicidal ideation, adolescents in the control condition evidenced similar improvement. Research on ABFT is ongoing, including attempts to identify factors of the adolescent and/or family that suggest greatest benefit of ABFT.

Connect

Connect is a group-based, caregiver-only program delivered over the course of ten 90-minute sessions that aims to improve conduct problems among adolescents (Moretti et al., 2018). Facilitators introduce a different attachment-relevant concept each session (e.g., meaning of behaviors, balancing autonomy and connection) with a goal of changing how caregivers perceive adolescent behavior and the manner in which they respond. In other words, the program is designed to improve caregiver reflective functioning, sensitive responding, and ability to cooperatively regulate emotions. Role plays are used throughout the intervention to help caregivers view different types of conflicts from the perspective of the youth and to practice alternative responses, all while receiving feedback from other group members and facilitators.

Initial results showed that parents reported improvements in their perceived competence and stress as well as reductions in internalizing and externalizing problems of the adolescents (Obsuth et al., 2006). These results were then replicated in a follow-up study that demonstrated superiority over a waitlist condition and sustained improvement at a 12-month follow-up assessment (Moretti & Obsuth, 2009). Pasalich and colleagues (in press) reported on the results of a community implementation project and found that adolescents with more significant externalizing problems, including C/U traits, demonstrated the most rapid improvement over the course of the Connect program. There is also emerging evidence that Connect may improve placement outcomes for youth residing in kinship care, suggesting potential child welfare applications (Pasalich et al., 2021).

INTEGRATING ATTACHMENT AND COGNITIVE BEHAVIORAL PERSPECTIVES

Numerous instances may arise in which a suitable caregiver is not available to participate in treatment for the benefit of an adolescent. Clinicians are often tasked with conducting individual therapy in such instances with little hope that environmental circumstances might be changed to aid the youth. Therefore, it is beneficial to consider the ways in which attachment theory and research might inform treatment during these times.

In postulating on the clinical relevance of attachment theory, Bowlby (1988) offered a number of practical suggestions. First, he argued that clinicians must serve as a secure base that will allow patients to explore troubling memories from the past. As such, rapport development is critically important, and skills such as empathic responding and active listening may be useful. Second, clinicians take an active role by encouraging patients to consider how their behavior within interpersonal relationships, including any relevant interactions with the clinician, are related to prior attachment experiences. The goal is to identify the makeup of the patient's internal working models (of the self, others, and interactional patterns) and connect them to prior experiences within attachment relationships. Third, clinicians assist patients in evaluating the validity of those internal working models. This process involves examining whether the models are supported by evidence in the present day and whether more adaptive models may be appropriate.

Bowlby's description of therapeutic method may sound strikingly similar to the cognitive therapy approach: develop effective rapport and help the patient evaluate and restructure current schemas that may be maintaining emotional or behavioral concerns. Indeed, Bowlby drew the comparison himself. In the third book of his attachment trilogy, Bowlby (1980) compared his approach with that of Aaron Beck, whose seminal *Cognitive Therapy of Depression* (Beck, 1979) was published just months earlier. Bowlby offered that the primary distinction between the two approaches is that attachment theory attempts to identify the developmental antecedents of maladaptive cognitions and use that understanding in treatment, whereas cognitive therapy prefers to focus on the patient's current context to derive disconfirming evidence and gives relatively less consideration to historical events in the person's life.

Another similarity between attachment and cognitive behavioral theories centers on the importance of developmental capacities, such as emotion regulation and impulse control. Attachment theory posits that early attachment experiences influence the development of these abilities and that constructs such as attachment scripts, states of mind, and mentalization are important in understanding one's ability to effectively tolerate and modulate emotions, control responses, and interact with others. CBT focuses treatment on directly training an individual in relaxation, emotion regulation, and social skills. As such, cognitive behavioral and attachment approaches exhibit numerous similarities in treatment goals and directives.

The parallels between attachment and CBT approaches provide an opportunity to integrate the two perspectives. Consider CBT interventions targeting adolescent depression. Meta-analytic results suggest that CBT protocols typically achieve a significantly weaker effect for depression than for other presenting concerns (e.g., Weisz et al., 2006). Bosmans (2016) argued that these findings may largely be because traditional CBT programs rarely target family relationships or apply learned skills to family conflict. Caregiver involvement in many CBT interventions is limited to encouraging the use of learned skills in the home. Bosmans contended that supplementing CBT interventions by integrating attachment-focused components, such as helping caregivers respond to youth in validating and sensitive ways and focusing on improving the adolescent's perception of the caregiver as supportive, may lead to enhanced treatment efficacy.

In short, attachment and CBT approaches both stress the importance of altering maladaptive cognitive structures, whether they be called schemas or internal working models, and the idea that improvement of one's ability to regulate emotions and behaviors is critical for treatment success. During individual treatment, with no caregiver available for inclusion, attachment theory suggests that examining prior attachment relationships may yield valuable information for challenging current schemas/internal working models. When a caregiver is available, the focus of attachment theory is on the interpersonal context, particularly within the adolescent–caregiver relationship, and this focus offers multiple opportunities to enhance traditional CBT approaches. For instance, clinicians may deliver a standard CBT treatment for depression while having caregivers participate in an attachment-based program, such as Connect. However, to date, no identified clinical trials are available to determine whether such an approach enhances treatment outcomes. Boxes 8.3 and 8.4 revisit the case studies of Jasmine and Michael, examining the use of CBT and attachment-based interventions. The case of Jasmine presents a scenario in which CBT might not be sufficient and it may be necessary to transition to ABFT, while Michael's case demonstrates how his CBT treatment and his mother's work with the Connect program can intersect with a common goal of improving his aggressive behavior.

BOX 8.3

THE CASE OF JASMINE, REVISITED

Following assessment, Jasmine and her parents both agreed to participate in treatment services. The clinician decided to begin a standard cognitive behavior therapy (CBT) program for Jasmine and attempted to integrate her parents into the protocol in numerous ways, including encouraging them to develop the same skills and practice them at home as well as to learn more about depression and how it influences Jasmine's perception of the family. The first two sessions occurred while she was in the inpatient facility, and treatment continued after she was discharged home. After six sessions, Jasmine seemed to be decompensating. The improved mood that was evident at the time of discharge from the inpatient facility gave way to a depressed affect, increased anger, and further discussion of suicide. The clinician attempted to troubleshoot with Jasmine the problems she was encountering. Although Jasmine demonstrated mastery of the learned coping skills, she reported not using them. Attempts to restructure maladaptive thoughts were often derailed by Jasmine turning the discussion to grievances with her parents.

BOX 8.3

THE CASE OF JASMINE, REVISITED (*Continued*)

The clinician decided that the treatment program was not effective and referred Jasmine to an Attachment-Based Family Therapy (ABFT) program in the community. Jasmine was unsure of participating in such a treatment because of her desire to separate from her parents; she did not think it was possible to improve her relationship with them. Nonetheless, she agreed to try and attended the first sessions. The ABFT clinician stressed that the focus of treatment was on understanding her perception of the caregivers, how it came to that point, and how it might be altered. Jasmine was encouraged by hearing of the collaborative nature of improving the relationship, as opposed to the previous intervention where she felt much of the burden for change rested on her. Her parents displayed less enthusiasm, as they were under the impression from their physician and previous therapists that the issue primarily resided with neurochemical imbalances and Jasmine's cognitions. The ABFT clinician empathized with the parents and framed the treatment as creating the opportunity for Jasmine to change her perceptions, which appeared to foster engagement from the caregivers.

Discussion Questions

1. Why do you think the initial treatment approach for Jasmine was unsuccessful? Why was ABFT an appropriate referral for Jasmine?
2. How did the manner in which the ABFT clinician presented the treatment to Jasmine and her parents promote engagement?
3. Suppose Jasmine had declined the referral and chose to stay with her CBT clinician. How might that clinician have implemented attachment-based principles in treatment?

BOX 8.4

THE CASE OF MICHAEL, REVISITED

After assessment with Michael, the clinician decided to begin individual treatment using a cognitive behavior therapy approach while referring Ms. Simpson to a Connect group recently initiated in the area. Michael initially began sessions with a quiet and difficult-to-engage demeanor. The clinician devoted significant time in the first four sessions to developing rapport and typically allowed Michael to choose the topics of conversation. Michael often discussed video games and football, and in these discussions he was able to provide coherent discussions of events that occurred, the reasons for their occurrence, and the way he responded. The clinician pointed out this structure to Michael and asked him to provide a similar account of a pleasurable experience with his mother. Michael smiled before telling of a time that he and his mother went shopping, enjoyed ice cream, and laughed at events that occurred that day. The clinician praised Michael's effort before asking him to do the same with an unpleasant event. Michael began to show difficulties with coherence, which the clinician pointed out. Michael understood the point the clinician was making and was able to connect these challenges with the emotional valence of the material.

The clinician taught Michael a number of emotion regulation skills (e.g., relaxation, positive imagery) and encouraged him to use these skills while recounting emotionally troubling experiences. Michael demonstrated an improved ability to discuss such topics in a coherent manner, prompting the clinician to make the experience more personal by asking specifically about past experiences of physical discipline delivered by his mother. Over the course of several sessions Michael was able to discuss, revise, and eventually provide a coherent account of one of these experiences, complete with his thoughts and feelings about the event.

Ms. Simpson progressed well through the Connect program. Although she found some aspects difficult to comprehend, particularly the components focused on examining how the past influences the present, she nonetheless completed the program. The clinician brought Ms. Simpson into session alone and reviewed how it would be beneficial for Michael to discuss his experiences with her as a way of demonstrating his improvement. Ms. Simpson agreed. The clinician reviewed the importance of using the skills learned in the Connect program to maintain an empathic and supportive stance and prepared her by letting her know that Michael planned to discuss his memories of prior physical discipline experiences. Ms. Simpson noted that it might be difficult to hear such memories and

BOX 8.4

THE CASE OF MICHAEL, REVISITED (*Continued*)

thoughts from Michael. The clinician empathized but stressed that engaging in such a discussion is important for building his view of her as a supportive individual he can turn to during times of distress. The clinician spent some time reviewing aspects of the Connect program and the ways that the conjoint session reflects an opportunity for her to practice these new skills.

Discussion Questions

1. What aspects of an attachment-based approach are visible in the individual treatment sessions implemented with Michael?
2. How might the clinician have involved Ms. Simpson in treatment if a Connect program was not available in the area?
3. Given that Michael was being treated because of problems with aggression, what might later treatment sessions entail?

CONCLUSION

Adolescence serves as a bridge between the caregiver-focused understanding of attachment and clinical intervention that pervades the childhood period and the individual-focused approaches that mark practice with adults. Understanding psychopathology among adolescents requires appreciating both the continued role of caregivers and the unique development of the individual's striving for autonomy. Because clinical interventions must consider the perspectives of both caregivers and adolescents as well as the interactional patterns between the dyads, many clinicians and researchers find it challenging to develop effective interventions. Much work remains, and the coming years are primed for an explosion of research on the clinical applications of attachment theory with adolescents.

BOX 8.5

DISCUSSIONS OF CASE STUDIES

Box 8.1: The Case of Jasmine

Question 1

It is obvious that Jasmine and her parents exhibit a difficult adolescent-parent relationship. Jasmine does not view her parents, especially her mother, as a source of support, and it appears likely that she has a preoccupied state of mind, given her level of anger and conflictual engagement with her mother. Her parents seem to have little understanding of their daughter's concerns or her perspective of the family. Their lack of parental reflective functioning serves to minimize the severity of her depression. There is also something curious about the parents' focus on Jasmine's poor academic functioning while their daughter is attempting to end her own life. This disconnect between the priorities of Jasmine and those of her parents may drive conflicts and Jasmine's perceptions of lack of support.

Question 2

The discrepancies between Jasmine and her parents point to a lack of agreement on the causes of the current problems. These disagreements may be partially attributed to differences in priorities, as discussed previously, but may also be due to problems with effective communication between the parents and the adolescent. These challenges likely will result in differences in perspective on the most appropriate treatment approach. Although it is tempting to many clinicians to determine which account is more supported by the evidence, that is not usually a fruitful avenue to explore. Rather, it can be clearly stated that Jasmine does not view her parents as supportive and this perception is probably maintaining or exacerbating her depression. All parties are likely to agree with this perspective, and the clinician can use this consensus as a launching point for planning treatment.

Question 3

It may be helpful to observe Jasmine and her parents interacting. What are the communication patterns exhibited? Do the parents demonstrate empathy and mutuality, or do they blame Jasmine and try to dictate the next steps? Does Jasmine engage with her caregivers first before turning to angry responses, or does she refuse even to begin a conversation? One cautionary note to make here is that many clinicians want to determine

BOX 8.5

DISCUSSIONS OF CASE STUDIES (*Continued*)

whether an overdose attempt is a legitimate suicide attempt or a self-injurious "cry for help." In terms of planning treatment, answering this question may not yield useful information. Regardless of the answer, safety planning should occur, and treatment should target improving parent-youth interactions, including attachment security and Jasmine's ability to regulate emotions.

Box 8.2: The Case of Michael

Question 1

Michael's responses to the questions seem to lack any coherent structure. He provides little evidence for the perceived slights of his peers and is unable to maintain focus on any given topic of conversation. He also contradicts himself when discussing his mother, first stating she enters his room without permission, which angers him, but later pivoting away from the topic by stating she does not do this very often. Michael would likely score low on coherence during the Child Attachment Interview or Adult Attachment Interview because he violates a number of Grice's (1975) maxims (see Chapter 5, this volume, for more detail). The state of mind he displays is less clear. His general approach to the interview may be suggestive of a dismissive state of mind, while his low level of coherence may reflect an unresolved state of mind. Although Ms. Simpson's comments suggest physical abuse occurred during Michael's childhood, we do not know the specific form of the physical discipline nor Michael's ability to discuss such events. Thus, an unresolved state of mind cannot be assumed.

Question 2

Whether in fact or in perception, Michael is confronted with a number of upsetting events at school. His low coherence suggests significant difficulty with attachment scripts, specifically how to resolve moments of distress, and poor internal working models of others and social interactions. As a result, Michael is unable to cognitively process effective solutions to these situations. In addition, the speed of escalation that occurs during these altercations suggests Michael possesses poor ability to tolerate and modulate negative emotion. These factors combine to create a predisposition to aggression for Michael.

(*continues*)

BOX 8.5

DISCUSSIONS OF CASE STUDIES (*Continued*)

Question 3

Ms. Simpson is generally unaware of the concerns confronting Michael, suggesting low parental reflective functioning and a lack of parent-adolescent engagement. Ms. Simpson displayed episodes of incoherence, blaming the school for the escalation in Michael's behaviors while being unable to express her responses to Michael's misbehavior. By the end of the vignette, it remains unclear what Ms. Simpson did upon learning of Michael's aggression at school. It seems she is unsure how to respond given that she believes physical discipline is not appropriate for an adolescent. This lack of clear direction suggests the possibility of intergenerational transmission of incoherence or, potentially, an unresolved state of mind.

Box 8.3: The Case of Jasmine, Revisited

Question 1

Jasmine clearly viewed her relationship with her parents as a significant source of her depression. The initial CBT protocol focused on teaching emotion regulation skills, which Jasmine learned and refused to implement, and on altering her maladaptive cognitions. It seems unlikely, however, that these cognitive restructuring techniques specifically focused on Jasmine's perceptions of her mother and father, whose involvement in treatment appeared limited to supporting Jasmine in her therapeutic work. Clearly, a family therapy intervention was indicated. ABFT was an appropriate referral because it brought the caregivers into more active involvement in treatment and focused specifically on improving Jasmine's perception of her caregivers. At the same time, the intervention helped Jasmine's parents develop a more adaptive view of Jasmine and consider how they might alter their parenting practices.

Question 2

The ABFT clinician did not assign blame to either Jasmine or her parents. Rather, the clinician presented the intervention as a collaborative process. To Jasmine, the intervention was an opportunity to directly discuss her perspective of the relationship with her parents and prior experiences in which she felt invalidated and dismissed. To the parents, the intervention was billed as an opportunity to provide Jasmine with disconfirming evidence that might challenge her perceptions of them as uncaring or critical. In this manner, the clinician appealed to the specific desires of each party.

BOX 8.5

DISCUSSIONS OF CASE STUDIES (*Continued*)

Question 3

If Jasmine had declined the ABFT referral, the clinician might have used attachment theory to guide examination of Jasmine's internal working models of her parents and their interactions. Presumably, significant evidence is available from past experiences that the clinician could have had Jasmine consider the ways in which prior interactions with her caregivers led to her current perceptions of them. The clinician might have used Jasmine's prior experiences as the basis for determining whether those interactions continued in the present day or were characteristic of a different developmental period. In addition, the clinician could have helped Jasmine consider how alternative responses may engender different reactions, allowing her to test different working models to determine which best fits the current evidence. The clinician could also have helped the parents understand the function of Jasmine's behavior, explore prior interactions that may have given rise to Jasmine's perceptions, and provide instruction on how to take an empathic and sensitive response to Jasmine's behaviors as a means of altering her view of them.

Box 8.4: The Case of Michael, Revisited

Question 1

Attachment-based components of treatment are evident throughout the individual sessions. First, the clinician attempted to improve Michael's ability to discuss negative emotions coherently. This process began by discussing emotionally neutral topics of Michael's choosing, then pleasant experiences, before turning to memories that caused unpleasant emotions. Second, the clinician taught Michael various skills that might improve his ability to regulate emotions when discussing upsetting events. Third, the clinician focused on relevant attachment experiences, specifically Ms. Simpson being both Michael's attachment figure and the one inflicting physical pain as a form of discipline. His ability to eventually discuss this experience in a coherent manner is a positive therapeutic sign.

Question 2

The Connect program provided focused instruction in understanding attachment behavior and needs, taking the perspective of the adolescent, responding in empathic and sensitive ways, and fostering autonomy while providing support. Although the group-based nature of Connect is viewed

(*continues*)

BOX 8.5

DISCUSSIONS OF CASE STUDIES (*Continued*)

as beneficial for allowing caregivers to receive feedback from others and to observe how various interactions might unfold, these skills can be implemented in an individual format. Depending on the constraints of clinical practice in a given area, the clinician may have needed to reduce the amount of time spent with Michael during each session to reserve time for Ms. Simpson or may have seen Ms. Simpson in separate individual sessions.

Question 3

Theoretically, Michael's improved ability to formulate cognitive responses to stressful stimuli and to regulate distressing emotions should generalize to other situations, including with peers at school. However, the clinician would be wise to provide focused practice in how to respond during such circumstances. This work may include developing coherent narratives pertaining to the previous incidents and allowing Michael to examine his responses and the evidence that supported them as well as to consider how different responses may have led to different outcomes. The clinician can stress the use of learned emotion regulation skills during these moments to prevent immediate reactions.

RESOURCES

Training Resources

- **Attachment-Based Family Therapy (ABFT):** Training in ABFT and further information is available at https://drexel.edu/familyintervention/attachment-based-family-therapy
- **Connect:** Training in Connect and further information is available at https://www.connectattachmentprograms.org/

9 ATTACHMENT AND CLINICAL PRACTICE WITH ADULTS

Applications to Individual and Couple Therapy

The application of attachment theory and research to clinical practice with adults is, by necessity, different in perspective than it is with infants, children, and adolescents. Adults are commonly independent, precluding the incorporation of caregiver-related techniques. While romantic partners may serve attachment functions, the relationship is typically one of mutuality rather than dependent caregiving. This shift in perspective opens the door for exploring how attachment concepts might be applied in both individual and couple therapy.

ATTACHMENT PROCESSES AND ADULT PSYCHOPATHOLOGY

Complicating clinical work with adults are findings demonstrating weak and/or inconsistent relationships between early attachment experiences and many forms of psychopathology in adulthood. As a result, attachment-based clinical applications with adults rely on established concurrent associations between various forms of psychopathology and adult attachment constructs

https://doi.org/10.1037/0000333-010
The Science and Clinical Practice of Attachment Theory: A Guide From Infancy to Adulthood, by B. Allen

and/or theoretical assumptions of the relationship between attachment constructs and the therapeutic process.

Mood and Anxiety Disorders

Historically, attachment researchers hypothesized links between insecure forms of attachment behavior during infancy and the likelihood of mood and anxiety disorders throughout one's life. While there is some evidence for this connection with children and adolescents, the available longitudinal studies do not suggest that this relationship extends into adulthood. However, there is ample support that the loss of a caregiver during childhood and/or retrospective reports of the caregiving received are related to depression and anxiety in adulthood (e.g., Nickerson et al., 2013). These same studies also document that the caregiving received after losing a caregiver plays a significant role in determining one's later display of depression or anxiety, underlining the principle that a multitude of influences occur between infancy and adulthood and that one is typically well served by giving more weight to the role of proximal factors than of distal ones.

Studies examining the relationship of attachment state of mind to depression often yield inconsistent results. Some found a preoccupied state of mind predicted depression (e.g., Borelli et al., 2010), but this finding is not uniform, and evidence suggests that the relationship may be dependent on the type of depression (e.g., major depressive disorder, dysthymia; Fonagy et al., 1996). Although one may assume unresolved states of mind are more predictive of depression than other forms of insecurity are, results on this proposition are mixed.

Similarly, the relationship of states of mind to anxiety-related disorders is unclear. Fonagy and colleagues (1996) found unresolved states of mind were common among individuals with anxiety disorders (86%), while van Emmichoven et al. (2003) found that only 11% of patients with an anxiety disorder were classified unresolved, although 39% were dismissing. Across studies, a preoccupied state of mind appears most closely linked to anxiety in adulthood when compared with the other states of mind (Dagan et al., 2020).

Theoretically, one may presume that different forms of insecurity are related to depression and anxiety through different mechanisms. For instance, an unresolved state of mind stemming from a previous loss may predispose one to fear losing current loved ones, while a dismissive state of mind may result in difficulty accessing social support. Indeed, Stovall-McClough and Dozier (2016) suggested that much of the inconsistency across studies may be accounted for by issues of comorbidity and by the diversity of presentations subsumed under the categories of depression and anxiety. Nonetheless, the relationship of attachment state of mind to depressive and anxiety disorders is unclear at the current time.

Emerging evidence suggests that poor mentalization, particularly ineffective reflective functioning, may predispose an individual to both depression and anxiety (e.g., Ballespí et al., 2019; Rothschild-Yakar et al., 2019). In other words, the inability of an individual to accurately reflect on the mental states of others and/or place one's own decision making in the context of environmental and situational demands may predispose the individual to depression or anxiety. This relationship is likely the result of maladaptive mentalization leading to conclusions characterized by self-blame, helplessness, and/or shame. Of course, this approach emphasizing mentalization leaves much to explore, and research is only beginning to examine the many facets of the construct and its interaction with the social context.

From a social psychological perspective, a relatively large number of studies have examined the relationships among self-reported attachment anxiety and avoidance and depression and anxiety symptoms. Most findings point to the conclusion that attachment anxiety and avoidance are strongly related to both depression (e.g., Rosenthal et al., 2014) and anxiety (e.g., Neumann et al., 2015). Interpreting such results are comparatively straightforward when one remembers that attachment security from the social psychological perspective equates to self-perceptions of comfort within interpersonal relationships. Individuals who worry about placing trust in others or tend to engage in shallow intimate relationships are likely to exhibit problems seeking out social support, which is a well-established risk factor for the onset of both depression and anxiety.

Posttraumatic Stress Disorder and Dissociation

Phenomenological similarities between the unresolved state of mind (i.e., avoidance of traumatic memories, difficulty coherently discussing trauma) and trauma-related conditions, such as posttraumatic stress disorder (PTSD) and dissociation, led to examination of the ways in which the constructs relate. Across several studies of samples diagnosed with PTSD (e.g., combat veterans, survivors of child abuse), states of mind were predominantly unresolved. However, preoccupied and dismissive states of mind were not related to trauma and PTSD (Bakermans-Kranenburg & van IJzendoorn, 2009). Some evidence suggests that this association may be the specific result of avoidance of trauma-related memories (Stovall-McClough & Cloitre, 2006).

Using self-report measures, evidence suggests a modest correlation between attachment anxiety and PTSD, but this relationship is significantly stronger if the individual reports elevated attachment avoidance as well (Woodhouse et al., 2015).

Mary Main hypothesized that dissociation is a key component underlying both disorganized attachment behavior and the unresolved state of mind (Duschinsky, 2020). Dissociation as a clinical phenomenon refers to problems with the integration of cognitive functions, such as memory, consciousness, and identity. Longitudinal evidence suggests infant disorganization, thought to be the result of repeated fear-inducing experiences (see Chapter 2, this volume), is related to the experience of dissociation in childhood and adolescence (E. A. Carlson, 1998). In addition, unresolved states of mind related to trauma are associated concurrently with dissociation (Riggs et al., 2007), but findings are mixed as to whether self-reported attachment anxiety and avoidance are related to dissociation (Nilsson et al., 2011; Riggs et al., 2007). Box 9.1 presents a case example involving a 34-year-old male combat veteran whose marriage is in trouble.[1]

Substance Use

If attachment is intimately related to emotion regulation and interpersonal relationships, as theory and research suggest, then one may expect to find insecure attachment related to maladaptive forms of coping, such as substance use. Dozens of studies have examined this contention and document convincing evidence that insecure attachment is modestly associated with higher rates of concurrently assessed substance use (Fairbairn et al., 2018). Studies examining the temporal sequence of this association find that attachment insecurity earlier in the lifespan is a significant, although weak, predictor of problems with substance use. While studies in this area commonly use self-report measures, similar results are obtained using narrative measures (e.g., Adult Attachment Interview). These findings suggest treatments for substance use disorders may benefit from techniques aiming to improve attachment constructs. However, this work is just beginning, and many of the available applications are focused on improving mentalization and attachment representations among mothers with substance use disorders (e.g., Suchman et al., 2018).

---

[1]To protect patient confidentiality, proper steps have been taken to disguise the identities of the individuals in this chapter's case examples.

BOX 9.1

THE CASE OF MARCUS

Marcus is a 34-year-old African American man who contacted the clinic because of recurring nightmares related to combat experience some years in the past. In addition, he reported persistent irritability that results in angry outbursts and constantly feeling "on edge" and hypervigilant. These concerns result in frequent outbursts directed toward his wife, who has threatened to leave him if he does not receive treatment. When the clinician asked for details about his military service, Marcus displayed notable difficulty discussing the topic and could relate only that he served in the army and was involved in a pitched firefight in which an unspecified number of his comrades died. Marcus refused to provide a developmental history, noting that his childhood was unimportant to his current problems. After the clinician explained that we learn to handle stress as we grow up, Marcus began discussing his mother but then became quiet and appeared to stare blankly out the window. The clinician tried for several minutes to reinitiate the conversation. Eventually, Marcus reengaged but did not recall the topic of conversation.

Discussion Questions

1. What clinical concerns are evident in Marcus's presentation?
2. What are your initial impressions of Marcus's attachment processes?
3. How might the attachment processes you have identified influence treatment?

Borderline Personality Disorder

Given that problems with interpersonal relatedness, identity, and emotion regulation are the core features of borderline personality disorder (BPD), etiological theories of the condition commonly employ an attachment framework. Although data linking attachment behavior during infancy and middle childhood to adult BPD are modest (Brumariu et al., 2020; E. A. Carlson et al., 2009; Lyons-Ruth et al., 2013), evidence suggests that unresolved and preoccupied states of mind are overrepresented in samples of individuals with BPD (Bakermans-Kranenburg & van IJzendoorn, 2009). In addition, self-report measures indicate that the combination of elevated scores for attachment anxiety and avoidance is predictive of a BPD diagnosis (Smith & South, 2020).

Trying to understand the relationship between attachment security and BPD on a more mechanistic level has led to two different approaches. The first employs the developmental psychopathology perspective and examines factors that may mediate the relationship between attachment and BPD. From this approach, negative attachment experiences in early childhood predispose one to develop features characteristic of BPD (e.g., emotion dysregulation, identity disturbance). For instance, Brumariu and colleagues (2020) found that caregiver insensitivity and maternal depression throughout childhood significantly predicted the display of borderline personality features by age 15 and that infant attachment behavior was no longer associated with BPD once caregiving factors were controlled. In a similar vein, E. A. Carlson et al. (2009) found a modest correlation between attachment disorganization during the first 18 months of life and BPD symptoms at 28 years of age; however, after accounting for maternal hostility and maternal life stress, attachment disorganization was no longer predictive of BPD. In addition, they found that representational measures (i.e., internal working model of the self) mediated the relationship between attachment behavior and BPD symptoms. In short, disorganized attachment behavior may be an early marker of future BPD symptoms because it suggests poor quality attachment relationships and aberrant development of important intrapersonal and interpersonal skills.

The second approach to understanding the link between attachment and BPD focuses on the role of mentalization. Studies paradoxically document difficulties mentalizing among individuals with BPD (Fonagy & Luyten, 2009) and above-average mentalizing capabilities (Dinsdale & Crespi, 2013). In confronting this seeming contradiction, Luyten and colleagues (2020) attempted to unpack the complexities of the mentalization construct. They surmised that the evidence suggests individuals with BPD are prone to rely on automatic forms of mentalization that occur quickly and often fail to attend to the complexity of the interpersonal situation. In some situations this process provides accurate and adaptive responses, resulting in individuals with BPD appearing acutely attuned to a given situation. However, the failure to initiate effortful forms of mentalization more frequently leads to misunderstanding the intentions of others and results in ineffective and poorly conceived emotional responses. The case reviewed in Box 9.2 explores the case of a 26-year-old woman admitted to an inpatient facility.

BOX 9.2

THE CASE OF ARIELLA

Ariella is a 26-year-old Latina woman admitted to an inpatient program following a suicide attempt. During the first meeting with the clinician, she denied that the cutting on her arms was an attempt at suicide and described it as an attempt "to feel something." The clinician empathized with her response, which prompted Ariella immediately to tell the clinician, "You are the only one who has ever understood me." Concerned by this response, the clinician inquired about her mother and father. Ariella rolled her eyes, sighed heavily, and said that her parents are not worth discussing. The clinician probed further, at which time Ariella launched into a nearly 7-minute-long diatribe vacillating between angrily criticizing her parents and asserting that they "are good people." When the clinician attempted to ask follow-up questions to clarify, Ariella became irritated and began accusing the clinician of taking her parents' side. Confused by the statement, the clinician reassured Ariella that she was merely trying to get a sense of the problems being faced and the people who might be supportive in her life. Ariella apologized for her comments and asked if the clinician still planned to work with her.

Discussion Question

1. Based on this brief vignette, what diagnostic picture emerges?
2. Ariella provides clues to her state of mind regarding attachment. What are those clues? How might you expect Ariella to perform on the Adult Attachment Interview or report on the Experiences in Close Relationships-Revised (see Chapter 5 for a discussion of these measures)?
3. What indications are present regarding Ariella's mentalizing ability?

ATTACHMENT PROCESSES IN INDIVIDUAL THERAPY

Researchers and clinicians have examined multiple applications of attachment concepts during individual therapy with adults, such as how such constructs might affect the therapeutic process or predict who benefits from a particular intervention. For multiple reasons, the research on therapeutic uses of attachment theory with adults remains in its infancy. Nonetheless, the field is progressing in a multitude of directions.

The Therapeutic Process

As discussed in more detail in Chapter 8 of this volume, Bowlby (1988) opined that a therapist should serve as a secure base that enables the patient to explore painful memories and the ways in which they influence current relationships. Although all major systems of psychotherapy recognize the importance of the therapeutic alliance, psychodynamic approaches emphasize examining the relationship between the patient and the therapist as a vehicle for change (i.e., transference and countertransference). Near the end of the 20th century, many psychodynamic theorists revisited Bowlby's ideas in a sort of rapprochement that led to new insights on how attachment theory and research might inform their practice, with an emphasis on application to the patient–therapist relationship (Slade, 2016).

A growing body of research converges on the conclusion that higher ratings of attachment anxiety and/or avoidance predict lower patient ratings of therapeutic alliance quality (Bernecker et al., 2014). Although the sizes of these relationships are typically small, they provide important considerations for therapeutic models that place a heavy emphasis on developing and interpreting the working alliance for therapeutic content. On the one hand, clinicians must consider that patients with insecure attachment styles may prove challenging and care must be taken during the interactions to foster the growth of the alliance. On the other hand, given the overrepresentation of insecure attachment among clinical populations, it is likely the case that clinical experience and intervention research are suitable sources for guiding interactions with such patients.

If a primary goal of treatment is for the therapist to serve as a secure base for the patient, the question then emerges as to whether a patient views the therapist as an attachment figure. Drawing on the conceptualization of attachment security with infants, "attachment to the therapist" reflects a patient's perception of the therapist as someone who provides a sense of psychological security and facilitates the confrontation of threatening or upsetting clinical material (Mallinckrodt et al., 1995). Not surprisingly, individuals scoring lower on attachment anxiety and avoidance reported a more secure attachment to therapist, while greater levels of anxiety and/or avoidance characterized either a preoccupied or avoidant attachment to the therapist (Mallinckrodt & Jeong, 2015). Collectively, these findings suggest that patients with insecure attachment styles may present difficulties with establishing a therapeutic alliance and, more specifically, may find it difficult to use the therapist as a secure base.

Given that the therapist is placed in the role of serving as an attachment figure for the patient, studies sought to determine whether a therapist's attachment style predicts quality of the therapeutic alliance. The general conclusion is that therapists who themselves have secure attachments tend to foster high-quality therapeutic alliances with patients and to judge patients' perspectives accurately (e.g., Dinger et al., 2009). In addition, some evidence suggests that therapist and client attachment styles interact to predict quality of the therapeutic alliance (Petrowski et al., 2011). However, the clinical implications of this body of knowledge regarding the impact of therapist attachment are unclear (Slade, 2016).

With compelling evidence that the therapeutic alliance is a critical factor in treatment retention and eventual outcome (Flückiger et al., 2020), finding ways to enhance the development and maintenance of therapeutic alliance is an important issue for clinical research. Extant findings suggest that attachment theory may have much to offer to those endeavors. However, several important issues require addressing. For instance, with few notable exceptions, practically all the research examining the influence of attachment on therapeutic alliance uses self-report measures derived from the social psychology field. While there are many benefits in this approach, important attachment constructs with potential relevance to this question (e.g., attachment scripts, states of minds) remain largely unexamined. In addition, much of the available research examined the role of attachment processes in the conduct of psychodynamically oriented therapy, and it is unclear whether findings generalize to other forms of intervention with less emphasis on examining the therapeutic alliance, such as cognitive-behavioral therapies. Box 9.3 illustrates these concepts by presenting the case of a 61-year-old woman who exhibits depression following the death of her husband.

Attachment as an Outcome, Moderator, and Mediator

Surprisingly, one question that has received relatively little attention is whether attachment constructs in adulthood can be changed through intervention. The first known attempt to examine this issue was carried out by Peter Fonagy and his colleagues (1996), who compared intake Adult Attachment Interview (AAI) classifications of individuals admitted for inpatient treatment to a second AAI completed 1 year after discharge. While all 35 patients were classified insecure at the first assessment, 40% of the cases moved to secure status by the second administration. A decade later Levy et al. (2006) reported on the results of a randomized controlled trial in which 60 patients with BPD received either Transference-Focused Psychotherapy, a psychodynamic intervention that aims to modify representations by leveraging the therapeutic alliance to effect change, dialectical behavior therapy

BOX 9.3

THE CASE OF ESTHER

Esther is a 61-year-old White woman who sought treatment for depression that has recurred several times over the past 3 years. She identified the original onset occurring after the death of her husband from heart failure. While discussing her late husband, she displayed sadness as well as episodes of anger. She faulted him for not taking better care of his health when he was alive and believes a better diet and more exercise may have prevented his death. Since his passing, she finds it difficult to open herself emotionally to others and had a series of romantic relationships that she described as shallow and short-lived. Treatment progressed well in the initial stages. The therapeutic alliance appeared strong, and Esther engaged with the clinician in focused discussions of her thought processes, particularly her views on living alone and whether she would ever be able to love another man. However, little improvement was noted in her depressive symptoms. Esther enjoyed attending therapy but began to question whether the treatment was helpful. She decided to broach the topic during the next session and began the discussion by asking the clinician what she saw as the next steps in treatment.

Discussion Questions

1. What evidence is present in the vignette regarding the quality of the therapeutic alliance? Is the clinician effective as a secure base for Esther?
2. Esther questions the effectiveness of treatment. Why do you think symptoms have not abated, and what attachment-informed directions might you propose?
3. From an attachment perspective, what factors may be limiting treatment progress?

(DBT), a cognitive behavioral intervention focused on the development of emotion regulation and interpersonal skills, or a supportive therapy condition. Only three of the patients were classified secure on the AAI at the beginning of treatment. At the end of treatment, nine individuals were classified secure, a small but statistically significant effect. Interestingly, all six patients who moved from insecure to secure received Transference-Focused Psychotherapy.

Fearon and Mansell (2001) argued that the psychological mechanisms of unresolved states of mind and PTSD are similar in that both are characterized by difficulty structuring a coherent autobiographical account of one's traumatic experience because of distress elicited by reminders of the trauma and the subsequent desire to avoid such reminders. Theoretically, then, well-established exposure-based interventions for PTSD that involve construction of a detailed narrative of one's traumatic experience should be effective for altering unresolved states of mind. Stovall-McClough and Cloitre (2003) examined a small sample ($n = 18$) of women with PTSD who were randomized to receive either an exposure-based therapy or affective and interpersonal skills training. Of the individuals unresolved on the AAI at the beginning of treatment ($n = 13$), the majority were no longer unresolved at the end of treatment ($n = 8$), and improvement was more pronounced in the exposure therapy condition. There were indications this improvement was associated with decreases in PTSD symptoms. Across conditions, the proportion of the sample classified secure by the end of treatment increased (11% at pretreatment, 50% at posttreatment). However, Madigan and colleagues (2015) found no indication that exposure therapy for PTSD improved unresolved states of mind among a sample of pregnant adolescents when compared to individuals in a parenting skills control condition.

Reflecting the literature relating attachment to psychopathology, many clinical trials examining attachment as an outcome use self-report measures. Unfortunately, these studies provide conflicting results. For instance, B. M. Strauss et al. (2011) did not find changes in self-rated attachment security for patients with personality disorders following inpatient treatment, although significant improvements were found among women receiving cognitive behavior therapy (CBT) to treat panic disorder (Zalaznik et al., 2019). It is possible that differences in outcomes may be attributed to conditions being treated or the interventions applied. For example, Strauß and colleagues (2018) found that a CBT intervention was superior to both a psychodynamic treatment and a waitlist control for reducing attachment anxiety and avoidance for patients diagnosed with social anxiety disorder. However, Fonagy et al. (2020) found significant improvement on both attachment anxiety and avoidance for patients diagnosed with depression, and no differences were detected between CBT and dynamic interpersonal therapy. Clearly, there is much work left to do on this topic, and definitive conclusions are not yet available.

The true value of attachment constructs for adult psychotherapy may lie in helping determine the types of individuals most likely to benefit from different forms of interventions (i.e., as a moderator of outcome). For example,

McBride et al. (2006) found that patients who scored high on a measure of self-reported attachment avoidance evidenced greater benefit from CBT than from interpersonal therapy in the treatment of depression. However, a direct replication of this trial failed to find any role of attachment security in predicting differential treatment outcomes (Bernecker et al., 2016). In a meta-analysis including 36 studies and more than 3,000 patients, Levy et al. (2018) concluded that higher pretreatment attachment security predicted greater levels of improvement by the end of treatment on various forms of psychiatric symptoms (e.g., anxiety, depression); however, the analysis did not find that attachment security predicted personality outcomes. In addition, patients with secure attachment benefited more from interventions deemed "non-interpersonal" (e.g., CBT), while those low in attachment security fared better with "interpersonal" (e.g., psychodynamic) forms of intervention.

An associated finding in the Levy et al. (2018) review was that improvements in attachment security coincide with improvements in psychiatric symptoms. Such findings suggest potential benefit in targeting attachment security as a mechanism through which to improve clinical outcomes (i.e., mediator). However, examinations of the directionality of improvements provide mixed conclusions. Zalaznik et al. (2019) found some evidence that improvements in attachment security preceded changes in panic disorder symptoms during a course of CBT, but considerably more evidence suggested improved attachment security resulted from reductions in clinical symptoms. Similar results are reported elsewhere (e.g., A-Tjak et al., 2020), but at present, it is not clear whether changes in attachment security predict changes in clinical outcomes or vice versa.

Mentalization-Based Therapy

Drawing on findings related to problematic mentalizing ability among patients with BPD, Bateman and Fonagy (2004) devised mentalization-based therapy (MBT). A predominantly psychodynamic form of treatment, MBT stresses the importance of the therapist leveraging the therapeutic alliance to challenge the patient's view of the self and interpersonal interactions. The therapist attempts to understand the patient's emotional experience and clearly relay that perception back to the patient, potentially using interpretations of interpersonal interactions as evidence, including those occurring within the therapeutic alliance. Through this process the therapist encourages the patient to further mentalize on their own perspectives and feelings as well as those expressed by others. The patient may be asked to clarify their reactions to interpersonal situations, to elaborate on the reasoning for emotional responses, and to consider how previous exchanges informed feelings and behaviors in a given interaction. It is not uncommon for MBT to include individual and group therapy sessions, particularly when delivered during an inpatient setting, to allow practice in the use of mentalization skills within various interpersonal experiences.

Initial findings suggested that MBT integrated into a partial hospitalization program was more effective than services-as-usual in treating patients with BPD (Bateman & Fonagy, 1999), with sustained improvement at a 5-year follow-up (Bateman & Fonagy, 2008). A series of trials since this initial test similarly demonstrate superiority of MBT over control conditions in the treatment of BPD (e.g., Bateman et al., 2021). A recent nonrandomized trial comparing MBT versus DBT for the treatment of patients with BPD found that the two interventions achieved comparable results for most outcomes, although the DBT group showed a steeper rate of decline of self-harming behaviors and emotion dysregulation (Barnicot & Crawford, 2019). However, the DBT group displayed a higher rate of dropout, and pretreatment differences between the two groups were noted (e.g., emotion dysregulation).

Beyond MBT, efforts to improve mentalization abilities among caregivers, particularly parental reflective functioning, are receiving increased attention from researchers. For instance, Minding the Baby is an in-home, caregiver-focused intervention initiated during the final trimester of pregnancy and continuing throughout the first 2 years of the child's life (Sadler et al., 2013). The program is geared toward first-time mothers considered at risk for poor psychosocial outcomes, particularly individuals with prior trauma exposure. The clinician works with the mother to consider the multitude of reasons her child might display different behaviors as well as to reflect on her own responses. The goal is for the mother to develop an enhanced ability to understand her child's mental states and, thereby, to respond in a more nurturing and sensitive manner. Although favorable results for parental reflective functioning and attachment security are available for specific interventions, such as Minding the Baby (Slade et al., 2020; see also the parent-training interventions discussed in Chapter 7, this volume), a meta-analysis reviewing the handful of available studies on mentalization-based parenting interventions found inconclusive evidence for the effectiveness of these protocols (Barlow et al., 2021).

ATTACHMENT-BASED COUPLE THERAPY

The work of attachment researchers, particularly those from the social psychological perspective, has been applied more recently to the practice of couple therapy. Attachment theory's emphasis on the systemic nature of behavior, including seeking out support from an attachment figure under moments of distress, is directly relevant to conceptualizing and intervening with couples facing relationship challenges (Johnson, 2021). One's internal working model of relationships or self-reported attachment style may dictate the manner and conditions under which support is sought from the partner, who is generally considered an attachment figure. Similarly, attachment processes may dictate the response provided by the individual in the supportive role and may provide important feedback to the partner regarding availability and support. Given that relationships commonly are confronted with challenges on a regular basis, ranging from minor (e.g., upsetting day at work) to significant (e.g., miscarriage), these attachment processes affect relationships often. In short, from an attachment perspective, relationship dysfunction occurs when emotional signals and overtures for support are poorly communicated by one partner and/or misunderstood or ignored by the other (Brassard & Johnson, 2016).

A clinician working with a couple from an attachment perspective seeks to identify the dynamics occurring within the relationship. It may be beneficial to determine the extent to which one views the other as a reliable partner during challenging times (i.e., safe haven). Similarly, it may be informative to identify whether the partners support one another in exploring the causes of their relationship struggles (i.e., secure base). An avoidant individual may refuse to discuss relationship issues, assuming the partner will not be receptive or may be critical. An individual with an anxious attachment style may be emotionally volatile and accusatory toward the partner. It is often possible to directly observe these attachment concepts in session through naturally occurring interactional styles or to elicit them by asking the couple to discuss a situation creating strain in their relationship.

The therapist is tasked with helping the partners understand how their interpersonal styles contribute to the relationship difficulties and take steps toward changing the way they relate to one another. By serving as a dispassionate observer and a secure base the therapist can call attention to responses from each partner and the ways that they are perceived. For instance, the clinician may point out that one partner disengaged from the discussion upon hearing something upsetting and that this response may be perceived by the partner as refusing to work toward a solution. For an avoidant individual, such a comment may prompt a reconsideration of the behavior displayed toward the partner. Alternatively, the therapist may note the emotion in the room and its impact on the discussion and may encourage both partners to reflect on how such an atmosphere interferes with creating an environment that is conducive to seeking out and providing support.

Couple therapy provides the opportunity for adults to engage in adaptive attachment experiences by relying on their romantic partner. While this goal may partially be achieved through greater self-awareness and perspective-taking (i.e., mentalization), attachment theory also promotes the development of effective emotion regulation and conflict resolution skills. Such efforts may take many forms, but the essential element in the couple therapy setting is that the skills are practiced in the dyadic format. Through repeated experience of resolving conflict, working through tensions together as a couple, and gaining increased confidence in the support of the partner, it is hypothesized that each member of the couple will evidence improved attachment security and be better situated to support the other in the future. As a result, concerns related to intimacy and abandonment should dissipate (Davila, 2003). The case study in Box 9.4 looks at a husband and wife who are on the brink of divorce and exhibit potential attachment issues that may be affecting their relationship.

Emotion-Focused Couple Therapy

Emotion-focused therapy (EFT) is an approach to couple therapy that derives its techniques from the principles of attachment theory while integrating several humanistic tenets (Johnson, 2018). Therapists guide couples through three distinct stages: (a) stabilization, in which the challenges faced in the relationship are viewed as a systemic problem; (b) restructuring the attachment, with couples examining their own forms of relating and working to improve their responses toward the partner; and (c) consolidation, during which the couple reflects on their new relationship and how it will operate going forward. Throughout these stages, a premium is placed on identifying upsetting emotions and creating an atmosphere in session in which these emotions can be safely processed. The therapist is expected to serve as a secure base for both partners, to encourage exploration of relevant relationship-specific emotions (e.g., betrayal, disappointment, anger), and to ensure that partners express their own perspectives while listening to and considering the perspectives of the other. A specific focus is on addressing incidents that weaken trust and may confirm the fears of an insecure partner (e.g., extramarital affairs, unavailability following the death of a loved one). Addressing such "attachment injuries" is at the heart of EFT and constitutes a primary aspect of the second stage of treatment (i.e., restructuring the attachment).

A recent review of the randomized controlled trial literature found that EFT achieved a moderate-sized effect in improving relationship distress

BOX 9.4

THE CASE OF SARAH AND NATHAN

Sarah and Nathan, both in their mid-30s, were married for 6 years when they first sought therapy to improve their marriage. Both reported they argue frequently, are dissatisfied with their relationship, and are considering divorce. Before taking that drastic step, they decided to try therapy. The therapist began the initial session by asking the couple to identify the largest strain on their relationship. Nathan sat back in his chair, folded his arms, and looked at Sarah. The therapist noted Nathan's behavior and asked if he had a perspective to share. Nathan responded, "I'll let Sarah talk. She always has a lot to say." Sarah responded by pointing out Nathan's persistent negative attitude and that she feels she is forced to do the talking because Nathan shuts down.

The therapist asked Nathan to comment on Sarah's belief that he frequently refuses to discuss the issues confronting them, to which Nathan agreed. However, he clarified that the reason he does not speak is that whatever he says tends to elicit anger from Sarah and serves only to escalate the situation. Upon hearing this, Sarah began to cry and expressed frustration that Nathan turns whatever she does into a criticism of her. She went on to say she believes Nathan no longer loves her and that his behavior is just an attempt to drive her away. Nathan began shaking his head and mumbled quietly, "That's not true." Sarah gave no indication that she heard Nathan's comment.

Discussion Questions

1. What attachment dynamics are present in the interactions between Sarah and Nathan? How might each of them score on the Experiences in Close Relationships-Revised (ECR-R) scale?
2. What strengths, if any, can the therapist identify for the couple that might be leveraged to improve communication?
3. How might the therapist use the results of the ECR-R to foster a dialogue between Nathan and Sarah? How might the concept of a secure base be helpful?

and that these results were maintained at 6-month follow-up (Rathgeber et al., 2019). Interestingly, this review showed that the effect for EFT was comparable to that for behavioral couple therapy, although the effects of EFT did not dissipate after 6 months while those of the behavioral interventions did. Improved attachment security amongst individuals receiving EFT predicts improvements with relationship satisfaction (e.g., Burgess Moser et al., 2016). Further, change toward attachment security predicted maintenance of treatment gains 2 years after completing treatment (Wiebe et al., 2017). More recently, EFT has been applied with encouraging results to situations in which one partner is experiencing a psychiatric disorder, such as PTSD (Weissman et al., 2018), or a terminal medical condition (McLean et al., 2013). The premise is that enhancing attachment security toward a partner may help cope with the distress of these challenges.

CONCLUSION

The clinical applications of attachment theory and research with adults received a boon with the introduction of the social psychological approach to conceptualizing attachment. Self-report measures are easily administered in practice and provide important information about the interpersonal style of patients and may be used for treatment purposes. However, by their nature, social psychologists are not clinicians, and many researchers examining the application of attachment to clinical practice historically relied on developmental metrics. The result is that attachment theory is viewed primarily as a lens through which to address clinical problems as opposed to a definable treatment approach. This perspective to practice, combined with the ease of administration of valid and reliable self-report measures, yields significant portability of attachment theory to clinical practice. Consequently, it is increasingly common to see attachment constructs investigated for their role in the onset and maintenance of various forms of psychopathology as well as applied to a variety of treatment models for adults.

BOX 9.5

DISCUSSIONS OF CASE STUDIES

Box 9.1: The Case of Marcus

Question 1

Marcus displays classic symptoms of posttraumatic stress disorder (PTSD), including avoidance of reminders (e.g., memories) of his traumatic experience, hypervigilance, irritability, and nightmares. Near the end of the vignette Marcus appears to display a form of dissociation: He abruptly stops speaking about his mother and looks out the window. This response did not appear to be voluntary, as Marcus had no recollection of the question the clinician asked or what he was discussing prior to looking out the window. The clinician also made several attempts to restart the conversation with Marcus, who seemingly did not hear the clinician.

Question 2

Marcus first attempted to avoid discussing his childhood and described it as "unimportant." Once given a rationale about why his upbringing might be relevant, Marcus began discussing his mother but stopped abruptly. It is telling that the dissociative experience occurred when discussing memories of his mother and not when attempting to recount his combat experiences. Such behavior is reflective of unresolved responses on the Adult Attachment Interview and reflects extremely poor narrative coherence. Although his state of mind cannot be stated with certainty, the vignette includes two noted attempts by the clinician to learn about Marcus's childhood. He responded to the first by trying to avoid the topic, and the second attempt prompted the onset of the apparent dissociative experience. It seems likely that significant negative attachment-related experiences, potentially of a traumatic nature, occurred in Marcus's past.

Question 3

The likelihood that Marcus experienced troubling attachment experiences in his past coupled with his current marital problems suggests potential limitations with his ability to effectively use social support. It may be emotionally difficult for Marcus to relay the details of his traumatic experiences to his wife or other support person, particularly early in treatment when he is struggling to confront distressing memories. In addition, Marcus may display challenges coherently providing a narrative of his trauma experience. Use of standard exposure-based therapies for PTSD may be challenging if such difficulty with narrative coherence is not appreciated and addressed during treatment.

BOX 9.5

DISCUSSIONS OF CASE STUDIES (*Continued*)

Box 9.2: The Case of Ariella

Question 1

Ariella reported using self-injurious behavior as a form of emotion regulation (i.e., "to feel something"). In addition, emotional lability is present: Ariella demonstrated significant anger toward her parents that then transferred to the clinician. Relationship stability also appears tenuous, as Ariella quickly assigned a significant level of trust to the clinician, describing her as the most understanding person in her life, before displaying anger toward the clinician and finally a fear of being abandoned by her. Ariella presented with symptoms of borderline personality disorder.

Question 2

Ariella's responses when asked about her parents are telling. She initially displayed contempt by rolling her eyes, sighing, and suggesting that they are irrelevant factors in her life. However, she then talked at length about her parents, often in an angry manner. Her behaviors are suggestive of a preoccupied state of mind on the AAI. Her notable fear of being abandoned by the clinician, combined with her ambivalence regarding her relationship with her parents, is suggestive of a high level of anxiety concerning interpersonal relationships. However, she does not appear to avoid discussing such relationships; her initial refusal to discuss her parents appears more driven by contempt than by a true desire to not discuss them. On the Experiences in Close Relationships-Revised, assuming a valid report, one might expect her to score high for anxiety and low for avoidance.

Question 3

Ariella displays a relative inability to mentalize effectively, which is most evident in relation to her interactions with the therapist. First, she assumes the therapist understands her perspective simply because the therapist empathized with her use of cutting as an emotion regulation technique. In actuality, the therapist knows very little of Ariella's experiences or concerns. This exchange is reflective of Ariella's inability to comprehend the mental processes of the therapist and to understand them as separate from her own. Later, when the clinician asked follow-up questions after Ariella's tirade against her parents, Ariella was unable to appreciate that the clinician was seeking to learn more about her perspective. Instead, she misattributed hostile intent to the clinician's questions by accusing

(*continues*)

BOX 9.5

DISCUSSIONS OF CASE STUDIES (*Continued*)

her of taking the side of the parents. Given these considerations, it is likely that treatment with Ariella may be marked by moments of strained therapeutic alliance.

Box 9.3: The Case of Esther

Question 1

Esther's enjoyment of attending therapy and her willingness to share her thoughts about her husband and relationships with the therapist suggests the therapeutic alliance is strong. Although it is mentioned that her husband's passing is difficult for her, there is no indication that his death has been a focus of therapeutic discussions. Whether Esther views the therapist as a secure base for exploring these painful memories is difficult to ascertain at this point. It is promising that Esther feels comfortable enough to talk with the therapist about her concerns regarding treatment progress. This discussion may be difficult to have with a trusted individual, such as a therapist, and her ability to initiate this conversation suggests that Esther views the therapist as someone who can help address this troubling issue (i.e., secure base).

Question 2

Esther identified the death of an attachment figure (i.e., her husband) as the key etiological factor in the onset of her depression. In addition, Esther reported harboring some anger toward her husband and blamed him for his death. No therapeutic work is mentioned directly related to these attachment-related thoughts and feelings. It is possible that her inability to confront and process this loss effectively is the primary driver of her depressive symptoms as well as of her ineffective romantic relationships. The therapist may be well served encouraging Esther to confront the death of her husband directly, with a focus on processing maladaptive thoughts and feelings.

Question 3

It is curious the therapist in this case did not focus on the apparent troubling perception that Esther holds regarding the death of her husband. One possibility is that the therapist is uncomfortable discussing these issues, perhaps as a result of an insecure attachment on the part of the therapist. Such insecurity may make it difficult for the therapist to

BOX 9.5

DISCUSSIONS OF CASE STUDIES (*Continued*)

discuss the loss of attachment figures. Alternatively, the therapist may be focused on changing thoughts and feelings by examining current context and future goals. In such a circumstance, the therapist fails to take account of the ways that prior experiences impede current functioning. Attachment theory encourages recognizing the impact of previous attachment relationships, including the loss of those relationships. Regardless of the cause, Esther clearly offered her perception of the reasoning for her concerns, and the therapist failed to address those concerns effectively during therapy.

Box 9.4: The Case of Sarah and Nathan

Question 1

Nathan's responses are difficult to interpret. Certainly, withdrawing from heated arguments is not altogether unusual, but his responses suggest the potential for an avoidant interpersonal style. His initial behavior of leaning back in the chair and folding his arms was in response to the clinician asking a question, not a comment by Sarah. Later, while Sarah was crying and in obvious emotion distress, he could only speak softly and nod his head instead of giving a more direct response. Nathan's response on the Experiences in Close Relationships-Revised (ECR-R), especially the avoidant scale, may be helpful in clarifying his interpersonal style. As for Sarah, she was quick to display an extreme emotional response that included both anger and apparent sadness. These emotions appear largely the result of feeling her attempts at being closer to Nathan are failing and he is rejecting her. Such an approach is characteristic of an anxious attachment style. However, they may be the result of learned helplessness, given the longstanding nature of their arguments. Her responses on the ECR-R should help clarify whether these are situational or characterological.

Question 2

Two primary strengths are evident. First, each partner appears committed to staying in the relationship if it can be improved. They mutually agreed to try therapy as an attempt to prevent divorce, suggesting a level of commitment to one another remains. Second, there are indications of love and caring between Sarah and Nathan. Sarah displays emotional distress

(*continues*)

BOX 9.5

DISCUSSIONS OF CASE STUDIES (*Continued*)

at the possibility of their marriage falling apart, including feeling hurt that her attempts are rebuffed by Nathan. For his part, Nathan denied Sarah's allegation that he no longer loves her, though he quietly whispered, and it is unclear whether Sarah heard his response.

Question 3

The use of the ECR-R may be helpful for assessment and conceptualization purposes, but it may also serve a direct treatment function. Assuming Nathan scores high on the avoidance scale, the clinician may discuss what such a score implies about Nathan's comfort during interpersonal interactions. This approach can prompt a discussion of how he responds to Sarah when she attempts to have an intimate conversation about their relationship. The same goes for Sarah's responses to the ECR. If she reports high levels of attachment anxiety, the clinician may ask her to consider how such a style affects the way she engages Nathan in emotionally laden conversations. The clinician can provide practical examples of these dynamics by invoking the concept of the secure base. Sarah and Nathan can be asked to consider how their styles influence situations in which one partner wishes to discuss an important topic with the other. Given the situation that occurred in the vignette, the clinician can point out the opportunity for each to serve as a secure base for the other. However, Nathan's avoidant style resulted in Sarah believing that Nathan was not listening to her and was blaming her for their problems, whereas Sarah's interpersonal anxiety encouraged Nathan to remain quiet and not risk upsetting her. Once these dynamics are visible to each partner, the clinician can guide the couple through exercises designed to improve their ability to listen to and support one another.

RESOURCES

Training Resources

- **Mentalization-Based Therapy (MBT):** Training in MBT and further information is available at https://www.annafreud.org/training/
- **Emotion-Focused Couple Therapy (EFT):** Training in EFT and further information is available at https://iceeft.com/

Suggested Further Reading

Wallin, D. J. (2007). *Attachment and psychotherapy.* Guilford Press.

This volume includes in-depth discussion of the application of attachment principles to individual therapy with adults. Topics range from how to consider patients' various attachment experiences to appreciating the role of mentalizing ability to the implications of the different states of mind. The volume is not focused on treating any one type of psychopathology but rather considers attachment as a lens through which to conduct treatment in general.

Holmes J., & Slade, A. (2017). *Attachment in therapeutic practice.* Sage.

This volume presents reviews of various attachment principles and highlights their clinical relevance. It concludes with discussion of different models of therapeutic change and applying the concepts to various clinical presentations.

PART III QUESTIONS AND CONTROVERSIES

10 "ATTACHMENT DISORDER," "ATTACHMENT THERAPY," AND THE REDEMPTION OF A CLINICAL THEORY

Scientific efforts over the past 5 decades have documented the role of attachment processes in human development, most notably in the social–emotional realm, as well as in the etiology of various clinical conditions. However, such insights are rarely acknowledged, or are outright dismissed, in various academic quarters. There are two primary culprits for this animosity. First is the partitioning of the clinical field into opposing camps wedded to a "theoretical orientation." Attachment theory having roots in psychoanalysis is sufficient cause for many to discount the whole body of knowledge. The strengths and weaknesses of the theoretical orientation concept already receive significant attention in contemporary debate and are not discussed further.

The second cause is related neither to scientific credentials nor to theoretical allegiances but rather to a profound and persistent misunderstanding of the clinical applications of attachment theory. Throughout the 1980s and the 1990s, attachment researchers defined the developmental tenets of the neophyte field, and applications to clinical practice were rarely discussed, a fact lamented by John Bowlby (1988) shortly before his death. However,

https://doi.org/10.1037/0000333-011
The Science and Clinical Practice of Attachment Theory: A Guide From Infancy to Adulthood, by B. Allen

a small cadre of clinicians, most with little experience conducting or critiquing scientific research, believed they understood the clinical implications of the emerging attachment science and marketed their ideas directly to the public. They misdiagnosed maltreated children with behavioral issues as having "attachment disorders," and their approaches to treatment, unethical and dangerous, were labeled "attachment therapy." When the reckoning inevitability came, the result was widespread public and professional skepticism of any clinician advocating an attachment-based perspective to practice.

"ATTACHMENT DISORDER"

Shortly after Bowlby visited Harry Harlow's laboratory in 1958 (see Chapter 1, this volume), Harlow welcomed another visitor, Bruno Bettelheim, the director of a home for children with emotional and behavioral difficulties. Like Bowlby, Bettelheim viewed emotional disturbances among children as resulting from problems within the parent–child relationship. However, while Bowlby viewed clinical symptoms in Harlow's monkeys as the result of an inability to access a caregiver for support during times of distress, Bettelheim argued that the monkeys displayed autism and saw the value of the experiments as demonstrating maternal deprivation as the cause. Though he had no formal training in psychology or psychiatry, Bettelheim (1967) produced a full-length volume proposing that autism was the result of emotional neglect, particularly from the mother. He relied on a psychoanalytic idea that the child turned inward on the self to escape the pain of maternal frigidness, popularizing the "refrigerator mother" hypothesis of autism. Although Bowlby and Harlow were repulsed by Bettelheim's ideas and believed he misconstrued the results of Harlow's studies (van Rosmalen et al., 2020), Bettelheim nonetheless became a noted autism expert, lectured widely, and appeared on numerous television programs.

Robert Zaslow, a psychologist in California, decided to build off Bettelheim's hypothesis (Zaslow & Menta, 1975). He reviewed Bowlby and Ainsworth's early work documenting various types of social referencing (e.g., eye contact, smiling) as initial forms of attachment behavior and suggested that the lack of such responses among children with autism points toward a problem of attachment. Specifically, he proposed that "autism is a developmental fixation at the infancy level due to a breakdown in the species-specific attachment process between mother and infant" (Zaslow & Menta, 1975, p. 90). In other words, a lack of normative social behavior, the hallmark symptom of autism, reflects a form of arrested development in which the child is stuck in a state of infancy because of inadequate attachment-related experiences. Therefore, Zaslow concluded, "I consider the autistic child to be the most unattached of children" (p. 214).

Zaslow similarly explained other symptoms of autism. Relying on psychoanalytic theory, he proposed that children with autism develop defenses to ward off perceived threats. Notable among these defenses is repression of the rage a child inherently feels toward the parent for providing deficient forms of caregiving. Consequently, children may appear nonverbal, resist interactions with others, and find it difficult to trust adults. In short, children with autism retreat into their inner world because of poor attachment experiences and then erect multiple layers of defense to protect themselves, all while harboring a growing sense of anger and resentment.

One of the individuals who heard Zaslow describe autism in this fashion was psychiatrist Foster Cline. It seemed to Cline (1979) that this etiological argument might generalize to other presentations, and he quickly published his own thoughts, suggesting maltreated children with severe behavioral problems may be understood from the same perspective. He proposed that these children maintain a reservoir of repressed rage toward their parents/abusers that manifests in violent outbursts. Over the following decade Cline (1992), among others, expanded on this conceptualization and came to view abuse within attachment relationships as effectively creating an inability for the child to trust other adults, resulting in a failure to develop empathy or a conscience. For Cline, the fundamental problem of maltreated children displaying conduct problems and callous/unemotional traits is the acquired inability to form an attachment with a caregiver, and he began referring to this presentation as "attachment disorder" (AD).

AD did not exist in the diagnostic taxonomy; however, reactive attachment disorder (RAD) was in the American Psychiatric Association's *Diagnostic and Statistical Manual of Mental Disorders*. Importantly, the criteria in the *DSM-III-R* (American Psychiatric Association, 1987) described the indiscriminate social behavior of disinhibited RAD as marked by a shallow, nongenuine affect, a presentation easily portrayed by Cline and others as reflecting psychopathic tendencies. The *DSM-IV* (American Psychiatric Association, 1994) description of disinhibited RAD emphasized "diffuse attachments," which were presented as a child's inability to attach to a specific caregiver. Proponents of the AD concept developed checklists purported to assess AD, often terming the condition "RAD" to provide clinicians with an eligible *DSM* diagnosis. These measures included items assessing a wide range of concerns, such as conduct problems (e.g., harming animals, aggression), questionable parent–child relational issues (e.g., not affectionate on caregiver's terms), learning disabilities, posttraumatic stress symptoms, ill-defined cognitive concerns (e.g., lack of cause-and-effect thinking, persistent nonsense questions), and false allegations of abuse, among others (Hughes, 1997; Randolph, 2000).[1]

The AD construct lacked empirical validity, and the developed measures performed poorly during independent evaluations (e.g., Cappelletty et al., 2005), but proponents of AD did not seek recognition from the scientific community. Rather, their primary audience became foster and adoptive families and the organizations that serve them. Many foster and adopted children enter their new homes with significant difficulty regulating emotions and behaviors as a result of their maltreatment experiences (see Juffer et al., 2011). For many parents, the child's behavioral problems cause significant strain in the family, and it may be difficult to develop the type of relationship intended when they decided to take in the child. The conclusion often reached is that some factor internal to the child is preventing improvement. Cline and his adherents offered that the factor in question was AD, a conceptualization that makes intuitive sense to many in the foster and adoption communities. The caregivers, who often have successfully raised other biological or adopted children, are absolved from responsibility for the child's problems or for the poor quality of the parent–child relationship, as the real culprit is the child's defenses prohibiting formation of an attachment to the caregiver.

The concept of AD began to take on a life of its own. Adopted children with severe conduct problems were diagnosed with AD or RAD, and preplacement experiences were deemed pathological solely because they necessitated out-of-home placement. For instance, substandard prenatal care became an etiological cause, as some AD adherents believed it created the inability to attach to a caregiver. Searching for a stronger theoretical basis, many AD proponents began citing Bowlby's (1944b) early suggestion that problems in the attachment relationship cause "affectionless characters," neglecting to mention that Bowlby later retracted the idea (Bowlby et al., 1956; see Chapter 1, this volume). Attempts followed to develop an empirical basis for the construct of AD. As explained by B. Allen (2018), these studies generally relied on circular reasoning, in which clinicians diagnose maltreated children with RAD based on the AD conceptualization and then interpret elevated scores on measures of externalizing concerns as evidence that children with

[1]The *DSM-IV* encouraged clinicians to separate RAD from concerns such as conduct disorder and oppositional defiant disorder and explicitly stated that "no direct link between Reactive Attachment Disorder and 'affectionless psychopathy' has been established" (American Psychiatric Association, 1994, p. 130). Cline and his adherents failed to mention this caveat.

RAD demonstrate severe conduct problems (e.g., Hall & Geher, 2003). Nonetheless, lower tier academic outlets published such reports, which allowed AD proponents to argue that their ideas were supported by studies in peer-reviewed journals.

While the AD construct was gaining momentum in the clinical arena, there was a noticeable silence on these issues from the scientific community. The RAD criteria in the *DSM-III* (American Psychiatric Association, 1980), *DSM-III-R* (American Psychiatric Association, 1987), and *DSM-IV* (American Psychiatric Association, 1994) were considered by most attachment and clinical researchers as poorly crafted and lacking a theoretical and empirical basis (see Chapter 6). In addition, RAD, as specified in the *DSM*, was rare in community settings and largely restricted to institutions, and thus researchers had little impetus to invest time and resources in developing assessment and treatment approaches. To compound the matter, foster and adoption communities rarely received attention from researchers (although the work of Mary Dozier and her colleagues is a notable exception; see Chapter 6). As a result, clinicians advocating for AD appeared to be the only ones who understood the challenges faced by foster and adoptive caregivers and the only ones offering specialized clinical interventions.

The propositions of Foster Cline and other AD advocates found an audience among well-meaning clinicians who were largely unaware that the construct of AD significantly diverged from *DSM*-defined RAD. Generations of clinicians received training during graduate school and in postgraduate supervision that RAD is the appropriate diagnosis for maltreated children, particularly those in foster or adoptive care, who display conduct problems and/or psychopathic traits. This misunderstanding continues to this day. Woolgar and Baldock (2015) reviewed 100 consecutive referrals to a specialized clinic in the United Kingdom serving foster and adopted children. The referring clinician or caseworker identified AD or RAD as a presenting issue in 31 of the cases. After assessment in the specialty clinic using *DSM-IV* (American Psychiatric Association, 1994) or *International Statistical Classification of Diseases and Related Health Problems* (10th ed.; *ICD-10*; World Health Organization, 1993) criteria and published diagnostic guidelines, only three cases qualified as RAD while 18 individuals were diagnosed with conduct disorder. B. Allen and Schuengel (2020) replicated these findings using *DSM-5* (American Psychiatric Association, 2013) criteria. Of 100 consecutive referrals of foster or adopted children to a specialty clinic in the United States, 39 presented with a diagnostic history of AD, RAD, or disinhibited social engagement disorder (DSED). Following assessment with a semistructured interview, three of these cases qualified for DSED, and none met criteria for

RAD. Further, the strongest correlate of a previous AD or RAD diagnosis was an elevated score on a measure assessing conduct problems.

"ATTACHMENT THERAPY"

The dissemination and popularization of the AD/RAD concept was accompanied by an assortment of purported treatments for the condition. Indeed, specification of the diagnosis was often an important step before explaining the various treatment ideas that came to be subsumed under the umbrella of "attachment therapy." Not surprisingly, the increased acceptance of the AD/RAD construct created a market for "attachment therapy" and numerous clinicians sought training to provide such treatment. As a broad class of techniques, "attachment therapy" has no guiding principle or common factor beyond the belief that these methods can break through the child's defenses and thereby create the capacity for attaching to a caregiver. Consequently, it is best to consider the different approaches in turn, although they are commonly used in conjunction.

"Rage Reduction" and Holding Therapy

Zaslow and Menta (1975) described an intervention for children with autism designed to elicit and discharge the repressed anger believed to underlie their condition, hence the approach commonly being referred to as "rage reduction" therapy. The child is placed in the lap of the therapist "in a position similar to that of the typical mother–infant holding position" from which the therapist is then directed to "manipulate and apply counter-pressure to the tense and motoric resistant parts of the body" (Zaslow & Menta, 1975, p. 91). In practice, the clinician holds the child like an infant, potentially with the assistance of other therapists, and intentionally pokes, rubs, or otherwise physically irritates the child to elicit "high arousal reactions (e.g., kicking, screaming, thrashing)" that signify the child is passing through the "rage barrier" (p. 91). Any movement by the child while in the holding position, such as twitching or squirming, is taken as resistance and an indication that holding must continue. The session ends when the child is calm.

Because Zaslow viewed autism as a severe form of attachment problem and social referencing was believed key to the development of attachment, he considered it critical for the success of rage reduction treatment that the child maintain eye contact until anger subsided (Zaslow & Menta, 1975). Averting the eyes was a sign of continued resistance. He acknowledged this process induced a significant level of distress for the child but argued that the stress–relaxation cycle experienced was necessary for developing attachment. Zaslow hypothesized that the process teaches the child to trust adults and to view them as wiser and stronger, resulting in fewer behavioral concerns. It was considered the ultimate sign of trust for the child to lie peacefully in the arms of another individual, the desired end state of a treatment session.

Cline (1979, 1992) applied Zaslow's treatment to the care of maltreated and adopted children, similarly believing in the need to break through their defenses to release repressed anger and teach them that adults are in control. Verbal confrontation, such as angrily yelling in the face of the child and ordering the child to repeat phrases the therapist believes represent the child's thoughts (e.g., "I would like to kill you"), was added to the physical restraint and coercion.[2] Cline established the Attachment Center at Evergreen (Colorado), which became widely regarded as the epicenter of "attachment therapy," providing intensive multiweek treatment programs based on his methods, publishing books and treatment materials, and training clinicians from around the country.[3] Variations on holding therapy later appeared, such as Martha Welch's (1989) "holding time" approach of teaching caregivers to use holding techniques in the home. Daniel Hughes (1997) promoted holding therapy but believed in the delivery of other techniques as well and advocated a more integrative approach to treatment.

Age Regression

One of the treatment ideas that Hughes (1997) thought might suitably complement holding techniques, particularly with adopted children, is allowing the child "to regress and to relate to his new parent as if he were a much younger child" (p. 89). For instance, although the child may be of school age, the caregiver may implement rocking, bottle feeding, and/or cutting food and feeding it to the child. The logic of these "age regression" techniques relies on the same psychoanalytic idea of developmental fixation employed by Zaslow. In essence, the development of attachment was stunted or halted at some prior point in life, likely during infancy for many adopted children,

[2]Videos of these sessions are available online, including on video sharing sites such as YouTube. Be cautioned, however, that some videos are graphic and disturbing.

[3]The Attachment Center at Evergreen was later renamed the Institute for Attachment and Child Development, which remained in operation until 2021. Two therapists who worked closely under Cline, Michael Orlans and Terry Levy, established their own programs, called Evergreen Psychotherapy Center and Attachment Treatment and Training Institute, which remain in operation.

and treatment requires allowing the child to experience those attachment-nurturing experiences of which they were deprived. Hughes (1997) cautioned, however, that

> for regression to have a significant effect on child functioning, it needs to be both comprehensive and of a long duration. Thus, if the 6-year-old boy is to be raised as if he were 2 years old, the parent will have to be prepared to provide him with the extensive supervision and involvement that she would actually give her 2-year-old. (p. 211)

Age regression taken to the extreme, and integrated with holding therapy ideas, resulted in the development of an intervention labeled "rebirthing therapy." In this approach, the child is wrapped in blankets while adults position themselves on top to apply pressure. The child is directed to free themself by fighting through the compressions to the end of the blanket where the parent is waiting to receive them. The hypothesis is that this process allows the child to start anew by receiving nurturance from the caregiver at the point of a psychological rebirth. For a larger discussion of the techniques of rebirthing therapy, see Mercer et al. (2003).

Power-Assertive Parenting

Alongside the directives for treatment sessions came guidance for caregivers on how to parent a child with AD/RAD. The traditional concept of caregiver sensitivity is perceived as fostering and enabling a manipulative child who will take advantage of the caregiver's kindness. Instead, parents are directed in a heavy-handed approach to demonstrate to the child that the power rests with the parents. The most well-known figure in "attachment parenting"[4] is Nancy Thomas, an adoptive mother who worked for a time with Foster Cline at the Attachment Center at Evergreen. Thomas's (1997) notable book, *When Love Is Not Enough: Parenting a Child With RAD*, directs parents to exert total control over the life of the child. As she stated, "Your

[4]The term "attachment parenting" is used colloquially in several ways. The power-assertive parenting techniques discussed here are often labeled "attachment parenting," as are "pop psychology" recommendations such as co-sleeping with an infant and breastfeeding into the preschool years. Although proponents of these ideas suggest that the promoted techniques improve the parent–child attachment, they are rarely supported by attachment research or theory. In fact, it is rare for reputable attachment researchers to use the term "attachment parenting," as they are prone to use more clearly definable terms based in the empirical literature, such as "caregiver sensitivity" (see Chapter 2).

child should learn to ask for everything. . . . When it starts to feel like they must ask to breathe, you are on the right track" (p. 52). Recommended techniques include placing an alarm on the child's door to prevent leaving the room without permission, assigning physical exercises (e.g., pushups) for perceived misbehavior, providing affection only on the parent's terms and timing, withholding pleasurable food and using it as a reward for desired behavior, and prohibiting the child from speaking. The child is expected to ask permission for all activities, including hugging the caregiver or going to the restroom. For repeated violation of these rules, the child may be removed to a respite home and allowed to return only when their behavior improves.

"Attachment Therapy" Organizes and Expands

In 1990, several prominent "attachment therapists" established a professional organization to advocate for the acceptance and use of "attachment therapy," the Association for Treatment and Training of Attachment in Children (ATTACh). They counted among their members Foster Cline and Nancy Thomas and sanctioned trainings and promoted the use of holding therapy, age regression, and power-assertive parenting approaches. ATTACh organized an annual conference, marketing specifically to the foster and adoption communities, and members actively recruited clinicians to fill the ranks, arguing that "attachment therapy and holding therapy are the only therapies that have proven to be effective with Attachment Disordered children" (N. Thomas, 1997, p. 21). Helping to spread the message, ATTACh members included adoptive parents and child welfare caseworkers.

"Attachment therapists" became more visible throughout the 1990s, partially because of the networking and coordination offered through ATTACh but also as a result of a concerted campaign of publishing books, which helped establish the appearance of a professional consensus on the acceptance of AD as a diagnosis and "attachment therapy" as the treatment of choice. Treatment centers modeled on the Attachment Center at Evergreen were established in multiple areas of the United States as well as internationally, bringing with them a wide reach of training opportunities and access to a specialized form of treatment unavailable from standard mental health clinicians. The advent of the internet led to websites from ATTACh and other organizations, including support groups for adoptive families, disseminating the AD/RAD concept, the assortment of checklists developed to assess the condition, and the importance of "attachment therapy" for saving such children.

A RECKONING AND A REDEMPTION

The "attachment therapy" field was rocked in 2000 by the death of Candace Newmaker, a 10-year-old adopted girl diagnosed with AD/RAD. She and her adoptive mother traveled from North Carolina to Colorado to undergo a 2-week intensive treatment program that included various "attachment therapy" techniques, including rebirthing therapy. The weight of the adults coupled with difficulty breathing while wrapped in a blanket proved too much for young Candace; she died the following day as a result of neurological damage caused by asphyxiation. Her death made nationwide headlines, with newspapers and magazines asking how a young child died during a therapy session (see Mercer et al., 2003).

A little over 2 years later, Cassandra Killpack, a 4-year-old girl in Utah who was diagnosed with RAD, was forced by her adoptive parents to drink more than a gallon of water as a consequence for sneaking a sip of her sibling's drink. The abundance of water in Cassandra's body caused a dangerous drop in her electrolyte levels, which induced brain swelling and eventual death. The parents claimed they were directed by her therapist at the Cascade Center for Family Growth to implement this punishment, an allegation the director of the program denied (Fattah, 2002). However, the case drew additional attention to "attachment therapy" practices, as such power-assertive parenting techniques were commonly associated with these approaches and the Cascade Center was known to provide rage reduction and other forms of holding therapy. A series of other cases emerged throughout the 2000s in which children were injured or killed because of methods linked to "attachment therapy" either directly as a result of therapist directives or indirectly through caregivers attending workshops or reading books by "attachment therapists."

The "attachment therapy" field was left scrambling. In a report prepared for ATTACh, V. J. Kelly (2003) argued that "the use of therapeutic holding (as a specific intervention or as a position in which to conduct other interventions) may be one of the many tools in the process of attachment therapy" (p. 1). She specified that the use of holding therapy does not inherently suggest physical coercion or intentional provocation of angry responses, a seeming attempt to step away from the rage reduction approach while not specifically shunning its use. She also suggested that holding therapy desensitizes the child to caregiver embraces and, therefore, serves to improve the relationship between the parent and child. Hughes (2003) published a commentary similarly walking back his earlier endorsements of holding therapy: "In looking for treatment strategies that are congruent with how secure attachments are facilitated, it is immediately obvious that the 'holding and coercive therapies' . . . have no place" (p. 272).

The Scientific Community Responds

For many in the scientific community, the death of Candace Newmaker was the first they heard of rebirthing therapy, holding therapy, or "attachment therapy." The death of Cassandra Killpack shortly thereafter removed the possibility that Newmaker's death was an isolated incident related to one or two unethical and misguided clinicians. It became clear that "attachment therapy" was a system of treatment that had taken hold among a certain segment of the clinical community. It could not be ignored and demanded a professional response.

Attachment researchers were among the first to respond. In a 2003 special issue of the flagship journal *Attachment and Human Development*, prominent developmental and clinical scientists took turns demonstrating the innumerable ways that AD and "attachment therapy" fail to coincide with the extant attachment research. For instance, AD does not attempt to diagnose a problem of attachment but rather attempts to invoke an attachment explanation for the onset of conduct problems. This tactic is akin to a psychodynamic clinician conceptualizing conduct problems as an object-relational disorder or a behavioral clinician calling it an operant-conditioning disorder. Critics pointed out that attachment is best conceived within a developmental psychopathology framework and that suggesting that conduct problems are the direct result of early attachment experiences is indefensible. As for treatment, various commentators noted that attachment theory and research promote the improvement of developmental trajectories by enhancing caregiver sensitivity and responsiveness, which directly contradicts the use of age regression, holding therapy, rage reduction therapy, and power-assertive parenting techniques. In short, the commenters agreed on one general conclusion: AD and the various techniques labeled as "attachment therapy" are not supported by attachment theory or research.

Professional organizations soon joined in the discussion. The American Academy of Child and Adolescent Psychiatry (Boris et al., 2005) developed a practice parameter on the treatment of RAD, cautioning against coercive forms of treatment, and the National Association of Social Workers (2005) passed a resolution that explicitly identified physically coercive treatment practices as unethical and dangerous. The American Professional Society on the Abuse of Children (APSAC) commissioned a task force that concluded

> Treatment techniques or attachment parenting techniques involving physical coercion, psychologically or physically enforced holding, physical restraint, physical domination, provoked catharsis, ventilation of rage, age regression, humiliation, withholding or forcing food or water intake, prolonged social isolation, or assuming exaggerated levels of control and domination over a child

BOX 10.1

THE CASE OF JANAE

Ms. Harrison is a child welfare caseworker who contacted the clinic to ask for recommended treatment directions and potentially a referral. Her client is Janae, a 7-year-old African American girl living with a foster mother (Ms. Barrow) who intends to adopt her. Since coming into the home Janae has displayed a series of dangerous behaviors, including pulling knives out of a drawer, hitting her younger biological sibling who also resides in the home, and making threatening comments toward Ms. Barrow. Ms. Harrison is deeply concerned because Ms. Barrow is considering stopping the adoption process and asking for Janae to be moved to another home. Ms. Harrison conducted an internet search and believes Janae has reactive attachment disorder (RAD). She also recently found a psychological evaluation from 2 years prior that diagnosed her with RAD. Her understanding is that Janae would benefit most from attachment therapy, but she has been unable to find an attachment therapist and is confused about the most appropriate services. She has asked if the clinic provides attachment therapy.

Discussion Questions

1. Do you believe that Janae has RAD? Why?
2. How do you respond to Ms. Harrison's question regarding the provision of attachment therapy at the clinic?

> are contraindicated because of risk of harm and absence of proven benefit and should not be used. (Chaffin et al., 2006, p. 86)

Division 37 of the American Psychological Association (Society for Child and Family Practice and Policy) endorsed the APSAC report (Chaffin et al., 2006). Some states passed laws prohibiting rebirthing and holding therapies, resulting in reduced availability of "attachment therapy" services. In addition, widely cited papers explicitly described holding therapy as a potentially harmful treatment (e.g., Lilienfeld, 2007). Box 10.1 examines a case example of a 7-year-old girl in foster care displaying aggressive behavior and a caseworker desperately trying to identify appropriate clinical services.[5]

[5]To protect patient confidentiality, proper steps have been taken to disguise the identities of the individuals in this chapter's case examples.

The "attachment therapy" community faced a crossroads. ATTACh realized their previous statement was insufficient to stem the tide of public and professional backlash. They drafted a white paper that explicitly shunned the use of rage reduction techniques in therapy, although they qualified the statement by suggesting the point at which "appropriate therapeutic confrontation" ends and coercive techniques begin is a "gray area" (Association for the Treatment and Training in the Attachment of Children, 2007, p. 4). Figureheads of the field stepped away. Foster Cline surrendered his license following an injury to a child and devoted his energies to disseminating his Parenting with Love and Logic program (Mercer, 2015). Daniel Hughes distanced himself from his former techniques and reformulated his ideas into a treatment he termed "dyadic developmental psychotherapy" (DDP).

Those who formerly promoted "attachment therapy" attempted to develop new professional identities, largely by associating with the burgeoning field of trauma. ATTACh changed its name to the Association for Training on Trauma and Attachment of Children, which allowed them to maintain their acronym. Some now discuss AD/RAD as a special case of developmental trauma disorder or argue that it denotes an older child displaying the social–emotional functioning of an infant or preschooler (Becker-Weidman, 2009). To disassociate themselves from "attachment therapy," holding therapy, and age regression—all of which had acquired pejorative meanings—clinicians began referring to their interventions as "attachment-focused," including Hughes with his DDP. These approaches include a vast array of techniques, ranging from nondirective play therapy and sandtray therapy to holding approaches that omit the physical coercion and forced eye contact. Nonetheless, these clinicians continue to advocate their approaches as the only effective treatment approach for children with AD/RAD or "trauma-attachment disorders." Box 10.2 provides an in-depth look at the history of developmental trauma disorder as a concept and the ways in which some former "attachment therapists" reconcile their approaches with this idea.

It is difficult to determine how popular "attachment therapy" was at its zenith in the 1990s, although estimates of more contemporary usage are available. In a 2010 survey of 240 clinicians serving maltreated children in the United States, B. Allen et al. (2012) found that only six clinicians reported being trained to use holding therapy and only two clinicians endorsed implementing it in practice. Similar results were found for DDP, with six clinicians reporting prior training and four clinicians regularly using the intervention. Implementation of "attachment therapy" techniques, such as age regression and forcing eye contact during caregiver holding, was also uncommon (B. Allen & Crosby, 2014). Going along with this clinical shunning is the current

BOX 10.2

A CLOSER LOOK: DEVELOPMENTAL TRAUMA DISORDER

In the 1980s, several clinicians and researchers working in the emerging field of trauma and traumatic stress suggested that the posttraumatic stress disorder (PTSD) diagnosis as found in the *Diagnostic and Statistical Manual of Mental Disorders* was inadequate for capturing the symptom presentation of patients with severe emotional, dissociative, and interpersonal concerns stemming from chronic traumatic experiences (e.g., childhood abuse). They proposed calling this presentation "complex PTSD" and later used the term "disorders of extreme stress not otherwise specified." Advocates of the diagnosis conducted a field trial of the criteria, hoping for its inclusion in the *DSM-IV* (Roth et al., 1997); the efforts were unsuccessful. In the mid-2000s the proponents revised their conceptualization to focus on the impact of prolonged trauma on the social-emotional development of children. They termed the condition "developmental trauma disorder" (DTD) and conducted another field trial (van Der Kolk et al., 2019). Again, the conceptualization and data failed to impress the committee, and DTD was left out of the *DSM-5*.

No one doubts that early maltreatment and trauma exert significant and pervasive impacts on the development of the child. The concern for opponents of the DTD diagnosis is that it focuses on the experience of trauma instead of the presenting concerns of the patient. For instance, a common criticism of the diagnosis is that the symptoms significantly overlap with those of borderline personality disorder (BPD) and that recognition of a new diagnosis may prompt clinicians to neglect validated treatments for BPD in search of new treatments for the new disorder. Indeed, an assortment of interventions are now marketed for DTD, complex PTSD, and/or "trauma-attachment disorders." Proponents of DTD include reformed "attachment therapists" who describe "attachment disorder"/reactive attachment disorder as a special case of DTD. It is not uncommon to hear "attachment-focused" treatment approaches described as treatments for DTD. Associating themselves with this more mainstream diagnostic concept gives the appearance of acceptance and credibility to those who distanced themselves from their "attachment therapy" pasts.

scientific consensus that techniques such as rebirthing, holding therapy, and withholding food and water as a discipline technique are thoroughly discredited (Koocher et al., 2015).

Nonetheless, children continue to be diagnosed with AD/RAD (B. Allen & Schuengel, 2020; Woolgar & Baldock, 2015), and child welfare caseworkers and clinicians continue to seek out "attachment therapy" as the presumed treatment, often unsure of what such a treatment entails or who provides it. Occasionally, a case of "attachment therapy" and the damage it caused to a child misdiagnosed with RAD makes headlines (e.g., USA Today, 2014), but the response from the professional community is a collective shaking of the head. Zeanah and Guyon-Harris (2020) recently opined that the increasing consensus among researchers as to the core symptoms of RAD is not effectively disseminated to clinicians and advocated for the development of portable and psychometrically valid assessment metrics, specifically observational paradigms and structured interviews. B. Allen (2016) suggested that the only permanent solutions may be to remove RAD from the *DSM* or to rename the condition an unrelated term to preclude clinicians from diagnosing it and receiving reimbursement for its treatment. Such an approach may also force allied professions, such as child welfare and adoption agencies, to ask questions regarding treatment services that they have not broached in decades.

CONCLUSION

Although "attachment therapy" is often an afterthought in the mind of many clinicians and researchers today, the damage caused by this unfortunate episode to legitimate interventions based in attachment theory and research is immense and has proven difficult to shake. To their credit, reputable attachment researchers were the first to call out such dangerous treatment practices when they came to their attention. Nonetheless, discussion of attachment-based approaches to assessment and intervention continue to be treated with skepticism by many in the academic arena, particularly outside of the infancy and young childhood age range.

BOX 10.3
DISCUSSION OF CASE STUDY

Box 10.1: The Case of Janae

Question 1

No, Janae does not display reactive attachment disorder (RAD), at least not according to the *DSM-5* or the *ICD-11*. Rather, Janae is displaying conduct problems. It is likely that Ms. Harrison concluded from her internet searches that Janae has RAD because a seemingly endless number of resources online describe the condition as severe conduct problems among maltreated children. Given the confusion regarding the diagnostic criteria, it is also likely that a previous psychologist diagnosed her with RAD. The challenge in this case is to focus on treating the presenting concerns as Ms. Harrison has relayed them, as opposed to finding treatment for an erroneously diagnosed disorder.

Question 2

The response to Ms. Harrison must be handled delicately. Simply stating that you do not provide "attachment therapy" may inadvertently convey to Ms. Harrison that you do not have the expertise or the knowledge to treat Janae. Conversely, trying to provide copious amounts of education to Ms. Harrison on attachment and treatment may be overwhelming and, ultimately, ineffective. Rather, you may briefly explain to Ms. Harrison why she was unable to identify an "attachment therapist," given the history of that term and what it suggests. Then, you may be able to reorient the conversation to focus on the problems Janae is presenting. If you are trained in an intervention for disruptive behavior disorders, you may discuss how such an intervention may effectively treat the problems. In addition, you may be able to describe how such an intervention may improve the attachment relationship between Janae and Ms. Barlow (see Chapters 6 and 7 in this volume).

RESOURCES

Training Resources

- **Effective Child Therapy:** This website, maintained by the Society of Clinical Child and Adolescent Psychology, provides a compendium of evidence-based interventions for children and adolescents with various presenting concerns, as well as training resources: https://effectivechildtherapy.org/

11 FREQUENTLY ASKED QUESTIONS

1. What is attachment theory?

Attachment theory is a lifespan model of human development that emphasizes the central role of discriminated individuals who provide a sense of safety and security (i.e., attachment figures). A person signals to the attachment figure a need for comfort and/or protection (i.e., attachment behavior) and, once this sense of security is obtained, is confident engaging with threatening stimuli and/or exploring the environment (i.e., exploratory behavior). These experiences with an attachment figure are considered critical for the development of a cognitive understanding of oneself, others, and social interactions (i.e., internal working models) as well as emotion regulation skills, social competence, and other self-regulatory abilities. As such, attachment theory is most commonly associated with social–emotional development, though it does intersect with the realms of cognitive and physical development as well.

2. How are "attachment" and "parent–child relationship" different?

"Parent–child relationship" is a broad term that implies a multitude of related concepts, including communication patterns, shared or disparate

https://doi.org/10.1037/0000333-012
The Science and Clinical Practice of Attachment Theory: A Guide From Infancy to Adulthood, by B. Allen

interests, and discipline techniques, among many others. "Attachment" refers specifically to the child's understanding of the caregiver as someone who can be relied upon to provide comfort during times of distress (i.e., safe haven), which thereby allows the child to feel safe exploring the environment and testing new skills (i.e., secure base). Although attachment theory proposes that this safe haven–secure-base provision is vitally important for development, it does not refute that other aspects of the parent–child relationship are important and, in many ways, complementary. However, reducing the broad and complex term "parent–child relationship" to the more specific construct of "attachment" is ill-advised and overly simplistic.

3. Isn't attachment theory related primarily to infants?

No, attachment theory is conceived as a model of human development "from the cradle to the grave," to borrow a phrase from John Bowlby. While it is true the majority of attachment research examines children under the age of 3, this is rapidly changing. The general hypothesis is that early parent–child relationships lay the foundations for human development, but change is possible throughout the lifespan and primarily occurs as a result of later interpersonal interactions. In short, later experiences can confirm or disconfirm the cognitive representations formed from one's initial interpersonal experiences (i.e., parent–child interactions during infancy). Attachment research increasingly examines various attachment constructs during childhood, adolescence, and adulthood.

4. What is the difference between attachment security and attachment organization?

Attachment *security* refers to an individual's confidence that an attachment figure will respond effectively to comfort-seeking behavior under moments of distress. For instance, an infant displaying secure attachment may seek out a caregiver with the expectation that the caregiver will understand the signals being implemented and offer a comforting response. On the other hand, an infant who believes the caregiver will be critical, or perhaps walk away, has little confidence in the effectiveness of the caregiver's response (i.e., insecure) and is likely to maintain distance when under distress (i.e., avoidant). Attachment *organization* refers to the coherence of one's strategy or pattern of comfort-seeking behavior under moments of distress. The two just-mentioned examples (i.e., secure, insecure-avoidant) are considered organized, as they demonstrate an understandable and goal-corrected form of behavior. For instance, insecure-avoidant behavior serves to maintain availability of the caregiver because proximity-seeking behavior may serve to increase the distance between the infant and caregiver. Disorganized behavior is marked by an apparent approach–avoidance conflict that may resemble a child displaying contradictory, odd, or disoriented behavior. This child appears to have no coherent concept of how to respond to distress (see Chapter 2).

5. How are attachment behavior, representations, and internal working models related?

Attachment *behavior* refers specifically to overt and observable behavioral responses directed toward an attachment figure under moments of distress. Research examining attachment behavior is most commonly associated with the Strange Situation Procedure. Attachment *representations* refer to one's cognitive understanding of the caregiver as providing a safe haven–secure base and are believed to underlie the observable attachment behavior implemented under moments of distress. *Internal working models* (IWMs), however, are higher level cognitive structures that incorporate attachment representations as well as multiple other sources of information to derive an understanding of oneself, other people, and social interactions. These IWMs, similar in many ways to Piaget's concept of the schema, are then implemented during assorted interactions and experiences (see Chapter 3).

6. Are "attachment classifications" and "attachment styles" the same thing?

No, the term "attachment classifications" refers to patterns of observable behavior defined using the Strange Situation Procedure. Some methods of categorizing patterns of responses on measures of attachment representations also use the same general scheme and are referred to as "attachment classifications" (see Chapters 2 and 3). However, "attachment style" refers to the scores one receives on self-report measures constructed by social psychologists. In other words, it is one's perception of how they interact with others (see Chapter 5 in this volume).

7. Is attachment theory a psychoanalytic theory?

The answer is a qualified "no." John Bowlby, the originator of attachment theory, was a trained psychoanalyst. However, Bowlby was disillusioned with what he believed was the rejection of empirical findings by his psychoanalytic colleagues. He integrated research on animal behavior and ethology, cybernetics, developmental psychology, and developmental biology with his psychoanalytic understanding of mental structures to derive the first iteration of attachment theory. By the time Mary Ainsworth began her structured observations of parent–child interactions in the 1960s, Bowlby had left the psychoanalytic community, and attachment theory more closely resembled an interpersonal form of learning theory than anything being discussed in psychoanalytic circles. Bowlby found similarities between his ideas and those of

Aaron Beck and, by the turn of the 21st century, attachment theory was rarely associated in academic writings with psychoanalytic thought. While some from the psychoanalytic community have attempted a form of rapprochement in recent decades, attachment theory is best viewed as a freestanding model of human development that shares many tenets with cognitive and behavioral theories and, to a lesser extent, psychoanalytic theory (see Chapter 1).

8. Did Bowlby say that parental separation causes psychopathy/ antisocial behavior?

Yes and no. Bowlby's original hypothesis from his clinical observations was that a mother who was absent or emotionally inept served as an etiological cause for criminal behavior, including the development of "affectionless characters." However, he recognized that his clinical observations were limited by the fact that they identified individuals with criminal behavior and looked backward. In 1956, he published a study that identified children experiencing parental separation early in life and examined how they appeared later in childhood. To his surprise, children undergoing parental separation were no more likely to display conduct problems than children without such separations. In reporting the results, Bowlby explicitly walked back his earlier hypothesis, going so far as to cite his previous observations and calling them "mistaken." He never again made this argument (see Chapter 1). Research since Bowlby demonstrates that infant attachment behavior is weakly related to callous–unemotional traits (see Chapter 8 in this volume).

9. Is reactive attachment disorder (RAD) a real condition?

Yes, although it was not derived from attachment theory or research. RAD was first defined in the *Diagnostic and Statistical Manual of Mental Disorders* (3rd ed.; *DSM-III*; American Psychiatric Association, 1980) and described nonorganic failure to thrive among infants. Only with the *DSM-5* (American Psychiatric Association, 2013) did the RAD diagnosis correspond with attachment theory and research. Even then, the condition describes a complete lack of discernible attachment behavior toward a caregiver and is exceptionally rare in community practice (see Chapter 6, this volume). Unfortunately, many people believe RAD to be the display of severe conduct problems secondary to maltreatment. This conceptualization never coincided with the diagnostic criteria defined within the *DSM* or the *International Statistical Classification of Diseases and Related Health Problems* (e.g., World Health Organization, 2019) and was popularized by clinicians who promoted dangerous and unethical forms of treatment (see Chapter 10, this volume).

10. Can children with maltreatment histories form attachments with new caregivers?

Yes. A rather sizable empirical literature documents that maltreated children living in foster or adoptive homes typically form attachment relationships with their new caregivers. This finding is well established among adoptive infants and is even documented with youth who first came to live with their new families as adolescents (see Chapter 6). This misconception among those unfamiliar with attachment theory is common as they confuse significant behavioral problems directed toward a caregiver with a lack of attachment. In actuality, the child may demonstrate attachment behavior toward a caregiver under moments of distress and concurrently struggle with behavior problems that significantly strain the parent–child relationship (see Question 2).

11. Are attachment-based interventions empirically supported?

Yes and no. A number of interventions designed for use with infants and young children are demonstrated in multiple clinical trials to improve outcomes. However, in these instances, the outcomes of interest are typically attachment behavior or caregiver sensitivity, not a diagnosable condition (see Chapter 6). There are no current attachment-based interventions with school-age children that one may consider empirically supported (see Chapter 7), and the available evidence for attachment-based interventions with adolescents is promising but not overwhelming (see Chapter 8). With adults, there is promising evidence for the efficacy of mentalization-based therapy and emotion-focused couple therapy, which both have roots in attachment theory (see Chapter 9).

12. What is "attachment therapy?"

"Attachment therapy" is not a unified treatment approach but rather a collection of different techniques that were promoted by clinicians with relatively little knowledge or training in attachment theory and research. They believed, erroneously, that attachment theory suggests that children who experience abuse and neglect early in life are unable to form attachments with caregivers because they have developed defense mechanisms, and as a result they develop severe conduct problems. The goal of their treatment techniques, then, was to break through the child's defenses and thereby create the ability for the child to form an attachment with the current caregiver, often an adoptive parent. These techniques commonly included coerced holding of the child, intentional provocation of anger, age regression (i.e., treating the child as if significantly younger in age), and power-assertive parenting techniques, such as withholding food or water as punishment for misbehavior. After the deaths and injuries of children, attachment researchers led the charge in showing how these techniques and their underlying rationale were not supported by attachment theory or research. Multiple professional organizations condemned these ideas, and it is rare now in contemporary practice to hear clinicians speak about providing "attachment therapy" (see Chapter 10).

References

Abrams, K. Y., Rifkin, A., & Hesse, E. (2006). Examining the role of parental frightened/frightening subtypes in predicting disorganized attachment within a brief observational procedure. *Development and Psychopathology, 18*(2), 345–361. https://doi.org/10.1017/S0954579406060184

Adam, K. S., Sheldon-Keller, A. E., & West, M. (1996). Attachment organization and history of suicidal behavior in clinical adolescents. *Journal of Consulting and Clinical Psychology, 64*(2), 264–272. https://doi.org/10.1037/0022-006X.64.2.264

Ahnert, L. (2021). Attachment to child care providers. In R. A. Thompson, J. A. Simpson, & L. J. Berlin (Eds.), *Attachment: The fundamental questions* (pp. 31–38). Guilford Press.

Ahnert, L., Pinquart, M., & Lamb, M. E. (2006). Security of children's relationships with nonparental care providers: A meta-analysis. *Child Development, 77*(3), 664–679. https://doi.org/10.1111/j.1467-8624.2006.00896.x

Ainsworth, M., Boston, M., Bowlby, J., & Rosenbluth, D. (1956). The effects of mother–child separation: A follow-up study. *The British Journal of Medical Psychology, 2–9*(3-4), 211–247. https://doi.org/10.1111/j.2044-8341.1956.tb00915.x

Ainsworth, M. D. S. (1964). Patterns of attachment behavior shown by the infant in interaction with his mother. *Merrill-Palmer Quarterly, 10*, 51–58.

Ainsworth, M. D. S. (1967). *Infancy in Uganda: Infant care and the growth of love*. Johns Hopkins University Press.

Ainsworth, M. D. S. (1989). Attachments beyond infancy. *American Psychologist, 44*(4), 709–716. https://doi.org/10.1037/0003-066X.44.4.709

Ainsworth, M. D. S., Bell, S. M., & Stayton, D. J. (1972). Individual differences in the development of some attachment behaviors. *Merrill-Palmer Quarterly, 18*, 123–143.

Ainsworth, M. D. S., Blehar, M. C., Waters, E., & Wall, S. N. (2015). *Patterns of attachment: A psychological study of the strange situation.* Taylor & Francis. https://doi.org/10.4324/9780203758045 (Original work published 1978)

Ainsworth, M. D. S., & Bowlby, J. (1953). *Research strategy in the study of mother–child separation*. Courrier de la Centre International de l'Enfance.

Ainsworth, M. D. S., & Bowlby, J. (1991). An ethological approach to personality development. *American Psychologist, 46*(4), 333–341. https://doi.org/10.1037/0003-066X.46.4.333

Ainsworth, M. D. S., & Wittig, B. A. (1969). Attachment and exploratory behavior of one-year-olds in a strange situation. In B. M. Foss (Ed.), *Determinants of infant behavior* (Vol. 4, pp. 113–136). Methuen.

Allen, B. (2011a). The use and abuse of attachment theory in clinical practice with maltreated children, part I: Diagnosis and assessment. *Trauma, Violence & Abuse, 12*(1), 3–12. https://doi.org/10.1177/1524838010386811

Allen, B. (2011b). The use and abuse of attachment theory in clinical practice with maltreated children, part II: Treatment. *Trauma, Violence & Abuse, 12*(1), 13–22. https://doi.org/10.1177/1524838010386974

Allen, B. (2016). A RADical idea: A call to eliminate "attachment disorder" and "attachment therapy" from the clinical lexicon. *Evidence-Based Practice in Child and Adolescent Mental Health, 1*(1), 60–71. https://doi.org/10.1080/23794925.2016.1172945

Allen, B. (2018). Misperceptions of reactive attachment disorder persist: Poor methods and unsupported conclusions. *Research in Developmental Disabilities, 77*, 24–29. https://doi.org/10.1016/j.ridd.2018.03.012

Allen, B., Bendixsen, B., Babcock Fenerci, R., & Green, J. (2018). Assessing disorganized attachment representations: A systematic psychometric review and meta-analysis of the Manchester Child Attachment Story Task. *Attachment & Human Development, 20*(6), 553–577. https://doi.org/10.1080/14616734.2018.1429477

Allen, B., & Brown, M. P. (2021). *Attachment security as an outcome of trauma-focused cognitive–behavioral therapy among maltreated children with posttraumatic stress* [Unpublished manuscript]. Penn State University School of Medicine.

Allen, B., Cramer, R. J., Harris, P. B., & Rufino, K. A. (2013). Borderline personality symptomatology as a mediator of the link between child maltreatment and adult suicide potential. *Archives of Suicide Research, 17*(1), 41–51. https://doi.org/10.1080/13811118.2013.748413

Allen, B., & Crosby, J. W. (2014). Treatment beliefs and techniques of clinicians serving child maltreatment survivors. *Child Maltreatment, 19*(1), 49–60. https://doi.org/10.1177/1077559513518097

Allen, B., Gharagozloo, L., & Johnson, J. C. (2012). Clinician knowledge and utilization of empirically-supported treatments for maltreated children. *Child Maltreatment, 17*(1), 11–21. https://doi.org/10.1177/1077559511426333

Allen, B., & Lauterbach, D. (2007). Personality characteristics of adult survivors of childhood trauma. *Journal of Traumatic Stress, 20*(4), 587–595. https://doi.org/10.1002/jts.20195

Allen, B., & Schuengel, C. (2020). Attachment disorders diagnosed by community practitioners: A replication and extension. *Child and Adolescent Mental Health, 25*(1), 4–10. https://doi.org/10.1111/camh.12338

Allen, B., Timmer, S. G., & Urquiza, A. J. (2014). Parent–Child Interaction Therapy as an attachment-based intervention: Theoretical rationale and pilot data with adopted children. *Children and Youth Services Review, 47*, 334–341. https://doi.org/10.1016/j.childyouth.2014.10.009

Allen, B., Timmer, S. G., & Urquiza, A. J. (2016). Parent–Child Interaction Therapy for sexual concerns of maltreated children: A preliminary investigation. *Child Abuse & Neglect, 56*, 80–88. https://doi.org/10.1016/j.chiabu.2016.04.008

Allen, J. P. (2021). Beyond stability: Toward understanding the development of attachment beyond childhood. In R. A. Thompson, J. A. Simpson, & L. J. Berlin (Eds.), *Attachment: The fundamental questions* (pp. 161–168). Guilford Press.

Allen, J. P., Grande, L., Tan, J., & Loeb, E. (2018). Parent and peer predictors of change in attachment security from adolescence to adulthood. *Child Development, 89*(4), 1120–1132. https://doi.org/10.1111/cdev.12840

Allen, J. P., McElhaney, K. B., Land, D. J., Kuperminc, G. P., Moore, C. W., O'Beirne-Kelly, H., & Kilmer, S. L. (2003). A secure base in adolescence: Markers of attachment security in the mother–adolescent relationship. *Child Development, 74*(1), 292–307. https://doi.org/10.1111/1467-8624.t01-1-00536

Allen, J. P., & Miga, E. M. (2010). Attachment in adolescence: A move to the level of emotion regulation. *Journal of Social and Personal Relationships, 27*(2), 181–190. https://doi.org/10.1177/0265407509360898

Allen, J. P., Porter, M., McFarland, C., McElhaney, K. B., & Marsh, P. (2007). The relation of attachment security to adolescents' paternal and peer relationships, depression, and externalizing behavior. *Child Development, 78*(4), 1222–1239. https://doi.org/10.1111/j.1467-8624.2007.01062.x

Allen, J. P., & Tan, J. S. (2016). The multiple facets of attachment in adolescence. In J. Cassidy & P. R. Shaver (Eds.), *Handbook of attachment: Theory, research, and clinical implications* (3rd ed., pp. 399–415). Guilford Press.

Almas, A. N., Papp, L. J., Woodbury, M. R., Nelson, C. A., Zeanah, C. H., & Fox, N. A. (2020). The impact of caregiving disruptions of previously institutionalized children on multiple outcomes in late childhood. *Child Development, 91*(1), 96–109. https://doi.org/10.1111/cdev.13169

American Psychiatric Association. (1980). *Diagnostic and statistical manual of mental disorders* (3rd ed.).

American Psychiatric Association. (1987). *Diagnostic and statistical manual of mental disorders* (3rd ed., rev.).

American Psychiatric Association. (1994). *Diagnostic and statistical manual of mental disorders* (4th ed.).

American Psychiatric Association. (2000). *Diagnostic and statistical manual of mental disorders* (4th ed., text rev.).

American Psychiatric Association. (2013). *Diagnostic and statistical manual of mental disorders* (5th ed.). https://doi.org/10.1176/appi.books.9780890425596

Arnott, B., & Meins, E. (2007). Links among antenatal attachment representations, postnatal mind-mindedness, and infant attachment security: A preliminary study of mothers and fathers. *Bulletin of the Menninger Clinic, 71*(2), 132–149. https://doi.org/10.1521/bumc.2007.71.2.132

Association for the Treatment and Training in the Attachment of Children. (2007). *Coercion in treatment* [White paper]. Retrieved March 5, 2009, from http://www.attach.org/WhitePaper.pdf

A-Tjak, J. G. L., Morina, N., Boendermaker, W. J., Topper, M., & Emmelkamp, P. M. G. (2020). Explicit and implicit attachment and the outcomes of acceptance and commitment therapy and cognitive behavioral therapy for depression. *BMC Psychiatry, 20*(1), Article 155. https://doi.org/10.1186/s12888-020-02547-7

Atkinson, L. (2019). Reactive attachment disorder and attachment theory from infancy to adolescence: Review, integration, and expansion. *Attachment & Human Development, 21*(2), 205–217. https://doi.org/10.1080/14616734.2018.1499214

Atkinson, L., Niccols, A., Paglia, A., Coolbear, J., Parker, K. C. H., Poulton, L., Guger, S., & Sitarenios, G. (2000). A meta-analysis of time between maternal sensitivity and attachment assessments: Implications for internal working models in infancy/toddlerhood. *Journal of Social and Personal Relationships, 17*, 791–810. https://doi.org/10.1177/0265407500176005

Atkinson, L., Paglia, A., Coolbear, J., Niccols, A., Parker, K. C. H., & Guger, S. (2000). Attachment security: A meta-analysis of maternal mental health correlates. *Clinical Psychology Review, 20*(8), 1019–1040. https://doi.org/10.1016/S0272-7358(99)00023-9

Bakermans-Kranenburg, M. J., & van IJzendoorn, M. H. (2009). The first 10,000 Adult Attachment Interviews: Distributions of adult attachment representations in clinical and non-clinical groups. *Attachment & Human Development, 11*(3), 223–263. https://doi.org/10.1080/14616730902814762

Bakermans-Kranenburg, M. J., & van IJzendoorn, M. H. (2016). Attachment, parenting, and genetics. In J. Cassidy & P. R. Shaver (Eds.), *Handbook of attachment: Theory, research, and clinical implications* (3rd ed., pp. 155–179). Guilford Press.

Bakermans-Kranenburg, M. J., van IJzendoorn, M. H., & Juffer, F. (2003). Less is more: Meta-analyses of sensitivity and attachment interventions in early childhood. *Psychological Bulletin, 129*(2), 195–215. https://doi.org/10.1037/0033-2909.129.2.195

Ballespí, S., Vives, J., Sharp, C., Tobar, A., & Barrantes-Vidal, N. (2019). Hypermentalizing in social anxiety: Evidence for a context-dependent relationship.

Frontiers in Psychology, *10*, Article 1501. https://doi.org/10.3389/fpsyg.2019.01501

Barlow, J., Sleed, M., & Midgley, N. (2021). Enhancing parental reflective functioning through early dyadic interventions: A systematic review and meta-analysis. *Infant Mental Health Journal*, *42*(1), 21–34. https://doi.org/10.1002/imhj.21896

Barnicot, K., & Crawford, M. (2019). Dialectical behaviour therapy *v.* mentalisation-based therapy for borderline personality disorder. *Psychological Medicine*, *49*(12), 2060–2068. https://doi.org/10.1017/S0033291718002878

Barone, L. (2003). Developmental protective and risk factors in borderline personality disorder: A study using the Adult Attachment Interview. *Attachment & Human Development*, *5*(1), 64–77. https://doi.org/10.1080/1461673031000078634

Barry, R. A., Kochanska, G., & Philibert, R. A. (2008). G × E interaction in the organization of attachment: Mothers' responsiveness as a moderator of children's genotypes. *Journal of Child Psychology and Psychiatry, and Allied Disciplines*, *49*(12), 1313–1320. https://doi.org/10.1111/j.1469-7610.2008.01935.x

Bartholomew, K., & Horowitz, L. M. (1991). Attachment styles among young adults: A test of a four-category model. *Journal of Personality and Social Psychology*, *61*(2), 226–244. https://doi.org/10.1037/0022-3514.61.2.226

Bateman, A., Constantinou, M. P., Fonagy, P., & Holzer, S. (2021). Eight-year prospective follow-up of mentalization-based treatment versus structured clinical management for people with borderline personality disorder. *Personality Disorders*, *12*(4), 291–299. https://doi.org/10.1037/per0000422

Bateman, A., & Fonagy, P. (1999). Effectiveness of partial hospitalization in the treatment of borderline personality disorder: A randomized controlled trial. *The American Journal of Psychiatry*, *156*(10), 1563–1569. https://doi.org/10.1176/ajp.156.10.1563

Bateman, A., & Fonagy, P. (2004). *Psychotherapy for borderline personality disorder: Mentalization based treatment*. Oxford University Press. https://doi.org/10.1093/med:psych/9780198527664.001.0001

Bateman, A., & Fonagy, P. (2008). 8-year follow-up of patients treated for borderline personality disorder: Mentalization-based treatment versus treatment as usual. *The American Journal of Psychiatry*, *165*(5), 631–638. https://doi.org/10.1176/appi.ajp.2007.07040636

Bates, B. C., & Dozier, M. (2002). The importance of maternal state of mind regarding attachment and infant age at placement to foster mother's representations of their foster infants. *Infant Mental Health Journal*, *23*(4), 417–431. https://doi.org/10.1002/imhj.10022

Beck, A. T. (1979). *Cognitive therapy of depression*. Guilford Press.

Becker-Stoll, F., Delius, A., & Scheitenberger, S. (2001). Adolescents' nonverbal emotional expressions during negotiation of a disagreement with their mothers: An attachment approach. *International Journal of Behavioral Development*, *25*(4), 344–353. https://doi.org/10.1080/01650250143000102

Becker-Weidman, A. (2009). Effects of early maltreatment on development: A descriptive study using the Vineland Adaptive Behavior Scales-II. *Child Welfare, 88*(2), 137–161.

Bell, S. M., & Ainsworth, M. D. S. (1972). Infant crying and maternal responsiveness. *Child Development, 43*(4), 1171–1190. https://doi.org/10.2307/1127506

Belsky, J. (1996). Parent, infant, and social-contextual determinants of attachment security. *Developmental Psychology, 32*(5), 905–913. https://doi.org/10.1037/0012-1649.32.5.905

Belsky, J. (1997). Theory testing, effect-size evaluation, and differential susceptibility to rearing influence: The case of mothering and attachment. *Child Development, 68*(4), 598–600. https://doi.org/10.2307/1132110

Belsky, J. (2005). Attachment theory and research in ecological perspective: Insights from the Pennsylvania Infant and Family Development Project and the NICHD Study of Early Child Care. In K. E. Grossmann, K. Grossmann, & E. Waters (Eds.), *Attachment from infancy to adulthood: The major longitudinal studies* (pp. 71–97). Guilford Press.

Belsky, J., Campbell, S. B., Cohn, J. F., & Moore, G. (1996). Instability of infant–parent attachment security. *Developmental Psychology, 32*(5), 921–924. https://doi.org/10.1037/0012-1649.32.5.921

Berger, L. E., Jodl, K. M., Allen, J. P., McElhaney, K. B., & Kuperminc, G. P. (2005). When adolescents disagree with others about their symptoms: Differences in attachment organization as an explanation of discrepancies between adolescent, parent, and peer reports of behavior problems. *Development and Psychopathology, 17*(2), 509–528. https://doi.org/10.1017/S0954579405050248

Bernard, K., Dozier, M., Bick, J., Lewis-Morrarty, E., Lindhiem, O., & Carlson, E. (2012). Enhancing attachment organization among maltreated children: Results of a randomized clinical trial. *Child Development, 83*(2), 623–636. https://doi.org/10.1111/j.1467-8624.2011.01712.x

Bernard, K., Hostinar, C. E., & Dozier, M. (2015). Intervention effects on diurnal cortisol rhythms of Child Protective Services-referred infants in early childhood: Preschool follow-up results of a randomized clinical trial. *JAMA Pediatrics, 169*(2), 112–119. https://doi.org/10.1001/jamapediatrics.2014.2369

Bernard, K., Nissim, G., Vaccaro, S., Harris, J. L., & Lindhiem, O. (2018). Association between maternal depression and maternal sensitivity from birth to 12 months: A meta-analysis. *Attachment & Human Development, 20*(6), 578–599. https://doi.org/10.1080/14616734.2018.1430839

Bernecker, S. L., Constantino, M. J., Atkinson, L. R., Bagby, R. M., Ravitz, P., & McBride, C. (2016). Attachment style as a moderating influence on the efficacy of cognitive-behavioral and interpersonal psychotherapy for depression: A failure to replicate. *Psychotherapy, 53*(1), 22–33. https://doi.org/10.1037/pst0000036

Bernecker, S. L., Levy, K. N., & Ellison, W. D. (2014). A meta-analysis of the relation between patient adult attachment style and the working alliance.

Psychotherapy Research, 24(1), 12–24. https://doi.org/10.1080/10503307.2013.809561

Bernier, A., & Dozier, M. (2003). Bridging the attachment transmission gap: The role of maternal mind-mindedness. *International Journal of Behavioral Development, 27*(4), 355–365. https://doi.org/10.1080/01650250244000399

Bernier, A., Matte-Gagné, C., Bélanger, M.-E., & Whipple, N. (2014). Taking stock of two decades of attachment transmission gap: Broadening the assessment of maternal behavior. *Child Development, 85*(5), 1852–1865. https://doi.org/10.1111/cdev.12236

Bettelheim, B. (1967). *The empty fortress: Infantile autism and the birth of the self.* The Free Press.

Bick, J., & Dozier, M. (2013). The effectiveness of an attachment-based intervention in promoting foster mothers' sensitivity toward foster infants. *Infant Mental Health Journal, 34*(2), 95–103. https://doi.org/10.1002/imhj.21373

Bick, J., Dozier, M., & Perkins, E. (2012). Convergence between attachment classifications and natural reunion behavior among children and parents in a child care setting. *Attachment & Human Development, 14*(1), 1–10. https://doi.org/10.1080/14616734.2012.636645

Bigelow, A. E., & DeCoste, C. (2003). Sensitivity to social contingency from mothers and strangers in 2-, 4- and 6-month-old infants. *Infancy, 4*(1), 111–140. https://doi.org/10.1207/S15327078IN0401_6

Birnie, C., McClure, M. J., Lydon, J. E., & Holmberg, D. (2009). Attachment avoidance and commitment aversion: A script for relationship failure. *Personal Relationships, 16*(1), 79–97. https://doi.org/10.1111/j.1475-6811.2009.01211.x

Bohn, A., & Berntsen, D. (2013). The future is bright and predictable: The development of prospective life stories across childhood and adolescence. *Developmental Psychology, 49*(7), 1232–1241. https://doi.org/10.1037/a0030212

Bonache, H., Gonzalez-Mendez, R., & Krahé, B. (2017). Romantic attachment, conflict resolution styles, and teen dating violence victimization. *Journal of Youth and Adolescence, 46*(9), 1905–1917. https://doi.org/10.1007/s10964-017-0635-2

Booth, A. T., Macdonald, J. A., & Youssef, G. J. (2018). Contextual stress and maternal sensitivity: A meta-analytic review of stress associations with the Maternal Behavior Q-Sort in observational studies. *Developmental Review, 48*, 145–177. https://doi.org/10.1016/j.dr.2018.02.002

Booth-LaForce, C., Groh, A. M., Burchinal, M. R., Roisman, G. I., Owen, M. T., & Cox, M. J. (2014). The Adult Attachment Interview: Psychometrics, stability and change from infancy and developmental origins: V. Caregiving and contextual sources of continuity and change in attachment security from infancy to late adolescence. *Monographs of the Society for Research in Child Development, 79*(3), 67–84. https://doi.org/10.1111/mono.12114

Borelli, J. L., Goshin, L., Joestl, S., Clark, J., & Byrne, M. W. (2010). Attachment organization in a sample of incarcerated mothers: Distribution of classifications and associations with substance abuse history, depressive symptoms, perceptions of parenting competency and social support. *Attachment & Human Development, 12*(4), 355–374. https://doi.org/10.1080/14616730903416971

Boris, N. W., Zeanah, C. H., & Work Group on Quality Issues. (2005). Practice parameter for the assessment and treatment of children and adolescents with reactive attachment disorder of infancy and early childhood. *Journal of the American Academy of Child and Adolescent Psychiatry, 44*(11), 1206–1219. https://doi.org/10.1097/01.chi.0000177056.41655.ce

Bornstein, M., Arterberry, M., & Mash, C. (2004). Long-term memory for an emotional interpersonal interaction occurring at 5 months of age. *Infancy, 6*(3), 407–416. https://doi.org/10.1207/s15327078in0603_6

Bosmans, G. (2016). Cognitive behaviour therapy for children and adolescents: Can attachment theory contribute to its efficacy? *Clinical Child and Family Psychology Review, 19*(4), 310–328. https://doi.org/10.1007/s10567-016-0212-3

Bosmans, G., Bakermans-Kranenburg, M. J., Vervliet, B., Verhees, M. W. F. T., & van IJzendoorn, M. H. (2020). A learning theory of attachment: Unraveling the black box of attachment development. *Neuroscience and Biobehavioral Reviews, 113*, 287–298. https://doi.org/10.1016/j.neubiorev.2020.03.014

Bosmans, G., Braet, C., & Van Vlierberghe, L. (2010). Attachment and symptoms of psychopathology: Early maladaptive schemas as a cognitive link? *Clinical Psychology & Psychotherapy, 17*(5), 374–385. https://doi.org/10.1002/cpp.667

Bosmans, G., & Kerns, K. A. (2015). Attachment in middle childhood: Progress and prospects. In G. Bosmans & K. A. Kerns (Eds.), *Attachment in middle childhood: Theoretical advances and new directions in an emerging field* (pp. 1–14). Jossey-Bass. https://doi.org/10.1002/cad.20100

Bosmans, G., Van Vlierberghe, L., Bakermans-Kranenburg, M. J., Kobak, R., Hermans, D., & van IJzendoorn, M. H. (2022). Clinical translations of the learning theory of attachment: Attachment-focused intervention strategies for early and middle childhood. *Clinical Child and Family Psychology Review.* https://doi.org/10.1007/s10567-021-00377-x

Bowlby, J. (1940). The influence of early environment in the development of neurosis and neurotic character. *The International Journal of Psycho-Analysis, 21*, 154–178.

Bowlby, J. (1944a). Forty-four juvenile thieves: Their characters and home-life. *The International Journal of Psycho-Analysis, 25*, 19–53.

Bowlby, J. (1944b). Forty-four juvenile thieves: Their characters and home-life (II). *The International Journal of Psycho-Analysis, 25*, 107–128.

Bowlby, J. (1952). *Maternal care and mental health* (2nd ed.). World Health Organization.

Bowlby, J. (1953). Some pathological processes set in train by early mother–child separation. *The Journal of Mental Science, 99*(415), 265–272. https://doi.org/10.1192/bjp.99.415.265

Bowlby, J. (1958). The nature of the child's tie to his mother. *The International Journal of Psycho-Analysis, 39*(5), 350–373.

Bowlby, J. (1960a). Grief and mourning in infancy and early childhood. *The Psychoanalytic Study of the Child, 15*(1), 9–52. https://doi.org/10.1080/00797308.1960.11822566

Bowlby, J. (1960b). Separation anxiety. *The International Journal of Psycho-Analysis, 41*, 89–113.

Bowlby, J. (1973). *Separation: Anxiety and anger*. Basic Books.

Bowlby, J. (1980). *Loss: Sadness and depression*. Basic Books.

Bowlby, J. (1982). *Attachment*. Basic Books. (Original work published 1969)

Bowlby, J. (1988). *A secure base*. Basic Books.

Bowlby, J. (2020). Psychological problems of evacuation. In R. Duschinsky & K. White (Eds.), *Trauma and loss: Key texts from the John Bowlby archives* (pp. 117–133). Routledge. (Original work published ca. 1939–1942)

Bowlby, J. (2020). Loss, detachment, and defense. In R. Duschinsky & K. White (Eds.), *Trauma and loss: Key texts from the John Bowlby archives* (pp. 66–96). Routledge. (Original work published 1962)

Bowlby, J. (2020). The role of the psychotherapist's personal resources in the treatment situation. In R. Duschinsky & K. White (Eds.), *Trauma and loss: Key texts from the John Bowlby archives* (pp. 214–223). Routledge. (Original work published 1985)

Bowlby, J., Ainsworth, M., Boston, M., & Rosenbluth, D. (1956). The effects of mother–child separation: A follow-up study. *British Journal of Medical Psychology, 29*, 169–201.

Bowlby, J., & Robertson, J. (1953). A two-year old goes to hospital. *Proceedings of the Royal Society of Medicine, 46*(6), 425–427. https://doi.org/10.1177/003591575304600603

Bowlby, J., & Smuts, A. (2020). Interview with Alice Smuts. In R. Duschinsky & K. White (Eds.), *Trauma and loss: Key texts from the John Bowlby archives* (pp. 187–213). Routledge. (Original work published 1977)

Branger, M. C. E., Emmen, R. A. G., Woudstra, M. J., Alink, L. R. A., & Mesman, J. (2019). Context matters: Maternal and paternal sensitivity to infants in four settings. *Journal of Family Psychology, 33*(7), 851–856. https://doi.org/10.1037/fam0000562

Brassard, A., & Johnson, S. M. (2016). Couple and family therapy: An attachment perspective. In J. Cassidy & P. R. Shaver (Eds.), *Handbook of attachment: Theory, research, and clinical applications* (3rd ed., pp. 805–823). Guilford Press.

Brennan, K. A., Clark, C. L., & Shaver, P. R. (1998). Self-report measurement of adult attachment: An integrative overview. In J. A. Simpson & W. S. Rholes (Eds.), *Attachment theory and close relationships* (pp. 46–76). Guilford Press.

Brennan, K. A., & Shaver, P. R. (1995). Dimensions of adult attachment, affect regulation, and romantic relationship functioning. *Personality and Social Psychology Bulletin, 21*(3), 267–283. https://doi.org/10.1177/0146167295213008

Bretherton, I. (2003). Mary Ainsworth: Insightful observer and courageous theoretician. In G. A. Kimble & M. Wertheimer (Eds.), *Portraits of pioneers in psychology* (Vol. 5, pp. 317–331). Lawrence Erlbaum Associates and American Psychological Association.

Bretherton, I. (2005). In pursuit of the internal working model construct and its relevance to attachment relationships. In K. E. Grossmann, K. Grossmann, & E. Waters (Eds.), *Attachment from infancy to adulthood: The major longitudinal studies* (pp. 13–47). Guilford Press.

Bretherton, I., & Ainsworth, M. D. S. (1973). Responses of one-year-olds to a stranger in a strange situation. In M. Lewis & L. A. Rosenblum (Eds.), *The origins of fear* (pp. 131–164). Wiley.

Bretherton, I., Ridgeway, D., & Cassidy, J. (1990). Assessing internal working models of the attachment relationship. In M. T. Greenberg, D. Cicchetti, & E. M. Cummings (Eds.), *Attachment in the preschool years: Theory, research, and intervention* (pp. 273–308). University of Chicago Press.

Bronfman, E., Parsons, E., & Lyons-Ruth, K. (1993). *Atypical Maternal Behavior Instrument for Assessment and Classification (AMBIANCE): Manual for coding disrupted affective communication* [Unpublished manuscript]. Cambridge Hospital.

Brown, G. L., Gustafsson, H. C., Mills-Koonce, W. R., & Cox, M. J. (2017). Associations between early caregiving and rural, low-SES, African-American children's representations of attachment relationships. *Attachment & Human Development*, *19*(4), 340–363. https://doi.org/10.1080/14616734.2017.1318935

Brumariu, L. E., & Kerns, K. A. (2010). Parent–child attachment and internalizing symptoms in childhood and adolescence: A review of empirical findings and future directions. *Development and Psychopathology*, *22*(1), 177–203. https://doi.org/10.1017/S0954579409990344

Brumariu, L. E., & Kerns, K. A. (2013). Pathways to anxiety: Contributions of attachment history, temperament, peer competence, and ability to manage intense emotions. *Child Psychiatry and Human Development*, *44*(4), 504–515. https://doi.org/10.1007/s10578-012-0345-7

Brumariu, L. E., Madigan, S., Giuseppone, K. R., Movahed Abtahi, M., & Kerns, K. A. (2018). The Security Scale as a measure of attachment: Meta-analytic evidence of validity. *Attachment & Human Development*, *20*(6), 600–625. https://doi.org/10.1080/14616734.2018.1433217

Brumariu, L. E., Owen, M. T., Dyer, N., & Lyons-Ruth, K. (2020). Developmental pathways to BPD-related features in adolescence: Infancy to age 15. *Journal of Personality Disorders*, *34*(Suppl. B), 104–129. https://doi.org/10.1521/pedi_2020_34_480

Buchman-Schmitt, J. M., Chiurliza, B., Chu, C., Michaels, M. S., & Joiner, T. E., Jr. (2014). Suicidality in adolescent populations: A review of the extant literature through the lens of the interpersonal theory of suicide. *International Journal of Behavioral and Consultation Therapy*, *9*(3), 26–34. https://doi.org/10.1037/h0101637

Buckner, J. D., Lopez, C., Dunkel, S., & Joiner, T. E., Jr. (2008). Behavior management training for the treatment of reactive attachment disorder. *Child Maltreatment, 13*(3), 289–297. https://doi.org/10.1177/1077559508318396

Burgess Moser, M., Johnson, S. M., Dalgleish, T. L., Lafontaine, M.-F., Wiebe, S. A., & Tasca, G. A. (2016). Changes in relationship-specific attachment in emotionally-focused couple therapy. *Journal of Marital and Family Therapy, 42*(2), 231–245. https://doi.org/10.1111/jmft.12139

Busch, A. L., Cowan, P. A., & Cowan, C. P. (2008). Unresolved loss in the Adult Attachment Interview: Implications for marital and parenting relationships. *Development and Psychopathology, 20*(2), 717–735. https://doi.org/10.1017/S0954579408000345

Cadman, T., Diamond, P. R., & Fearon, P. (2018). Reassessing the validity of the attachment Q-sort: An updated meta-analysis. *Infant and Child Development, 27*(1), Article e2034. https://doi.org/10.1002/icd.2034

Cappelletty, G. G., Brown, M. M., & Shumate, S. E. (2005). Correlates of the Randolph Attachment Disorder Questionnaire (RADQ) in a sample of children in foster care. *Child & Adolescent Social Work Journal, 22*(1), 71–84. https://doi.org/10.1007/s10560-005-2556-2

Card, N. A., & Little, T. D. (2006). Proactive and reactive aggression in childhood and adolescence: A meta-analysis of differential relations with psychosocial adjustment. *International Journal of Behavioral Development, 30*(5), 466–480. https://doi.org/10.1177/0165025406071904

Carlson, E. A. (1998). A prospective longitudinal study of attachment disorganization/disorientation. *Child Development, 69*(4), 1107–1128. https://doi.org/10.1111/j.1467-8624.1998.tb06163.x

Carlson, E. A., Egeland, B., & Sroufe, L. A. (2009). A prospective investigation of the development of borderline personality symptoms. *Development and Psychopathology, 21*(4), 1311–1334. https://doi.org/10.1017/S0954579409990174

Carlson, V., Cicchetti, D., Barnett, D., & Braunwald, K. (1989). Disorganized/disoriented attachment relationships in maltreated infants. *Developmental Psychology, 25*(4), 525–531. https://doi.org/10.1037/0012-1649.25.4.525

Cassidy, J. (2016). The nature of the child's ties. In J. Cassidy & P. R. Shaver (Eds.), *Handbook of attachment: Theory, research, and clinical applications* (3rd ed., pp. 3–24). Guilford Press.

Cassidy, J., Brett, B. E., Gross, J. T., Stern, J. A., Martin, D. R., Mohr, J. J., & Woodhouse, S. S. (2017). Circle of Security–Parenting: A randomized controlled trial in Head Start. *Development and Psychopathology, 29*(2), 651–673. https://doi.org/10.1017/S0954579417000244

Cassidy, J., & Kobak, R. (1988). Avoidance and its relation to other defensive processes. In J. Belsky & T. Neworski (Eds.), *Clinical implications of attachment* (pp. 300–323). Lawrence Erlbaum.

Cassidy, J., Marvin, R. S., & the MacArthur Attachment Working Group. (1992). *Attachment organization in preschool children: Coding guidelines* (4th ed.) [Unpublished manuscript]. University of Virginia.

Cassidy, J., Woodhouse, S. S., Sherman, L. J., Stupica, B., & Lejuez, C. W. (2011). Enhancing infant attachment security: An examination of treatment efficacy and differential susceptibility. *Development and Psychopathology, 23*(1), 131–148. https://doi.org/10.1017/S0954579410000696

Chaffin, M., Hanson, R., Saunders, B. E., Nichols, T., Barnett, D., Zeanah, C., Berliner, L., Egeland, B., Newman, E., Lyon, T., LeTourneau, E., & Miller-Perrin, C. (2006). Report of the APSAC task force on attachment therapy, reactive attachment disorder, and attachment problems. *Child Maltreatment, 11*(1), 76–89. https://doi.org/10.1177/1077559505283699

Chaffin, M., Silovsky, J. F., Funderburk, B., Valle, L. A., Brestan, E. V., Balachova, T., Jackson, S., Lensgraf, J., & Bonner, B. L. (2004). Parent–Child Interaction Therapy with physically abusive parents: Efficacy for reducing future abuse reports. *Journal of Consulting and Clinical Psychology, 72*(3), 500–510. https://doi.org/10.1037/0022-006X.72.3.500

Chisholm, K. (1998). A three-year follow-up of attachment and indiscriminate friendliness in children adopted from Romanian orphanages. *Child Development, 69*(4), 1092–1106. https://doi.org/10.1111/j.1467-8624.1998.tb06162.x

Chisholm, K., Carter, M. C., Ames, E. W., & Morison, S. J. (1995). Attachment security and indiscriminately friendly behavior in children adopted from Romanian orphanages. *Development and Psychopathology, 7*(2), 283–294. https://doi.org/10.1017/S0954579400006507

Cicchetti, D. (1984). The emergence of developmental psychopathology. *Child Development, 55*(1), 1–7. https://doi.org/10.2307/1129830

Cicchetti, D., & Rogosch, F. A. (1996). Equifinality and multifinality in developmental psychopathology. *Development and Psychopathology, 8*(4), 597–600. https://doi.org/10.1017/S0954579400007318

Cicchetti, D., Rogosch, F. A., Toth, S. L., & Sturge-Apple, M. L. (2011). Normalizing the development of cortisol regulation in maltreated infants through preventive interventions. *Development and Psychopathology, 23*(3), 789–800. https://doi.org/10.1017/S0954579411000307

Cline, F. W. (1979). *Understanding and treating the severely disturbed child.* EC Publications.

Cline, F. W. (1992). *Hope for high risk and rage filled children*. EC Publications.

Colonnesi, C., Draijer, E. M., Jan J M Stams, G., Van der Bruggen, C. O., Bögels, S. M., & Noom, M. J. (2011). The relation between insecure attachment and child anxiety: A meta-analytic review. *Journal of Clinical Child and Adolescent Psychology, 40*(4), 630–645. https://doi.org/10.1080/15374416.2011.581623

Connell, D. B. (1977). *Individual differences in attachment behavior: Long-term stability and relationships to language development* [Unpublished doctoral dissertation]. Syracuse University.

Cooke, J. E., Kochendorfer, L. B., Stuart-Parrigon, K. L., Koehn, A. J., & Kerns, K. A. (2019). Parent–child attachment and children's experience and regulation of emotion: A meta-analytic review. *Emotion, 19*(6), 1103–1126. https://doi.org/10.1037/emo0000504

Cooke, J. E., Stuart-Parrigon, K. L., Movahed-Abtahi, M., Koehn, A. J., & Kerns, K. A. (2016). Children's emotion understanding and mother–child attachment: A meta-analysis. *Emotion, 16*(8), 1102–1106. https://doi.org/10.1037/emo0000221

Coppola, G., Vaughn, B. E., Cassibba, R., & Costantini, A. (2006). The attachment script representation procedure in an Italian sample: Associations with adult attachment interview scales and with maternal sensitivity. *Attachment & Human Development, 8*(3), 209–219. https://doi.org/10.1080/14616730600856065

Crowell, J. A. (2021). The Adult Attachment Interview: A guide for new researchers and research consumers. In E. Waters, B. E. Vaughn, & H. S. Waters (Eds.), *Measuring attachment: Developmental assessment across the lifespan* (pp. 297–337). Guilford Press.

Crowell, J. A., Treboux, D., Gao, Y., Fyffe, C., Pan, H., & Waters, E. (2002). Assessing secure base behavior in adulthood: Development of a measure, links to adult attachment representation and relations to couples' communication and reports of relationships. *Developmental Psychology, 38*(5), 679–693. https://doi.org/10.1037/0012-1649.38.5.679

Crowell, J. A., & Waters, E. (1994). Bowlby's theory grown up: The role of attachment in adult love relationships. *Psychological Inquiry, 5*(1), 31–34. https://doi.org/10.1207/s15327965pli0501_4

Cyr, C., Euser, E. M., Bakermans-Kranenburg, M. J., & van IJzendoorn, M. H. (2010). Attachment security and disorganization in maltreating and high-risk families: A series of meta-analyses. *Development and Psychopathology, 22*(1), 87–108. https://doi.org/10.1017/S0954579409990289

Dadds, M. R., Gale, N., Godbee, M., Moul, C., Pasalich, D. S., Fink, E., & Hawes, D. J. (2016). Expression and regulation of attachment-related emotions in children with conduct problems and callous-unemotional traits. *Child Psychiatry and Human Development, 47*(4), 647–656. https://doi.org/10.1007/s10578-015-0598-z

Dadds, M. R., & Tully, L. A. (2019). What is it to discipline a child: What should it be? A reanalysis of time-out from the perspective of child mental health, attachment, and trauma. *American Psychologist, 74*(7), 794–808. https://doi.org/10.1037/amp0000449

Dagan, O., Facompré, C. R., Nivison, M. D., Roisman, G. I., & Bernard, K. (2020). Preoccupied and dismissing representations are differentially associated with anxiety in adolescence and adulthood: A meta-analysis. *Clinical Psychological Science, 8*(4), 614–640. https://doi.org/10.1177/2167702620917455

Dagan, O., Groh, A. M., Madigan, S., & Bernard, K. (2021). A lifespan development theory of insecure attachment and internalizing symptoms: Integrating meta-analytic evidence via a testable evolutionary mis/match hypothesis. *Brain Sciences, 11*(9), Article 1226. https://doi.org/10.3390/brainsci11091226

Dagan, O., Schuengel, C., Verhage, M. L., van IJzendoorn, M. H., Sagi-Schwartz, A., Madigan, S., Duschinsky, R., Roisman, G. I., Bernard, K., Bakermans-Kranenburg, M., Bureau, J.-F., Volling, B. L., Wong, M. S., Colonnesi, C.,

Brown, G. L., Eiden, R. D., Pasco Fearon, R. M., Oosterman, M., Aviezer, O., Cummings, E. M., & The Collaboration on Attachment to Multiple Parents and Outcomes Synthesis. (2021). Configurations of mother–child and father–child attachment as predictors of internalizing and externalizing behavioral problems: An individual participant data (IPD) meta-analysis. *New Directions for Child and Adolescent Development, 2021*(180), 67–94. https://doi.org/10.1002/cad.20450

Davila, J. (2003). Attachment processes in couple therapy: Informing behavioral models. In S. M. Johnson & V. E. Whiffen (Eds.), *Attachment processes in couple and family therapy* (pp. 124–143). Guilford Press.

De Wolff, M. S., & van IJzendoorn, M. H. (1997). Sensitivity and attachment: A meta-analysis on parental antecedents of infant attachment. *Child Development, 68*(4), 571–591. https://doi.org/10.1111/j.1467-8624.1997.tb04218.x

Del Giudice, M. (2011). Sex differences in romantic attachment: A meta-analysis. *Personality and Social Psychology Bulletin, 37*(2), 193–214. https://doi.org/10.1177/0146167210392789

Deneault, A.-A., Bakermans-Kranenburg, M. J., Groh, A. M., Fearon, P. R. M., & Madigan, S. (2021). Child–father attachment in early childhood and behavior problems: A meta-analysis. *New Directions for Child and Adolescent Development, 2021*(180), 43–66. https://doi.org/10.1002/cad.20434

Diamond, G. S., Diamond, G. M., & Levy, S. A. (2014). *Attachment-Based Family Therapy for depressed adolescents*. American Psychological Association. https://doi.org/10.1037/14296-000

Diamond, G. S., Kobak, R. R., Krauthamer Ewing, E. S., Levy, S. A., Herres, J. L., Russon, J. M., & Gallop, R. J. (2019). A randomized controlled trial: Attachment-based family and nondirective supportive treatments for youth who are suicidal. *Journal of the American Academy of Child & Adolescent Psychiatry, 58*(7), 721–731. https://doi.org/10.1016/j.jaac.2018.10.006

Diamond, G. S., Reis, B. F., Diamond, G. M., Siqueland, L., & Isaacs, L. (2002). Attachment-Based Family Therapy for depressed adolescents: A treatment development study. *Journal of the American Academy of Child & Adolescent Psychiatry, 41*(10), 1190–1196. https://doi.org/10.1097/00004583-200210000-00008

Diamond, G. S., Wintersteen, M. B., Brown, G. K., Diamond, G. M., Gallop, R., Shelef, K., & Levy, S. (2010). Attachment-Based Family Therapy for adolescents with suicidal ideation: A randomized controlled trial. *Journal of the American Academy of Child & Adolescent Psychiatry, 49*(2), 122–131.

Diamond, L. M., Fagundes, C. P., & Butterworth, M. R. (2012). Attachment style, vagal tone, and empathy during mother–adolescent interactions. *Journal of Research on Adolescence, 22*(1), 165–184. https://doi.org/10.1111/j.1532-7795.2011.00762.x

Dickmann, C. R., & Allen, B. (2017). Parent–Child Interaction Therapy for the treatment of disinhibited social engagement disorder: A case report. *Evidence-Based Practice in Child and Adolescent Mental Health, 2*(1), 19–29. https://doi.org/10.1080/23794925.2017.1286959

Dinger, U., Strack, M., Sachsse, T., & Schauenburg, H. (2009). Therapists' attachment, patients' interpersonal problems and alliance development over time in inpatient psychotherapy. *Psychotherapy*, *46*(3), 277–290. https://doi.org/10.1037/a0016913

Dinsdale, N., & Crespi, B. J. (2013). The borderline empathy paradox: Evidence and conceptual models for empathic enhancements in borderline personality disorder. *Journal of Personality Disorders*, *27*(2), 172–195. https://doi.org/10.1521/pedi.2013.27.2.172

Dozier, M., & Bernard, K. (2019). *Coaching of parents of vulnerable infants: The Attachment and Biobehavioral Catch-Up approach*. Guilford Press.

Dozier, M., Stovall, K. C., Albus, K. E., & Bates, B. (2001). Attachment for infants in foster care: The role of caregiver state of mind. *Child Development*, *72*(5), 1467–1477. https://doi.org/10.1111/1467-8624.00360

Dubois-Comtois, K., Bernier, A., Tarabulsy, G. M., Cyr, C., St-Laurent, D., Lanctôt, A.-S., St-Onge, J., Moss, E., & Béliveau, M.-J. (2015). Behavior problems of children in foster care: Associations with foster mothers' representations, commitment, and the quality of mother–child interaction. *Child Abuse & Neglect*, *48*, 119–130. https://doi.org/10.1016/j.chiabu.2015.06.009

Dubois-Comtois, K., Cyr, C., & Moss, E. (2011). Attachment behavior and mother–child conversations as predictors of attachment representations in middle childhood: A longitudinal study. *Attachment & Human Development*, *13*(4), 335–357. https://doi.org/10.1080/14616734.2011.584455

Dubois-Comtois, K., Moss, E., Cyr, C., & Pascuzzo, K. (2013). Behavior problems in middle childhood: The predictive role of maternal distress, child attachment, and mother–child interactions. *Journal of Abnormal Child Psychology*, *41*(8), 1311–1324. https://doi.org/10.1007/s10802-013-9764-6

Duschinsky, R. (2020). *Cornerstones of attachment research*. Oxford University Press.

Duschinsky, R., Bakkum, L., Mannes, J. M. M., Skinner, G. C. M., Turner, M., Mann, A., Coughlan, B., Reijman, S., Foster, S., & Beckwith, H. (2021). Six attachment discourses: Convergence, divergence and relay. *Attachment & Human Development*, *23*(4), 355–374. https://doi.org/10.1080/14616734.2021.1918448

Dykas, M. J., & Cassidy, J. (2011). Attachment and the processing of social information across the life span: Theory and evidence. *Psychological Bulletin*, *137*(1), 19–46. https://doi.org/10.1037/a0021367

Dykas, M. J., Woodhouse, S. S., Cassidy, J., & Waters, H. S. (2006). Narrative assessment of attachment representations: Links between secure base scripts and adolescent attachment. *Attachment & Human Development*, *8*(3), 221–240. https://doi.org/10.1080/14616730600856099

Dykas, M. J., Woodhouse, S. S., Jones, J. D., & Cassidy, J. (2014). Attachment-related biases in adolescents' memory. *Child Development*, *85*(6), 2185–2201. https://doi.org/10.1111/cdev.12268

Egeland, B., & Farber, E. A. (1984). Infant–mother attachment: Factors related to its development and changes over time. *Child Development*, *55*(3), 753–771. https://doi.org/10.2307/1130127

Erickson, M. F., Sroufe, L. A., & Egeland, B. (1985). The relationship between quality of attachment and behavior problems in preschool in a high-risk sample. *Monographs of the Society for Research in Child Development, 50*(1-2), 147–166. https://doi.org/10.2307/3333831

Facompré, C. R., Bernard, K., & Waters, T. E. A. (2018). Effectiveness of interventions in preventing disorganized attachment: A meta-analysis. *Development and Psychopathology, 30*(1), 1–11. https://doi.org/10.1017/S0954579417000426

Fagot, B. I., & Kavanagh, K. (1990). The prediction of antisocial behavior from avoidant attachment classifications. *Child Development, 61*(3), 864–873. https://doi.org/10.2307/1130970

Fairbairn, C. E., Briley, D. A., Kang, D., Fraley, R. C., Hankin, B. L., & Ariss, T. (2018). A meta-analysis of longitudinal associations between substance use and interpersonal attachment security. *Psychological Bulletin, 144*(5), 532–555. https://doi.org/10.1037/bul0000141

Fattah, G. (2002, September 18). Couple blames therapy advice for girl's death. *The Deseret News*. https://www.deseretnews.com/dn/view/0,1249,405031545,00.html

Fearon, R. M., van IJzendoorn, M. H., Fonagy, P., Bakermans-Kranenburg, M. J., Schuengel, C., & Bokhorst, C. L. (2006). In search of shared and nonshared environmental factors in security of attachment: A behavior-genetic study of the association between sensitivity and attachment security. *Developmental Psychology, 42*(6), 1026–1040. https://doi.org/10.1037/0012-1649.42.6.1026

Fearon, R. M. P., & Mansell, W. (2001). Cognitive perspectives on unresolved loss: Insights from the study of PTSD. *Bulletin of the Menninger Clinic, 65*(3), 380–396. https://doi.org/10.1521/bumc.65.3.380.19845

Fearon, R. P., Bakermans-Kranenburg, M. J., van IJzendoorn, M. H., Lapsley, A. M., & Roisman, G. I. (2010). The significance of insecure attachment and disorganization in the development of children's externalizing behavior: A meta-analytic study. *Child Development, 81*(2), 435–456. https://doi.org/10.1111/j.1467-8624.2009.01405.x

Feeney, J. A., Noller, P., & Hanrahan, M. (1994). Assessing adult attachment. In M. B. Sperling & W. H. Berman (Eds.), *Attachment in adults: Clinical and developmental perspectives* (pp. 128–152). Guilford Press.

Fish, M. (2004). Attachment in infancy and preschool in low socioeconomic status rural Appalachian children: Stability and change and relations to preschool and kindergarten competence. *Development and Psychopathology, 16*(2), 293–312. https://doi.org/10.1017/S0954579404044529

Flückiger, C., Rubel, J., Del Re, A. C., Horvath, A. O., Wampold, B. E., Crits-Christoph, P., Atzil-Slonim, D., Compare, A., Falkenström, F., Ekeblad, A., Errázuriz, P., Fisher, H., Hoffart, A., Huppert, J. D., Kivity, Y., Kumar, M., Lutz, W., Muran, J. C., Strunk, D. R., . . . Barber, J. P. (2020). The reciprocal relationship between alliance and early treatment symptoms: A two-stage individual participant data meta-analysis. *Journal of Consulting and Clinical Psychology, 88*(9), 829–843. https://doi.org/10.1037/ccp0000594

Fonagy, P., Leigh, T., Steele, M., Steele, H., Kennedy, R., Mattoon, G., Target, M., & Gerber, A. (1996). The relation of attachment status, psychiatric classification, and response to psychotherapy. *Journal of Consulting and Clinical Psychology, 64*(1), 22–31. https://doi.org/10.1037/0022-006X.64.1.22

Fonagy, P., Lemma, A., Target, M., O'Keeffe, S., Constantinou, M. P., Ventura Wurman, T., Luyten, P., Allison, E., Roth, A., Cape, J., & Pilling, S. (2020). Dynamic interpersonal therapy for moderate to severe depression: A pilot randomized controlled and feasibility trial. *Psychological Medicine, 50*(6), 1010–1019. https://doi.org/10.1017/S0033291719000928

Fonagy, P., & Luyten, P. (2009). A developmental, mentalization-based approach to the understanding and treatment of borderline personality disorder. *Development and Psychopathology, 21*(4), 1355–1381. https://doi.org/10.1017/S0954579409990198

Fonagy, P., Luyten, P., Allison, E., & Campbell, C. (2016). Reconciling psychoanalytic ideas with attachment theory. In J. Cassidy & P. R. Shaver (Eds.), *Handbook of attachment: Theory, research, and clinical applications* (3rd ed., pp. 780–804). Guilford Press.

Fonagy, P., Steele, M., Steele, H., Moran, G. S., & Higgitt, A. C. (1991). The capacity for understanding mental states: The reflective self in parent and child and its significance for security of attachment. *Infant Mental Health Journal, 12*(3), 201–218. https://doi.org/10.1002/1097-0355(199123)12:3<201::AID-IMHJ2280120307>3.0.CO;2-7

Forslund, T., Granqvist, P., van IJzendoorn, M. H., Sagi-Schwartz, A., Glaser, D., Steele, M., Hammarlund, M., Schuengel, C., Bakermans-Kranenburg, M. J., Steele, H., Shaver, P. R., Lux, U., Simmonds, J., Jacobvitz, D., Groh, A. M., Bernard, K., Cyr, C., Hazen, N. L., Foster, S., . . . Duschinsky, R. (2022). Attachment goes to court: Child protection and custody issues. *Attachment & Human Development, 24*(1), 1–52. https://doi.org/10.1080/14616734.2020.1840762

Fortuna, K., & Roisman, G. I. (2008). Insecurity, stress, and symptoms of psychopathology: Contrasting results from self-reports versus interviews of adult attachment. *Attachment & Human Development, 10*(1), 11–28. https://doi.org/10.1080/14616730701868571

Fox, N. A., Kimmerly, N. L., & Schafer, W. D. (1991). Attachment to mother/attachment to father: A meta-analysis. *Child Development, 62*(1), 210–225. https://doi.org/10.2307/1130716

Fraiberg, S. (1980). *Clinical studies in infant mental health*. Tavistock.

Fraley, R. C., Gillath, O., & Deboeck, P. R. (2021). Do life events lead to enduring changes in adult attachment styles? A naturalistic longitudinal investigation. *Journal of Personality and Social Psychology, 120*(6), 1567–1606. https://doi.org/10.1037/pspi0000326

Fraley, R. C., Hudson, N. W., Heffernan, M. E., & Segal, N. (2015). Are adult attachment styles categorical or dimensional? A taxometric analysis of general and relationship-specific attachment orientations. *Journal of Personality and Social Psychology, 109*(2), 354–368. https://doi.org/10.1037/pspp0000027

Fraley, R. C., Roisman, G. I., Booth-LaForce, C., Owen, M. T., & Holland, A. S. (2013). Interpersonal and genetic origins of adult attachment styles: A longitudinal study from infancy to early adulthood. *Journal of Personality and Social Psychology, 104*(5), 817–838. https://doi.org/10.1037/a0031435

Fraley, R. C., Roisman, G. I., & Haltigan, J. D. (2013). The legacy of early experiences in development: Formalizing alternative models of how early experiences are carried forward over time. *Developmental Psychology, 49*(1), 109–126. https://doi.org/10.1037/a0027852

Fraley, R. C., & Spieker, S. J. (2003). Are infant attachment patterns continuously or categorically distributed? A taxometric analysis of strange situation behavior. *Developmental Psychology, 39*(3), 387–404. https://doi.org/10.1037/0012-1649.39.3.387

Fraley, R. C., Waller, N. G., & Brennan, K. A. (2000). An item response theory analysis of self-report measures of adult attachment. *Journal of Personality and Social Psychology, 78*(2), 350–365. https://doi.org/10.1037/0022-3514.78.2.350

Frick, M. A., Darling Rasmussen, P., & Brocki, K. C. (2022). Can attachment predict core and comorbid symptoms of attention-deficit/hyperactivity disorder beyond executive functions and emotion regulation? *British Journal of Clinical Psychology, 61*(1), 93–111. https://doi.org/10.1111/bjc.12317

Frigerio, A., Ceppi, E., Rusconi, M., Giorda, R., Raggi, M. E., & Fearon, P. (2009). The role played by the interaction between genetic factors and attachment in the stress response in infancy. *Journal of Child Psychology and Psychiatry, and Allied Disciplines, 50*(12), 1513–1522. https://doi.org/10.1111/j.1469-7610.2009.02126.x

Gallo, L. C., & Smith, T. W. (2001). Attachment style in marriage: Adjustment and responses to interaction. *Journal of Social and Personal Relationships, 18*(2), 263–289. https://doi.org/10.1177/0265407501182006

Gambin, M., Wozniak-Prus, M., & Sharp, C. (2018). Attachment and psychopathic traits in inpatient female and male adolescents. *Comprehensive Psychiatry, 81*, 73–80. https://doi.org/10.1016/j.comppsych.2017.11.008

George, C., Kaplan, N., & Main, M. (1996). *Adult Attachment Interview* (3rd ed.) [Unpublished manuscript]. University of California at Berkeley.

George, C., & Solomon, J. (2011). Caregiving helplessness: The development of a screening measure for disorganized maternal caregiving. In J. Solomon & C. George (Eds.), *Disorganized attachment and caregiving* (pp. 133–166). Guilford Press.

Gleason, M. M., Fox, N. A., Drury, S., Smyke, A., Egger, H. L., Nelson, C. A., III, Gregas, M. C., & Zeanah, C. H. (2011). Validity of evidence-derived criteria for reactive attachment disorder: Indiscriminately social/disinhibited and emotionally withdrawn/inhibited types. *Journal of the American Academy of*

Child & Adolescent Psychiatry, 50(3), 216–231.e3. https://doi.org/10.1016/j.jaac.2010.12.012

Gloger-Tippelt, G., & Kappler, G. (2016). Narratives of attachment in middle childhood: Do gender, age, and risk-status matter for the quality of attachment? *Attachment & Human Development, 18*(6), 570–595. https://doi.org/10.1080/14616734.2016.1194440

Graham, J. M., & Unterschute, M. S. (2015). A reliability generalization meta-analysis of self-report measures of adult attachment. *Journal of Personality Assessment, 97*(1), 31–41. https://doi.org/10.1080/00223891.2014.927768

Granqvist, P. (2016). Observations of disorganized behaviour yield no magic wand: Response to Shemmings. *Attachment & Human Development, 18*(6), 529–533. https://doi.org/10.1080/14616734.2016.1189994

Granqvist, P., Sroufe, L. A., Dozier, M., Hesse, E., Steele, M., van IJzendoorn, M., Solomon, J., Schuengel, C., Fearon, P., Bakermans-Kranenburg, M., Steele, H., Cassidy, J., Carlson, E., Madigan, S., Jacobvitz, D., Foster, S., Behrens, K., Rifkin-Graboi, A., Gribneau, N., . . . Duschinsky, R. (2017). Disorganized attachment in infancy: A review of the phenomenon and its implications for clinicians and policy-makers. *Attachment & Human Development, 19*(6), 534–558. https://doi.org/10.1080/14616734.2017.1354040

Green, J., Stanley, C., Smith, V., & Goldwyn, R. (2000). A new method of evaluating attachment representations in young school-age children: The Manchester Child Attachment Story Task. *Attachment & Human Development, 2*(1), 48–70. https://doi.org/10.1080/146167300361318

Grice, H. P. (1975). Logic and conversation. In P. Cole & J. L. Morgan (Eds.), *Syntax and semantics: Vol. III. Speech acts* (pp. 41–58). Academic Press.

Groh, A. M., Fearon, R. P., Bakermans-Kranenburg, M. J., van IJzendoorn, M. H., Steele, R. D., & Roisman, G. I. (2014). The significance of attachment security for children's social competence with peers: A meta-analytic study. *Attachment & Human Development, 16*(2), 103–136. https://doi.org/10.1080/14616734.2014.883636

Groh, A. M., Narayan, A. J., Bakermans-Kranenburg, M. J., Roisman, G. I., Vaughn, B. E., Fearon, R. M. P., & van IJzendoorn, M. H. (2017). Attachment and temperament in the early life course: A meta-analytic review. *Child Development, 88*(3), 770–795. https://doi.org/10.1111/cdev.12677

Groh, A. M., Roisman, G. I., Booth-LaForce, C., Fraley, R. C., Owen, M. T., Cox, M. J., & Burchinal, M. R. (2014). The Adult Attachment Interview: Psychometrics, stability and change from infancy and developmental origins: IV. Stability of attachment security from infancy to late adolescence. *Monographs of the Society for Research in Child Development, 79*(3), 51–66. https://doi.org/10.1111/mono.12113

Groh, A. M., Roisman, G. I., van IJzendoorn, M. H., Bakermans-Kranenburg, M. J., & Fearon, R. P. (2012). The significance of insecure and disorganized attachment for children's internalizing symptoms: A meta-analytic study. *Child Development, 83*(2), 591–610. https://doi.org/10.1111/j.1467-8624.2011.01711.x

Grossmann, K., Grossmann, K. E., & Kindler, H. (2005). Early care and the roots of attachment and partnership representations: The Bielefeld and Regensburg Longitudinal Studies. In K. E. Grossmann, K. Grossmann, & E. Waters (Eds.), *Attachment from infancy to adulthood: The major longitudinal studies* (pp. 98–136). Guilford Press.

Guyon-Harris, K. L., Humphreys, K. L., Degnan, K., Fox, N. A., Nelson, C. A., & Zeanah, C. H. (2019). A prospective longitudinal study of Reactive Attachment Disorder following early institutional care: Considering variable- and person-centered approaches. *Attachment & Human Development, 21*(2), 95–110. https://doi.org/10.1080/14616734.2018.1499208

Hadden, B. W., Smith, C. V., & Webster, G. D. (2014). Relationship duration moderates associations between attachment and relationship quality: Meta-analytic support for the temporal adult romantic attachment model. *Personality and Social Psychology Review, 18*(1), 42–58. https://doi.org/10.1177/1088868313501885

Hall, S. E. K., & Geher, G. (2003). Behavioral and personality characteristics of children with reactive attachment disorder. *The Journal of Psychology, 137*(2), 145–162. https://doi.org/10.1080/00223980309600605

Hanf, C., & Kling, J. (1973). *Facilitating parent–child interaction: A two-stage training model* [Unpublished manuscript]. University of Oregon Medical School.

Harlow, H. F. (1958). The nature of love. *American Psychologist, 13*(12), 673–685. https://doi.org/10.1037/h0047884

Harlow, H. F., & Zimmermann, R. R. (1958). The development of affectional responses in infant monkeys. *Proceedings of the American Philosophical Society, 102*, 501–509.

Hart, J. R., Venta, A., & Sharp, C. (2017). Attachment and thought problems in an adolescent inpatient sample: The mediational role of theory of mind. *Comprehensive Psychiatry, 78*, 38–47. https://doi.org/10.1016/j.comppsych.2017.07.002

Hawkins, E., Madigan, S., Moran, G., & Pederson, D. R. (2015). Mediating and moderating processes underlying the association between maternal cognition and infant attachment. *Journal of Applied Developmental Psychology, 39*, 24–33. https://doi.org/10.1016/j.appdev.2015.04.001

Haydon, K. C., Roisman, G. I., Owen, M. T., Booth-LaForce, C., & Cox, M. J. (2014). The Adult Attachment Interview: Psychometrics, stability and change from infancy and developmental origins: VII. Shared and distinctive antecedents of Adult Attachment Interview state-of-mind and inferred-experience dimensions. *Monographs of the Society for Research in Child Development, 79*(3), 108–125. https://doi.org/10.1111/mono.12116

Hazan, C., & Shaver, P. (1987). Romantic love conceptualized as an attachment process. *Journal of Personality and Social Psychology, 52*(3), 511–524. https://doi.org/10.1037/0022-3514.52.3.511

Hesse, E. (1999). The Adult Attachment Interview: Historical and current perspectives. In J. Cassidy & P. R. Shaver (Eds.), *Handbook of attachment: Theory, research, and clinical applications* (pp. 395–433). Guilford Press.

Hesse, E. (2016). The Adult Attachment Interview: Protocol, method of analysis, and selected empirical studies: 1985–2015. In J. Cassidy & P. R. Shaver (Eds.), *Handbook of attachment: Theory, research, and clinical applications* (3rd ed., pp. 553–597). Guilford Press.

Hesse, E., & Main, M. (2000). Disorganized infant, child, and adult attachment: Collapse in behavioral and attentional strategies. *Journal of the American Psychoanalytic Association, 48*(4), 1097–1127. https://doi.org/10.1177/00030651000480041101

Hinde, R. (1989). Continuities and discontinuities: Conceptual issues and methodological considerations. In M. Rutter (Ed.), *Studies of psychosocial risk: The power of longitudinal data* (pp. 367–384). Cambridge University Press.

Hoffman, K. T., Marvin, R. S., Cooper, G., & Powell, B. (2006). Changing toddlers' and preschoolers' attachment classifications: The Circle of Security intervention. *Journal of Consulting and Clinical Psychology, 74*(6), 1017–1026. https://doi.org/10.1037/0022-006X.74.6.1017

Hsiao, C., Koren-Karie, N., Bailey, H., & Moran, G. (2015). It takes two to talk: Longitudinal associations among infant–mother attachment, maternal attachment representations, and mother–child emotion dialogues. *Attachment & Human Development, 17*(1), 43–64. https://doi.org/10.1080/14616734.2014.981671

Huber, A., McMahon, C. A., & Sweller, N. (2015). Efficacy of the 20-week Circle of Security Intervention: Changes in caregiver reflective functioning, representations, and child attachment in an Australian clinical sample. *Infant Mental Health Journal, 36*(6), 556–574. https://doi.org/10.1002/imhj.21540

Hudson, J., & Nelson, K. (1986). Repeated encounters of a similar kind: Effects of familiarity on children's autobiographical memory. *Cognitive Development, 1*(3), 253–271. https://doi.org/10.1016/S0885-2014(86)80004-1

Hughes, D. (1997). *Facilitating developmental attachment*. Jason Aronson.

Hughes, D. A. (2003). Psychological interventions for the spectrum of attachment disorders and intrafamilial trauma. *Attachment & Human Development, 5*(3), 271–277. https://doi.org/10.1080/14616730310001596142

Huth-Bocks, A. C., Muzik, M., Beeghly, M., Earls, L., & Stacks, A. M. (2014). Secure base scripts are associated with maternal parenting behavior across contexts and reflective functioning among trauma-exposed mothers. *Attachment & Human Development, 16*(6), 535–556. https://doi.org/10.1080/14616734.2014.967787

Jacobson, J. L., & Wille, D. E. (1984). Influence of attachment and separation experience on separation distress at 18 months. *Developmental Psychology, 20*(3), 477–484. https://doi.org/10.1037/0012-1649.20.3.477

Jenkins-Guarnieri, M. A., Wright, S. L., & Hudiburgh, L. M. (2012). The relationships among attachment style, personality traits, interpersonal competency, and Facebook use. *Journal of Applied Developmental Psychology, 33*(6), 294–301. https://doi.org/10.1016/j.appdev.2012.08.001

Johnco, C. J., Magson, N. R., Fardouly, J., Oar, E. L., Forbes, M. K., Richardson, C., & Rapee, R. M. (2021). The role of parenting behaviors in the bidirectional and intergenerational transmission of depression and anxiety between parents and early adolescent youth. *Depression and Anxiety, 38*(12), 1256–1266. https://doi.org/10.1002/da.23197

Johnson, S. M. (2018). *Attachment theory in practice: Emotionally focused therapy (EFT) with individuals, couples, and families*. Guilford Press.

Johnson, S. M. (2021). Attachment principles as a guide to therapeutic change: The example of Emotionally Focused Therapy. In R. A. Thompson, J. A. Simpson, & L. J. Berlin (Eds.), *Attachment: The fundamental questions* (pp. 332–338). Guilford Press.

Joiner, T. E., Jr., Van Orden, K. A., Witte, T. K., Selby, E. A., Ribeiro, J. D., Lewis, R., & Rudd, M. D. (2009). Main predictions of the interpersonal-psychological theory of suicidal behavior: Empirical tests in two samples of young adults. *Journal of Abnormal Psychology, 118*(3), 634–646. https://doi.org/10.1037/a0016500

Jones, J. D., Cassidy, J., & Shaver, P. R. (2015). Parents' self-reported attachment styles: A review of links with parenting behaviors, emotions, and cognitions. *Personality and Social Psychology Review, 19*(1), 44–76. https://doi.org/10.1177/1088868314541858

Jones, J. D., Ehrlich, K. B., Brett, B. E., Gross, J. T., Mohr, J. J., Hopper, E. A., Dinh, J. V., Malanchuk, O., Peck, S. C., Brodish, A. B., Adam, E. K., Eccles, J. S., Kemeny, M. E., & Cassidy, J. (2017). Perceptions of parental secure base support in African American adolescents and young adults: A preliminary study of predictive links to adult C-reactive protein. *Journal of Social and Personal Relationships, 34*(8), 1168–1185. https://doi.org/10.1177/0265407516670532

Jones, J. D., Fraley, R. C., Ehrlich, K. B., Stern, J. A., Lejuez, C. W., Shaver, P. R., & Cassidy, J. (2018). Stability of attachment style in adolescence: An empirical test of alternative developmental processes. *Child Development, 89*(3), 871–880. https://doi.org/10.1111/cdev.12775

Joseph, M. A., O'Connor, T. G., Briskman, J. A., Maughan, B., & Scott, S. (2014). The formation of secure new attachments by children who were maltreated: An observational study of adolescents in foster care. *Development and Psychopathology, 26*(1), 67–80. https://doi.org/10.1017/S0954579413000540

Juffer, F., Bakermans-Kranenburg, M. J., & van IJzendoorn, M. H. (2005). The importance of parenting in the development of disorganized attachment: Evidence from a preventive intervention study in adoptive families. *Journal of Child Psychology and Psychiatry, and Allied Disciplines, 46*(3), 263–274. https://doi.org/10.1111/j.1469-7610.2004.00353.x

Juffer, F., Bakermans-Kranenburg, M. J., & van IJzendoorn, M. H. (Eds.). (2008). *Promoting positive parenting: An attachment-based intervention.* Taylor & Francis.

Juffer, F., Palacios, J., Le Mare, L., Sonuga-Barke, E. J. S., Tieman, W., Bakermans-Kranenburg, M. J., Vorria, P., van IJzendoorn, M. H., & Verhulst, F. C. (2011). The Adult Attachment Interview: Psychometrics, stability and change from infancy and developmental origins: II. Development of adopted children with histories of early adversity. *Monographs of the Society for Research in Child Development, 76*(4), 31–61. https://doi.org/10.1111/j.1540-5834.2011.00627.x

Kawabata, Y., Alink, L. R. A., Tseng, W.-L., van IJzendoorn, M. H., & Crick, N. R. (2011). Maternal and paternal parenting styles associated with relational aggression in children and adolescents: A conceptual analysis and meta-analytic review. *Developmental Review, 31*(4), 240–278. https://doi.org/10.1016/j.dr.2011.08.001

Keller, H., & Bard, K. A. (Eds.). (2017). *The cultural nature of attachment*. MIT Press. https://doi.org/10.7551/mitpress/9780262036900.001.0001

Kelly, K., Slade, A., & Grienenberger, J. F. (2005). Maternal reflective functioning, mother–infant affective communication, and infant attachment: Exploring the link between mental states and observed caregiving behavior in the intergenerational transmission of attachment. *Attachment & Human Development, 7*(3), 299–311. https://doi.org/10.1080/14616730500245963

Kelly, V. J. (2003). *Theoretical rationale for the treatment of disorders of attachment*. Retrieved March 5, 2009, from http://www.attach.org/theorational.htm

Kerns, K. A., Klepac, L., & Cole, A. (1996). Peer relationships and preadolescents' perceptions of security in the child–mother relationship. *Developmental Psychology, 32*(3), 457–466. https://doi.org/10.1037/0012-1649.32.3.457

Kerns, K. A., Tomich, P. L., & Kim, P. (2006). Normative trends in children's perceptions of availability and utilization of attachment figures in middle childhood. *Social Development, 15*(1), 1–22. https://doi.org/10.1111/j.1467-9507.2006.00327.x

Khan, F., Chong, J. Y., Theisen, J. C., Fraley, R. C., Young, J. F., & Hankin, B. L. (2020). Development and change in attachment: A multiwave assessment of attachment and its correlates across childhood and adolescence. *Journal of Personality and Social Psychology, 118*(6), 1188–1206. https://doi.org/10.1037/pspi0000211

Kisilevsky, B. S., Hains, S. M. J., Lee, K., Xie, X., Huang, H., Ye, H. H., Zhang, K., & Wang, Z. (2003). Effects of experience on fetal voice recognition. *Psychological Science, 14*(3), 220–224. https://doi.org/10.1111/1467-9280.02435

Klagsbrun, M., & Bowlby, J. (1976). Responses to separation from parents: A clinical test for young children. *British Journal of Projective Psychology & Personality Study, 21*, 7–27.

Klein, M. (1932). *The psycho-analysis of children*. Hogarth.

Kobak, R., Cole, H., Ferenz-Gillies, R., Fleming, W., & Gamble, W. (1993). Attachment and emotional regulation during mother–teen problem solving: A control theory analysis. *Child Development, 59*, 135–146. https://doi.org/10.2307/1131448

Kobak, R., Rosenthal, N., & Serwik, A. (2005). The attachment hierarchy in middle childhood: Conceptual and methodological issues. In K. A. Kerns & R. A. Richardson (Eds.), *Attachment in middle childhood* (pp. 71–88). Guilford Press.

Kobak, R., Zajac, K., & Smith, C. (2009). Adolescent attachment and trajectories of hostile-impulsive behavior: Implications for the development of personality disorders. *Development and Psychopathology, 21*(3), 839–851. https://doi.org/10.1017/S0954579409000455

Köber, C., Facompré, C. R., Waters, T. E. A., & Simpson, J. A. (2019). Autobiographical memory stability in the context of the Adult Attachment Interview. *Cognition, 191*, Article 103980. https://doi.org/10.1016/j.cognition.2019.05.017

Koehn, A. J., & Kerns, K. A. (2018). Parent–child attachment: Meta-analysis of associations with parenting behaviors in middle childhood and adolescence. *Attachment & Human Development, 20*(4), 378–405. https://doi.org/10.1080/14616734.2017.1408131

Kondo-Ikemura, K., Behrens, K. Y., Umemura, T., & Nakano, S. (2018). Japanese mothers' prebirth Adult Attachment Interview predicts their infants' response to the Strange Situation Procedure: The strange situation in Japan revisited three decades later. *Developmental Psychology, 54*(11), 2007–2015. https://doi.org/10.1037/dev0000577

Koocher, G. P., McMann, M. R., Stout, A. O., & Norcross, J. C. (2015). Discredited assessment and treatment methods used with children and adolescents: A Delphi poll. *Journal of Clinical Child and Adolescent Psychology, 44*(5), 722–729. https://doi.org/10.1080/15374416.2014.895941

Labov, W., & Waletsky, J. (1967). Narrative analysis: Oral versions of personal experience. In J. Helms (Ed.), *Essays on the verbal and visual arts* (pp. 12–44). University of Washington Press.

Lecompte, V., & Moss, E. (2014). Disorganized and controlling patterns of attachment, role reversal, and caregiving helplessness: Links to adolescents' externalizing problems. *American Journal of Orthopsychiatry, 84*(5), 581–589. https://doi.org/10.1037/ort0000017

Leijten, P., Scott, S., Landau, S., Harris, V., Mann, J., Hutchings, J., Beecham, J., & Gardner, F. (2020). Individual participant data meta-analysis: Impact of conduct problem severity, comorbid attention-deficit/hyperactivity disorder and emotional problems, and maternal depression on parenting program effects. *Journal of the American Academy of Child & Adolescent Psychiatry, 59*(8), 933–943. https://doi.org/10.1016/j.jaac.2020.01.023

Lemche, E., Kreppner, J. M., Joraschky, P., & Klann-Delius, G. (2007). Attachment organization and the early development of internal state language: A longitudinal perspective. *International Journal of Behavioral Development, 31*(3), 252–262. https://doi.org/10.1177/0165025407076438

Levendosky, A. A., Bogat, G. A., Huth-Bocks, A. C., Rosenblum, K., & von Eye, A. (2011). The effects of domestic violence on the stability of attachment from infancy to preschool. *Journal of Clinical Child and Adolescent Psychology, 40*(3), 398–410. https://doi.org/10.1080/15374416.2011.563460

Levi-Belz, Y., Gvion, Y., Horesh, N., & Apter, A. (2013). Attachment patterns in medically serious suicide attempts: The mediating role of self-disclosure and loneliness. *Suicide & Life-Threatening Behavior, 43*(5), 511–522. https://doi.org/10.1111/sltb.12035

Levy, K. N., Kivity, Y., Johnson, B. N., & Gooch, C. V. (2018). Adult attachment as a predictor and moderator of psychotherapy outcome: A meta-analysis. *Journal of Clinical Psychology, 74*(11), 1996–2013. https://doi.org/10.1002/jclp.22685

Levy, K. N., Meehan, K. B., Kelly, K. M., Reynoso, J. S., Weber, M., Clarkin, J. F., & Kernberg, O. F. (2006). Change in attachment patterns and reflective function in a randomized control trial of Transference-Focused Psychotherapy for borderline personality disorder. *Journal of Consulting and Clinical Psychology, 74*(6), 1027–1040. https://doi.org/10.1037/0022-006X.74.6.1027

Li, T., & Chan, D. K.-S. (2012). How anxious and avoidant attachment affect romantic relationship quality differently: A meta-analytic review. *European Journal of Social Psychology, 42*(4), 406–419. https://doi.org/10.1002/ejsp.1842

Lieberman, A. F., & Van Horn, P. (2008). *Psychotherapy with infants and young children: Repairing the effects of stress and trauma on early attachment*. Guilford Press.

Lieberman, A. F., Van Horn, P., & Ghosh Ippen, C. G. (2005). Toward evidence-based treatment: Child–Parent Psychotherapy with preschoolers exposed to marital violence. *Journal of the American Academy of Child & Adolescent Psychiatry, 44*(12), 1241–1248. https://doi.org/10.1097/01.chi.0000181047.59702.58

Lieberman, A. F., Weston, D. R., & Pawl, J. H. (1991). Preventive intervention and outcome with anxiously attached dyads. *Child Development, 62*(1), 199–209. https://doi.org/10.2307/1130715

Lilienfeld, S. O. (2007). Psychological treatments that cause harm. *Perspectives on Psychological Science, 2*(1), 53–70. https://doi.org/10.1111/j.1745-6916.2007.00029.x

Lind, T., Bernard, K., Yarger, H. A., & Dozier, M. (2020). Promoting compliance in children referred to child protective services: A randomized clinical trial. *Child Development, 91*(2), 563–576. https://doi.org/10.1111/cdev.13207

Lind, T., Lee Raby, K., Goldstein, A., Bernard, K., Caron, E. B., Yarger, H. A., Wallin, A., & Dozier, M. (2021). Improving social-emotional competence in internationally adopted children with the Attachment and Biobehavioral Catch-up intervention. *Development and Psychopathology, 33*(3), 957–969. https://doi.org/10.1017/S0954579420000255

Lindhiem, O., & Dozier, M. (2007). Caregiver commitment to foster children: The role of child behavior. *Child Abuse & Neglect, 31*(4), 361–374. https://doi.org/10.1016/j.chiabu.2006.12.003

Lionetti, F., Pastore, M., & Barone, L. (2015). Parenting stress: The roles of attachment states of mind and parenting alliance in the context of adoption. *Parenting: Science and Practice, 15*(2), 75–91. https://doi.org/10.1080/15295192.2015.1020142

Loeb, E. L., Stern, J. A., Costello, M. A., & Allen, J. P. (2021). With(out) a little help from my friends: Insecure attachment in adolescence, support-seeking, and adult negativity and hostility. *Attachment & Human Development, 23*(5), 624–642. https://doi.org/10.1080/14616734.2020.1821722

Lorenz, K. (1952). *King Solomon's ring*. Methuen Publishing.

Lucassen, N., Tharner, A., van IJzendoorn, M. H., Bakermans-Kranenburg, M. J., Volling, B. L., Verhulst, F. C., Lambregtse-Van den Berg, M. P., & Tiemeier, H. (2011). The association between paternal sensitivity and infant–father attachment security: A meta-analysis of three decades of research. *Journal of Family Psychology, 25*(6), 986–992. https://doi.org/10.1037/a0025855

Luijk, M. P. C. M., Roisman, G. I., Haltigan, J. D., Tiemeier, H., Booth-Laforce, C., van IJzendoorn, M. H., Belsky, J., Uitterlinden, A. G., Jaddoe, V. W., Hofman, A., Verhulst, F. C., Tharner, A., & Bakermans-Kranenburg, M. J. (2011). Dopaminergic, serotonergic, and oxytonergic candidate genes associated with infant attachment security and disorganization? In search of main and interaction effects. *Journal of Child Psychology and Psychiatry, and Allied Disciplines, 52*(12), 1295–1307. https://doi.org/10.1111/j.1469-7610.2011.02440.x

Luyten, P., Campbell, C., Allison, E., & Fonagy, P. (2020). The mentalizing approach to psychopathology: State of the art and future directions. *Annual Review of Clinical Psychology, 16*(1), 297–325. https://doi.org/10.1146/annurev-clinpsy-071919-015355

Lyons-Ruth, K., Bureau, J. F., Holmes, B., Easterbrooks, A., & Brooks, N. H. (2013). Borderline symptoms and suicidality/self-injury in late adolescence: Prospectively observed relationship correlates in infancy and childhood. *Psychiatry Research, 206*(2-3), 273–281. https://doi.org/10.1016/j.psychres.2012.09.030

Lyons-Ruth, K., Connell, D. B., Grunebaum, H. U., & Botein, S. (1990). Infants at social risk: Maternal depression and family support services as mediators of infant development and security of attachment. *Child Development, 61*(1), 85–98. https://doi.org/10.2307/1131049

Lyons-Ruth, K., Yellin, C., Melnick, S., & Atwood, G. (2003). Childhood experiences of trauma and loss have different relations to maternal Unresolved and Hostile-Helpless states of mind on the AAI. *Attachment & Human Development, 5*(4), 330–352. https://doi.org/10.1080/14616730310001633410

Lyons-Ruth, K., Zeanah, C. H., Benoit, D., Madigan, S., & Mills-Koonce, W. R. (2014). Disorder and risk for disorder during infancy and toddlerhood. In E. J. Mash & R. A. Barkley (Eds.), *Child psychopathology* (3rd ed., pp. 673–736). Guilford Press.

Macfie, J., Fitzpatrick, K. L., Rivas, E. M., & Cox, M. J. (2008). Independent influences upon mother–toddler role reversal: Infant–mother attachment disorganization and role reversal in mother's childhood. *Attachment & Human Development, 10*(1), 29–39. https://doi.org/10.1080/14616730701868589

Macfie, J., McElwain, N. L., Houts, R. M., & Cox, M. J. (2005). Intergenerational transmission of role reversal between parent and child: Dyadic and family systems internal working models. *Attachment & Human Development, 7*(1), 51–65. https://doi.org/10.1080/14616730500039663

Madigan, S., Atkinson, L., Laurin, K., & Benoit, D. (2013). Attachment and internalizing behavior in early childhood: A meta-analysis. *Developmental Psychology, 49*(4), 672–689. https://doi.org/10.1037/a0028793

Madigan, S., Bakermans-Kranenburg, M. J., van IJzendoorn, M. H., Moran, G., Pederson, D. R., & Benoit, D. (2006). Unresolved states of mind, anomalous parental behavior, and disorganized attachment: A review and meta-analysis of a transmission gap. *Attachment & Human Development, 8*(2), 89–111. https://doi.org/10.1080/14616730600774458

Madigan, S., Brumariu, L. E., Villani, V., Atkinson, L., & Lyons-Ruth, K. (2016). Representational and questionnaire measures of attachment: A meta-analysis of relations to child internalizing and externalizing problems. *Psychological Bulletin, 142*(4), 367–399. https://doi.org/10.1037/bul0000029

Madigan, S., Moran, G., Schuengel, C., Pederson, D. R., & Otten, R. (2007). Unresolved maternal attachment representations, disrupted maternal behavior, and disorganized attachment in infancy: Links to toddler behavior problems. *Journal of Child Psychology and Psychiatry, and Allied Disciplines, 48*(10), 1042–1050. https://doi.org/10.1111/j.1469-7610.2007.01805.x

Madigan, S., Vaillancourt, K., McKibbon, A., & Benoit, D. (2012). The reporting of maltreatment experiences during the Adult Attachment Interview in a sample of pregnant adolescents. *Attachment & Human Development, 14*(2), 119–143. https://doi.org/10.1080/14616734.2012.661230

Madigan, S., Vaillancourt, K., McKibbon, A., & Benoit, D. (2015). Trauma and traumatic loss in pregnant adolescents: The impact of trauma-focused cognitive behavior therapy on maternal unresolved states of mind and posttraumatic stress disorder. *Attachment & Human Development, 17*(2), 175–198. https://doi.org/10.1080/14616734.2015.1006386

Main, M., & Cassidy, J. (1988). Categories of response to reunion with the parent at age 6: Predictable from the infant attachment classifications and stable over a 1-month period. *Developmental Psychology, 24*(3), 415–426. https://doi.org/10.1037/0012-1649.24.3.415

Main, M., & Goldwyn, R. (1984). Predicting rejection of her infant from mother's representation of her own experience: Implications for the abused–abusing intergenerational cycle. *Child Abuse & Neglect, 8*(2), 203–217. https://doi.org/10.1016/0145-2134(84)90009-7

Main, M., Goldwyn, R., & Hesse, E. (1984–2003). *Adult attachment rating and classification systems* [Unpublished manuscript]. University of California at Berkeley.

Main, M., & Hesse, E. (1990). Parents' unresolved traumatic experiences are related to infant disorganized attachment status: Is frightened and/or frightening parental behavior the linking mechanism? In M. T. Greenberg, D. Cicchetti, & E. M. Cummings (Eds.), *Attachment in the preschool years: Theory, research, and intervention* (pp. 161–182). University of Chicago Press.

Main, M., Hesse, E., & Kaplan, N. (2005). Predictability of attachment behavior and representational processes at 1, 6, and 19 years of age: The Berkeley Longitudinal Study. In K. E. Grossmann, K. Grossmann, & E. Waters (Eds.), *Attachment from infancy to adulthood: The major longitudinal studies* (pp. 245–304). Guilford Press.

Main, M., Kaplan, N., & Cassidy, J. (1985). Security in infancy, childhood, and adulthood: A move to the level of representation. In I. Bretherton & E. Waters (Eds.), Growing points in attachment theory and research. *Monographs of the Society for Research in Child Development, 50* (1-2, Serial No. 209), 66–104. https://doi.org/10.2307/3333827

Main, M., & Solomon, J. (1986). Discovery of a new, insecure-disorganized/disoriented attachment behavior. In M. Yogman & T. B. Brazelton (Eds.), *Affective development in infancy* (pp. 95–124). Ablex.

Main, M., & Solomon, J. (1990). Procedures for identifying infants as disorganized/disoriented during the Ainsworth Strange Situation. In M. T. Greenberg, D. Cicchetti, & E. M. Cummings (Eds.), *Attachment in the preschool years: Theory, research, and intervention* (pp. 121–160). University of Chicago Press.

Main, M., & Weston, D. R. (1981). The quality of the toddler's relationship to mother and to father: Related to conflict behavior and the readiness to establish new relationships. *Child Development, 52*(3), 932–940. https://doi.org/10.2307/1129097

Mallinckrodt, B., Gantt, D. L., & Coble, H. M. (1995). Attachment patterns in the psychotherapy relationship: Development of the Client Attachment to Therapist Scale. *Journal of Counseling Psychology, 42*(3), 307–317. https://doi.org/10.1037/0022-0167.42.3.307

Mallinckrodt, B., & Jeong, J. (2015). Meta-analysis of client attachment to therapist: Associations with working alliance and client pretherapy attachment. *Psychotherapy, 52*(1), 134–139. https://doi.org/10.1037/a0036890

Manthos, M., Owen, J., & Fincham, F. D. (2014). A new perspective on hooking up among college students: Sexual behavior as a function of distinct groups. *Journal of Social and Personal Relationships, 31*(6), 815–829. https://doi.org/10.1177/0265407513505932

Markiewicz, D., Lawford, H., Doyle, A. B., & Haggart, N. (2006). Developmental differences in adolescents' and young adults' use of mothers, fathers, best friends, and romantic partners to fulfill attachment needs. *Journal of Youth and Adolescence, 35*(1), 121–134. https://doi.org/10.1007/s10964-005-9014-5

Martin, J., Raby, K. L., Labella, M. H., & Roisman, G. I. (2017). Childhood abuse and neglect, attachment states of mind, and non-suicidal self-injury.

Attachment & Human Development, 19(5), 425–446. https://doi.org/10.1080/14616734.2017.1330832

Martin, M. J., Sturge-Apple, M. L., Davies, P. T., & Gutierrez, G. (2019). Attachment behavior and hostility as explanatory factors linking parent–adolescent conflict and adolescent adjustment. *Journal of Family Psychology, 33*(5), 586–596. https://doi.org/10.1037/fam0000529

Matias, C., O'Connor, T. G., Futh, A., & Scott, S. (2014). Observational attachment theory-based parenting measures predict children's attachment narratives independently from social learning theory-based measures. *Attachment & Human Development, 16*(1), 77–92. https://doi.org/10.1080/14616734.2013.851333

McBride, C., Atkinson, L., Quilty, L. C., & Bagby, R. M. (2006). Attachment as moderator of treatment outcome in major depression: A randomized control trial of interpersonal psychotherapy versus cognitive behavior therapy. *Journal of Consulting and Clinical Psychology, 74*(6), 1041–1054. https://doi.org/10.1037/0022-006X.74.6.1041

McClure, M. J., & Lydon, J. E. (2014). Anxiety doesn't become you: How attachment anxiety compromises relational opportunities. *Journal of Personality and Social Psychology, 106*(1), 89–111. https://doi.org/10.1037/a0034532

McCormick, M. P., O'Connor, E. E., & Barnes, S. P. (2016). Mother–child attachment styles and math and reading skills in middle childhood: The mediating role of children's exploration and engagement. *Early Childhood Research Quarterly, 36*, 295–306. https://doi.org/10.1016/j.ecresq.2016.01.011

McGoron, L., Gleason, M. M., Smyke, A. T., Drury, S. S., Nelson, C. A., III, Gregas, M. C., Fox, N. A., & Zeanah, C. H. (2012). Recovering from early deprivation: Attachment mediates effects of caregiving on psychopathology. *Journal of the American Academy of Child & Adolescent Psychiatry, 51*(7), 683–693. https://doi.org/10.1016/j.jaac.2012.05.004

McLean, L. M., Walton, T., Rodin, G., Esplen, M. J., & Jones, J. M. (2013). A couple-based intervention for patients and caregivers facing end-stage cancer: Outcomes of a randomized controlled trial. *Psycho-Oncology, 22*(1), 28–38. https://doi.org/10.1002/pon.2046

McNeil, C. B., & Hembree-Kigin, T. L. (2011). *Parent–Child Interaction Therapy* (2nd ed.). Springer.

Meins, E., & Fernyhough, C. (1999). Linguistic acquisitional style and mentalising development: The role of maternal mind-mindedness. *Cognitive Development, 14*(3), 363–380. https://doi.org/10.1016/S0885-2014(99)00010-6

Meins, E., Fernyhough, C., Wainwright, R., Clark-Carter, D., Das Gupta, M., Fradley, E., & Tuckey, M. (2003). Pathways to understanding mind: Construct validity and predictive validity of maternal mind-mindedness. *Child Development, 74*(4), 1194–1211. https://doi.org/10.1111/1467-8624.00601

Mercer, J. (2015). Attachment therapy. In S. O. Lilienfeld, S. J. Lynn, & J. M. Lohr (Eds.), *Science and pseudoscience in clinical psychology* (2nd ed., pp. 466–499). Guilford Press.

Mercer, J., Sarner, L., & Rosa, L. (2003). *Attachment therapy on trial: The torture and death of Candace Newmaker*. Praeger.

Mesman, J., van IJzendoorn, M. H., & Sagi-Schwartz, A. (2016). Cross-cultural patterns of attachment: Universal and contextual dimensions. In J. Cassidy & P. R. Shaver (Eds.), *Handbook of attachment: Theory, research, and clinical implications* (3rd ed., pp. 852–877). Guilford Press.

Miga, E. M., Hare, A., Allen, J. P., & Manning, N. (2010). The relation of insecure attachment states of mind and romantic attachment styles to adolescent aggression in romantic relationships. *Attachment & Human Development, 12*(5), 463–481. https://doi.org/10.1080/14616734.2010.501971

Mikulincer, M., Florian, V., & Tolmacz, R. (1990). Attachment styles and fear of personal death: A case study of affect regulation. *Journal of Personality and Social Psychology, 58*(2), 273–280. https://doi.org/10.1037/0022-3514.58.2.273

Mikulincer, M., & Shaver, P. R. (2016). *Attachment in adulthood: Structure, dynamics, and change* (2nd ed.). Guilford Press.

Mistry, J. J., & Lange, G. W. (1985). Children's organization and recall of information in scripted narratives. *Child Development, 56*(4), 953–961. https://doi.org/10.2307/1130107

Moretti, M. M., & Obsuth, I. (2009). Effectiveness of an attachment-focused manualized intervention for parents of teens at risk for aggressive behaviour: The Connect Program. *Journal of Adolescence, 32*(6), 1347–1357. https://doi.org/10.1016/j.adolescence.2009.07.013

Moretti, M. M., Pasalich, D. S., & O'Connell, K. A. (2018). Connect: An attachment-based program for parents of teens. In H. Steele & M. Steele (Eds.), *Handbook of attachment-based interventions* (pp. 375–400). Guilford Press.

Moss, E., Bureau, J. F., Cyr, C., Mongeau, C., & St-Laurent, D. (2004). Correlates of attachment at age 3: Construct validity of the preschool attachment classification system. *Developmental Psychology, 40*(3), 323–334. https://doi.org/10.1037/0012-1649.40.3.323

Moss, E., Cyr, C., & Dubois-Comtois, K. (2004). Attachment at early school age and developmental risk: Examining family contexts and behavior problems of controlling-caregiving, controlling-punitive, and behaviorally disorganized children. *Developmental Psychology, 40*(4), 519–532. https://doi.org/10.1037/0012-1649.40.4.519

Moss, E., & Lecompte, V. (2015). Attachment and socioemotional problems in middle childhood. In G. Bosmans & K. A. Kerns (Eds.), *Attachment in middle childhood: Advances and new directions in an emerging field* (pp. 63–76). Jossey-Bass. https://doi.org/10.1002/cad.20095

National Association of Social Workers. (2005, August). *Resolution against the physical restraint of children.* Unanimously passed at the National Association of Social Workers Delegate Assembly, Washington, DC.

Neumann, E., Sattel, H., Gündel, H., Henningsen, P., & Kruse, J. (2015). Attachment in romantic relationships and somatization. *Journal of Nervous and Mental Disease, 203*(2), 101–106. https://doi.org/10.1097/NMD.0000000000000241

NICHD Early Child Care Research Network. (1997). The effects of infant child care on infant–mother attachment security: Results of the NICHD Study of Early Child Care. *Child Development, 68*(5), 860–879.

NICHD Early Child Care Research Network. (2001). Child-care and family predictors of preschool attachment and stability from infancy. *Developmental Psychology, 37*(6), 847–862. https://doi.org/10.1037/0012-1649.37.6.847

Nickerson, A., Bryant, R. A., Aderka, I. M., Hinton, D. E., & Hofmann, S. G. (2013). The impacts of parental loss and adverse parenting on mental health: Findings from the National Comorbidity Survey-Replication. *Psychological Trauma: Theory, Research, Practice, and Policy, 5*(2), 119–127. https://doi.org/10.1037/a0025695

Nievar, M. A., & Becker, B. J. (2008). Sensitivity as a privileged predictor of attachment: A second perspective on De Wolff and van IJzendoorn's meta-analysis. *Social Development, 17*(1), 102–114. https://doi.org/10.1111/j.1467-9507.2007.00417.x

Nilsson, D., Holmqvist, R., & Jonson, M. (2011). Self-reported attachment style, trauma exposure and dissociative symptoms among adolescents. *Attachment & Human Development, 13*(6), 579–595. https://doi.org/10.1080/14616734.2011.609004

Nock, M. K. (2009). Why do people hurt themselves? New insights into the nature and functions of self-injury. *Current Directions in Psychological Science, 18*(2), 78–83. https://doi.org/10.1111/j.1467-8721.2009.01613.x

Obsuth, I., Moretti, M. M., Holland, R., Braber, K., & Cross, S. (2006). Conduct disorder: New directions in promoting effective parenting and strengthening parent–adolescent relationships. *Journal of the Canadian Academy of Child and Adolescent Psychiatry, 15*(1), 6–15.

O'Connor, T. G., Matias, C., Futh, A., Tantam, G., & Scott, S. (2013). Social learning theory parenting intervention promotes attachment-based caregiving in young children: Randomized clinical trial. *Journal of Clinical Child and Adolescent Psychology, 42*(3), 358–370. https://doi.org/10.1080/15374416.2012.723262

Oldmeadow, J. A., Quinn, S., & Kowert, R. (2013). Attachment style, social skills, and Facebook use amongst adults. *Computers in Human Behavior, 29*(3), 1142–1149. https://doi.org/10.1016/j.chb.2012.10.006

Opie, J. E., McIntosh, J. E., Esler, T. B., Duschinsky, R., George, C., Schore, A., Kothe, E. J., Tan, E. S., Greenwood, C. J., & Olsson, C. A. (2021). Early childhood attachment stability and change: A meta-analysis. *Attachment & Human Development, 23*(6), 897–930. https://doi.org/10.1080/14616734.2020.1800769

Overall, N. C., Simpson, J. A., & Struthers, H. (2013). Buffering attachment-related avoidance: Softening emotional and behavioral defenses during conflict discussions. *Journal of Personality and Social Psychology, 104*(5), 854–871. https://doi.org/10.1037/a0031798

Pace, C. S., Di Folco, S., Guerriero, V., Santona, A., & Terrone, G. (2015). Adoptive parenting and attachment: Association of the internal working models between adoptive mothers and their late-adopted children during adolescence. *Frontiers in Psychology, 6,* Article 1433. https://doi.org/10.3389/fpsyg.2015.01433

Pace, C. S., Muzi, S., & Steele, H. (2020). Adolescents' attachment: Content and discriminant validity of the Friends and Family Interview. *Journal of Child and Family Studies, 29*(4), 1173–1186. https://doi.org/10.1007/s10826-019-01654-8

Pallini, S., Chirumbolo, A., Morelli, M., Baiocco, R., Laghi, F., & Eisenberg, N. (2018). The relation of attachment security status to effortful self-regulation: A meta-analysis. *Psychological Bulletin, 144*(5), 501–531. https://doi.org/10.1037/bul0000134

Pallini, S., Morelli, M., Chirumbolo, A., Baiocco, R., Laghi, F., & Eisenberg, N. (2019). Attachment and attention problems: A meta-analysis. *Clinical Psychology Review, 74,* Article 101772. https://doi.org/10.1016/j.cpr.2019.101772

Pasalich, D. S., Craig, S. G., Goulter, N., O'Donnell, K. A., Hernandez, C. S., & Moretti, M. M. (in press). Patterns and predictors of different youth responses to attachment-based parenting intervention. *Journal of Clinical Child and Adolescent Psychology.*

Pasalich, D. S., Dadds, M. R., Hawes, D. J., & Brennan, J. (2012). Attachment and callous-unemotional traits in children with early-onset conduct problems. *Journal of Child Psychology and Psychiatry, and Allied Disciplines, 53*(8), 838–845. https://doi.org/10.1111/j.1469-7610.2012.02544.x

Pasalich, D. S., Moretti, M. M., Hassall, A., & Curcio, A. (2021). Pilot randomized controlled trial of an attachment- and trauma-focused intervention for kinship caregivers. *Child Abuse & Neglect, 120,* 105178. https://doi.org/10.1016/j.chiabu.2021.105178

Pears, K. C., Bruce, J., Fisher, P. A., & Kim, H. K. (2010). Indiscriminate friendliness in maltreated foster children. *Child Maltreatment, 15*(1), 64–75. https://doi.org/10.1177/1077559509337891

Petrowski, K., Nowacki, K., Pokorny, D., & Buchheim, A. (2011). Matching the patient to the therapist: The roles of the attachment status and the helping alliance. *Journal of Nervous and Mental Disease, 199*(11), 839–844. https://doi.org/10.1097/NMD.0b013e3182349cce

Phillips, P., & Mychailyszyn, M. (2021). A review of Parent–Child Interaction Therapy: Applications for youth anxiety. *Children and Youth Services Review, 125,* Article 105986. https://doi.org/10.1016/j.childyouth.2021.105986

Pinquart, M., Feussner, C., & Ahnert, L. (2013). Meta-analytic evidence for stability in attachments from infancy to early adulthood. *Attachment & Human Development, 15*(2), 189–218. https://doi.org/10.1080/14616734.2013.746257

Porter, R. H., & Winberg, J. (1999). Unique salience of maternal breast odors for newborn infants. *Neuroscience and Biobehavioral Reviews, 23*(3), 439–449. https://doi.org/10.1016/S0149-7634(98)00044-X

Powell, B., Cooper, G., Hoffman, K., & Marvin, B. (2014). *The Circle of Security Intervention: Enhancing attachment in early parent–child relationships*. Guilford Press.

Psouni, E., & Apetroaia, A. (2014). Measuring scripted attachment-related knowledge in middle childhood: The Secure Base Script Test. *Attachment & Human Development, 16*(1), 22–41. https://doi.org/10.1080/14616734.2013.804329

Raby, K. L., Cicchetti, D., Carlson, E. A., Cutuli, J. J., Englund, M. M., & Egeland, B. (2012). Genetic and caregiving-based contributions to infant attachment: Unique associations with distress reactivity and attachment security. *Psychological Science, 23*(9), 1016–1023. https://doi.org/10.1177/0956797612438265

Raby, K. L., Fraley, R. C., & Roisman, G. I. (2021). Categorical or dimensional measures of attachment? Insights from factor-analytic and taxometric research. In R. A. Thompson, J. A. Simpson, & L. J. Berlin (Eds.), *Attachment: The fundamental questions* (pp. 70–77). Guilford Press.

Raby, K. L., Verhage, M. L., Fearon, R. M. P., Fraley, R. C., Roisman, G. I., van IJzendoorn, M. H., Schuengel, C., Madigan, S., Oosterman, M., Bakermans-Kranenburg, M. J., Bernier, A., Ensink, K., Hautamäki, A., Mangelsdorf, S., Priddis, L. E., Wong, M. S., & The Collaboration on Attachment Transmission Synthesis. (2022). The latent structure of the Adult Attachment Interview: Large sample evidence from the collaboration on attachment transmission synthesis. *Development and Psychopathology, 34*(1), 307–319. https://doi.org/10.1017/S0954579420000978

Randolph, E. M. (2000). *Manual for the Randolph Attachment Disorder Questionnaire* (3rd ed.). The Attachment Center Press.

Rathgeber, M., Bürkner, P.-C., Schiller, E.-M., & Holling, H. (2019). The efficacy of emotionally focused couples therapy and behavioral couples therapy: A meta-analysis. *Journal of Marital and Family Therapy, 45*(3), 447–463. https://doi.org/10.1111/jmft.12336

Richters, M. M., & Volkmar, F. R. (1994). Reactive attachment disorder of infancy or early childhood. *Journal of the American Academy of Child & Adolescent Psychiatry, 33*(3), 328–332. https://doi.org/10.1097/00004583-199403000-00005

Riggs, S. A., Paulson, A., Tunnell, E., Sahl, G., Atkison, H., & Ross, C. A. (2007). Attachment, personality, and psychopathology among adult inpatients: Self-reported romantic attachment style versus Adult Attachment Interview states of mind. *Development and Psychopathology, 19*(1), 263–291. https://doi.org/10.1017/S0954579407070149

Robertson, J. (1952). *A two-year-old goes to hospital* [Film]. The Tavistock Child Development Research Unit.

Roisman, G. I., & Fraley, R. C. (2008). A behavior-genetic study of parenting quality, infant attachment security, and their covariation in a nationally representative sample. *Developmental Psychology, 44*(3), 831–839. https://doi.org/10.1037/0012-1649.44.3.831

Roisman, G. I., Haltigan, J. D., Haydon, K. C., & Booth-LaForce, C. (2014). The Adult Attachment Interview: Psychometrics, stability and change from infancy and developmental origins: VI. Earned-security in retrospect: Depressive symptoms, family stress, and maternal and paternal sensitivity from early childhood to mid-adolescence. *Monographs of the Society for Research in Child Development, 79*(3), 85–107. https://doi.org/10.1111/mono.12115

Roisman, G. I., Holland, A., Fortuna, K., Fraley, R. C., Clausell, E., & Clarke, A. (2007). The Adult Attachment Interview and self-reports of attachment style: An empirical rapprochement. *Journal of Personality and Social Psychology, 92*(4), 678–697. https://doi.org/10.1037/0022-3514.92.4.678

Roisman, G. I., Rogosch, F. A., Cicchetti, D., Groh, A. M., Haltigan, J. D., Haydon, K. C., Holland, A. S., & Steele, R. D. (2017). Attachment states of mind and inferred childhood experiences in maltreated and comparison adolescents from low-income families. *Development and Psychopathology, 29*(2), 337–345. https://doi.org/10.1017/S0954579417000025

Rosenthal, H. E. S., Somers, N., Fleming, P., & Walsh, J. (2014). The contributions of interpersonal attachment and friendship group identification to depressive symptoms in a nonclinical sample. *Journal of Applied Social Psychology, 44*(6), 409–414. https://doi.org/10.1111/jasp.12232

Rosenthal, N. L., & Kobak, R. (2010). Assessing adolescents' attachment hierarchies: Differences across developmental periods and associations with individual adaptation. *Journal of Research on Adolescence, 20*(3), 678–706. https://doi.org/10.1111/j.1532-7795.2010.00655.x

Roth, S., Newman, E., Pelcovitz, D., van der Kolk, B., & Mandel, F. S. (1997). Complex PTSD in victims exposed to sexual and physical abuse: Results from the *DSM-IV* Field Trial for Posttraumatic Stress Disorder. *Journal of Traumatic Stress, 10*(4), 539–555. https://doi.org/10.1002/jts.2490100403

Rothbaum, F., Weisz, J., Pott, M., Miyake, K., & Morelli, G. (2000). Attachment and culture. Security in the United States and Japan. *American Psychologist, 55*(10), 1093–1104. https://doi.org/10.1037/0003-066X.55.10.1093

Rothschild-Yakar, L., Stein, D., Goshen, D., Shoval, G., Yacobi, A., Eger, G., Kartin, B., & Gur, E. (2019). Mentalizing self and other and affect regulation patterns in anorexia and depression. *Frontiers in Psychology, 10*, Article 2223. https://doi.org/10.3389/fpsyg.2019.02223

Rutter, M., Colvert, E., Kreppner, J., Beckett, C., Castle, J., Groothues, C., Hawkins, A., O'Connor, T. G., Stevens, S. E., & Sonuga-Barke, E. J. S. (2007). Early adolescent outcomes for institutionally-deprived and non-deprived adoptees. I: Disinhibited attachment. *Journal of Child Psychology and Psychiatry, and Allied Disciplines*, *48*(1), 17–30. https://doi.org/10.1111/j.1469-7610.2006.01688.x

Rutter, M., & Shaffer, D. (1980). *DSM-III*: A step forward or back in terms of the classification of child psychiatric disorders? *Journal of the American Academy of Child Psychiatry, 19*(3), 371–394. https://doi.org/10.1016/S0002-7138(09)61060-8

Sadler, L. S., Slade, A., Close, N., Webb, D. L., Simpson, T., Fennie, K., & Mayes, L. C. (2013). Minding the Baby: Enhancing reflectiveness to improve early health and relationship outcomes in an interdisciplinary home visiting program. *Infant Mental Health Journal, 34*(5), 391–405. https://doi.org/10.1002/imhj.21406

Sagi, A., Lamb, M. E., Lewkowicz, K. S., Shoham, R., Dvir, R., & Estes, D. (1985). Security of infant–mother, –father, and –metapelet attachments among kibbutz-reared Israeli children. *Monographs of the Society for Research in Child Development, 50*(1-2), 257–275. https://doi.org/10.2307/3333837

Sagi, A., van IJzendoorn, M. H., Aviezer, O., Donnell, F., & Mayseless, O. (1994). Sleeping out of home in a Kibbutz communal arrangement: It makes a difference for infant–mother attachment. *Child Development, 65*(4), 992–1004. https://doi.org/10.2307/1131299

Schuengel, C., Verhage, M. L., & Duschinsky, R. (2021). Prospecting the attachment research field: A move to the level of engagement. *Attachment & Human Development, 23*(4), 375–395. https://doi.org/10.1080/14616734.2021.1918449

Seay, B., Hansen, E., & Harlow, H. F. (1962). Mother–infant separation in monkeys. *Journal of Child Psychology and Psychiatry, and Allied Disciplines, 3*(3-4), 123–132. https://doi.org/10.1111/j.1469-7610.1962.tb02047.x

Sheftall, A. H., Mathias, C. W., Furr, R. M., & Dougherty, D. M. (2013). Adolescent attachment security, family functioning, and suicide attempts. *Attachment & Human Development, 15*(4), 368–383. https://doi.org/10.1080/14616734.2013.782649

Shemmings, D., & Shemmings, Y. (2011). *Understanding disorganized attachment: Theory and practice for working with children and adults*. Jessica Kingsley Publishers.

Sherman, L. J., Rice, K., & Cassidy, J. (2015). Infant capacities related to building internal working models of attachment figures: A theoretical and empirical review. *Developmental Review, 37*, 109–141. https://doi.org/10.1016/j.dr.2015.06.001

Shlafer, R. J., Raby, K. L., Lawler, J. M., Hesemeyer, P. S., & Roisman, G. I. (2015). Longitudinal associations between adult attachment states of mind and parenting quality. *Attachment & Human Development, 17*(1), 83–95. https://doi.org/10.1080/14616734.2014.962064

Shmueli-Goetz, Y., Target, M., Fonagy, P., & Datta, A. (2008). The Child Attachment Interview: A psychometric study of reliability and discriminant validity. *Developmental Psychology, 44*(4), 939–956. https://doi.org/10.1037/0012-1649.44.4.939

Siegel, D., & Bryson, T. P. (2014, September 23). 'Time-outs' are hurting your child. *Time*. https://time.com/3404701/discipline-time-out-is-not-good/

Simpson, J. A. (1990). Influence of attachment styles on romantic relationships. *Journal of Personality and Social Psychology, 59*(5), 971–980. https://doi.org/10.1037/0022-3514.59.5.971

Skerry, A. E., & Spelke, E. S. (2014). Preverbal infants identify emotional reactions that are incongruent with goal outcomes. *Cognition, 130*(2), 204–216. https://doi.org/10.1016/j.cognition.2013.11.002

Slade, A. (2016). Attachment and adult psychotherapy: Theory, research, and practice. In J. Cassidy & P. R. Shaver (Eds.), *Handbook of attachment: Theory, research, and clinical implications* (3rd ed., pp. 759–779). Guilford Press.

Slade, A., Holland, M. L., Ordway, M. R., Carlson, E. A., Jeon, S., Close, N., Mayes, L. C., & Sadler, L. S. (2020). *Minding the Baby*®: Enhancing parental reflective functioning and infant attachment in an attachment-based, interdisciplinary home visiting program. *Development and Psychopathology*, *32*(1), 123–137. https://doi.org/10.1017/S0954579418001463

Slagt, M., Dubas, J. S., Deković, M., & van Aken, M. A. G. (2016). Differences in sensitivity to parenting depending on child temperament: A meta-analysis. *Psychological Bulletin*, *142*(10), 1068–1110. https://doi.org/10.1037/bul0000061

Smith, M., & South, S. (2020). Romantic attachment style and borderline personality pathology: A meta-analysis. *Clinical Psychology Review*, *75*, Article 101781. https://doi.org/10.1016/j.cpr.2019.101781

Smyke, A. T., Dumitrescu, A., & Zeanah, C. H. (2002). Attachment disturbances in young children. I: The continuum of caretaking casualty. *Journal of the American Academy of Child & Adolescent Psychiatry*, *41*(8), 972–982. https://doi.org/10.1097/00004583-200208000-00016

Smyke, A. T., Zeanah, C. H., Gleason, M. M., Drury, S. S., Fox, N. A., Nelson, C. A., & Guthrie, D. (2012). A randomized controlled trial comparing foster care and institutional care for children with signs of reactive attachment disorder. *The American Journal of Psychiatry*, *169*(5), 508–514. https://doi.org/10.1176/appi.ajp.2011.11050748

Solomon, J., George, C., & de Jong, A. (1995). Children classified as controlling at age six: Evidence of disorganized representational strategies and aggression at home and at school. *Development and Psychopathology*, *7*(3), 447–463. https://doi.org/10.1017/S0954579400006623

Spitz, R. A. (1953). Aggression: Its role in the establishment of object relations. In R. M. Loewenstein (Ed.), *Drives, affects, behavior* (pp. 126–138). International Universities Press. https://doi.org/10.1037/10633-006

Spitz, R. A., & Wolf, K. M. (1947). *Grief: A peril in infancy* [Film]. United States National Library of Medicine.

Spruit, A., Goos, L., Weenink, N., Rodenburg, R., Niemeyer, H., Stams, G. J., & Colonnesi, C. (2020). The relation between attachment and depression in children and adolescents: A multilevel meta-analysis. *Clinical Child and Family Psychology Review*, *23*(1), 54–69. https://doi.org/10.1007/s10567-019-00299-9

Sroufe, L. A., Carlson, E. A., Levy, A. K., & Egeland, B. (1999). Implications of attachment theory for developmental psychopathology. *Development and Psychopathology*, *11*(1), 1–13. https://doi.org/10.1017/S0954579499001923

Sroufe, L. A., Egeland, B., Carlson, E. A., & Collins, W. A. (2005a). *The development of the person: The Minnesota Study of Risk and Adaptation from birth to adulthood*. Guilford Press.

Sroufe, L. A., Egeland, B., Carlson, E., & Collins, W. A. (2005b). Placing early attachment experiences in developmental context: The Minnesota Longitudinal Study. In K. E. Grossmann, K. Grossmann, & E. Waters (Eds.), *Attachment from infancy to adulthood: The major longitudinal studies* (pp. 48–70). Guilford.

Sroufe, L. A., & Rutter, M. (1984). The domain of developmental psychopathology. *Child Development, 55*(1), 17–29. https://doi.org/10.2307/1129832

Sroufe, L. A., & Waters, E. (1977). Heart rate as a convergent measure in clinical and developmental research. *Merrill-Palmer Quarterly, 23*, 3–27.

Stacks, A. M., Muzik, M., Wong, K., Beeghly, M., Huth-Bocks, A., Irwin, J. L., & Rosenblum, K. L. (2014). Maternal reflective functioning among mothers with childhood maltreatment histories: Links to sensitive parenting and infant attachment security. *Attachment & Human Development, 16*(5), 515–533. https://doi.org/10.1080/14616734.2014.935452

Stayton, D. J., & Ainsworth, M. D. S. (1973). Individual differences in infant responses to brief, everyday separations as related to other infant and maternal behaviors. *Developmental Psychology, 9*(2), 226–235. https://doi.org/10.1037/h0035089

Stayton, D. J., Ainsworth, M. D. S., & Main, M. B. (1973). Development of separation behavior in the first year of life: Protest, following, and greeting. *Developmental Psychology, 9*(2), 213–225. https://doi.org/10.1037/h0035090

Steele, H., & Steele, M. (2005). The construct of coherence as an indicator of attachment security in middle childhood: The Friends and Family Interview. In K. A. Kerns & R. A. Richardson (Eds.), *Attachment in middle childhood* (pp. 137–160). Guilford Press.

Steele, H., & Steele, M. (2008). *Clinical applications of the Adult Attachment Interview*. Guilford Press.

Steele, H., & Steele, M. (Eds.). (2018). *Handbook of attachment-based interventions*. Guilford Press.

Steele, H., & Steele, M. (2021). Categorical assessments of attachment: On the ontological relevance of group membership. In R. A. Thompson, J. A. Simpson, & L. J. Berlin (Eds.), *Attachment: The fundamental questions* (pp. 63–69). Guilford Press.

Steele, R. D., Waters, T. E. A., Bost, K. K., Vaughn, B. E., Truitt, W., Waters, H. S., Booth-LaForce, C., & Roisman, G. I. (2014). Caregiving antecedents of secure base script knowledge: A comparative analysis of young adult attachment representations. *Developmental Psychology, 50*(11), 2526–2538. https://doi.org/10.1037/a0037992

Stovall, K. C., & Dozier, M. (2000). The development of attachment in new relationships: Single subject analyses for 10 foster infants. *Development and Psychopathology, 12*(2), 133–156. https://doi.org/10.1017/S0954579400002029

Stovall-McClough, K. C., & Cloitre, M. (2003). Reorganization of unresolved childhood traumatic memories following exposure therapy. *Annals of the New York Academy of Sciences, 1008*(1), 297–299. https://doi.org/10.1196/annals.1301.036

Stovall-McClough, K. C., & Cloitre, M. (2006). Unresolved attachment, PTSD, and dissociation in women with childhood abuse histories. *Journal of Consulting and Clinical Psychology*, *74*(2), 219–228. https://doi.org/10.1037/0022-006X.74.2.219

Stovall-McClough, K. C., & Dozier, M. (2004). Forming attachments in foster care: Infant attachment behaviors during the first 2 months of placement. *Development and Psychopathology*, *16*(2), 253–271. https://doi.org/10.1017/S0954579404044505

Stovall-McClough, K. C., & Dozier, M. (2016). Attachment states of mind and psychopathology in adulthood. In J. Cassidy & P. R. Shaver (Eds.), *Handbook of attachment: Theory, research, and clinical implications* (3rd ed., pp. 715–738). Guilford Press.

Strauß, B., Altmann, U., Manes, S., Tholl, A., Koranyi, S., Nolte, T., Beutel, M. E., Wiltink, J., Herpertz, S., Hiller, W., Hoyer, J., Joraschky, P., Nolting, B., Ritter, V., Stangier, U., Willutzki, U., Salzer, S., Leibing, E., Leichsenring, F., & Kirchmann, H. (2018). Changes of attachment characteristics during psychotherapy of patients with social anxiety disorder: Results from the SOPHO-Net trial. *PLoS One*, *13*(3), Article e0192802. https://doi.org/10.1371/journal.pone.0192802

Strauss, B. M., Mestel, R., & Kirchmann, H. A. (2011). Changes of attachment status among women with personality disorders undergoing inpatient treatment. *Counselling & Psychotherapy Research*, *11*(4), 275–283. https://doi.org/10.1080/14733145.2010.548563

Strauss, C., Morry, M. M., & Kito, M. (2012). Attachment styles and relationship quality: Actual, perceived, and ideal partner matching. *Personal Relationships*, *19*(1), 14–36. https://doi.org/10.1111/j.1475-6811.2010.01333.x

Suchman, N. E., DeCoste, C., Borelli, J. L., & McMahon, T. J. (2018). Does improvement in maternal attachment representations predict greater maternal sensitivity, child attachment security and lower rates of relapse to substance use? A second test of Mothering from the Inside Out treatment mechanisms. *Journal of Substance Abuse Treatment*, *85*, 21–30. https://doi.org/10.1016/j.jsat.2017.11.006

Suomi, S. J., Harlow, H. F., & McKinney, W. T., Jr. (1972). Monkey psychiatrists. *The American Journal of Psychiatry*, *128*(8), 927–932. https://doi.org/10.1176/ajp.128.8.927

Suomi, S. J., van der Horst, F. C. P., & van der Veer, R. (2008). Rigorous experiments on monkey love: An account of Harry F. Harlow's role in the history of attachment theory. *Integrative Psychological & Behavioral Science*, *42*(4), 354–369. https://doi.org/10.1007/s12124-008-9072-9

Takahashi, K. (1986). Examining the Strange Situation Procedure with Japanese mothers and 12-month-old infants. *Developmental Psychology*, *22*(2), 265–270. https://doi.org/10.1037/0012-1649.22.2.265

Tarabulsy, G. M., Bernier, A., Provost, M. A., Maranda, J., Larose, S., Moss, E., Larose, M., & Tessier, R. (2005). Another look inside the gap: Ecological contributions to the transmission of attachment in a sample of adolescent mother–infant dyads. *Developmental Psychology, 41*(1), 212–224. https://doi.org/10.1037/0012-1649.41.1.212

Tarabulsy, G. M., Larose, S., Bernier, A., Trottier-Sylvain, K., Girard, D., Vargas, M., & Noël, C. (2012). Attachment states of mind in late adolescence and the quality and course of romantic relationships in adulthood. *Attachment & Human Development, 14*(6), 621–643. https://doi.org/10.1080/14616734.2012.728358

Taubner, S., White, L. O., Zimmermann, J., Fonagy, P., & Nolte, T. (2013). Attachment-related mentalization moderates the relationship between psychopathic traits and proactive aggression in adolescence. *Journal of Abnormal Child Psychology, 41*(6), 929–938. https://doi.org/10.1007/s10802-013-9736-x

Teufl, L., Deichmann, F., Supper, B., & Ahnert, L. (2020). How fathers' attachment security and education contribute to early child language skills above and beyond mothers: Parent–child conversation under scrutiny. *Attachment & Human Development, 22*(1), 71–84. https://doi.org/10.1080/14616734.2019.1589063

Thomas, N. (1997). *When love is not enough: Parenting a child with RAD*. NT Press.

Thomas, R., Abell, B., Webb, H. J., Avdagic, E., & Zimmer-Gembeck, M. J. (2017). Parent–Child Interaction Therapy: A meta-analysis. *Pediatrics, 140*(3), Article e20170352. https://doi.org/10.1542/peds.2017-0352

Thomas, R., & Zimmer-Gembeck, M. J. (2012). Parent–Child Interaction Therapy: An evidence-based treatment for child maltreatment. *Child Maltreatment, 17*(3), 253–266. https://doi.org/10.1177/1077559512459555

Thompson, L. A., & Trevathan, W. R. (2008). Cortisol reactivity, maternal sensitivity, and learning in 3-month-old infants. *Infant Behavior and Development, 31*(1), 92–106. https://doi.org/10.1016/j.infbeh.2007.07.007

Thompson, L. A., & Trevathan, W. R. (2009). Cortisol reactivity, maternal sensitivity, and infant preference for mother's familiar face and rhyme in 6-month-old infants. *Journal of Reproductive and Infant Psychology, 27*(2), 143–167. https://doi.org/10.1080/02646830801918463

Timmer, S. G., Ho, L. K. L., Urquiza, A. J., Zebell, N. M., Fernandez Y Garcia, E., & Boys, D. (2011). The effectiveness of Parent–Child Interaction Therapy with depressive mothers: The changing relationship as the agent of individual change. *Child Psychiatry and Human Development, 42*(4), 406–423. https://doi.org/10.1007/s10578-011-0226-5

Tinbergen, N. (1951). *The study of instinct*. Clarendon Press.

Tizard, B., & Rees, J. (1975). The effect of early institutional rearing on the behaviour problems and affectional relationships of four-year-old children. *The Journal of Child Psychology & Psychiatry, 16*(1), 61–73. https://doi.org/10.1111/j.1469-7610.1975.tb01872.x

Toth, S. L., Maughan, A., Manly, J. T., Spagnola, M., & Cicchetti, D. (2002). The relative efficacy of two interventions in altering maltreated preschool children's representational models: Implications for attachment theory.

Development and Psychopathology, *14*(4), 877–908. https://doi.org/10.1017/S095457940200411X

Toth, S. L., Michl-Petzing, L. C., Guild, D., & Lieberman, A. F. (2018). Child–Parent Psychotherapy: Theoretical bases, clinical applications, and empirical support. In H. Steele & M. Steele (Eds.), *Handbook of attachment-based interventions* (pp. 296–317). Guilford Press.

Toth, S. L., Rogosch, F. A., Manly, J. T., & Cicchetti, D. (2006). The efficacy of toddler-parent psychotherapy to reorganize attachment in the young offspring of mothers with major depressive disorder: A randomized preventive trial. *Journal of Consulting and Clinical Psychology*, *74*(6), 1006–1016. https://doi.org/10.1037/0022-006X.74.6.1006

Tracy, R. L., Lamb, M. E., & Salter Ainsworth, M. D. (1976). Infant approach behavior as related to attachment. *Child Development*, *47*(3), 571–578. https://doi.org/10.2307/1128170

Tran, S., & Simpson, J. A. (2009). Prorelationship maintenance behaviors: The joint roles of attachment and commitment. *Journal of Personality and Social Psychology*, *97*(4), 685–698. https://doi.org/10.1037/a0016418

USA Today. (2014, August 12). Oregon board suspends psychologist's license. *USA Today*. https://www.usatoday.com/story/news/nation/2014/08/12/oregon-psychologist-license/13976251/

Vaish, A., & Woodward, A. (2010). Infants use attention but not emotions to predict others' actions. *Infant Behavior and Development*, *33*(1), 79–87. https://doi.org/10.1016/j.infbeh.2009.11.003

van den Dries, L., Juffer, F., van IJzendoorn, M. H., & Bakermans-Kranenburg, M. J. (2009). Fostering security? A meta-analysis of attachment in adopted children. *Children and Youth Services Review*, *31*(3), 410–421. https://doi.org/10.1016/j.childyouth.2008.09.008

van der Kolk, B., Ford, J. D., & Spinazzola, J. (2019). Comorbidity of developmental trauma disorder (DTD) and post-traumatic stress disorder: Findings from the DTD field trial. *European Journal of Psychotraumatology*, *10*(1), 1562841. https://doi.org/10.1080/20008198.2018.1562841

van Emmichoven, I. A., van IJzendoorn, M. H., de Ruiter, C., & Brosschot, J. F. (2003). Selective processing of threatening information: Effects of attachment representation and anxiety disorder on attention and memory. *Development and Psychopathology*, *15*(1), 219–237. https://doi.org/10.1017/S0954579403000129

van IJzendoorn, M. H. (1995). Adult attachment representations, parental responsiveness, and infant attachment: A meta-analysis on the predictive validity of the Adult Attachment Interview. *Psychological Bulletin*, *117*(3), 387–403. https://doi.org/10.1037/0033-2909.117.3.387

van IJzendoorn, M. H., & Bakermans-Kranenburg, M. J. (1996). Attachment representations in mothers, fathers, adolescents, and clinical groups: A meta-analytic search for normative data. *Journal of Consulting and Clinical Psychology*, *64*(1), 8–21. https://doi.org/10.1037/0022-006X.64.1.8

van IJzendoorn, M. H., & Bakermans-Kranenburg, M. J. (2006). DRD4 7-repeat polymorphism moderates the association between maternal unresolved loss or trauma and infant disorganization. *Attachment & Human Development, 8*(4), 291–307. https://doi.org/10.1080/14616730601048159

van IJzendoorn, M. H., & Bakermans-Kranenburg, M. J. (2014). Confined quest for continuity: The categorical versus continuous nature of attachment. *Monographs of the Society for Research in Child Development, 79*(3), 157–167. https://doi.org/10.1111/mono.12120

van IJzendoorn, M. H., & Bakermans-Kranenburg, M. J. (2015). Genetic differential susceptibility on trial: Meta-analytic support from randomized controlled experiments. *Development and Psychopathology, 27*(1), 151–162. https://doi.org/10.1017/S0954579414001369

van IJzendoorn, M. H., & Bakermans-Kranenburg, M. J. (2019). Bridges across the intergenerational transmission of attachment gap. *Current Opinion in Psychology, 25*, 31–36. https://doi.org/10.1016/j.copsyc.2018.02.014

van IJzendoorn, M. H., Bakermans-Kranenburg, M. J., & Juffer, F. (2005). Why less is more: From the dodo bird verdict to evidence-based interventions on sensitivity and early attachments. In L. J. Berlin, Y. Ziv, L. Amaya-Jackson, & M. T. Greenberg (Eds.), *Enhancing early attachments: Theory, research, intervention, and policy* (pp. 297–312). Guilford Press.

van IJzendoorn, M. H., & De Wolff, M. S. (1997). In search of the absent father—meta-analyses of infant–father attachment: A rejoinder to our discussants. *Child Development, 68*(4), 604–609. https://doi.org/10.1111/j.1467-8624.1997.tb04223.x

van IJzendoorn, M. H., Dijkstra, J., & Bus, A. G. (1995). Attachment, intelligence, and language: A meta-analysis. *Social Development, 4*(2), 115–128. https://doi.org/10.1111/j.1467-9507.1995.tb00055.x

van IJzendoorn, M. H., Schuengel, C., & Bakermans-Kranenburg, M. J. (1999). Disorganized attachment in early childhood: Meta-analysis of precursors, concomitants, and sequelae. *Development and Psychopathology, 11*(2), 225–250. https://doi.org/10.1017/S0954579499002035

van IJzendoorn, M. H., Schuengel, C., Wang, Q., & Bakermans-Kranenburg, M. J. (2022). Improving parenting, child attachment, and externalizing behaviors: Meta-analysis of the first 25 randomized controlled trials on the effects of Video-feedback Intervention to promote Positive Parenting and Sensitive Disciplines. *Development and Psychopathology*, 1–16. https://doi.org/10.1017/S0954579421001462

van IJzendoorn, M. H., Vereijken, C. M. J. L., Bakermans-Kranenburg, M. J., & Riksen-Walraven, J. M. (2004). Assessing attachment security with the Attachment Q Sort: Meta-analytic evidence for the validity of the observer AQS. *Child Development, 75*(4), 1188–1213. https://doi.org/10.1111/j.1467-8624.2004.00733.x

van Rosmalen, L., van der Horst, F. C. P., & van der Veer, R. (2016). From secure dependency to attachment: Mary Ainsworth's integration of Blatz's security theory into Bowlby's attachment theory. *History of Psychology, 19*(1), 22–39. https://doi.org/10.1037/hop0000015

van Rosmalen, L., van der Veer, R., & van der Horst, F. (2015). Ainsworth's Strange Situation Procedure: The origin of an instrument. *Journal of the History of the Behavioral Sciences, 51*(3), 261–284. https://doi.org/10.1002/jhbs.21729

van Rosmalen, L., van der Veer, R., & van der Horst, F. C. P. (2020). The nature of love: Harlow, Bowlby and Bettelheim on affectionless mothers. *History of Psychiatry, 31*(2), 227–231. https://doi.org/10.1177/0957154X19898997

Vandesande, S., Bosmans, G., Sterkenburg, P., Schuengel, C., Van Den Noortgate, W., & Maes, B. (2020). Comfort provided by parents versus strangers after eliciting stress in children with severe or profound intellectual disabilities: Does it make a difference? *Attachment & Human Development, 22*(4), 425–447. https://doi.org/10.1080/14616734.2019.1659835

Vaughn, B., Egeland, B., Sroufe, L. A., & Waters, E. (1979). Individual differences in infant–mother attachment at twelve and eighteen months: Stability and change in families under stress. *Child Development, 50*(4), 971–975. https://doi.org/10.2307/1129321

Vaughn, B. E., Coppola, G., Verissimo, M., Monteiro, L., Santos, A. J., Posada, G., Carbonell, O. A., Plata, S. J., Waters, H. S., Bost, K. K., McBride, B., Shin, N., & Korth, B. (2007). They quality of maternal secure-base scripts predicts children's secure-base behavior at home in three sociocultural groups. *International Journal of Behavioral Development, 31*(1), 65–76. https://doi.org/10.1177/0165025407073574

Vaughn, B. E., & Waters, E. (1990). Attachment behavior at home and in the laboratory: Q-sort observations and strange situation classifications of one-year-olds. *Child Development, 61*(6), 1965–1973. https://doi.org/10.2307/1130850

Vaughn, B. E., Waters, T. E. A., Steele, R. D., Roisman, G. I., Bost, K. K., Truitt, W., Waters, H. S., & Booth-Laforce, C. (2016). Multiple domains of parental secure base support during childhood and adolescence contribute to adolescents' representations of attachment as a secure base script. *Attachment & Human Development, 18*(4), 317–336. https://doi.org/10.1080/14616734.2016.1162180

Venta, A., Hatkevich, C., Mellick, W., Vanwoerden, S., & Sharp, C. (2017). Social cognition mediates the relation between attachment schemas and post-traumatic stress disorder. *Psychological Trauma, 9*(1), 88–95. https://doi.org/10.1037/tra0000165

Venta, A., Sharp, C., Shmueli-Goetz, Y., & Newlin, E. (2015). An evaluation of the construct of earned security in adolescents: Evidence from an inpatient sample. *Bulletin of the Menninger Clinic, 79*(1), 41–69. https://doi.org/10.1521/bumc.2015.79.1.41

Venta, A., Shmueli-Goetz, Y., & Sharp, C. (2014). Assessing attachment in adolescence: A psychometric study of the child attachment interview. *Psychological Assessment, 26*(1), 238–255. https://doi.org/10.1037/a0034712

Verhage, M. L., Schuengel, C., Madigan, S., Fearon, R. M. P., Oosterman, M., Cassibba, R., Bakermans-Kranenburg, M. J., & van IJzendoorn, M. H. (2016).

Narrowing the transmission gap: A synthesis of three decades of research on intergenerational transmission of attachment. *Psychological Bulletin, 142*(4), 337–366. https://doi.org/10.1037/bul0000038

Vicedo, M. (2017). Putting attachment in its place: Disciplinary and cultural contexts. *European Journal of Developmental Psychology, 14*(6), 684–699. https://doi.org/10.1080/17405629.2017.1289838

Vonderlin, R., Kleindienst, N., Alpers, G. W., Bohus, M., Lyssenko, L., & Schmahl, C. (2018). Dissociation in victims of childhood abuse or neglect: A meta-analytic review. *Psychological Medicine, 48*(15), 2467–2476. https://doi.org/10.1017/S0033291718000740

Waddington, C. H. (1957). *The strategy of the genes*. Allen & Unwin.

Walczak, M., Esbjørn, B. H., & Breinholst, S. (2017). Attachment as a predictor of non response to CBT treatment in children with anxiety disorders. *Attachment & Human Development, 19*(6), 635–653. https://doi.org/10.1080/14616734.2017.1339099

Wartner, U. G., Grossmann, K., Fremmer-Bombik, E., & Suess, G. (1994). Attachment patterns at age six in south Germany: Predictability from infancy and implications for preschool behavior. *Child Development, 65*(4), 1014–1027. https://doi.org/10.2307/1131301

Waters, E. (1978). The reliability and stability of individual differences in infant–mother attachment. *Child Development, 49*(2), 483–494. https://doi.org/10.2307/1128714

Waters, E., Crowell, J., Elliott, M., Corcoran, D., & Treboux, D. (2002). Bowlby's secure base theory and the social/personality psychology of attachment styles: Work(s) in progress. *Attachment & Human Development, 4*(2), 230–242. https://doi.org/10.1080/14616730210154216

Waters, E., & Deane, K. (1985). Defining and assessing individual differences in attachment relationships: Q-methodology and the organization of behavior in infancy and early childhood. *Monographs of the Society for Research in Child Development, 50*(1/2), 41–65. https://doi.org/10.2307/3333826

Waters, E., Merrick, S., Treboux, D., Crowell, J., & Albersheim, L. (2000). Attachment security in infancy and early adulthood: A twenty-year longitudinal study. *Child Development, 71*(3), 684–689. https://doi.org/10.1111/1467-8624.00176

Waters, H. S., & Waters, E. (2006). The attachment working models concept: Among other things, we build script-like representations of secure base experiences. *Attachment & Human Development, 8*(3), 185–197. https://doi.org/10.1080/14616730600856016

Waters, T. E. A. (2021). Representational measures of attachment: A secure base script perspective. In R. A. Thompson, J. A. Simpson, & L. J. Berlin (Eds.), *Attachment: The fundamental questions* (pp. 78–85). Guilford Press.

Waters, T. E. A., Bosmans, G., Vandevivere, E., Dujardin, A., & Waters, H. S. (2015). Secure base representations in middle childhood across two Western cultures: Associations with parental attachment representations and maternal reports of behavior problems. *Developmental Psychology, 51*(8), 1013–1025. https://doi.org/10.1037/a0039375

Waters, T. E. A., Brockmeyer, S. L., & Crowell, J. A. (2013). AAI coherence predicts caregiving and care seeking behavior: Secure base script knowledge helps explain why. *Attachment & Human Development, 15*(3), 316–331. https://doi.org/10.1080/14616734.2013.782657

Waters, T. E. A., & Facompré, C. R. (2021). Measuring secure base script knowledge in the Adult Attachment Interview. In E. Waters, B. E. Vaughn, & H. S. Waters (Eds.), *Measuring attachment: Developmental assessment across the lifespan* (pp. 338–373). Guilford Press.

Waters, T. E. A., Facompré, C. R., Dujardin, A., Van De Walle, M., Verhees, M., Bodner, N., Boldt, L. J., & Bosmans, G. (2019). Taxometric analysis of secure base script knowledge in middle childhood reveals categorical latent structure. *Child Development, 90*(3), 694–707. https://doi.org/10.1111/cdev.13229

Waters, T. E. A., Facompré, C. R., Van de Walle, M., Dujardin, A., De Winter, S., Heylen, J., Santens, T., Verhees, M., Finet, C., & Bosmans, G. (2019). Stability and change in secure base script knowledge during middle childhood and early adolescence: A 3-year longitudinal study. *Developmental Psychology, 55*(11), 2379–2388. https://doi.org/10.1037/dev0000798

Waters, T. E. A., Fraley, R. C., Groh, A. M., Steele, R. D., Vaughn, B. E., Bost, K. K., Veríssimo, M., Coppola, G., & Roisman, G. I. (2015). The latent structure of secure base script knowledge. *Developmental Psychology, 51*(6), 823–830. https://doi.org/10.1037/dev0000012

Waters, T. E. A., Raby, K. L., Ruiz, S. K., Martin, J., & Roisman, G. I. (2018). Adult attachment representations and the quality of romantic and parent–child relationships: An examination of the contributions of coherence of discourse and secure base script knowledge. *Developmental Psychology, 54*(12), 2371–2381. https://doi.org/10.1037/dev0000607

Waters, T. E. A., & Roisman, G. I. (2019). The secure base script concept: An overview. *Current Opinion in Psychology, 25*, 162–166. https://doi.org/10.1016/j.copsyc.2018.08.002

Waters, T. E. A., Ruiz, S. K., & Roisman, G. I. (2017). Origins of secure base script knowledge and the developmental construction of attachment representations. *Child Development, 88*(1), 198–209. https://doi.org/10.1111/cdev.12571

Weinfield, N. S., Sroufe, L. A., & Egeland, B. (2000). Attachment from infancy to early adulthood in a high-risk sample: Continuity, discontinuity, and their correlates. *Child Development, 71*(3), 695–702. https://doi.org/10.1111/1467-8624.00178

Weissman, N., Batten, S. V., Rheem, K. D., Wiebe, S. A., Pasillas, R. M., Potts, W., Barone, M., Brown, C. H., & Dixon, L. B. (2018). The effectiveness of emotionally focused couples therapy with veterans with PTSD: A pilot study. *Journal of Couple & Relationship Therapy, 17*(1), 25–41. https://doi.org/10.1080/15332691.2017.1285261

Weisz, J. R., McCarty, C. A., & Valeri, S. M. (2006). Effects of psychotherapy for depression in children and adolescents: A meta-analysis. *Psychological Bulletin, 132*(1), 132–149. https://doi.org/10.1037/0033-2909.132.1.132

Welch, M. G. (1989). *Holding time*. Fireside.

Wiebe, S. A., Johnson, S. M., Burgess Moser, M., Dalgleish, T. L., & Tasca, G. A. (2017). Predicting follow-up outcomes in emotionally focused couple therapy: The role of change in trust, relationship-specific attachment, and emotional engagement. *Journal of Marital and Family Therapy, 43*(2), 213–226. https://doi.org/10.1111/jmft.12199

Wilkins, D. (2012). Disorganized attachment indicates maltreatment: How is this link useful for child protection social workers? *Journal of Social Work Practice, 26*(1), 15–30. https://doi.org/10.1080/02650533.2011.598228

Wilkins, D. (2017). Using Q methodology to understand how child protection social workers use attachment theory. *Child & Family Social Work, 22*, 70–80. https://doi.org/10.1111/cfs.12276

Wilkins, D. (2021). Disorganized attachment does not indicate child maltreatment. *Journal of Social Work Practice, 35*(2), 219–220. https://doi.org/10.1080/02650533.2020.1787364

Willoughby, M. T., Mills-Koonce, W. R., Gottfredson, N. C., & Wagner, N. (2014). Erratum to: Measuring callous unemotional behaviors in early childhood: Factor structure and the prediction of stable aggression in middle childhood. *Journal of Psychopathology and Behavioral Assessment, 36*(1), 43–46. https://doi.org/10.1007/s10862-013-9379-9

Wong, M., Bost, K. K., Shin, N., Veríssomo, M., Maia, J., Monteiro, L., Silva, F., Coppola, G., Costantini, A., & Vaughn, B. E. (2011). Preschool children's mental representations of attachment: Antecedents in their secure base behaviors and maternal attachment scripts. *Attachment & Human Development, 13*(5), 489–502. https://doi.org/10.1080/14616734.2011.602256

Woo, J., Wrath, A. J., & Adams, G. C. (2020). The relationship between attachment and self-injurious behaviors in the child and adolescent population: A systematic review of the literature. *Archives of Suicide Research*. Advance online publication. https://doi.org/10.1080/13811118.2020.1804024

Woodhouse, S., Ayers, S., & Field, A. P. (2015). The relationship between adult attachment style and post-traumatic stress symptoms: A meta-analysis. *Journal of Anxiety Disorders, 35*, 103–117. https://doi.org/10.1016/j.janxdis.2015.07.002

Woolgar, M., & Baldock, E. (2015). Attachment disorders versus more common problems in looked after and adopted children: Comparing community and expert assessments. *Child and Adolescent Mental Health, 20*(1), 34–40. https://doi.org/10.1111/camh.12052

World Health Organization. (1993). *International statistical classification of diseases and related health problems* (10th ed.).

World Health Organization. (2019). *International statistical classification of diseases and related health problems* (11th ed.).

Yap, M. B. H., Allen, N. B., & Sheeber, L. (2007). Using an emotion regulation framework to understand the role of temperament and family processes in risk for adolescent depressive disorders. *Clinical Child and Family Psychology Review, 10*(2), 180–196. https://doi.org/10.1007/s10567-006-0014-0

Yarger, H. A., Bernard, K., Caron, E. B., Wallin, A., & Dozier, M. (2020). Enhancing parenting quality for young children adopted internationally: Results of a randomized controlled trial. *Journal of Clinical Child and Adolescent Psychology, 49*(3), 378–390. https://doi.org/10.1080/15374416.2018.1547972

Zalaznik, D., Weiss, M., & Huppert, J. D. (2019). Improvement in adult anxious and avoidant attachment during cognitive behavioral therapy for panic disorder. *Psychotherapy Research, 29*(3), 337–353. https://doi.org/10.1080/10503307.2017.1365183

Zaslow, R. W., & Menta, M. (1975). *The psychology of the Z-process: Attachment and activation* (2nd ed.). San Jose State University Press.

Zeanah, C. H., & Boris, N. W. (2000). Disturbances and disorders of attachment in early childhood. In C. H. Zeanah (Ed.), *Handbook of infant mental health* (2nd ed., pp. 353–368). Guilford Press.

Zeanah, C. H., & Gleason, M. M. (2015). Annual research review: Attachment disorders in early childhood—clinical presentation, causes, correlates, and treatment. *Journal of Child Psychology and Psychiatry, and Allied Disciplines, 56*(3), 207–222. https://doi.org/10.1111/jcpp.12347

Zeanah, C. H., & Guyon-Harris, K. L. (2020). Commentary: Increasing diagnostic precision in reactive attachment disorder—a commentary on Allen & Schuengel (2019). *Child and Adolescent Mental Health, 25*(1), 11–12. https://doi.org/10.1111/camh.12357

Zeanah, C. H., & Smyke, A. T. (2009). Attachment disorders. In C. H. Zeanah (Ed.), *Handbook of infant mental health* (3rd ed., pp. 421–434). Guilford Press.

Zeegers, M. A. J., Colonnesi, C., Stams, G. J. M., & Meins, E. (2017). Mind matters: A meta-analysis on parental mentalization and sensitivity as predictors of infant–parent attachment. *Psychological Bulletin, 143*(12), 1245–1272. https://doi.org/10.1037/bul0000114

Zephyr, L., Cyr, C., Monette, S., Archambault, M., Lehmann, S., & Minnis, H. (2021). Meta-analyses of the associations between disinhibited social engagement behaviors and child attachment insecurity or disorganization. *Research on Child and Adolescent Psychopathology, 49*(7), 949–962. https://doi.org/10.1007/s10802-021-00777-1

ZERO TO THREE. (2020). *DC:0-5: Diagnostic classification of mental health and developmental disorders of infancy and early childhood* (Version 2.0). (Original work published 2016)

ZERO TO THREE. (2005). *DC: 0-3R, Diagnostic classification of mental health and developmental disorders of infancy and early childhood (Revised edition).*

Zimmer-Gembeck, M. J., Kerin, J. L., Webb, H. J., Gardner, A. A., Campbell, S. M., Swan, K., & Timmer, S. G. (2019). Improved perceptions of emotion regulation and reflective functioning in parents: Two additional positive outcomes of Parent–Child Interaction Therapy. *Behavior Therapy, 50*(2), 340–352. https://doi.org/10.1016/j.beth.2018.07.002

Zimmermann, P., & Iwanski, A. (2019). Attachment Disorder behavior in early and middle childhood: Associations with children's self-concept and observed signs of negative internal working models. *Attachment & Human Development, 21*(2), 170–189. https://doi.org/10.1080/14616734.2018.1499212

Zimmermann, P., Maier, M. A., Winter, M., & Grossmann, K. E. (2001). Attachment and adolescents' emotion regulation during a joint problem-solving task with a friend. *International Journal of Behavioral Development, 25*(4), 331–343. https://doi.org/10.1080/01650250143000157

Zimmermann, P., Mohr, C., & Spangler, G. (2009). Genetic and attachment influences on adolescents' regulation of autonomy and aggressiveness. *Journal of Child Psychology and Psychiatry, and Allied Disciplines, 50*(11), 1339–1347. https://doi.org/10.1111/j.1469-7610.2009.02158.x

Zisk, A., Abbott, C. H., Ewing, S. K., Diamond, G. S., & Kobak, R. (2017). The Suicide Narrative Interview: Adolescents' attachment expectancies and symptom severity in a clinical sample. *Attachment & Human Development, 19*(5), 447–462. https://doi.org/10.1080/14616734.2016.1269234

Index

A

E

Q

R

T

U

About the Author

Brian Allen, PsyD, is a clinical psychologist who currently serves as the director of mental health services at the Penn State Children's Hospital's Center for the Protection of Children. He also is an associate professor of pediatrics and psychiatry and behavioral health in the Penn State College of Medicine and core faculty in the Child Maltreatment Solutions Network at Penn State University. Dr. Allen conducts research on the developmental impact of childhood trauma and maltreatment, the effectiveness and implementation of clinical interventions for children, and problematic sexual behavior among preteen children. His research is funded by the National Institutes of Health, the Children's Miracle Network, and other public and private agencies. To date, he has published more than 50 scientific papers and book chapters. Dr. Allen currently serves on the editorial boards of multiple scientific journals and is an associate board member of the Society for Emotion and Attachment Studies.